I0831845

VAN CORTLANDT

Family Papers

VOLUME FOUR

Map of Croton Point and Croton River, 1867. For most of the 19th century, waterpower remained a basic source of energy for mill operations. The Croton River was an ideal site because of an abundant fall of water, as well as a proximity to the major marketplace of New York City. The Van Cortlandts obtained significant revenues from leased properties along the River used for various manufacturing purposes. When New York City increasingly began to tap the upper reaches of the Croton River for its water supply, the usefulness of the River for manufacturing purposes would dissipate. Note the location of the Van Cortlandt homesite along the northern bank of the Croton. (from: F.W. Beers, *Atlas of New York and Vicinity*, New York, 1867).

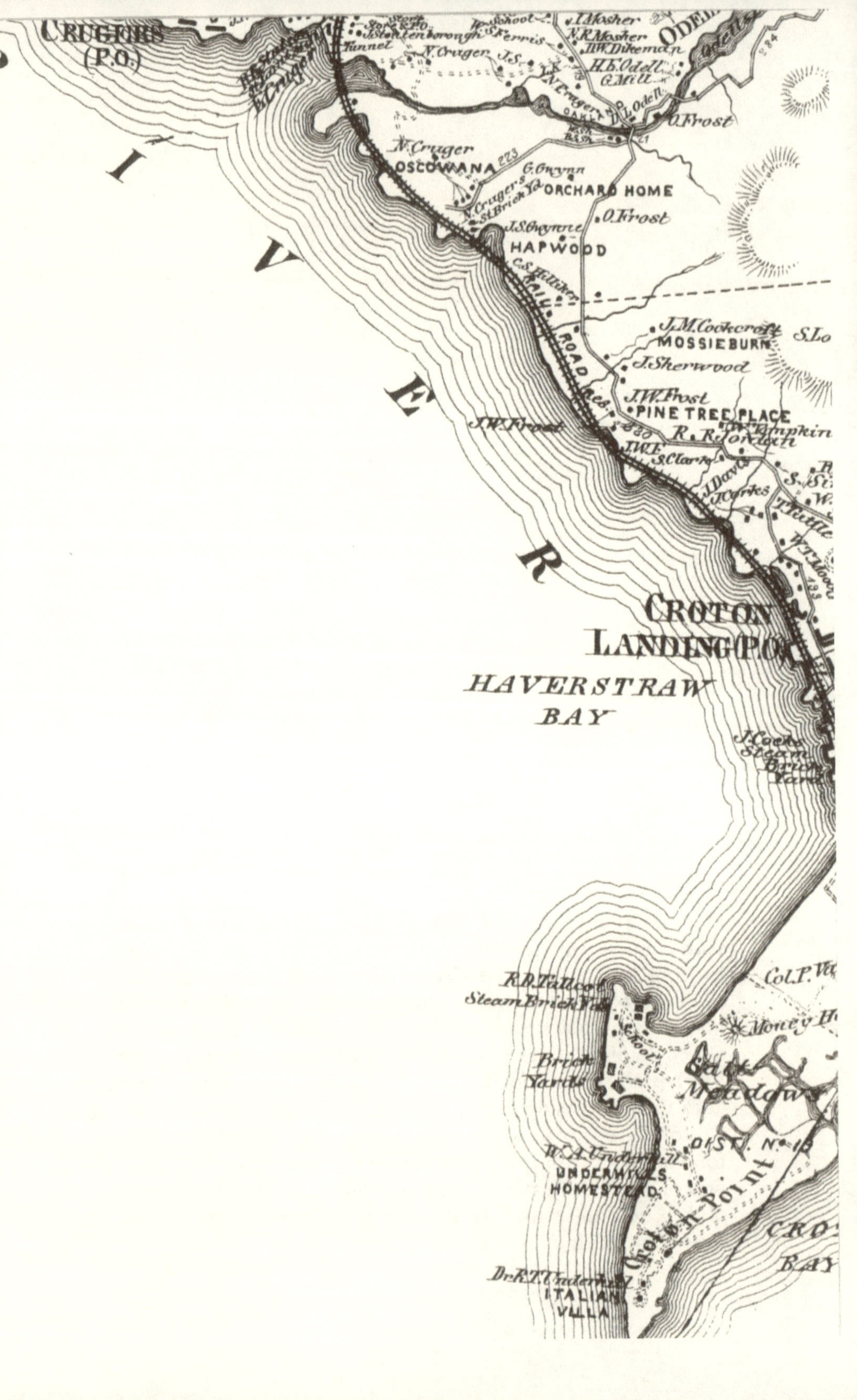

CRUGERS
(P.O.)
R
I
V
E
R
ODELL
J.I. Mosher
N.R. Mosher
J.W. Dikeman
H.E. Odell
G. Mill
D.L. Odell
O. Frost
Tunnel
N. Cruger
OAKLAND
N. Cruger
OSCOWANA
G. Gwynn
N. Cruger's St. Brick Yd.
ORCHARD HOME
O. Frost
J.S. Gwynne
HAPWOOD
C.S. Hilliker
J.M. Cockcroft
MOSSIEBURN
J. Sherwood
J.W. Frost
PINE TREE PLACE
J.W. Frost
R. R. Jordan
S. Clark
J. Davis
J. Carks
CROTON
LANDING (P.O.)
HAVERSTRAW
BAY
J. Cocks
Steam
Brick
Yard
R.D. Tallcot
Steam Brick Yd.
Brick
Yards
Salt
Meadows
Col. P. Va
Money H
W.A. Underhill
DIST. N° 13
UNDERHILLS
HOMESTEAD
Croton Point
Dr. R.T. Underhill
ITALIAN
VILLA
CRO
BAY

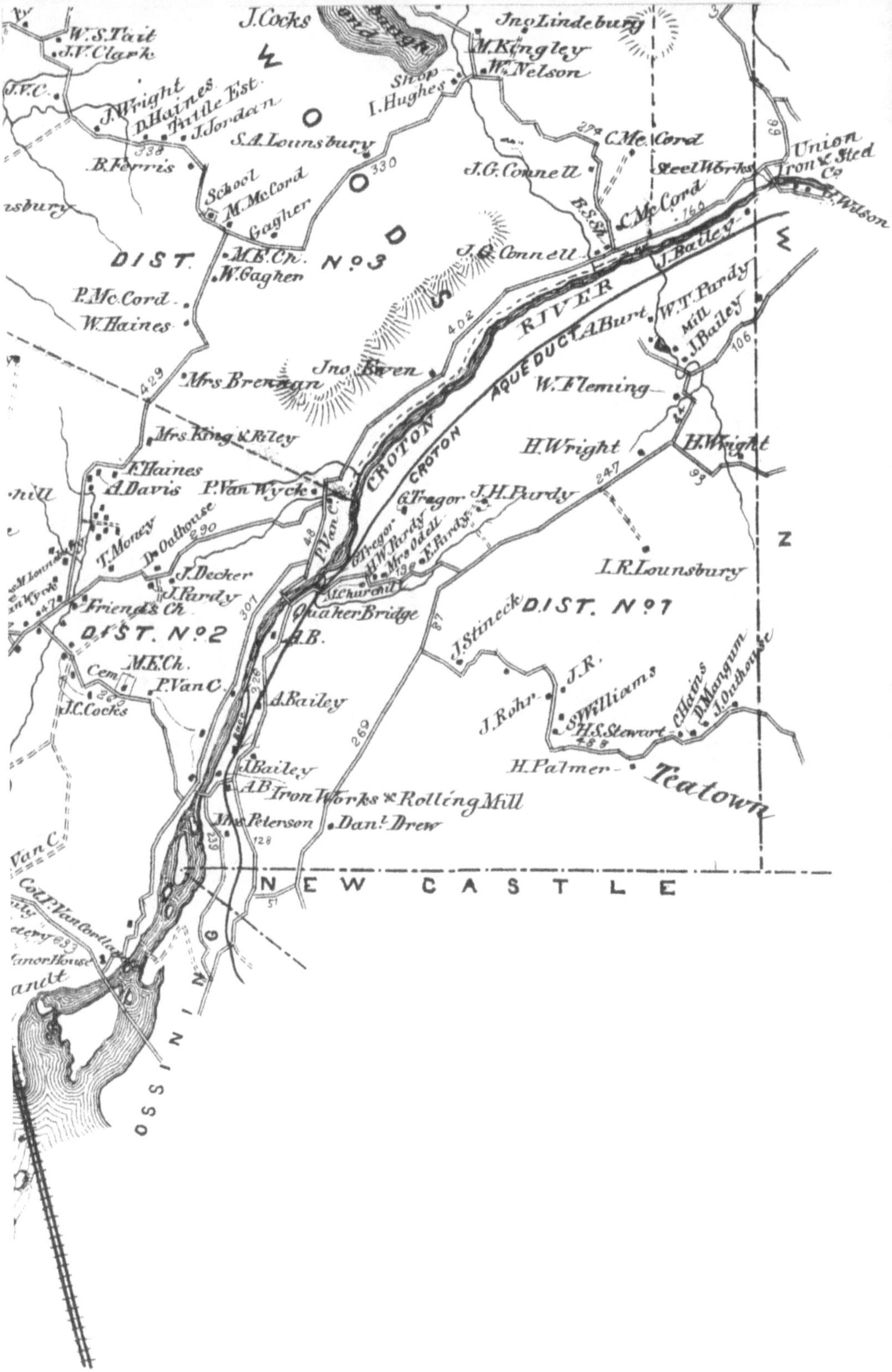

J. Cocks
Jno Lindeburg
M. Kingley
Wm Nelson
W. S. Tait
J. V. Clark
J. V. C.
J. Wright
D. Haines
Tuttle Est.
J. Jordan
Shop
I. Hughes
S. A. Lounsbury
B. Ferris
School
M. McCord
Gagher
W O O D S
C. McCord
J. G. Connell
Steel Works
Union Iron & Steel Co.
B. S. Sh.
C. McCord
H. Wilson
J. Bailey
J. G. Connell
DIST. No 3
M. E. Ch.
W. Gagher
P. McCord
W. Haines
RIVER
W. T. Purdy
Mill
J. Bailey
A. Burt
CROTON AQUEDUCT
Mrs Brennan
Jno Ewen
W. Fleming
Mrs King & Riley
CROTON
H. Wright
H. Wright
F. Haines
A. Davis
P. Van Wyck
G. Tregor
J. H. Purdy
T. Money
D. Outhouse
P. Van C.
G. Tregor
H. W. Purdy
Mrs Odell
F. Purdy
I. R. Lounsbury
J. Decker
J. Purdy
M. Churchill
Friends Ch.
Quaker Bridge
J. Stineck
DIST. No 1
DIST. No 2
A. B.
M. E. Ch.
Cem.
P. Van C.
J. C. Cocks
A. Bailey
J. R.
J. Rohr
S. Williams
C. Hains
D. Mangum
J. Outhouse
H. S. Stewart
J. Bailey
H. Palmer
Teatown
A. B.
Iron Works & Rolling Mill
Mrs Peterson
Danl Drew
NEW CASTLE
Van C.
Col. P. Van Cortlandt
Manor House
OSSINING

Van Cortlandt Manor House. The Van Cortlandt family maintained a continued presence in this structure from the time Pierre Van Cortlandt moved from New York City in 1749 until its sale during World War II. It served as the residence for Pierre (1721–1814), his two sons, Philip (1749–1831), and Pierre, Jr. (1762–1848), his daughter, Ann (1766–1855), and subsequent generations following Pierre, III (1815–1884).

In its present form, the Manor House is a restored and preserved historic site owned and operated by SLEEPY HOLLOW RESTORATIONS.

Correspondence
of the
Van Cortlandt Family
of
Cortlandt Manor
1815–1848

Compiled and Edited
by
Jacob Judd

SLEEPY HOLLOW PRESS

SLEEPY HOLLOW RESTORATIONS
Tarrytown, New York

First Printing

For information, address the publisher:
Sleepy Hollow Press
Tarrytown, New York 10591

Library of Congress Cataloging in Publication Data
Main entry under title:
Correspondence of the Van Cortlandt family
of Cortlandt Manor, 1815–1848.

(The Van Cortlandt family papers; v. 4)
Bibliography: p.
Includes index.
1. Van Cortlandt family.
2. Van Cortlandt, Philip, 1749–1831.
3. Van Cortlandt, Pierre, 1762–1848.
I. Judd, Jacob, 1929–
II. Series: Van Cortlandt family papers; v. 4.
CS71.V224 1976, vol. 4 929'.2'0973 80-22763

ISBN 0-912882-41-7

DESIGNED BY RAY FREIMAN

Contents

Maps & Illustrations

ILLUSTRATIONS ON JACKET: (top) Pierre Van Cortlandt (1721–1814), by John Wesley Jarvis from the Collections of Sleepy Hollow Restorations; (center) Philip Van Cortlandt (1749–1831) by Ezra Ames, from The Metropolitan Museum of Art, Gift of Christian A. Zabriskie, 1940; (bottom) Pierre Van Cortlandt, Jr. (1762–1848) by Ezra Ames, from the Collections of Sleepy Hollow Restorations.

Editorial Apparatus

THE MANUSCRIPT MATERIALS presented in this collection have been transcribed in a form as close as is reasonable to the originals. The orthography, grammatical usage and paragraphing follow practices used in the original letters. Misspelled proper names have been corrected in the notes but not in the body of the manuscripts. Similarly, raised letters and abbreviations have been retained in the transcriptions, including the use of the ampersand, &. Only in those instances where the meaning is unclear, has additional information been included in brackets [ ]. For example, W.P. appears W[hite] P[lains].

Punctuation markings of the original manuscripts have been followed. After reading several letters, the natural pauses will become apparent to today's reader, and the absence of periods will not create comprehension difficulties.

In most cases strike-overs have been deleted. However, in those instances where they have been thought interesting, they have been retained. In short, nothing has been arbitrarily deleted from the documents except for strike-overs.

Where material has been lost or destroyed it will be so noted. In a few instances, where a word remains unclear, an educated guess has been made and is marked off in brackets with an added question mark.

The source of each selected manuscript has been identified. Letters have been characterized as to whether they are letters or documents, drafts autographed or printed, signed or unsigned.

The annotations following a selection identify individuals, places and events mentioned in the manuscript. Wherever deemed necessary, editorial comments have been added to clarify issues discussed in the correspondence.

The annotations serve two main purposes: (1) they provide identifications which supply background data for the material, and (2) they guide the reader to additional sources of information. A policy has been adopted to keep them as concise as possible even though many of the subjects easily lent themselves to development as treatises on outstanding events.

Map showing Salisbury Island and Cortlandt Manor tenants in Peekskill region. North of Peekskill, mountain ranges rise on both sides of the Hudson River. Not only did the Van Cortlandts control desirable lands along the eastern bank of the Hudson River, but owned valuable acreage on small islands located between Westchester and Rockland counties. This manuscript map contains the names of many of the tenant farmers whose rent and business accounts are included in this volume. (Sleepy Hollow Restorations Collections).

Rock Land County

Turnpike Road

Island

Anthony's Nose

Dunderberg

Caldwells

Cooks Island

No. X

Seth Conklin farm 200 Acres

Turnpike Road

Nath. Philips House

Horton about 150

Travis about 150

Moores

Belknaps

John McCoys 300 Acres

Peeks Creek

about 300

about 100

Old Abr

Putnam County Line

River

Lot No. IX

farm about 300 acres

339 Acres P.V.C.

130 acres

170 acres

John

Abbreviations & Short Titles

&	And
&c	Etcetera
AD	Autograph Document
ADf	Autograph Draft
ADfs	Autograph Draft Signed
ADS	Autograph Document Signed
AL	Autograph Letter
ALS	Autograph Letter Signed
Df	Draft
Dfs	Draft Signed
DS	Document Signed
HSP	Historical Society of Pennsylvania
inst.	instant; of this month
Lbc	Letter Book Copy
LC	Library of Congress
MHS	Massachusetts Historical Society
NYHS	The New-York Historical Society
NYPL	The New York Public Library
NYSHA	New York State Historical Association
NYSL	New York State Library
SHR	Sleepy Hollow Restorations
ulto.	ultimo; of last month

Alexander	DeAlva S. Alexander. *A Political History of the State of New York* (Port Washington, N.Y., reprint 1969), 4 vols.
Appleton's Cyclopaedia	James G. Wilson and John Fiske, eds. *Appleton's Cyclopaedia of American Biography* (New York, 1887–1889), 6 vols.

Biographical Directory American Congress	U.S. Senate. *Biographical Directory of the American Congress 1774–1971* (Washington, D.C., 1971).
"Council of Appointment, Civil"	"Council of Appointment, Civil, for the Years 1801–1815," New York State Library.
Council of Appointment, Military	Hugh M. Hastings, ed. *Military Minutes of the Council of Appointment of the State of New York, 1783–1821* (Albany, NY, 1901–1902), 4 vols.
DAB	Dumas Malone, ed. *Dictionary of American Biography* (New York, 1922–1937), 22 vols.
French	J. H. French, ed. *Gazetteer of the State of New York: Embracing A Comprehensive View of the Geography, Geology, and General History of the State . . .* (Syracuse, NY, 1860).
Heads of Families 1790	U.S. Bureau of Census. *Heads of Families at the First Census of the United States Taken in the Year 1790: New York* (Baltimore, 1971).
Niles' Weekly Register	Henry Niles, ed. *The Weekly Register* (Baltimore, 1811–1815).
OED	Oxford University Press. *The Compact Edition of the Oxford English Dictionary* (New York, 1971), 2 vols.
Scharf	J. Thomas Scharf, ed. *History of Westchester County, New York . . .* (Philadelphia, 1886), 2 vols.
VCFP, I, II, III	Jacob Judd, ed. Volumes I, II, III of *The Van Cortlandt Family Papers* (Tarrytown, NY, 1976–78).
Werner	Edgar A. Werner, comp. *Civil List and Constitutional History of the Colony and State of New York* (Albany, NY, 1883, 1886, 1888, 1889).

In footnote references, when only the author's name is listed, please consult the Bibliography. When several books by the same author are employed, dates in parentheses distinguish between titles.

Introduction

THE 330 DOCUMENTS published in this volume bring to a close the Van Cortlandt Family Papers series. Beginning with the *Revolutionary War Memoir* of Philip Van Cortlandt in the first volume, the family saga has been traced from the relatively placid times of mid-eighteenth century provincial America to the eve of the Civil War. Originally of Dutch origin, the Van Cortlandts easily accommodated themselves to the English occupation of what originally had been New Netherland, and rose to economic and political prominence under the later Stuart and Hanoverian reigns prior to the American Revolution.

Commencing with the pre-Revolutionary era and continuing into the early days of the Republic, several members of the family distinguished themselves for their revolutionary ideology, administrative capacities, and willingness to sacrifice possessions and their lives, if necessary, in the cause of American freedom. Outstanding in this period were Pierre Van Cortlandt (1721–1814) and his two sons, Philip (1749–1831) and Pierre, Jr. (1762–1848).

The father gained prominence as a member of New York's Provincial Assembly, advocated the American cause in the Provincial Congresses, was chosen President of the Provincial Congress and then served for seventeen years as New York's first Lieutenant-Governor under George Clinton. The oldest son, Philip, meanwhile joined the Continental Army in 1775 and served under the military commands of

Washington, Clinton, Sullivan, Putnam, and Lafayette. After a distinguished military career, he soon entered Congress and sat in that body during the presidencies of Washington, Adams, and Jefferson.

While the younger brother, Pierre, Jr., only sat in Congress one term, he maintained a close liaison with the Jefferson administration through his father-in-law, Vice-President George Clinton. Originally ardent Jeffersonians in their politics, they soon cooled to James Madison and Dolley. As their ardor dimmed for the national party continually headed by Virginians, they increasingly turned their attention to local politics and agricultural pursuits.

This volume begins at a point where the War of 1812 was drawing to a close and the nation found itself poised on the verge of a giant leap forward into major transportation improvements, into manufacturing, and into a rapid exploitation of its seemingly unlimited natural resources.

In the period covered by this volume (1815–1848), the family members underwent rapid political transformations from Jeffersonianism, to becoming Democrats, shifting to Whiggism for a brief period, and finally, upon reexamining their true beliefs, a return to an earlier Democratic allegiance. Such political wanderings were direct reflections upon the shifting political sands of politics in ante-bellum America.

The half-century which intervened between the American Revolution and the rise of Jacksonianism found a quite different nation emerging so soon after the successful culmination of its struggle for political independence. Aristocrats, but revolutionaries at the same time, the Van Cortlandts bridged the gap from the pre-Revolutionary War days through Jacksonianism and the rise of Whig opposition to "King Andrew." Their correspondence reflects some of the subtle changes in sentiment occurring in the nation as well as in this family of aristocratic mien.

In the person of Philip Van Cortlandt, a living bridge was maintained from the Revolution to Jacksonianism. Being the highest ranking survivor of the American Continental forces, Philip was given the honor of escorting the revered French hero of the American Revolution, the Marquis de Lafayette, on part of his triumphant journey through New York in 1824–25. While this stirring event was in process, Philip and his brother, Pierre, Jr., were receiving vivid first-hand descriptions of Andrew Jackson and life in Nashville, Tennessee from their nephew, Abraham Van Wyck.

Other manifestations of a democratic shift in sentiment can be found in the family's embrace of Methodism and their move to manumit their remaining slaves. No longer the possessors of vast manorial estates, the Van Cortlandts soon accommodated themselves to the modern ways of business enterprise in nineteenth-century America.

Throughout this volume an emphasis on the business and commercial aspects of land ownership in eighteenth- and nineteenth-century America can be found. The once proud possessors of one of the great Hudson Valley estates, the Van Cortlandts maintained their remaining properties as business entities until the eve of the American Civil War. The Van Cortlandt family correspondence and related business documents help to exemplify the transformation in politics, agriculture, and land practices which obtained from the time of the American Revolution into the turbulent 1850's.

Also included in this final volume is an addendum of eighteenth-century family correspondence, a glossary of business terms, and an index.

Jacob Judd
Tarrytown, New York

Calendar of Correspondence

1

Pierre, Jr. to [Clarissa Gilbert ?][1] **ALS**
SHR

Albany June 25, 1815.

[torn] bert

I wrote you by the last [torn] that Mrs Van Cortlandts Breast continued very painful, yesterday it was so extremely painful that the Doctor opened it, She is more free from pain now but yet at times it is great & is very weak,[2] She will not be able to return home this week, and will write you by every mail how She is and I hope by the next will be able to fix the time when M^{r} McCoy can come up for us, that is if She will be able to come, I was to write [torn] by this mail however Billy can let him know the Contents of this which will answer as well — Mrs V. Cortlandt as usual send her Love to you & the Family Pierre grows finely —

Your freind
Pierre Van Cortlandt

---

1. Clarissa Gilbert apparently served Pierre as a housekeeper. See *VCFP,* III, 452, 623.

2. Ann had given birth to Pierre III on April 25. She may have been suffering from a postpartum infection.

"Monies paid for the late George Clinton by Pierre Van Cortlandt." ADS
NYPL

[ca. July 7, 1815.]

Dr.

1811		
Decr. 14	To Harden & Hodges for repairing Carriage	$10.00
26	To Patrick Rogers for do. Harness	24.58½
Febr. 2	To Joshua Lodder Blacksmith for shoeing horses	4.37½
1812	To Hunt & Johnson Blacksm. for shoeing horses from Jany 1812 to 28th April	15.00
May 2 & March 19	To Henry Dunlap for repairing Carriage.	14.28½
	To John Barnes for Liquor from Novr. 4.1811 to March 20–1812	23.85
	During the sickness of the Vice President for himself & those sitting up with him 3 Gallons Wine	15.00
	and 2 Gallons Brandy	6.00
	Paid for Apples Biskets &c &c for V. Presdt.	3.00
April 20	To James Calder & Son for mourning suits for the Two Servants of the Vice President	78.57
	Paid Jeweller at George Town, by request of Miss Clinton $18 for two breast pins with her Father's hair for Col. Gilman & Mr. ONeale	18.00
	Paid for a black handkerchief for James $1.25 And a pair of black	

	stockings for Powers 1.75 by request of Miss Clinton to complete their mourning suit	3.00
	Paid for Crape for Miss Clinton & her sister Tallmadge	8.00
May 4	Paid Henry Ingle for hire of a bed Chair	2.00
8	Paid Sanderson for soldering the Coffin at Night	8.00
2	Paid Matilda Henson (Wash woman)	12.50
		$246.16

1812		
April 27	Paid Doctor Elizey, bill for Medical Attendance on the Vice President during his illness	$57.00
27	Paid Doctor Sim for d^o^ d^o^	50.00
28	Paid Doctor Worthington for d^o^ d^o^	150.00
May 9	Paid William O Neale for Robert Baileys board	51.18½
	Paid Robert Bailey for his & Miss Clintons Expenses to Washington from New York	51.40
	Paid Robert Bailey for drivers return	10.00
April 29	Paid Doctor May for Medical Attendance	11.00
27	Paid John Ott, Druggist for Medicine	22.95
29	Paid James Hickey (hair dresser)	22.72
March 29	Paid Honore Sullivan (Confectioner) for Jellies for V. President	1.50
27	Paid Jacob Leonard (watch Maker) for rep^r^. & cl^g^. Watch	2.50
May 9	Paid William O Neale for board for himself his daughter Maria, his Nurse[,] James his body Servant & for Coachman &c &c	663.70
9	Paid Mrs Burris — his Nurse	38.00

8	Paid Mrs Kartright for boarding Coachman		45.00
14	Paid Genl. Cummings for a Coachee Horses & Driver to go from Newark to the City of Washington with Miss Clinton &c &c and return		82.50
	Paid travelling Expences from City Washington to New York returning with Miss Clinton &c		89.42
	Paid for James (the black Servant) returning by Water Stages from Washington to New York with Baggage &c of Vice President		23.00
			1371.87
1812 May	Paid Henry Hammon for keeping the late Vice Presidents horses to rights & Blacksmiths bill for shoeing them in New York		17.50
May 15	Paid Hugh Wishart for 2 silver Cake Baskets made by directions of the late Vice President for me[2]		156.00
April 24	Paid Maria Clinton at Washington		100.00
May	Paid Doctor Sim for Medical Assistance to Miss Clinton		6.00
	Paid for James The Body servant which was in part of his wages due him from the late Vice Prest., viz.		
some time in Jany.	A Coat at George Town	$10.50	
	1 Shirt	1.50	
	Cash $2	2.00	
May 1	Cash $6	6.00	20.00
1812 April 30	Paid Powers (Coachman) Viz — $30.00		

May 8	Paid Powers	$16.00	
18	Paid Powers at New York	2.50	
July 20	Paid for Powers to Rachel Bates	.50	
	To Paye for him	2.75	
	Paid Mrs Clinton for 3pr Nankeen	2.44	
	To Mrs Clinton for Shoes Powers had but charged to her acct. at Pougkeepsie	3.12½	
	To Mrs Clinton she paid for the freight of Powers trunk	.50	
	Paid Bogardus & Dering for Powers	.33	
			58.14½

1814 June 21	Paid Joshua Hayes $3.75 for Horse Shoes made for the late V. Prest. in 1811	3.75
		$361.94

1811 July 5	Paid John Thorp (blacksmith) at Wappingers Creek for Vice President	$ 2.31
1804	Paid Nathan Westcott for a Sett of harness, silver plated for a coachee	100.00
		$102.31

1st Page	246.16
2d	1371.87
3d	361.94
4.	102.31
	$2082.28

Copy Sent to Mr. Emmot July 7–1815

Calendar of Correspondence

Ommissions &
Errors Excepted Pierre Van Cortlandt

---

1. The dispute concerning George Clinton's estate still remained unresolved as of 1815. Matthias B. Tallmadge continued to question every statement and bill submitted by Pierre on behalf of his late father-in-law's account. See *VCFP,* III, 514–515, 539–540, 542–546, 549–554, and *passim.;* Pierre, Jr. to Elisha Williams, August 30, 1816 (No. 12).

2. Included in this list of expenditures, involving medical fees, nursing, the purchase of fruits and sweets, etc., is the acquisition of two silver cake baskets made for Pierre by Hugh Wishart, one of the great New York silversmiths. *Antiques* (June, 1970), p. 909. The names and addresses of Patrick Rodgers, Nathan Wescott, Jacob Leonard, Dr. Fredrick May, Sanderson the plumber, and Henry Dunlap all appear in the pages of Judah Delano's *The Washington Directory,* published in the nation's capital in 1822.

Nathaniel Gilman[1] to Pierre, Jr. ALS
NYPL

Exeter Sept: 25th 1815.

Dear Sir.

I have now before me your polite & very affectionate letter of Augt. 8th. 1814, the Receipt of which I ought to have acknowledged more than twelve Months since — Believe me when I assure you that the delay has not arrisen from a careless inattention on my part, but rather from causes which I will not State — About the time your Letter came to hand we were threatened with an attack by the enemy in Portsmouth,[2] and living within 14 miles of that place obliged us to be constantly on the alert — two of my sons with my hired men took the field — After the alarm had in some measure subsided, and finding I had neglected your letter for several Months, determined you should not hear from me untill I could gratify your wishes with the portrait of our mutual friend[3] — Not having his likeness, except one taken with a pencil, a number of years since, I anticipated a difficulty of getting the expression, but finally found a young man, of this town, who discovered a great natural genius for painting and who had taken several likenesses I had hope, with the assistance of my family, to obtain one from him, but finding he was just going to Boston to perfect himself in that art thought best to postpone the business untill his Return — he went, and after being there about one Month was taken with a feaver & died. — This month I took M^rs^. Gilman, with several of my Children to Boston and by the assistance we gave the Artist have been able to obtain something of the similitude of our dec^d^. friend — I have to lament we could not obtain a better likeness. —

I have requested my friends Messrs. Cornelius Coolidge & Co., of Boston, to have the portrait box'd up & ship'd to New-York, direct to the care of the Honble DeWitt Clinton, which hope will come safe to hand.

I shall feel myself highly remunerated for any expence or trouble, that may have accrued, by having the portrait placed by the side of that truly venerable & highly respected patriot for whom I know my dec^d^. Brother (as also for the different branches of your family) held the warmest affection.

One of my sons mentioned to me, a few days since, that M^r^. Langdon, of Portsmouth, observed to him that you inquired Respecting a mare that formerly belonged to my brother — that animal I now own & has been in my care for a Number of years, it is one that my bro^r^. was much attached to and would formerly have commanded the first price in any market — I have no particular wish to part with her, neither would I in this part of the Country, least [lest] I should see her abused — Although she knows what service is, yet has never been injured, every limb perfectly sound with all the activity of a pony — she has had one Colt only, which came last July, and was thought to be a very beautiful creature, but unfortunately, when ab[t]. three days old, fell from a bank by the side of a River and lay some time entangled among the roots of trees & was so bruised that it died in about one week — she took the Horse again last Month, but whither with foal or not I cannot say — I have a number of Horses on hand more than I want for use and should any person be travelling this way, that you have confidence in, if she should answer expectation, you shall have her at a fair price — she is this year 14 years old & no more, appears to possess a great constitution, has been in the family from three years old and to my knowledge has never been unwell a day. Believe me to be with great Respect, sir

Your Most Obed[t]Serv[t]
Nath[l]. Gilman

Hon[bl]. Pierre Van Cortlandt

---

1. Nathaniel Gilman was the brother of the late Senator Nicholas Gilman.

2. British naval commander Thomas M. Hardy sailed out of Halifax, Nova Scotia, in July, 1814, with an extensive military and naval force. He threatened the New England coastline during the month of August, with Portsmouth, New Hampshire, a likely target for attack. Benson J. Lossing, *The Field-Book of the War of 1812* . . . (New York, 1869), pp. 890–891.

3. Pierre, Jr. apparently sought a portrait of the late Senator Gilman, who had been a close friend of Vice President George Clinton.

4

Charles Clinton[1] to Pierre, Jr. ALS
SHR

New York 18th Octr 1815.

Dr Sir

I take the liberty to recommend to your attention the bearer, Mathew Corwin, who is an honest, industrious Man, in very indigent circumstances, with a large family — He has a disposition to better his Circumstances by removing to the Genessee Country, but is unable to proceed by reason of his poverty — He has received some Assistance from the Members of the Society to which he belongs, and from other charitable disposed persons, but is still much behind hand — I am Satisfied that your charity cannot be better placed than by relieving his necessities —

Accept of my respects for you
& family —
I am Sir Yours &c
Cha. Clinton

[Addressed]
Pierre Van Cortlandt, Esqr

Croton

Westchester
By Mr Mathew Corwin

---

1. Charles Clinton was DeWitt Clinton's brother. He seems to have been asking Pierre for some monetary assistance in aiding the indigent Mathew Corwin to move from New York City to the Genessee River region by way of the Hudson and Mohawk valleys.

5

John Peter DeLancey[1] to Philip. ALS
NYPL

Mamaroneck November 7th 1815.

Sir

In a conversation I had with judge Purdy a few days since, I understood from him that you had gone to Albany to ascertain if the quit rents now demanded for the manor of Courtland[2] had not already been paid, if not, on what part of the manor those demanded were due, and how the different proprietors are to proceed in estimating their respective proportions. as I am interested in a part of the manor, I will thank you for any information you can give on this subject. I hope you will excuse the trouble I give you, and beleive me Sir

Respectfully Yours
J.P. DeLancey

General Philip Van Cortlandt

[bottom of page]

Philip to John Peter DeLancey. ADf

Nov^{r}–29–1815.

Dr Sir

This day — On my return from Albany I was favored with yours of the 7th and am happy to inform you that I have Settled & paid up all the Q Rent of the Manor of Cortlandt and also Committed for all future — QR — in such manner as not to be obliged to call on any of the Proprieters Neither will any Tax be Necessary you may therefore rest perfectly Contented there remaind some undivided land which was sold to accomplish it —

& am with great respect y^{rs}

---

1. John Peter DeLancey (1753–1828) was the fourth son and eighth child of Lieutenant Governor James and Anne (Heathcote) DeLancey. Educated in England, he was a Loyalist, as was his family. In the Revolution he served as a major of a regiment of Pennsylvania Loyalists. After the war he fled to England. He returned to the United States in 1789 to make his home at Heathcote Hill in Mamaroneck, New York, with his wife, the former Elizabeth Floyd, daughter of Richard Floyd, a Suffolk County Loyalist. One of their eight children, Susan, married James Fenimore Cooper, the novelist. John DeLancey was related to the Van Cortlandts through his paternal grandmother, Anne (Van Cortlandt) DeLancey, the third daughter of Stephanus Van Cortlandt. This connection entitled him to the possession of some land rights in the Manor. D.A. Story, *The DeLanceys* (Toronto, 1931), pp. 18, 35–38; *VCFP,* III, xli–xliii, 8–9, 611.

2. The collection of quitrents was recognized under New York law from earliest colonial times until their abolition in 1846. For much of the period prior to the Revolution, the province hesitated to use this valid source of revenue because it ultimately enhanced the royal coffers. Once the Revolution occurred, and crown influence was eliminated, the legislature resorted to this revenue device.

   The rate varied, and collections were not carried out systematically. Therefore, from time to time landowners were given the option of settling accounts, both past and future, on a negotiated rate. Apparently this is what Philip achieved on his visit to Albany in November. Marshall Harris, *Origin of the Land Tenure System in the United States* (Ames, IA, 1953), p. 326; Beverley W. Bond, Jr., *The Quit-Rent System in the American Colonies* (New Haven, CT, 1919), pp. 283–285; O'Callaghan, *Documentary History New-York,* IV, 938–939.

6

Cornelia Beekman to Catharine Van Wyck. ALS
SHR

Decem^r 21, 1815.

Dear Sister

My Not being well Obliges Me to Stay at home and Not attend the Quartily Meeting. I Could wish to Join you in the Meeting, but health of Body for bids My Exposing My Self, at this Inclement Season, but beg you will remember your Sister that is absent —

Brother Phillip has Call here to See Me on purpose to See the Lease of Peeks Kill.[1] twise I have been put in an awkward possition Not having the Lease in My Possision, I was Constrained to tell him, that he Should See the Lease in welcome — but Not at this time, I beg he would Excuse My Not bringing it forward, but that the Next time he come here I would gratify him with the Sight of it, that I had My reasons why I Could Not now, I acknowledged that Our Dear father Delivered that Lease in My hands as Sacred to keep for us all, I am Mortifyed that Cousin Theodore has detained it out of my Possesson So Long, Sarah will Deliver this to you and I beg that you will give her the Lease — and She will bring it Safe to Me, Send it up and tell her it is of great Consiquence to Me, that She will be Cairfull of the Papers you intrust her with —

Remember Me Most affectionatly to Dear Cousin Mary[2] tell her that I feel most tenderly for her, theres scarsely an hour but I bear her in Mind and May the almighty of his infinite Goodness, Meet her, and bless her, in her Perilous hour — Am D^r

Sister your Most affectionatly
C. Beekman

NB Brother Pierre has Sent for the key of My Cubboard that is at P.Kills he wants to Move it out of the room, I have given Brother Phillip the key for him to do with the press as he

Pleases, will you Mention the Carpet and get it. Divide it and Send Me the one half

[Addressed]
Mrs. Catharine Van Wyck
Croton
Pr Sarah

[Endorsed]
Cornelia Beekman Order for the lease of the Land at Peeks kill — Granted by Gertruydt Beekman to Pierre Van Cortland deceased — this Letter &r dated Decemr 1815

---

1. The late Pierre, Sr. had received a significant legacy under the terms of the will of his aunt, Gertrude (Van Cortlandt) Beekman, and his heirs were in the process of determining who rightfully obtained shares in the estate. For the Beekman legacy, see Nos. 271–277 and the accompanying commentary.

2. The identification of "Cousin Mary" remains unresolved. There were numerous Marys related to the Van Wycks.

7

James W. Wilkin[1] to Pierre, Jr. ALS
SHR

Washington February 4th 1816.

Dear General

I have had no Public Documents lately that I could send you they print now but one copy for each Member or I should have ranked you among my first and best friends and made it manifest by my attention I have time to write but few letters other than those I am obliged to write home on business.

I send you herewith a news paper which has the whole

of the Correspondence of the Chevalier De Onis with Mr Monroe on our relations with Spain it is a Valuable Public Document & state paper.[2]

The house of Representatives have for a long time had under Consideration the report of the Committee of Ways and means on a System of Permanent Revinue which I presume you have seen.[3] I believe the house will concur with the Committee in their report generally. A bill was passed yesterday in our house to repeal the duties on all goods arms and merchandize manufactured within the United States I have no doubt it will soon pass the Senate and become a law.[4]

Mr John Randolph opposes the Report generally[.] he has spoken a great deal against it he occupied the floor for three days in succession and speaks about four hours on each day[.] he wandered very often from the subject he is however a fine speaker.[5]

I can not give you any certain account or information on the Presidential Question it now becomes rather the better opinion that Governor Tompkins will not get a Caucus nomination Mr Monroe is most likely (by what I can learn) to succeed at a Caucus Governor Tompkins may perhaps be nominated Vice President.[6] I have just heard that a legislative caucus of the Legislature of Pennsylvania have nominated Mr Monroe for Presdt & Governor Snyder for Vice Presdt.

As soon as I can get any better information I will write you again I will be very happy to hear from you —

I am very respectfully
your Humble Servt
Jas. W. Wilkin

Genl P. Van Cortland —

[Addressed]
Free Jas. W. Wilkin
Genl Pierre Van Cortland
Peeks Kill
Westchester County
N York

---

1. James W. Wilkin of Orange County had been a political correspondent of the Van Cortlandts as early as 1810. He had risen politically from the New York Senate and Assembly to the Congress. See *VCFP,* III, 325–326.

2. President James Madison transmitted to Congress late in January a series of letters which had passed between Secretary of State James Monroe and Spanish Minister Plenipotentiary Luis de Onis y Gonzales. This correspondence mainly concerned West Florida, and American involvement in the support of insurrectionary movements in Central and South America. *Niles' Weekly Register,* February 3, 1816, pp. 392–397; George Dangerfield, *The Awakening of American Nationalism 1815–1828* (New York, 1965), pp. 56–57.

3. Wilkin referred to a Ways and Means Committee report submitted to Congress on January 9. In it, the committee recommended increased tariff regulations as a device for raising adequate revenues in support of the federal government. *Niles' Weekly Register,* January 20, 1816, pp. 354–357.

4. Congress was in the midst of a debate as to whether it should repeal the wartime measure of January 18, 1815, whose aim had been to "provide additional revenues . . . by laying duties on various goods, wares and merchandise, manufactured within the United States." *Ibid.,* February 10, 1816, p. 418.

5. The Jeffersonian Republican warhorse John Randolph had a long affiliation with the Van Cortlandts and the Clinton family. In the course of the debate on this issue, Randolph introduced a motion to "reduce the military establishment of the United States." He had a reputation for being a brilliant but at times somewhat erratic speaker.

6. Wilkin was correct in his assumption that Monroe would be chosen by the Republican caucus on March 16 as the presidential candidate, and that Pierre's political nemesis Daniel D. Tompkins would be tapped for the vice presidency. Irwin, p. 208.

8

Pierre, Jr. to John Tayler.[1] ALS
NYSL

Peekskill Feb–19th–1816.

Dear Sir

Some time ago I received a Letter from Abraham Varick Esqr. mentioning that he had an Offer of five dollars 50/100 for 100 acres in Lot No. 38 Fonda's patent belonging to the Estate of G.W. Clinton and that Genl. Floyd had advised the Sale. I wrote Mr. Varick that if you & Col. N. Floyd approved of the Sale that I also consented[.] Yesterday I received another Letter from him, stating that he had offers for 100 Acres in No 65 Fonda's at Eight Dollars per Acre and 112 1/2 Acres in Lot No. 4 in Sumners patent at thirteen Dollars fifty five Cents per Acre,[2] (These Lands belonging to the same Estate of G.W. Clinton). He further mentions that Genl. Floyd and a Mr. Wright who advice the sale at that price — As I have never been in that part of the Country and unacquainted with the Value of Lands there, I have thought proper to address this Letter to you as a Co Executor with me — Whether it is best to sell the Childs real Property[3] now when there is certainly a depreciation of paper money owing to the multitude of Banks which are already incorporated, as well as from a deluge of Paper Currency issued by Swindlers without authority, whose Agents are hawking it about through the Country, than to keep the Land until confidence is again established in paper money[.] Or if this land is sold can it be replaced again by the purchase of Other Lands which will be increasing in Value as the Child grows up — These are Considerations which I think it prudent to enquire into before any further Sales take place of his Real Estate. I beg you to give me your Opinion as soon as convenient, that I write to Mr Varick —

Mrs Van Cortlandt unites with me in best regards to you Mrs Cooper & family & tell her that my little Pierre grows astonishingly & is a prodigious fine fellow

I am with much esteem your
Ob Serv[t]
Pierre Van Cortlandt

Hon John Tayler

---

1. John Tayler (1742–1829) had been a political ally of the late George Clinton and of Pierre, Sr. He was active in New York politics from 1776 through 1817, and became Acting Governor in February, 1817, when Governor Daniel D. Tompkins moved on to become Vice President.

2. The Fonda and Sumner patents adjoined each other in Montgomery County. "Map of State of New York" in Flick, V, endmap.

3. Pierre and John Tayler were co-executors of the estate of George Washington Clinton, son of former Vice President George Clinton. See *VCFP,* III, 569, and *passim;* George William Clinton to Pierre, Jr., August 26, 1831 (No. 140).

9

John Tayler to Pierre, Jr. ALS
NYPL

Albany 8th March 1816.

Dear Sir,

I received your two several favours it gave me much pleasure to hear from you & your Good wife a favourite of mine — an expression I presume (Circumstances & abilities considered) that will not be unpleasing — Varick has been here some time soliciting a grant of land for the Services of his Uncle Richard in the revolutionary war[1] — & mentioned the Sale of the two lots he had Conditionally agreed for. I expressed a Sentiment similar to yours on that Subject. that it would be improper to change real Estate of the infant to personal — as it would thereby be exposed to loss and depreciation. at the same time as his lots could not be of Moment if his Grand father & Uncle consented I could have no Objection but lots that were [in] hand ought to be retained even if the rents were not regularly paid — I presume that I expressed your Sentiments also on this Subject — as to the excise law as it is administred it is a great evil and as far as my Influence could extend I should have been happy to contribute in having it altered —

I sincerely lament that any difficulty should be in the way to prevent your uniting in support of the Republican cause. and I trust that the spirit of Conciliating jealousies & discord will soon overcome every obstacle — this Spirit will tend to unite all our friends I have great hope the period is not far distant in which this Object will be Effected[2] — If I am rightly informed the Governor utterly disclaims any interference in the Election in the County of Westchester — it would be pleasing indeed to see a union of Republicans in that respectable county. M^{r}. & M^{rs}. Cooper joins in our best wishes to you your Good Wife I pray kiss the boy for me and

believe me to be Yours most respectfully

John Tayler

Pierre V Cortlandt

---

1. Lawyer, military officer during the Revolution, assemblyman, and mayor of New York City, Richard Varick (1753–1831), an uncle to the Varick referred to in this letter, was a leading Federalist politician during the early years of the Republic. Kass, pp. 53–54; Benson J. Lossing, *History of New York City* . . . (New York, 1884), I, 202.

2. It was a presidential election year and the Republicans had high hopes of electing their slate of James Monroe for President and New York's Governor Daniel D. Tompkins for Vice President. Pierre was not a political admirer of Tompkins and it was feared that he would not work in support of the national slate.

10

Cornelia Beekman to Philip. ALS
SHR

April 1, 1816.

Dr Brother

Pr Post I received information that there was again taxes to be paid on the four Lots, Corner of North and Second Streets Corporation and U S taxes, the Amount ten Dollars, if not Paid this week (Say by thursday) thay will be sold for the taxes, they have been due upwards of Sixty days — I have Not got the Money, therefore am under the Necessity of Sending to you for it, and will be thankfull you will Send it Me by the bearer So that I Can Remit it tomorrow to have it Paid — Am Dr Brother your affectionate

Sister C. Beekman

April 1
1816

[Endorsed]
Sister Beekman
Sent for $10.00
to pay Taxes for
Bowery Lots
-1816-

11

Magdalen Stevenson[1] to Ann [Stevenson] Van Cortlandt. ALS
SHR

Abbay april 23 1816.

My Dearest Anne

I received your letter dated the 19 and was happy to hear Peirre was rather better may the Lord remove his complaint and may wee soon say wee hear he is better, we will be very happy to see you all and the sooner the better for my anxity about Walsh is great he is very weak, and quite absent, Short of memery. Sally Sent for me to day to know what She would do about Sending for a Doc^{tr} he does not complain and wont know he ails any, thing Sally very much Distresed I have Sent for George Manciies[2] to git him to speak him to Send for a Doc^{tr}, the Business of the Church has affected him much both families Join in love to you & M^{r} V Cortland, kiss little peirre for us

I remain My Dear Ann your
affectionate Mother
Magdalen Stevenson

[Addressed]
M^{rs}. Ann Van Cortlandt
Peekskill NY

---

1. Magdalena Stevenson was the wife of John Stevenson and the daughter of Volckert P. and Anna (DePeyster) Douw. Belknap, p. 22.

2. Possibly George W. Mancius, the son of Dr. Wilhelmus Mancius of Market Street (now Broadway) in Albany. He served as the city's postmaster in 1795. Howell and Tenney, pp. 208–209, 438, 667, 671.

12

Pierre, Jr. to Elisha Williams.[1] ADfs

NYPL

Albany Aug–30–1816.

Dear Sir

In 1796 Dirck Wynkoop of Kingston gave a Bond to Governor Clinton for £ 1172 which Bond Govr. Clinton in the autumn of 1801 assigned to me specifying for a valuable consideration the Whole Principal & the Interest then due and which should thereafter become due upon the said bond — Many Letters passed between me and the Executors of Judge Wynkoop upon the Subject they offering proposals by giving me real Estate upon certain Conditions which were rejected on my part — a year or two before the Death of Govr Clinton, He made a settlement with the Executrix (Mrs Sarah Smith) of Judge Wynkoop and gave her an Indemnification against that bond for $2000 — upon her paying at that time a certain sum of money & her bond for the residue which she has since paid to Stephen D. Beekman who married Govr. Clinton's youngest daughter Maria — The assigned Bond of Dirck Wynkoop has not been out of my possession since the Date of the Assignment nor do I think that he saw it from that time He however informed me that he had made such settlement with Mrs Smith, but that I must keep the bond, as the settlement was his loss & that he would pay me the whole amount of the Bond — this was a private Conversation between him & me — So it stands with respect to the Bond —

In October 1811 Govr. Clinton & I went to the City of Washington — When we left New York He told me that I must pay all the Expenses of the Journey and all the Expenses of his Horses & repairing his Carriage when there, to keep an Account of which & that he would repay me — All this I did — He fell sick & while sick he gave me a Check for

$ and an Order to receive what pay was due him from the U. States as Vice President — I received upwards of $3000 & paid at Washington certain sums of money for his Board his Two Servants Board, the keeping of his Horses, his Servants wages, bought mourning suits for his Two Servants by the request his Daughter Maria, Sent for his Daughter from NYork paid the Expences of her Journey to Washington together with the Expenses of Mr. Robt. Bailey who accompanied her, paid their Expenses at Washington and back again to NYork, Paid the Accounts of the Attendant Physicians, his Nurse's bill and a number of other Accounts — which Mat Tallmadge by his Attorney Js Talmadge has refused to allow me & have sent a person to Washington to prove he will return in time for the Circuit at Dutchess — The money I have paid out does not amount to as much as the Money I received at Washington, but the indorsed Bond of Dirck Wynkoop over balances it by several thousand Dollars —

I have every reason to believe that Govr. Clinton left a will, which was deposited in a trunk of his most valuable papers & left to the safe keeping of Mrs Bates who lived in One of his Houses near his mansion house at Caspers Kill, that trunk I wanted to open on my bringing Maria home, but she & her Brother opposed it alledging the recent death of their Father & promised most sacredly that it should remain untouched until my return from the City of Washington on my Summons upon the War Question, I had scarcely arrived at Washington before Mat Tallmadge got his Brother James with Washington Clinton & Washington Clinton's wife to open the trunk — and no will to be found — Mat Tallmadge has administred upon the Estate and brought a Suit against me for the monies Govr Clinton gave me at the City of Washington which is now noticed for trial at the Circuit of Dutchess the 16 of September — Mr Emmot has asked payment in a Letter by the Accounts of Money I have paid,[2] and the Bond of Dirck Wynkoop assigned to me — I have doubts whether it would not be best to leave it to reference [?] or to file a Bill in Chancery against Mat & James Tallmadge to compel them to make disclosure of the destruction of the will —

I go down this day with the Steam boat to Peeks kill, & shall hand this Letter to some Person going on ashore at Hudson —

I am yours with Esteem
Pierre Van Cortlandt

Elisha Williams Esq[r] —

D[r] Sir

I have just received a Letter from M[r] Smith mentioning that he had been served with a Countermand of Notice of Final injunction of Tallmadge against me —

[Addressed]
Elisha Williams Esq[r]
Hudson

---

1. Elisha Williams sat in the New York Assembly as early as 1800 and as late as 1828 as a representative from Columbia County. It is apparent that he was acting as an attorney in behalf of Pierre in the dispute with Matthias B. Tallmadge concerning George Clinton's estate. Werner, pp. 127, 322, 326, 329–330, 334, 339.

2. Pierre referred to the itemized statement labeled "Monies paid for the late George Clinton by Pierre Van Cortlandt" (No. 2). He was attempting to deduct these expenditures from the amount due him on a bond he held from the late Dirck Wynkoop.

13

Pierre, Jr. to Philip. ALS
SHR

PeeksKill October 10h—1816 —

Dear Brother

I send you an Account of the Places Rented on the West Side of the Sprout Creek together with the New House on this farm. I leave it with you to settle the Business with my Sisters — Only remarking that the affair of Stuyvesant is yet unsettled and if that should be revived and a Recovery had against me that I may [be] made secure —

The Ask Lot I wish to have sold, as I pay Sister Rensselaer Interest for the Land my Father directed I should pay for on the Farm Called the Gore —

The House David McCoy has built at the Turnpike bridge I am to pay for after which he is to allow me for Rent as much as the Interest of the money I pay with $15.00 — for the Lot —

The New Mill ought to be moved away, there are I think five good burr Stones in it which are valuable —

Ann joins me in Affectionate Remembrances to you and all with you And

Am Your Affectionate Brother
Pierre Van Cortlandt

Genl Ph.V.Cortlandt —

[Endorsed]
Octr.10.1816 —
brother Pierre
on his affairs
with his Sisters

[attached to previous letter]

James Sharrocks Lease for $150. per Annum.
$25. to be laid out in Stone Wall. This Lease

was conveyed by Sharrock to Millers by them to Belknaps & by them to John Mc.Coy. 6 or 7 Years unexpired — All the wood & timber is cut off	$125.00
Henry C Voght, Lease expired with my Fathers life — rent was $100 — per Annum half of which was to laid out in Stone wall —	50.00
Seth Conklin, Lease for my life	17.50
Nehemiah Horton Tenant at will very trifling rent I beleive five pounds per Annum	12.50
Old Abs. Cronk — $00.00 — his Father before him paid Nothing — his Sons Shameful wood theives	00.00
Abel Travis — Tenant at will as to give $25.00 but is so poor cannot pay any thing, when I get him off it ought to pay $50 after it was in repair	
David Mc. Coy — The House & farm Lewis Benedict had — $50 per year has had it three years & laid it out in Stone wall	$50.00
Turn pike Gate House	50.00
David McCoys Lot	15.00
Odells Farm was leased for three lives renewable at the expiration of either by paying $25.00. The Rent was $16. I purchased the Lease and have built two houses on it repaired the Barn with a New Roof and made several hundred Rods of Stone wall — My Father told me to purchase the Lease & gave it to me	
Joseph Hawes — The New House rented One half of it of my Father for $37.50 He alone occupies it — That House is a great Nuisance to me as the Person who ever occupies it is continually taking my wood and does me more injury than the rent is worth	
The Salisbury meadow —	
Only the ring is in my possession — Seth	

Conklin claims the right and has always. Cutt 5 Acres — and Sharrocks Lease wither 5 or 8 Acres — the remainder is very trifling — M[r] Terrel & Throgmorton served an Ejictment upon Wynants Park Monday, when they get it in possession it may be reclaimed & made valuable ——

14

Pierre Jr. to Timothy Pitkin.[1] ALS
HSP

Peekskill Nov[r]. 30–1816.

Dear Sir

John Paulding[2] who detected Major Andre as a spy has sent a Petition to Congress for an Increase of Pension, He is very poor and very infirm, has a numerous Family of small Children to support and his greatest dependance is the small pension awarded him by the Old Congress — I have written particularly to Gen[l]. Wilkins who will present the Petition & to Genl Smith of Maryland — If you think well of his petition I am confidant you will advocate it — & trully I do not know how he will support himself unless he obtains relief from Government — his farm is mortgaged to its value & I am informed there are several Executions against his personal property

I am with Esteem Your
Ob ser[t]
Pierre Van Cortlandt

Hon[ble]
Timothy Pitkin

---

1. Timothy Pitkin (1766–1847) was born in Farmington, Connecticut. Graduated from Yale in 1785, he was admitted to the bar in 1788 and commenced practice in Farmington. After

having served in the state legislature for several years, he was elected as a Federalist to the Ninth Congress and remained in that body until 1819. *Biographical Directory American Congress,* p. 1462; Reed, I, 428–429.

2. John Paulding (1758–1818) was one of the three captors of Major John André in 1780. The Van Cortlandts apparently had a special affection for him and sought to help him monetarily on a number of occasions. Paulding always seemed to be desperately short of funds. This petition led to an interesting interchange on the floor of Congress and in the newspapers concerning the merits of the case. In his petition Paulding declared that "he was one of the three persons who arrested Major John André, the Adjutant General of the British Army, during the Revolutionary War. That for his patriotic service they received the approbation of General Washington and the Congress, and also an annuity of two hundred dollars each. He states that he is now old, has a large family some of whom are infants; that he is very infirm, and incapable of hard labor." Paulding therefore requested Congress to "increase his allowance which he now has, or to grant him such further assistance as his faithful and patriotic services, and his infirmity and advanced age, may demand." *Annals of Congress,* Fourteenth Congress, 2nd Session, pp. 473–476; see also James W. Wilkin to Pierre, Jr., January 3, 1817 (No. 19), and Pierre's statements of January, 1817 (No. 21–23), and April 17, 1817 (No. 26).

15

Egbert Benson[1] to Philip. ALS
NYPL

New York Dec^{r}.3^{d}.1816 —

D^{r}. Sir,

I am preparing something like a Discourse for the Historical Society.[2] The Subject will chiefly be the Names of Places and I must request some Aid from Freinds in the way of Information — Did I understand you right that it was your Father's Opinion that <u>Croton</u> was an erroneous spelling of an Indian name proceeding from an erroneous pronunciation of it? — The Dutch Shippers formerly called the present Tellors Point, Sarah's Point — who was this Sarah? — Did you ever hear of a Blandina Bayard, an Indian Interpretess, as the Proprietor of it? — Will you let me hear from you as soon as conveniently may be?

Yours sincerely
Egb[t].Benson

[Addressed]
Gen[l]. Van Cortlandt
Croton River
WestChester County

[Endorsed]
Egbert Benson
Dec[r].3.18.6.
& answer. who
was Croton

---

1. See *VCFP,* II, 187, 202, 264–265, 444–445, 542–543.

2. Egbert Benson read a paper concerned with the place names of Indian, Dutch, English, and Spanish origin before the Historical Society of the State of New York on December 31, 1816. For Philip's reply to this letter, see No. 17.

In Benson's address, Philip's lengthy description of the origins of Croton was condensed to "the mispelling of the name of an Indian, probably the proprietor of the lands at the mouth of it." Of Teller's Point, he explained that the Indians had given it to William and Sarah Teller.

William Beauchamp described Croton as a "personal name applied to a place." Beauchamp also indicated that Blandina Bayard had bought several tracts of land in Rockland County in 1700. Egbert Benson, *Memoir Read Before the Historical Society of the State of New York,* 31st December 1816 (New York, 1817), pp. 13, 47; William M. Beauchamp, *Aboriginal Place Names of New York* (Albany, 1907), pp. 186–187, 245.

16

Samuel L. Mitchill[1] to Pierre, Jr. ALS
SHR

New York. 9th decr. 1816.

My dear sir

I have examined the animal specimen from your land of Anthony's Nose; and find it to be similar to several that, during the last summer, were found in digging a ditch on the south side of Staten island. In my opinion, they have belonged to an animal well known to veterinary surgeons. The Equus caballus[2] of the Naturalists, was the former proprietor of the Tooth. The individual probably ended his days on the mountain, and during the age of his vigour might have been a fleet & mettlesome Steed.

This may be truly called the age of inquiry. We are daily becoming better and better acquainted with our Country. The Sand Stone of Nyack [in] Rockland, overlays [torn] of eight feet, a stratum [containing?] the broken bones of Land animals. The Neversunk Hills in Monmouth County New Jersey are underlaid by the remains of Quadrupeds & marine creatures not now known to be alive. Of these, a Crocodile, an Elephant & a Rhinoceros, are some.

I have just finished a Memoir on these extinct animals; which I suppose that I have evidence to prove were at least twenty in number, I have no doubt there are many more; and that I am but beginning the extensive inquiry.

Geology will receive great aid from the facts disclosed in the Predrift[3] regions of North America. But they, as well as antiquarians must beware that they mistake not the Barber's labor for the [torn].

Adieu, my dear Sir. be assured of my goodwill & thanks.

Saml. L. Mitchill

[Addressed]
Col. Pierre Van Cortlandt Albany
(to be forwarded by Judge Miller)

---

1. Physician, teacher, naturalist, writer, lawyer, and politician, Samuel L. Mitchill (1764–1831) was a true disciple of the Enlightenment. While the Van Cortlandts and Mitchill may not always have agreed on political issues (he had supported Aaron Burr), they recognized him as an outstanding figure in contemporary New York society and as a man of science. Mitchill's study of New York City, published in 1807 under the title *The Picture of New-York; or The Traveller's Guide through the Commercial Metropolis of the United States,* served as the butt for Washington Irving's *A History of New York* (1809). Mitchill is alleged to have declared: "I know Great Britain from the Grampian Hills to the chalky cliffs of Dover; there is no need of my going to Europe, Europe now comes to me." Stanley T. Williams, *The Life of Washington Irving* (New York, 1935), I, 110–111.

2. The *equus caballus* was the ancestor of the horse.

3. Mitchill referred to the pre-glacial period in North America.

17

Philip to Egbert Benson. **ADFS**
NYPL

Dec[r].14.1816.

D[r]. Sir

Your favor of the 3[d]. was not received untill the 12th. Evening or I should have done myself the pleasure to have answered it before —

Croton wether properly Spelled or not I cannot assertain as I never heard my Fathers or any other persons opinion on that subject but supposed him to have been an Indian Chief and that he resided on the River near Tide Water[1] mostly on the flat lands near Sholes of Rapids where in the proper Seasons was taken large Quantities of Shad and Herren[2] and in the Hills find Vennison and other wild Game[.]it is also Supposed that he and his Tribe occasionly resided on kicktawonk Point which formed the Northwestly Penensula of Kicktawonk Bay or mouth of Croton river where they procured in its Vicinity mostly oysters as the Banks of Shells on the Point are a Sufficient Evidence[.]they had also in the Bay wild fowl in abundance Brant Geese and Ducks as well as fish in great plenty[.]The south Easterly-Side of the Bay was Called Parmirsink and Seperated from Singsink by a Brook of water all in the Vicinity of the Confluence of the waters of the Croton and Hudson Rivers, the Indians called the Bay Kicktawonk on account of the abundance of wild fowl freqenting it[.]This Information I rec^{d}. before the revolutionary War from one of the first white ~~when a youth partlygrow~~ Inhabitants of Parmirsink Francis Basley when he was near one hundred years old — it is also probable that the said Indian Chief Croton with his Family and Tribe from their affluent situation abounding in Luxurious Plenty were at times Obliged to Defend themselves against Hostile tribes of Indians who attempted to supplant them, for there is yet the remains of a Fortified Work of Earth made on my land as you advance toward the point in a Commanding Situation being flanked by a Salt Marsh on one Side and a Swamp on the Other[.] and as Evidence of Battles ~~have there taken place~~ Several graves some of large dementions and Hight was found near the work as well as Stone Harpoons for Points of arrows —

W^{m}. Tellor and Sarah his wife obtained permission from the Indians to Settle on the point and became Indian traders they it is Supposed made a purchace ~~and procured an Indian deed~~ on the Decease of Wil^{m}. his Widow Sarah Continued to reside and carry'd on the Trade not only with the indians but also as occasion presented Intertained the name of Sarah's Point — Two of her Sons John and Jacobus resided there after her Decease ~~in the days of my youth~~ as I well remember —

As for the Indian Interpretess you mention Blandina Bayard there might have been such a person but I have no knowledge thereof

[Addressed]
Hon[ble]. Egbert Benson
N.York

[in the hand of Philip]

Indian names for certain places in the Manor of Cortlandt as laid down on a map of the same made [by] Philip Verplank.

The Croton river was called	Kightewank
The Elbow near Bluetown	Keivightekwack
The Kiskow was called	Peuighting
The Titicus " "	Matigkticoos
Salsburg Island was called	Wanakawaghkin
Snakehole creek " "	Kenkapagh
The creek South of Snake hole	Assinapink

---

1. The Kitchawancs (Kitchawans, Kitchawaughs, Kicktawans) belonged to the Wappinger Confederacy of Algonquins. Their habitat extended from the region of Poughkeepsie south to New York Bay. No one is quite certain as to the origin of the name "Croton." Philip may have been right in believing that it derived from the name of an Indian chieftain.

   The Kitchawancs established a fortified village on Croton Point, a site they designated *Senasqua.* Many relics have been unearthed on Croton Point and within the current village of Croton-on-Hudson. Marian F. Graves, *Wampum Strings of the Kitchawancs* (Croton, N.Y., 1952), *passim.*

2. The Hudson River contained an abundance of fish. Among the varieties found were "anadromous fishes, which live in salt water but spawn in fresh, such as shad and herring, striped bass, sea sturgeon, and tomcod." Robert H. Boyle, *The Hudson River: A Natural and Unnatural History* (New York, 1969), pp. 109–111.

18

Philip to William Delanoy. ADS
SHR

January 1, 1817.

This Indenture made the first Day of January 1817 Between Philip Van Cortlandt of the Town of Cortlandt County of Westchester & State of New York Esqr. of the first part and William DeLanoy of the Town of Mount Pleasant County and State aforesaid of the Second part. Witnesseth That the said party of the first part for and in Consideration of the Rents and Covenants hereafter mentioned hath Leased unto the said party of the Second part and his Heirs all that fishing place Situate on the Hudsons River extending from the Land in the possession of Robert Underhill to the Old Dock near the House William A Lent has in possession for Seven years from the date hereof and the prevelidge to Cut Alder poles in the Swamps adjoining to dry his nets, and may pick up old wood in and about the said Swamps to burn in the Stoves, and may put up another Fish House which he may take away at the End of the Term The one already built is to be kept in repair and he so to leave it on the ground it being the property of the Said Philip he having paid for the materials of which it is built. And the Said William DeLanoy hereby promisses and binds himself and his heirs to pay the said Philip his Heirs or Assigns during Each fishing Season One Eighth part of all the fish which shall be taken by himself and the people fishing under him or his heirs Either in fish or the Value thereof in money, And ingages that at least one Seine shall fish during Every fishing season or this lease to be Void — And that Two Seines Shall fish Every Season unless it shall so happen that hands cannot be procured to fish with the Second Seine[1] — In witness whereof we have hereunto Set our hands & Seals the day and Year first above written —

Sealed and delivored
in the presents of
Ph G Van Wyck
Robert Height [?]

Ph. V. Cortlandt
William Delanoy

---

1. Fishing on the Hudson River was important from the time of the early Indian settlers to the current day. Shad was the most important catch. Robert Boyle declares that "In the mid 1880s, records show the fishery in relative decline. Then, toward the end of the nineteenth century, shad again became abundant; in 1889, the catch from the Hudson was 4,332,000 pounds, the all-time record." Fishermen primarily used a large net or seine, floated vertically in the water between "shad poles." When the net was drawn in it contained a multitude of shad, herring, carp, etc. The Van Cortlandts were traditionally entitled to a share of the fish taken from the rivers and streams adjoining their properties. Robert H. Boyle, *The Hudson River: A Natural and Unnatural History* (New York, 1969), pp. 111–112.

19

James W. Wilkin to Pierre, Jr. ALS
SHR

Washington Janr[y] 3rd 1817.

D[r] Sir

In answer to your letter relative to the Petitions of Paulding[1] I inform you that the Petition has been in the House of Representatives referrd to the Committee on Pensions and Revolutionary Claims — The Committee have not yet reported but by what I can learn from the Chairman the report will be against the Petition[.] M[r] Pitkin has endeavored with me to get a different report I fear however without success[.] What the house will do I can not say[.] We shall try to leave the report laid on the table so that when we are ready we can call it up —

I have no particular news to write you[.] the House is now engaged on a Report of the Committee of Elections on a Contested election between M[r] Easton & M[r] Scott from the Missouri Territory M[r] Scott is the sitting member[2]

I would be pleased to hear from you often on a subject you and I have always agreed on I want to know how Matters looks; whether for or against our views — And who is the most prominent Character to be opposed to our friend[.] I would like to hear from you at least twice a week after our Legislature meets.[3]

It is settled that Governor Tompkins will resign after the 3[d] March next & also give a previous notice of that intention as soon as he knows officially that he is to be [Vice] Presd[t] of the U.S.

We are engaged in the Ordinary business of Legislation — in haste

I am very respectfully your Humble Serv[t]
Jas,W,Wilkin

[Addressed]
The honble. Pierre Van Cortland
Albany —

---

1. See Pierre's letter of November 30, 1816 (No. 14).

2. Rufus Easton petitioned Congress for the right to be regarded as the delegate from the Missouri Territory in lieu of incumbent John Scott. Easton charged that the voting procedure in one district was illegal and, therefore, he was entitled to the seat. After a protracted debate, the House on January 4 moved to recommit Easton's petition to the Committee on Elections. The issue came before the House again on January 10, at which time it voted to declare the Missouri election invalid and the delegate's seat vacant for that term. *Niles' Weekly Register,* January 11, 1817, p. 334; January 18, 1817, p. 350. See also *VCFP,* III, 400.

3. Wilkin was concerned over the issue of the New York gubernatorial post. With Tompkins's impending resignation from that office to assume the vice presidency, the advocates of De-Witt Clinton became extremely active. Wilkin and the Van Cortlandts supported Clinton. Alexander, I, 247–248.

20

James W. Wilkin to Pierre, Jr. ALS
NYPL

Washington Jan^{ry} 8th 1817.

Dear Sir

I take the liberty to enclose to your care a letter to my friend Major James Faulkner of the Assembly of New York[1] it is on the Subject of who shall be our next Governour presuming that Govr. Thompkins will resign — I do not know the views of Major Faulkner on that subject he is a personal friend of mine & I hope he is favorable to our mutual friend — he is from orange is a plane but a sensible well informed Orange County farmer I mistake the man much if he is not to be depended on what wise course he may take on this Interesting Subject — I have requested an immediate answer to my letter I hope it will be Satisfactory I wish you to have my letter delivered to him on the first or second day of the Session I did intend to have seen him before I left home but I could not in that case we should have had an understanding on the subject of who shall be our next Governour.

I would be pleased if you would freely communicate with me on the Subject let me know the prospect of Success in procuring a nomination in the old & what we have always called the regular way.[2]

I hope our friends will act prudently and not be led away by pretentions & specious shews of friendship when none is meant or intended. Our friend has Subtle and powerful adversaries if I am well informed. — To meet and defeat these means much Wisdom & prudence is necessary to be alluded to. I am not well informed of the popular sentiment in the State but I believe that if M[r] C can get an equal start he will out run any man in the state who may be Opposed to him in the contest.

I have made the above Observations to commence a correspondence, which I hope you are willing to become one of the parties I will be unhappy if I do not hear every day or two what is going on at Albany I mean particular as incident to the nomination of a Candidate for Governor in haste

I am your friend & very humble Serv[t]
Jas, W, Wilkin

Pierre Van Cortland

[Addressed]

Free

Gen[l] Pierre Van Cortland
Albany

---

1. James Faulkner sat in the Fortieth Session of the state Assembly as a representative from Orange County. Werner, p. 331.

2. In March, 1817, Governor Daniel D. Tompkins was scheduled to become Vice President. The burning question in New York concerned the choice of his successor in the gubernatorial position. Martin Van Buren was the leading political force behind Tompkins in New York and he had no intention of losing control even though his protégé was moving up to a higher office.

   If the traditional Republican caucus had been followed, in which only Republicans sitting in the state legislature had the power to decide upon a party candidate, Van Buren's handpicked man would have been successful. His opponents proposed that all districts be represented, whether they had representatives in the legislature or not, in a general Republican state convention wherein all would have a voice in choosing a candidate. This gave rise to the concept of a state convention replacing the caucus.

DeWitt Clinton was the leading candidate of the anti-Van Buren wing of the New York Republicans. Clinton, then in the process of gaining state approval for his Erie Canal project, was painted by the Van Buren forces, including Tammany, as a secret Federalist who would prove to be a Republican Judas. Despite the combined efforts of Tammany and Van Buren, the convention chose Clinton as their candidate, and he went on to win overwhelmingly in the election. Alexander, I, 247–251; Hammond, I, 437–438.

21

Pierre, Jr.: Statement Concerning John Paulding. ADf
SHR

[January 21, 1817.]

Dr Sir

In overlooking the National Intelligencer I was extremely mortified to see the violent Philippic of Col Talmadge on the floor of Congress against John Paulding,[1] It is very strange that He Mr Tallmadge did not make this late communication 38 years since, but he does not profess to know any thing of the capture personally and relies upon his Memory for the conversation of Major Andre and his opinion of the men, who had withstood his offered bribe — I will not say Mr Tallmadge has wantonly traduced those three Patriots, yet I do say his remarks were ill timed and without that colour of proof which I should rely upon If I did not personally know the contrary I should not interested myself in this application; I have heard the story of the capture from Paulding 30 years ago and and repeatedly since and it was always uniform and never contradictory — Paulding was taken a prisoner by the British three times during the revolution. four Days before this capture he was a prisoner in the north church at New York, he leaped the fence one evening and got out of the city the next evening he crossed the North River in a small canoe near Bulls ferry from whence he went to our Army lying in the Neighboorhood of Tappan, recrossed the River at Verplancks point and immediately on his arrival at Crumpound in the manor of Cortland went with a party below to annoy the Refugees so called: Near Tarry town him and his two Collegues Van Wart & Williams detected Major Andre upon their stopping him (Andre) He asked them to what party they belonged, Paulding who was dressed in a British uniform coat which his freinds in New York had purchased for him to favor his desertion, answered, below my Dress shows that, Andre taken by surprise mentioned that he also belonged to the Lower party and was urgent to go on and not to be detained, Paulding replied if he was convinced that he belonged to the Lower party, He might pass but until he had assurances of that fact, he would detain him, to satisfy them he told them that He was a British Officer and that he had a plan of Fort west point and all its dependencies. Then it was they undecieved him, upon which Andre shewed them Arnolds pass, and said that he had only mentioned his being a british officer as a finesse least they might have belonged to the British army; They then took him to a piece of woods and examined him & in his Boots the papers were found; When Andre found himself detected he made offers to them to give them any Sum of money they would demand which offered bribe convinced them of the importance of his character and that he was a spy, They immediately took him to Col Jameson's at whose Quarters they arrived in the night and delivered him to Jameson with the detected papers — A few days afterwards General Washington sent for these three valuable men and showed them every mark of attention at Head Quarters, If they had been those depraved fellows

[a continuation has not been found]

---

1. To whom Pierre addressed this philippic remains unclear. He had been corresponding with Congressman James W. Wilkin concerning John Paulding's petition, but the tone of the letter

implies that it may have been in the nature of a "letter to the editor."

Benjamin Tallmadge (1754–1835), Revolutionary War officer and head of Washington's secret service, educator, businessman, and congressman, delivered a scathing attack on the floor of Congress in opposition to John Paulding's request for an increase in his pension. He asserted that Paulding, along with the other two captors of Major John André, had acted more from mercenary motives than from patriotic fervor. Tallmadge asserted that he was then commanding the advance guard of the American line when Major André was brought in disguised as "John Anderson," and that it was he who recognized that "Anderson" had a military bearing. Tallmadge declared that he remained with André until the latter's execution, and during that time André declared to Tallmadge that the only reason the three captors turned him over to American authorities was because he could not pay the amount of the bribe they sought for his release.

This attack by Tallmadge against the revered trio of captors launched a massive newspaper campaign to defend the reputations of Paulding, David Williams, and Isaac Van Wart. Pierre rushed into the fray and prepared a number of statements in support of Paulding (see also Nos. 22, 23, and 26.) Despite the furor, Paulding's request was denied.

As late as 1822 Tallmadge still felt it necessary to defend his earlier statement made on the floor of Congress. In a letter to Timothy Pickering dated September 17, 1822, Tallmadge declared that his remarks were "occasioned by a proposition to increase the pensions of *Paulding, Williams & Van Vert.* Knowing the Circumstances which related to the Capture of Major André, I felt it to be my Duty to state some facts, that the House might act accordingly on the occasion." Henry P. Johnston, ed., *Memoir of Colonel Benjamin Tallmadge* (New York, 1904), pp. 136–137; *DAB*, XVIII, 284–285; *Annals of Congress*, Fourteenth Congress, 2nd Session, pp. 473–476.

22

Pierre, Jr.: Statement Concerning John Paulding. ADf
SHR

Albany Jany. 22–1817—

Dear Sir

I wrote you yesterday immediately after I had read the calumny pronounced by Tallmadge on the floor of Congress against one of the most virtuous Patriots which this or any other country can boast of—What could have induced Tallmadge to utter those things is to me astonishing. If he had detailed the villanous conduct of the Smugglers and the robbing of the Inhabitants of Long Island during the Revolution he might have exposed some characters which now are from the situation they are placed called honorable men, But his relation I much doubt in every point of view, He says that Andre was not [out] of his sight from the time those young men delivered him up until the time of his Execution; They surrendered him to Col. Jameson and I think Capt. Hoogland had the charge of him to take to Head Quarters, but whether or not—Colonel Hamilton was with Andre Repeatedly if not all the time he was at Tappan, Andre would sooner confer with Hamilton, a pleasant intelligent sensible man who stood so high in the estimation of the Commander in Chief than with a Man little known in the Army either from his Talents as a Man of Letters or from any Services he had rendered his Country by his military Exploits, and if Andre had entertained that Opinion of these men He no doubt would have mentioned it to Hamilton & he to the Commander in Chief who then was paying them every Attention at Head Quarters—A general indignation is excited against Tallmadge in this city, and I suppose it is universal, it ought to be for this wanton abuse of men whom the whole United States have honored from their Patriotism, perhaps M^{r}. Tallmadge as his politic consequence is at End with the present Session of Congress wishes to leave something behind him not to be forgotten, and has taken this method to shew his patriotism to prevent an Old Man infirm and poor from receiving the just rewards of Merit[.] He took care of himself; by voting for the Compensation bill, proving that he was a lover of money,

But a fact which but from the violent attack of those three patriotic young men on the floor of Congress by Benjamin Tallmadge a representative from Connecticut might have remained a secret deserves to be told, which is this — That when Andre was delivered to Colonel Jameson by the Captures, Major Tallmadge (now the Honorable Benjamin Tallmadge a representative in Congress) urged the propriety of sending Andre immediately to Arnold, but Paulding who is represented by the Hon. Mr. Tallmadge as every thing which is base & mean remonstrated against it as a very improper act and advised not to let Arnold know any thing of the transaction until General Washington was apprised of it — notwithstanding all this Major Tallmadge did send a Dragoon Express to Arnold apprising him of the Event which information gave Arnold time to escape —

23

Pierre, Jr.: Statement Concerning John Paulding. ADf
SHR

[ca. January, 1817.]

John Paulding is of a very respectable family in the County of West Chester, He was taken Prisoner by the British three times during the Revolutionary War, Four days before he detected Major Andre he was a Prisoner in the North Church in the City of New York — The Prisoners were permitted by squads to walk in the yard, One evening just before the time of locking them up for the night, he watched his opportunity when the centinels back was towards him to leap the fence into the Yard of an Adjacent House from which he repaired to the House of a freind who secreted him for that night, purchased him a British uniform to favor his escape out of the city which he effected the following evening by crossing the Hudson in a small canoe from Bloomingdale to the Jersey shore and early the next morning found himself with our Army which were posted at the English Neighbourhood and at Tappan — He recrossed the Hudson at Verplancks Point and on his arrival at Crumpond in the Manor of Cortlandt joined a Party going below on a scout — When near Tarry Town in the manor of Philipsburgh these three young men took post on the Post roads to intercept marauding parties of the British —

The capture of Andre is detailed pretty accurately in Marshalls life of Washington which no doubt Judge Marshall must have found among General Washingtons papers, and the exalted character given by General Hamilton of those three young men who captured Andre in a Letter to his friend at the very time of the transaction must be conclusive of their disinterested patriotism — Hamilton was with Andre the greater part of his confinement, and it is highly presumable that Andre would sooner communicate his sentiments and opinion to him who was the accomplished scholar, the amiable and polished Gentleman in his manners, and endowed with so much wisdom and merited the confidence of the great Washington — rather than to a man little known in the army either for his Talents or for any services he had rendered his country by his military exploits, — If Andre had entertained that Opinion of those young men, no doubts he would have mentioned it to Hamilton, & he certainly would have communicated it to the Commander in Chief who was then paying them every Attention at Head Quarters, and dining them at his Table, indeed the Major Generals of our Army, Greene, Baron Steuben, Knox, La Fayette, &c &c were vying with each other who should have the honor of entertaining them — These were facts notorious at that day —

Tallmadge could have given a better narrative of the Arts practiced in smuggling British Goods within our Lines and the wanton depredations committed on the defenceless Inhabitants of Long Island — The Regiment to which he belonged was stationed the greater part of the war along the Sound and gave him an opportunity to know something of those transactions —

Paulding has fifteen living children, is very poor and so infirm owing to a fit of the Palsy some years since and other complaints as render him unfit for manual labor — One of his Sons, Hiram, was a midshipman with Commodore M^c.Donnough in the memorable action on Lake Champlain — and although only seventeen years old behaved with the utmost Gallantry and received three small wounds during the engagement —

[NB.] The British uniform Paulding procured to favor his escape from NYork, he wore the day he took Andre & which in a great measure deceived Andre —

24

Pierre, Jr. to William Miller.[1] ALS
SHR

Albany March 5, 1817.

William Miller

I wrote you a Letter which I intended to send by W. B. Howard but he went before the time he had appointed — I have Nothing particular to mention more than I told you when at home — I wish you to take Care that the Gammons are not smoked too much, better not enough than too much — be carefull of the Grain; and the potatoes which are in the Cellar had better be fed to the Hogs, I hope Mr Soper has made the Cutting Box — The Carriage Horses had better not be fed with Grain until the first of April — I fear the little Lambs have suffered from the extreme Cold — Nests ought to be made in the fowl house for the hens — Rails we shall want & wood at the Door — I wish you to measure the length of the Phaeton in Red Coach House that is from Spring to Spring–(   ) that I may have a Body made here — I shall return home with the first Steam Boat — Mrs Van Cortlandt is very Well and little Pierre tolerable he has had a very sore face and has now a Cold — He talks almost every thing

I will write you again in a day or two

Your Assured freind   Pierre Van Cortlandt

---

1. William Miller was the overseer of the Peekskill estate and appears frequently in Pierre's correspondence.

25

Stephen Van Rensselaer to Pierre, Jr. ALS
SHR

NewYork April 5th 1817.

My dear Sir

Accept my thanks for your friendly communication the Martlen men rediculed the idea of M^{r}. Clintons nomination & could not believe it till it was pronounced publickly[1] — I feel relievd from the state of suspense — I hope his administration will be the mean[s] of healing party animosities & promoting the public weal —
Present my regards to all our friends —

With Sincerity
Yours &c
SVRensselaer

[Addressed]
Genl. Pierre Van Cortlandt
Albany

---

1. See James W. Wilkin to Pierre, Jr., January 8, 1817 (No. 20). "Martlen men" is a reference to the so-called Martling Men, an anti-Clinton faction that customarily met at Abraham Martling's New York City tavern.

26

Pierre, Jr.: Statement Concerning John Paulding. ADf
SHR

April 16–1817

John Paulding in the year 1780 was a Sergeant under Lieutenant Peacock who was stationed with his Corps at Daniel Requa's on the Road leading from Tarry Town to Bedford, That Command was stationed on the Lines to protect the Inhabitants against the marauding Parties of the British Cow Thieves, and was in pay either from the State of New York or United States. That Lieutenant Peacocks Command at that place was between thirty and forty men — That early one morning they were surprised and attacked by Captain Totten with upwards of one hundred of the British Refugee Dragoons — That John Paulding with about twenty men of Peacocks Corps were taken Prisoner, some very much wounded besides that number old Daniel Requa & Thomas Dean — were also taken Prisoners and Daniel Requa very badly wounded, That John Paulding and the other Prisoners were immediately marched to New York and confined in the North Church — That John Paulding remained a Prisoner in the North Church about three months when he made his escape from the yard in Rear of the Church over a board fence while the Hessian Centinels back who was stationed there was towards him, into the yard of an Adjacent house, He was observed by a Black woman who favored his Escape into the Street; He then went to Nathaniel Leviness his friend who lived near the Jail, who furnished Paulding with some provisions and recommended to him to keep out of the Road as much as possible to Bloomingdale where he might see a small boat to get across the River, That Paulding followed his advice and went on near Bloomingdale where he espied a small boat aground — That he went in the Bushes and took a nap until the Tide rose high enough to float her, That just in the Dusk of the Evening he got in the Boat and paddled across the Hudson River and landed some where near Bulls ferry on the Jersey Shore — that He Then made the best of his way to the American Camp which were stationed in the English Neighbourhood, was carried to the Commanding Officer (whom he thinks was the Marquis De lafayette[)] who gave him a pass to return to West Chester County, That he travelled up and recrossed the Hudson River at West Point and went directly to Haight now Somers Town Plain in the Manor of Cortlandt — That Paulding was very anxious to see his mother who was then living at the House of old Peter Paulding at the Saw Mill River about three miles East of Tarry Town on the Road leading to the White Plains That his father was fearful to remain below and then resided in the manor of Cortlandt & shortly after moved his mother up — That Paulding and six others marched down from the manor of Cortlandt to Daniel Requas the Place where he had been taken Prisoner, That they heard of number of Horses being stole at Poughkeepsie and they divided their Party to intercept the Theives, if they should pass on to NYork four of the Party stationed themselves at old William Davids Esqr. on the Hill & the other three Paulding Van Wert and Williams stationed themselves along the Post roads at a small brook just above Tarry town in the Bushes — This was he thinks fourth days after he had escaped from the North Church

27

Commission of Pierre, Jr. as Major General of the 11th Militia Division. ADS

SHR

August 26, 1817.

The People of the State of New-York, by the Grace of God Free and Independent:

TO Pierre Van Cortlandt Esquire GREETING:

WE, reposing especial trust and confidence, as well in your patriotism, conduct and loyalty, as in your integrity and readiness to do us good and faithful service, HAVE appointed and constituted, and by these Presents DO appoint and constitute you the said Pierre Van Cortlandt Major General of the Eleventh Division of Infantry of our said State with rank from the 8th. day of July 1816. — You are therefore to take the said Division — into your care, as Major General thereof, and the Officers and Soldiers of that Division — are hereby commanded to obey and respect you as their Major General and you are also to observe and follow such orders and directions as you shall from time to time receive from our General and Commander in Chief of the Militia of our said State, or any other your superior officer, according to the Rules and Discipline of War, in pursuance of the trust reposed in you; and for so doing this shall be your Commission, for and during our good pleasure, to be signified by our Council of Appointment.

IN TESTIMONY WHEREOF, We have caused our Seal for Military Commissions to be hereunto affixed: WITNESS our trusty and well-beloved DeWitt Clinton Esquire, — Governor of our said State, General and Commander in Chief of all the Militia, and Admiral of the Navy of the same, by and with the advice and consent of our said Council of Appointment, at our City of Albany, the 26th–day of August in the year our Lord one thousand eight hundred and Seventeen and in the 42^{d}. year of our Independence.

DeWitt Clinton

Passed the Secretary's Office, the
29 day of August 1817
Arch^{d}. Campbell Dep. Secretary.

[Endorsed]
State of New York
Secretary's office —

I certify that Pierre Van Cortland within named was this day qualified according to law

Chas. D. Cooper Secretary

Albany 30th Augt. 1817

28

Elijah Crawford[1] to Pierre, Jr. ALS
SHR

September 17, 1817.

Dear Sir

You will be good enough to pardon me for Not Answering your request sooner, I rec^{d}. your letter in Court time with a bundle of other papers, & had it some time before I knew it or Opened it, had I have known it sooner I would have sent you some word respecting the same from Court.

I have now got through the press of business and am at liberty to give you a Statement — as you See above there was real difficulties to surmount in this town as well as in many Others, my republican friends reprobated my Naming M^{r}. D. Clinton as Governor, I answer^{d} them — the Nomination is a regular one Such as we have always contended for and thought our Selves in duty bound to Support, then I was told he is No republican, See the Accounts in the public prints, I answer^{d}. the public prints I was in the habbit of reading and was well satisfied that instead of being orricles [oracles] of Truth I found them Vehicles of Slander, my friends then determined to have me displaced as soon as the Counsel met, But I determined to do as I thought best, for I never could believe that Mr. Clinton was a Tory, or any of the Name belonging to that family[.]I told them that the Name of Clinton was dear to every friend to his country, — with Sentiments of respect — I am yours

Elijah Crawford

[Attached to previous letter]

West Chester County Election. 1817 —	Governor	Lt Governor	P.B. Porter	P.A. Jay	Barnum	J. Dayton (State Senator)	A. Odell (State Senator)	C.S. Riggs (State Senator)
W Plains	2	6	15	13	17	17		
Yonkers		38	38		37	37		
M Pleasant	68	94	28		93	94	3	3
Scarsedale	2	7	3		8	8		
Cortlandt	39	30	19		63	62	43	43
N Rochelle	5	21	17		19	19		
Greenburgh	47	46	25		28	28		
East Chester	5	25	31		27	27		
South Salem	38	36			33	33		
New Castle	28				1	1		
North Castle	25	39	40		39	39		
North Salem	6	50	1		52	52		
Mamaroneck		11	12		2	2		
Rye	18	20	14		17	17		
Bedford	90	35	5		32	33		
Harrison	10	37	31		31	31		
Poundridge	53	23			9	9		
York Town	31	14	1		26	26	33	41
Somers	36	10	1		19	17	55	53
West Chester	1	8	6		23	23		
Pelham	1	3	3		3	3		
	506	563	295		579	578		

P. VanCortlandt Esquire
Wplains. September 17th 1817

[Addressed]
Pierre VanCortlandt Esquire
Cortlandt Town

State Assemblyman							
Barker	Requa	Isaacs	Wallace	Anderson	Grison	Ward	Read
37	33	35	17	21	18		
8	8	7	45	45	45		
133	215	33	18	23		202	1
4	2	2	10	9	9		
76	75	68	94	96	96	24	24
27	25	27	24	23	23		
77	80	62	26	25	22	1	
17	13	17	30	33	30		
63	59	61	36	33	34		
47	37	36	1	2		11	
61	56	60	47	48	54		
7	6	6	65	69	63	1	
16	16	16	13	13	13		
30	26	29	28	31	26		
177	170	182	39	51	52		
22	4	13	33	56	38		2
54	66	47	40	32	35		
45	40	36	23	31	28	2	1
82	82	57	22	22	15	2	
19	18	18	35	34	35		
6	5	5	1	1	1		
1008	1036	817	657	698	633		

---

1. Serving as clerk of Westchester County, Elijah Crawford felt compelled to defend his support of DeWitt Clinton in the state gubernatorial election. Of interest is his inclusion of the election returns from the county. They demonstrate that Clinton and his running mate, John Tayler, outpolled the Tammany candidate, Peter B. Porter, almost two to one. The other candidates sought seats in the State Legislature. Stephen Barnum and Jonathan Dayton were elected to the Senate, while William Barker, Benjamin Isaacs and William Requa became Assemblymen. Hammond, I, 443–444. See James W. Wilkin to Pierre, Jr., January 8, 1817 (No. 20).

29

Eliza Treat[1] to Ann (Stevenson) Van Cortlandt. ALS
SHR

Albany October 28th 1817 —

My dear Friend,

I would have performed my promise before of giving you a particular account of Margaret and Pierre from the time you left them if I had not been prevented by unfortunately hurting my foot the very morning you went in consequence of which I have been obliged to stay at home untill this morning — I prevailed on Margaret to spend Thursday afternoon with me and was delighted with her behaviour she was as cheerful and looked as well as I have ever seen her — I am inclined to think that if she was among strangers entirely she would soon recover; because the constant anxiety which her relations express about her situation prevents her thoughts from taking another course, — if she was with strangers she would be obliged to talk upon indifferent subjects and her mind would be insensibly brought back to its natural state — she was not so lively this morning as I expected to find her but Catharine says she appears in a different character in the company of her <u>spouse elect</u>

which proves that she can be cheerful if she will only endeavor to be so[2] — Mrs Stevenson desired me to give her love to you and say that Pierre is a very good child — he is very little trouble to her — extravagantly fond of Catharine who understands managing as well as his mother — she is very attentive to him both night and day — I cannot flatter you by telling you how anxious he is to see you for strange as it may seem he has not asked for you at all, indeed he is so engaged with his horses and little Jack that he would not even speak to me — Whenever the weather is fine I will urge Margaret to walk with me and try to make her visit more than she has done. — My love to Mr. Van Courtlandt Marg. sends her love to you.

your affectionate friend Eliza

[Addressed]
Mrs Ann Van Cortlandt
Care of Gen. Pierre Van Courtlandt
Peekskill

---

1. Eliza (Elizabeth) Treat (1795–) was the daughter of Richard S. and Gertrude (Stringer) Treat. Her father served as a county judge, grand juror, and Albany alderman. Munsell, *Annals,* VIII, 146, 148.

2. Margaret Stuyvesant, the daughter of Petrus and Margaret (Livingston) Stuyvesant, neither recovered from her mysterious illness nor married her suitor, as she would die soon after the date of this letter. See No. 32.

30

Pierre, Jr., to William Miller. ALS
SHR

Coxsacki[1] Nov. 14 [1817?]

Wm Miller

On friday Evening We arrived safe at Albany — this morning I learnt that the Sloop was at this place & have rode down here — the slaying as fine as ever I saw it — to morrow the Sloop will be at Albany — I have only time to mention that I think it will be best for you to get all the Corn cut up & draw it in the Barn then it can be husked at leisure — take care of everything from freezing as well as you can — I shall be down next week Tell Soper that I will exact from him at least his Horse & Waggon his slay & Boat —

Your freind in
haste I am first
returning to Albany
Pierre Van Cortlandt

[Addressed]
Mr William Miller
PeeksKill

---

1. Pierre was writing from Coxsackie, a small hamlet on the west bank of the Hudson River just south of Albany.

31

Pierre, Jr. to William Miller. ALS
SHR

Albany Novem^{r}. 18, 1817.

Mr Wm Miller

I intended to have left Here this morning with the Steam Boat, but the rain is so great that I deferred it until Thursday next, when I will return home with the Chancellor, if the Weather is very Calm and clear you may let Jesse meet me at the Landing (Mrs Hunters) about Nine O Clock at night should I not be there before ten he need not wait. but come down the next morning — He had better come down with the Gig — I wish you would see that the Grape Vines in the Garden are covered first with Straw and then with ground to keep them from freezing —

Mrs Van Cortlandt is yet quite distressed at Margarets death — Pierre is very well —

I am your freind
[torn] Cortlandt

[Addressed]
Mr William Miller
at Gen Van Cortlandts
PeeksKill N.Y.

32

Nancy Jay[1] to Ann (Stevenson) Van Cortlandt. ALS
SHR

Bedford 19th of Nov. 1817.

However appearances have been against me, & may lead to a supposition that I had forgotten an early friendship, be assured dear Ann, I have never heard with indifference of any circumstance or event which would promote your happiness, or of the many & various afflictions with which you have been visited, without participating in your feelings — The weakness of my eyes has several times prevented my writing, when otherwise it would have been a pleasure — Now they are better & in the hope that you may derive satisfaction from considering yourself remembered & loved by an old friend, sharing in your feelings, & wishing to contribute to your consolation, willingly renew our long neglected intercourse — & rejoice that the same comforts which have supported me in trouble, have long been yours — At the same never-failing source, we have both sought, & found our chief happiness — Amidst your bereavements, may you be duly sensible of your blessings, among them, how great is that of knowing that those of your family from whom death has separated you for the present, had each chosen the paths of virtue & piety — & however painful to be parted for this life, you have a well grounded hope to meet again in that which is to come, where change & sorrow can never enter — Poor Margaret's death was no less regretted than unexpected.[2] A Mysterious Providence certainly wise, but beyond our comprehension — To her might be applied those beautiful lines of Young. "Early, bright, transient, chaste as morning dew, She sparkled, was exhal'd, & went to heav'n"[3] —

It is the assurance that she is there & that it was the will of her Heavenly Father to call her hence, that can alone reconcile you to her departure — your loss is her certain gain — To be also ready will be our wisdom — To her death at any time had lost his string — how dreadful to many to be summoned so suddenly —

Much care may now devolve upon you, & I am anxious to know if you will not find it necessary to reside with your sisters family — You must now look back with peculiar satisfaction to that devoted attention to them, which could not fail to excite in them a filial affection for you — we sympathize with your excellent mother — in her old age troubles have multiplied — But it is a comfort & encouragement to see how those who trust in God are supported through all — & are enabled to say "Thy will be done" — A rest remains for his people & many & precious are the promises they live on by the way — Please to remember me very affec^{ly}. to her —

26th I was interrupted by the arrival of an old friend of papa's & being prevented before the post went, from making an apology which I deemed necessary, for not visiting you last summer postponed sending my letter — Be assured my dear Ann it was my sincere wish, papa fully approved of my going, and W^{m} & sister Maria[4] were desirous to accompany me — But either the lameness of our carriage horses, W^{ms} absence from home, or the necessity of his attending to business at home, or some other substantial objection, continually prevented my having that pleasure — So much did I desire to see you that I proposed going with sister in the Gig[5] — but papa could not be persuaded to let us drive so far —I will hope we may meet next summer both at Peekskill & at Bedford — My best respects to Mrs Van Rensselaer & to the General[6] — Kiss your little darling for me & accept for yourself & yours

the best wishes of my dear Ann
your affec^{t}. friend
[torn] [Nancy]

M^{rs}. Van Cortlandt
Sister Sally desires to be kindly remembered —

[Addressed]
Mrs Van Cortlandt
To the care of James Stevenson Esqr. —
Albany —

---

1. Nancy Jay was the daughter of John and Sarah (Livingston) Jay, and Ann Jay's sister. Monaghan, p. 427.

2. Margaret Stuyvesant died sometime between October 28 and the date of this letter. No obituary has been located.

3. Nancy Jay was reciting from *Night Thoughts, Night the Fifth: The Relapse,* by the Reverend Edward Young (1683–1765). The complete stanza reads:

   And first, thy youth. What says it to grey hairs
   Narcissa, I'm become thy pupil now —
   Early, bright, transient, chaste, as morning dew
   She sparkled, was exhalted and went to heaven
   Time on this head has snow'd; yet still tis borne
   Aloft; nor thinks but anothers' grave
   Cover'd with shame I speak it age severe
   Old worn-out vice sets down for virtue fair;
   With graceless gravity, chastising youth,
   That youth chastised surpassing in a fault
   Father, of all, forgetfulness of death:
   As if, like objects pressing on the sight,
   Death had advanced too near us to be seen.

   Edward Young, *The Complaint: or, Night Thoughts* (Hartford, Conn., 1851 ed.), p. 112.

4. William Jay (1789–1859) was the second son of John and Sarah (Livingston) Jay. A Yale graduate, he read law in the Albany offices of John B. Henry and for many years served as a Westchester County judge. His sister, Maria Jay, married a Mr. Banyer of Albany; she suffered the tragedy of losing both her child and her husband by 1809. She afterward returned to the Jay homestead in Katonah to live with her father. Monaghan, pp. 430–431.

5. A gig is a light-weight, two-wheeled carriage drawn by a single horse. C.T. Onions, ed., *The Oxford Dictionary of English Etymology* (Oxford, 1966), p. 397.

6. "Mrs. Van Rensselaer" was Ann, the wife of Philip S. Van Rensselaer and the sister-in-law of Ann (Stevenson) Van Cortlandt. The "General" was Philip Van Cortlandt. *VCFP,* II, 23.

33

Pierre, Jr. to William Miller. ALS
SHR

Albany Dec^{r}.18–1817 Thursday noon —

Mr Wm Miller

I arrived here yesterday at two OClock found the Old Lady exceeding ill and so low that I am fearful She will not recover[1] — Mrs Van Cortlandt is almost wore down with distress and the want of sleep — When I arrived at Greenbush I met an Express sent after me, — Little Pierre is very well —

Let Gale make the fire place good in the kitchen & plaister it up warm I wish you to put the Lead above the Chimney on the roof of the New Room — I will write you often

Your freind
Pierre Van Cortlandt

Perhaps Gale had better mason up with mortar between the wall in the Cellar and the Sill of the House to keep out the cold and safe the potatoes and every thing else from freezing and also in the milk cellar & to mason up that back window in the milk cellar — Shut the window under the front Piazza in the Cellar — & secure the milk Cellar door to keep the frost up & the other Cellar door I would advice you always to keep Locked which will prevent the Cider drinkers going down there — Measure the window in the kitchen Garret & let Mabel make a sash for it — then get Glass & put in it and glass wherever it is wanting

[Addressed]
Mr William Miller
at Genl Van Cortlandts
Peeks Kill N.Y.

---

1. Pierre's mother-in-law, Magdalena (Douw) Stevenson, died on December 20, 1817.

34

Philip to [Archibald?] Mercer.[1] ALS
SHR

Croton Dec^{r}.24th. 1817.

D^{r}. Sir

I had to remain at Paulis Hook all the Day I left you, and untill monday Morning after breakfast, there being no Steam Boat to take me over, however when the Ice would permit one Came, and I had a fine run in a short time, and proceeded on to M^{r}. Augustus Van Cortlandt and found him in good health and very glad to see me. he was Rejoyced to hear you was so happy with your Charming Companion for life and Congratulates you all with much Sincerity.

Your letter to M^{r}. John Travis I will send to the care of Solomon Dingee as you directed, and have already writen to the man who wishes to purchase the farm in Pound Ridge where Enoch Harris Resides, when I have his answer I will do myself the pleasure to inform you of the Result.

With much Esteem and all
affectionate Reguards to Your
kind Mother M^{rs}. Mercer and
Your honoured Lady I am

Truly Yours
Ph.V.Cortlandt

P.S. Just this moment I have a letter from my brother who informs me of the Distressing affliction of his wife & friends occasied [occasioned] by the Death of Old M^{rs}. Stevenson his Wifes mother She Departed. the 20th in the Morning

---

1. The recipient of this letter may have been Archibald Mercer, who had married Catalina Sophia (Cuyler) Van Cortlandt (1766–1823), widow of John Van Cortlandt (1764–1793) of Second River, New Jersey. DeForest, n.p.

35

Pierre, Jr. to William Miller. ALS
SHR

Albany March 13, 1818.

Mr William Miller

I wrote to you a few days ago, this goes by Jacob Lent who has been here four weeks and for the service he has been, he might as well remained at home; When I will return must depend upon the River opening, but as soon as the Steam boat runs You may expect me — In my last I wrote you how ill Pierre has been with the Croup but thank God he is now very well again — The rest of the family are well Mrs Van Cortlandt's Aunt Ten Eyck is to be buried to morrow[1] — When I come down I will endeavour to bring with me some Summer Wheat to sew — But I wish your Uncle John would get me two Tons of Plaister and two Bushels of Clover Seed the first trip he makes to New York[.] I have mentioned that I have 500 boards here for fencing — and will want a Number of Parts for the Garden fence, Mr McCoy said there were a great many in the Clay fields which would answer — speak to him about them —

I wish you to save all the short dung you can for the Garden, — I want very much to be at home & long for the Ice to go out of the River —

remember us all at home and
am your freind
Pierre Van Cortlandt

Albany
March 13th, 1818

[Addressed]
Mr. William Miller
at Genl Van Cortlandts
Peekskill

---

1. Maria (Douw) Ten Eyck, widow of John DePeyster Ten Eyck, died on March 12, 1818. Ann Van Cortlandt's mother was Magdalena Douw, Maria's sister. Munsell, *Collections,* IV, 118; *New York Genealogical and Biographical Record,* LXIII (1932), 282–283.

36

Billy Hibbard, Jr. to Pierre, Jr. ALS
SHR

Canaan March 27. 1818.

Dear Sir

I have deferd. writing to you Sir till this time oweing to an expectation of receiving an answer to a letter Father wrote you soon after he returnd. from his journey to the West. but I am apprehensive that it has not reached you as the Mails were verry much impeded in their progress to & from Albany at that time — Father in his letter informd the General that the cause of his not waiting upon him on his return to Albany was the great pressure of business & a desire of knowing whether I would remain in Town for any length of time & whether I would be willing to accept the Appointment of Justice of the Peace which Gen. Courtlandt was so good as to offer his Influential services in obtaining for me[1] —

I have Sir maturely considered the Subject considering the Importance of the Office to Society & myself together with the Necessary business of the Office which is not Inconsiderable in this Neighborhood and which I am frequently calld. upon to execute — I have concluded if the appointment could be obtained — to accept it and execute the office to the best of my abilities — I have Sir drafted a petition or rather a recommendation which is inclosed & which is signed by the principal men of this Neighborhood to whom I have presented it — which Sir if expedient may be presented to the Hon. Council — I am Sir personally known to Mr. Peter R Livingston of the Council[2] who I presume will have no objections to My appointment if he does not make one from the difference there exists in our political Tenets which that Gentleman is well convinced of & I have not unfrequently had to receive a portion of the "Phials of Wrath he has pourd out without mixture"[3] upon those who have opposed the principles of the Livingston Dynasty. with due defference Sir to your better Judgment I submit the foregoing & the Inclosed to your management — being well convinced that the welfare & happiness of the State, to be of the utmost importance & the first concideration of its influential inhabitants

Mother desires to be remmembered with respect to the general

Accept Sir assurance of the highest consideration from your obt. humble Servt.

Billy Hibbard Junr.

Gen PVn Courtlandt Jr

[reverse side]

We the Subscribers Inhabitants of the Town of Canaan, County of Columbia, & State of New York, beleiving it to be Expedient & Necessary to have a Magistrate for the administration of Justice & for executing the business relative to his Office, in, this section of the Town — do for that purpose recommend — Billy Hibbard Jr. an Inhabitant of this Town, and to us well known, to the Honorable the Council of Appointment as a Person well qualified to fill the said office & relying as we do upon his ability & activity in discharging the duties of Justice of the Peace, we do the more Cheerfully recommend him to the Honorable Council for an appointment to Said Office — March 25th 1818

Amos Peabody
Joseph Norton
Matthew Brogue

John Brogue
Henry Hendrix
Josiah Shelton
Samuel Palmer
[end of page torn off]

[Addressed]
Gen. Pierre Van Courtlandt
Albany
NYork

[Written below address in Pierre, Jr.'s hand:]
Riker will come out as Bob McComb did
when he prosecuted Coleman —
He is wicked & base
I know an instance of his Conduct as base
& as corrupt as that Coleman mentions
at Peekskill where I live
all those fellows Tompkins appointed in New
York were a lot of Scoundrels[4]

---

1. Billy Hibbard, Jr. does not appear to have been appointed to the position of a local justice of the peace in Columbia County. He was the son of the famous itinerant minister Billy Hibbard, whose biography was published in 1843 as the *Memoirs of the Life and Travels of B. Hibbard, Minister of the Gospel . . .* The father traveled the western Massachusetts and Connecticut circuits during 1816 and 1817. Hibbard, p. 367.

2. Peter R. Livingston (1766–1847) was a Tammany leader who opposed DeWitt Clinton and the Erie Canal. *National Cyclopaedia of American Biography,* III, 380.

3. Hibbard was making a biblical reference to Chapter 16 of the Book of Revelation in the New Testament. Alexander Cruden, ed., *Cruden's Unabridged Concordance* (Grand Rapids, Mich., 1973), p. 536.

4. The circumstances surrounding this cryptic note in Pierre's hand remain unresolved. Pierre obviously was against some of former Governor Daniel D. Tompkins's appointees in Westchester County.

37

John and Margaretta Brown[1] to Philip. ALS
NYHS

General Philip Van Cortlandt Frankfort 15th. May 1818.
Sir

Please to pay unto the Bearer Mason Brown any Ballance remaining in your Hands of the price of the land you sold in our Behalf & oblige

Your obt Servt.
J. Brown
Margaretta Brown

---

1. See Mason Brown to Philip, August 13, 1818 (No. 39); *VCFP,* III, 338–339.

38

Eliza Treat to Ann (Stevenson) Van Cortlandt. ALS
SHR

Albany August 6th 1818.

Nothing gives me greater pleasure My dear Mrs Cortlandt than to hear from you and be entrusted with any commission you think me capable of executing — I can procure the silk and will send it with Mr Walsh but I do not think there is a piece of Canton Crape in town fit for the girls to wear — many persons buy the coloured crapes and have it dyed black — I think it far superior to that which comes originally black — if you wish I will get a piece and have it done for you directly — be kind enough to let me know immediately and how I must send it — Our family are all well Mama's health I think in general is better than it has been in several years — Aunt Lush[1] instead of having returned only expects to leave this on Monday next she is not well I am in hopes this jaunt will be of great benefit to her — M^{r} & Mrs James will remain to keep house during Aunt's absence they have given up the idea of living in New York and will only make a visit there this fall — I am very happy to hear that the children are all well and pleased with their situations it would give me great pleasure to see them but I do not think it probable that I shall leave home this season and consequently cannot accept of your kind invitation to pay you a visit at present — Remember me affectionately to all not forgetting Pierre in which request Mama and Rachel join[2] — Rachel has been spending three weeks at Claverack with Cath: Van Ness[3] — she saw the family at M^{r}. Van Rensellaers several times[4] — Mrs Lane was making them a visit[5] — they were all well — I have neither news nor scandal to tell you — every body is gone a jaunting and Albany is dull to a proverb — I should be very happy if either of the young ladies would honor me with a line I will answer them directly — with sincere wishes for your happiness believe me your affectionate friend

Eliza

[Addressed]
Mrs Ann Van Cortlandt
Care of Gen Pierre Van Cortlandt
Peekskill

---

1. The wife of the prominent Albany attorney and Columbia College graduate Stephen Lush, Lydia Lush was the daughter of

Dr. Samuel Stringer (1759–1841) and the sister of Gertrude (Stringer) Treat. Munsell, *Collections,* IV, 144.

2. A reference to Eliza's mother, Gertrude (Stringer) Treat, and to Eliza's sister, Rachel (1800–). *Ibid.,* 173.

3. Catharine Van Ness may have been the daughter of John P. and Margaret (Burns) Van Ness of Claverack, New York. Margaret Bayard Smith, *The First Forty Years of Washington Society* (repr. New York, 1965), pp. 135, 424.

4. Philip S. and Ann (Van Cortlandt) Van Rensselaer.

5. There was a Mrs. Mary Lane (1800–1857) in Albany at this time. Munsell, *Annals,* IX, 349.

39

Mason Brown[1] to Philip. ALS
NYHS

Yale College, August 13th 1818.

Dear Sir,

I received your favour of the 1st Inst. containing a check on the Manhatten Bank for one hundred dollars: and have availed myself of the present opportunity to acknowledge its arrival. I hope Sir, you will not put yourself to the least inconvenience, as it respects the payment of the remainder, but that you will consult your own convenience in every respect —

Any information you can give me relative to that portion of the land which remains unsold, and also of the taxes due upon it to the State, will be thankfully received — My Father expects to visit this country during the ensuing winter, and will then probably have the pleasure of paying you a visit. He desires me to remember him affectionately to you, and assure you of his continued friendship. Inclosed I send

you a receipt for the $100. contained in your last, and remain
Very respectfully

Yours

Mason Brown.

Gnr^{l} Philip Van Cortland —

[Enclosure]

Yale College August 13th. 1818.

Received of Gnr^{l} P.V. Cortlandt one hundred dollars, being the payment, of part of the money arising from the sale of lands, sold by him for John, and Margaretta Brown.
$100. Mason Brown —

---

1. Mason Brown (1799–1867) was the son of John and Margaretta (Mason) Brown. His father was acquainted with Philip Van Cortlandt through his service as a U.S. Senator from Kentucky. Mason Brown attended Yale and graduated in 1820. He later studied law and went into practice in Frankfort, Kentucky. Yale University, *Obituary Record of Graduates of Yale College from July, 1859 to July, 1870* (New Haven, Conn., 1870), pp. 238–239.

40

James Fenimore Cooper[1] to Pierre, Jr. ALS
SHR

Scarsdale. Sept. 23^{d}–1818.

Dear Sir

I had the honor to receive your communication of the 18th inst. yesterday and accept with pleasure the appointment, I beg you to receive my thanks for your polite attention to my request. I am at present so occuppied with workmen and business here having but just moved into my new house as to render it somewhat uncertain whether I can go to Town before the 5th — but I will endeavor to be equipt by that time and ready to attend to your orders. I have just heard that the parade on the 5th — will be at Underhills this is within two miles of my house which I beg you will make your own during your continuance in this part of the County I can give your aids a bed a piece without inconvenience and trust you will not hesitate to bring them along —

I am Sir very Respectfully
Yours
James Cooper

Major Gen Van Cortlandt —
Peekskill.

[Addressed]
Major-General Van Cortlandt
Peekskill
West-Chester Co

---

1. James Fenimore Cooper, the eminent American man of letters, and his wife, Susan Augusta (DeLancey), moved from Cooperstown, New York, to Westchester County in 1817. They built a home on a farm in Scarsdale, where Cooper became engaged in agricultural activities and the state militia. He was also heavily involved in land speculations. As a means of extricating himself from financial obligations, he soon turned to writing fiction. James F. Beard, *The Letters of James Fenimore Cooper* (Cambridge, Mass., 1960), I, 23–24.

41

Pierre, Jr. to John V. Henry and James McKown.[1] ALS
HSP

Oct 7–1818.

Gentlemen.

Nancy Gordon has been subpaeneed as a Witness in a suit pending at this Circuit now held in this City between James Jackson ex dem. Charles R Webster[,] George Pearson & William Caldwell Plaintiffs & William Easton & Samuel

Emmerson Defendants — It is very inconvenient for Nancy Gordon to leave the family (late M[r]. Walshs) until she is absolutely wanted in Court when the Cause is tried — & therefore beg you will be so obliging as to let me know whether it will be tried this day & if not this day, when it will be —

I am Gentlemen Your
ObSer[t]
Pierre Van Cortlandt

Mess[rs]. Henry & McKown —

---

1. John V. Henry (1765?–1829) and James McKown were two eminent attorneys practicing in Albany. Pierre apparently was involved in this litigation as an attorney. Howell and Tenny, pp. 133–134; Charles Edwards, *Pleasantries about Courts and Lawyers of the State of New York* (New York, 1867), p. 516.

42

Lemuel Wicker to Pierre, Jr. ALS
SHR

Ticonderoga 2 November 1818.

Dear General

I would inform you that frequently since you was here — I have been called upon by the setlers on your patent — for the purpose of settling difficulties existing between them — they occasionally trespass upon each other — although they are all trespassers themselves — they are frequently cutting the timber while others not wishing to have it done are complaining about it, one in particular has applied to me for the privilege of cutting some timber for a house — it is pine timber he says, but the trees are all dead — occasioned by the fire two years ago — I think it would do you no injury to have it done — and it may be well while those stay who are able to pay, to call on them for rent — if you have a mind to let me look to the business & see that they do what is about right between each other it would I have no doubt have a good effect

Yours with much esteem &c

Lemuel H. [?] Wicker

Gen. Pierre Van Courtlandt

P.S. I wish you to have the goodness to write me soon & particularly whether the man (one of the setlers) can cut a few of the trees as above described —

[Addressed]
General Pierre Van Courtlandt
Peek's Kill
Putnam formerly Duchess Cy.
N.Y.

43

Pierre, Jr. to William Miller. ALS
SHR

Albany Nov[r]. 24, 1818.

William Miller

Furman is to leave here this day I have written to you by him —

I shall leave here as soon as possible but as I intend going to New York before I leave Peeks Kill for here for the Winter perhaps in order to save time that I will go immediately from here to New York —

I mentioned in my Letter by Furman that if you could buy the Poney — Smith the Constable had belonging to John Fowler to buy him for me for forty Dollars if he was a Young horse — which I wish you would do —

I wish you to tell Sylvester Mandeville that as I have got 4 Guiney hens & am to have another pair from M[r] Verplanck that I will buy his as he cannot keep them from mine —

Your freind

Pierre Van Cortlandt

[Addressed]
M[r] William Miller
at Gen Van Cortlands
PeeksKill

44

John Van Rensselaer[1] to Philip. ALS
NYHS

BellVille Dec. 12, 1818.

D[r]. Sir

I Rece[d]. your letter of a few days since in which you inform[d] me that you have heard of the disagreeable news and barbarous treatment of James Van Cortlandt towards his wife it is a fact that he beat her in a shocking manner and draged her a cross the room by her hair and threatand to put her on the fire and swore that he would be death of her she fortunately made her escape from him and fled up stairs and locked herself up during this time the Servents came for me I had retired to bed. I got up very much alarmed and went over partly drest and found them in a most dredful situation James appear to be very much intoxicated and told me that he mant to be the death of her I conversed with him some time and after much persuation got him in bed and locked him up — I then whent up to Hetty and found her in a distressed situation I brought her over to my house she — remained in my family untill yesterday when she again returned to her husband very much against the approbaton of all her relations. how they make-out now I. am not able to inform you, Mrs. Murser Was not present at the time, she has sinç abused me and my family beyond all descripton Hetty stayd with ous three weeks

I. Remain your humble
Servent
John Van Rensselaer

BellVille Decr. 12th. 1818

[Addressed]
Genn. Phillip Van Cortlandt
Albany
State of New York

---

1. John Van Rensselaer was married to Elizabeth Van Cortlandt, daughter of Stephen and Catherine (Rutgers) Van Cortlandt. Elizabeth's sister, Hester, married her first cousin, James Van Cortlandt, associated with the Second River or Belleville, New Jersey, branch of the family. The mutual relationship with Philip was through Philip's great-grandfather, Stephanus.
   The letter provides ample evidence that wife abuse was manifested long before the family distresses of the twentieth century.

45

Pierre, Jr. to William Miller. ALS
SHR

Albany Janr 21, 1819.

William Miller

I have been coming home every day since New Year, which is the reason I have not written[.]One day we had every thing packed up and the Horses harnessed to set off when it began to Snow the next day it rained & after that the roads were ruff. We then expected Snow every day and Now as soon as there is slaying we shall embrace it & take a ride home. M[rs] Van Cortlandt continues to be very low spirited although I think her better than when I arrived here and a long ride might [be] of service to her to divert her mind — Pierre is very well —

I believe I forgot to mention to you about the Tax to M[r] Sands it is about $104 — I wish you to speak to your Uncle John M[c]Coy whether he cannot advance it — Ward B. Howard owes me $50 — for rent of the Saw mill place, if I do not come down soon I will send you an Order upon Him — I suppose it is now as good a time as will be to sell rye flour I therefore should advice to grind One hundred Bushels [as] Ward Hunter at the landing would purchase it, he told me he would give the highest price going — I wrote on the memorandum I left for you to get some flax for the Gi[rls] to spin, I suppose you have done it, there was [some] in the Garret, also to spin — I wish to speak to [torn] Others about PeeksKill before you order the flour grown — so that you may know where to get a market — There has not been the least Slaying whatever here —

Remember Us at Home and am
Your freind
Pierre Van Cortlandt

[Addressed]
M[r] William Miller
at Gen[l] Van Cortlandts
PeeksKill
N.Y.

46

Aaron Ward[1] to Pierre, Jr. ALS
SHR

Mount, Pleasant. 22^{d}. Jany. 1819.

Dear Genl.

I arrived in time to attend the meeting on that day. and found a very large and respectable assemblage. there were some few persons who attended as Spies, among the number was John Haff from New York,[2] he immediately wrote to Noah as I have been informed[3] — I and we may expect to see some satirical remark in his paper — should he attempt it, he shall be answered — I was agreeably surprised to find the meeting so unanimous — there was not a discenting voice, Delavan Came out boldly — indeed Genl. you have many friends in this quarter — it will be well in my opinion that you visit this county as soon as you can conveniently, and spend some time among your friends, we must be active since we have a host to Contend against, and as this will be their last struggle in this district we ought to be well prepared for them, If they die it will be with a terrible struggle —

I am in hopes that you receivd my letter Relative to the Incorporation of our Academy we expect much from your friendly interferance, let me know the result as soon as practicable

I am Dr Genl.

Respectfully
Yours &c
Aaron Ward

[Addressed]
Major Genl. Pierre Van Courtlandt
Albany

---

1. Aaron Ward (1790–1867) was a native of Westchester County. He served in a Westchester militia unit during the War of 1812 and rose to the rank of captain by 1815. He studied law and opened a practice in his community of Sing Sing (Ossining). He continued in the militia and was subsequently elevated to the rank of major general. In July, 1819, he was appointed as district attorney for Westchester County. Ward was active in politics as a Democrat and served several terms in Congress, 1825–1829, 1831–1837, 1841–1843. He was a trustee of the Mount Pleasant Academy, situated in Sing Sing, which advertised itself as "A Select Military Boarding School for Boys." *Biographical Directory American Congress,* p. 1878; French, pp. 744–745; "Council of Appointment, Civil," XII, 351.

2. Pierre was attempting a political comeback by running as a candidate for the state Senate on the DeWitt Clinton ticket. The Republican opposition was led by Clinton's nemesis, Martin Van Buren. John Haff was a known Van Burenite. Albany *Argus,* September 19, 1834.

3. Editor and publisher of the *National Advocate,* Mordecai M. Noah was an avowed supporter of Martin Van Buren. Noah sought to win New York City Federalist support for the Van Buren "Bucktail" slate. Noah also bitterly opposed Clinton's canal project. Kass, p. 118; Alexander, I, 262.

47

Aaron Ward to Pierre, Jr. ALS
SHR

Mount Pleasant. 4th. Febry. 1819.

Dear Genl.

Col Montross[1] called at my office yesterday and desired me to solicit you to issue the order for the Court Martial to meet as soon as possible,

The Col. begged me to refer you to the 17th sec. of the late Military Act by which he says "he is not enabled to ascertain whether it is the duty of the Genr^{l}. to point out by his order the several places where the Court must set or whether it is in the power of the Court to adjourn from place to place and from time to time as may be most convenient to them" If the former then he begged me to name the following places to be inserted in the order provided they meet your approbation, 1th at Ferrises, Pines Bridge and at Shf Cooks for Col. Montross's Reg^{t}. at Squire Woods for Col Meads Reg^{t}. at M^{rs}. Deans Tarry Town & Mr Willis's White Plains for Col. Hobby's Reg^{t}. at Bishop Underhills for Col. Varians Reg^{t}. at Yonkers for Rifle Corps. & at Tarry Town for Col. Hammonds, If however you should be of the latter opinion. then he wishes you to direct the meeting of the Court first at Ferris's.

Before I conclude allow me to acknowledge the receipt of yours of the 23^{d} inst. I am extremely apprehensive that we shall not have snow soon, I wish you was down in this County, your presence would be of essential Service in my opinion, however should it be inconvenient for you to attend you may rest assured that our attention to your concerns shall be faithful,

I have written to Rockland for my friends to call a meeting and approve of our nominations which I presime will be done,[2]

I should be glad to hear from you occasionally, — yesterday must have been a trying time to some of the Political Gentry in Albany, and to day they will receive their quietus[3] — you may recollect the number of Gent^{n}. called from N York on the Lottery question their chief business no doubt was to aid in Electioneering for the Council &^{c}.

Let me hear from you relative to our Academy — I hope you will succeed in getting it Incorporated. I wrote to you some time Since, and sent my letter by a private Conveyance and am rather apprehensive you have not receivd it — I feel more and more assured that we shall be enabled to give you an overwhelming Majority in this County — much can be done in Putnam and Rockland and it shall be attended to.

Very Respectfully
Yours
Aaron Ward

[Addressed]
Major Gen[l] Piere Van Courtlandt
Albany

Mail

---

1. Nathaniel Montross served under Pierre in the 15th Infantry Brigade of the New York militia. In 1820 Montross replaced Pierre as commander of the brigade upon the latter's promotion to major general. Montross was one of four inspectors of turnpikes for the County of Westchester. Furthermore, both men were running on the same political ticket in 1819, with Pierre seeking a state Senate seat and Montross an Assembly seat. *Council of Appointment, Military,* III, 2224; "Council of Appointment, Civil," XII, 210.

2. *Republican Nominations* [Broadside, April, 1819], SHR Collections.

3. New York Republicans were bitterly split between the opposing Martin Van Buren (Bucktail) and DeWitt Clinton camps. Not having openly come to a parting of the ways in 1819, they held a joint caucus to choose a candidate for the U.S. Senate. The Clintonians held a majority of the votes in the caucus and supported John C. Spencer, son of Ambrose Spencer. The Bucktails, however, placed Samuel Young's name before the group. The Clintonians were disorganized and caught unprepared by the concerted effort to thwart Spencer's nomination. Bitter words were exchanged and the caucus reached no decision.

   The matter was then placed before a joint legislative session on February 2. Spencer received sixty-four votes, Young fifty-seven, and Rufus King, the Federalist, thirty-four. Since they could not agree on a mutual candidate, as stipulated by the state constitution, the legislature moved to adjourn. This left

New York without a U.S. Senator. Alexander, I, 263–267; Hammond, I, 485–486.

48

Aaron Ward to Philip. ALS
NYPL

Mount Pleasant March 3d 1819.

Dear Genl.

Joseph W. Strang Esqr. of Peeks Kill called upon me the day after you left this County & pledged himself to support the present administration, he tells me that Birdsall the present Justice of the peace in that place is decidedly with us. Mr Strang will be pleased with the office of Commissioner.[1]

We ought to have some one appointed as a Master in Chancery in this County at present we have none. Ralsamon C. Austin Esqr. of Peekskill is a Counsellor at Law and would be glad to receive that appointment, you will therefore be pleased to recommend him for it.[2]

Every thing in the political way goes on well. the Tammany men at their meeting appointed Nelson, Purdy, White, Odell & Townsend as delegates each of those Gent. calculate upon receiving the nomination Consequently 4 of them must be disappointed.[3]

The Federal Meeting shall be put down. Lee is yet active. he is going thro the County urging the federalists to turn out & slandering your brother.[4] should he fail in obtaining the nomination he will assuredly go mad. Let me hear from you whenever convenient.

Very Respectfully
Yours &c.
Aaron Ward

[Addressed]
Genl Philip Van Cortlandt
Albany

---

1. Joseph W. Strong was rewarded for his loyalty to the Clintonians by being appointed as one of the Commissioners of Deeds in Westchester County on March 18. William Birdsall served as a local justice and was reappointed in March, 1819. "Council of Appointment, Civil," XII, 261–262.

2. Ralsamon C. Austin received the appointment as a Master in Chancery. *Ibid.*

3. Of these local men, Henry White held the most important county position, that of a surrogate. He was removed from office by the Council of Appointment in March. *Ibid.*

4. The Federalist spokesman "Lee" mentioned here and in the following letter remains unidentified.

49

Aaron Ward to Philip. ALS
SHR

Mount Pleasant 10th March 1819.

Dear Genl.

I have this moment been informed that Jesse Seaman one of the Justices of the Town of Bedford is exceedingly attached to our party, I know him personally and am clearly of the opinion that he ought to be continued in the place of Lancelot G. Mc Donald who is upon the list for that office and who is not aware that he is to receive the appointment.[1] I think it advisable at all events that McDonalds appt. should be deferred until some future day that we may be enabled to ascertain which appointment will be the most advisable.

You will have heard before or by the time this reaches you the result of Lee's county meeting thro' some other channel. It was in a measure put down by the force that we mustered from this place. Youngs had become soured because his appointment was not made on the day that Cooks was and had made up his mind to stay at home.[2] I called upon him and told him that unless he went to the meeting he might go to the D___l. that if I had any influence it should be exerted against him and that he might rest assured that he would never receive the App^{t}. that he ought at least to merit it, before he put in his claim, at length he yielded and I dispached Yoe with him[3] — had he acted agreeably to my advice there would have been an end to the meeting. But Munroe possesses so great an influence over him that he was prevailed upon to consent to an adjournment of the meeting. — Lee appeared on the ground aided by Doct. Quereau,[4] Tompkins, and two boys. T___s became convinced that the step taken by Lee was not advisable and deserted his cause, as I am told the united force of Munroe and Lee did not exceed Six Voters Owen was on the ground and done his duty — you may rest assured that those Gentlemen shall be put down — Youngs now declares that he will act boldly —

Respectfully
Yours &c.
Aaron Ward

[Endorsed]
Aaron Ward
10 March –1819–

---

1. Jesse Seaman was reappointed as a local justice on March 29. Apparently there was a McDonald mix-up; a John McDonald was appointed instead of an Allen. The name of Lancelot McDonald does not appear on the appointment lists at all. "Council of Appointment, Civil," XII, 274, 281.

2. Lyman Cook was appointed as a sheriff on March 2 and Samuel Youngs was appointed surrogate on July 8. *Ibid.*, 241, 344.

3. Charles Yoe served as both an auctioneer and as a justice of the peace. *Ibid.*, 260, 263.

4. Dr. Elias Queareau was a local physician with an extensive practice. He apparently carried on farming activities and dabbled in politics. *VCFP*, II, 561; III, 206, 296, 472.

50

Philip to John V. Henry. ALS
Morristown National Historic Park Library

Cortlandt Town. Jany. 10. 1820.

D^{r}. Sir

I am informed that the Chancellor has Refered Our Cause, with the Underhills, again to the court for the Correction of Errors — On Account of the Costs which it is said was not sufficiently Explained — how this is I am ignorant, and wish you to attend to it and whatever other matters you find to be Worthy of your attention in the Cause[1] —

I wish you will please to consult Pierre C. Van Wyck. I have written to him on the subject and if he should not go to Albany I Expect he will write to You but at any rate, I wish you will please to give the subject the necessary Attention both as to the Costs or any other Matters that may be intruduced —

and am with great Respect
Your Humble ser^{t}.
Ph.V.Cortlandt

John.V.Henry Esqr —

[Addressed]
John V. Henry Esqr.
Albany

---

1. The noted Albany attorney John V. Henry was serving as counsel for the family in their dispute with the Underhills over the use of mills and Croton River water rights. On this involved and lengthy litigation, see Nos. 180 and 182.

51

Philip to James Van Cortlandt.[1] ALS
SHR

Cortlandt Town Novr. 1. 1820.

D^{r}. Sir

I am sorry that I did not Receive your letter in time to meet you at mount pleasant — and am truly mortified to find that you should be so near and not call to see me — however when you will please to notify me by a line that you will be ready to make a final Settlement with me I will do myself the pleasure to attend when and where you shall direct and with my best Respects to your good Lady and friends I am with great Esteem yours truly

Ph.V.Cortlandt

James Van Cortlandt Esqr.

[Addressed]
James Van Cortlandt Esqr.
NewArk
Cortlandt Town S.N.Jersey
Nov 1st

---

1. This was the same James Van Cortlandt of New Jersey who had been accused of wife-beating (No. 44). The settlement possibly concerned family estates of which the late Pierre, Sr. had acted as executor.

52

Jacob R. LeRoy to Philip. ALS
NYPL

New York 21st Novr 1820

Sir

By the request of my Mother Mrs Robt LeRoy I take the liberty of writing you to know if you can give her any information respecting some property her Father owned near Wappingers Creek in which you were interested.

I would be much obliged to hear from you as soon as convenient.

I remain Sir
Your Obt.
Servt.
Jacob R. LeRoy

Gen. Philip Van Cortland
Croton

53

Philip to Jacob R. LeRoy. ADfs
NYPL

Novr. 27.–1820.

Copy of Answer

Jacob R. LeRoy

Dr Sir — in answer to yr favor of the 21 — in order to give information to yr mother respecting some property her Father owned near to Wappingers Creek I have to Observe that as far as that claim interfered with mine I made a purchase of Mr. Cuyler and have a deed dated the 13. of Octr. 1794. for the Consideration of £250 — for all the

Lands then in the possession of the tenants claiming under my right —

I believe there was some other part claimed by y^r. G. Father which I laid no Claim to, but how much I am not able to inform you[.] our [tenants] who had it then or now have it in possession the land I bought of y^r. G. father was about 200 acres the Deed was Executed by him for himself and by his [? for] Cornelius Cuyler as attorney for Cornelius Cuyler as Ex^{rs} to the last will & Test of Cornelius Cuyler I see by a letter in my files dated 6. March. 1797 sent to me by Henry Cuyler requesting information of the land in $poss^n$. of Henry Phillips which he concluded was a part of my claim but that farm was the property of Genl. Ph. Schuyler and it is probable I so informed him but have no copy of my answer[.] he said he had a suit depending with Phillips which was to be brought to Issue in poughkeepsie in that month[.] further I have not heard and am y^{rs}.

PVC —

J. LeRoy

54

Ann (Stevenson) Van Cortlandt to Pierre, Jr. ALS
SHR

December 9th. 1820.

My dear Husband

I was happy to hear by your letter from Hudson yesterday that you had arrived safe so far, I regreted you had come too late for the Steam Boat, I have not been so well for these two days past, but hope I will be better in a day or two the Measles prevail so much about & some of the Children at Pierre's school have taken it, I have thought best to keep him home have I done right, John is very attentive & has thought best to sleep here, he received a letter from James yesterday, who is quite in high life, he will be home next week, tell Sally I will send her the Muslin for the Valence she is making when you go down again, Should William come to Peekskill ask him if he can spare a shirt for a pattern then I will have them made for him[.]the weather has been very mild since you left us, this morning it snowed which has now turned to rain — the old Woman is here yet I have settled with her but she has begged so hard to stay I told her she could stay this week this morning she sent up begging to stay another week, but I dont think I will let her, I had to pay $5 a month a Colored Woman who formerly belonged to my cousin Mrs Lane & who has lived at Mrs Woodworth going on 3 years is coming here in a weeks time I have to give $5 & half for 1 month to try her — Mrs W gave her 6 in summer & $6–50 in winter, she has no husband & is honest & industrious I will write you again very soon — your truly affectionate Wife

Ann Van Cortlandt

I have just received your last letter & was happy to hear you had got on so well — Albany Dec. 9. 1820

[Addressed]
Genl. Pierre Van Cortlandt
Peekskill

55

Pierre, Jr. to Philip. ALS
SHR

Sunday Afternoon Feb.11.1821.

My dear Brother

My dear Wife is growing Weaker this day Mr Lacey administered the blessed Sacrament to her, Brother & Sister Rensselaer were here & partook it with her; I now have not the smallest encouragement that She will Recover, My dear little Pierre appears to Realize the Loss he is Shortly to experience already, at times he is inconsolable —

She leaves this World like a true Christian, having always lived a pious Religious Life, She is assured Soon to be with her dear Redeemer, The fear of Death is not on her, the Only Reluctance is to part with her Relatives & particularly her dear little Infant But She says She Resigns him to that God who is the Orphan's freind —

Your Affectionate
Brother Pierre —

[Endorsed]
Brother Pierre
11 Feby. 1821 —

56

Philip to Pierre, Jr. ALS
SHR

Feby. 18. 1821.[1]

Dr, Brother

Yours of last Thursday did not Arrive untill this morning owing to the great fall of snow and badness of the Roads. but it has revived our hopes and may the Lord be pleased to restore our Dear Sister again to health is my Sincere prayer for altho I trust she would be happy if taken away, yet for the sake of her friends who must Receive pious Empressions from her Example and Advice I hope and pray she may recover

This World is a place of probation Exhibiting Troubles, Sorrows, and Various perplexities — attended Sometimes with Immaginary pleasures and Comforts of short duration. therefore how very necessary it is to be attentive to the word of Our Lord Jesus Christ. be ye also ready for you know not the day or the hour when the Lord will call. Yes my Brother I do believe the scriptures in one God Father, Son, and Holy Ghost, and that without holiness no Soul will be received into happiness and that only through the merritts and Suffering of Our Lord and Savior Jesus Christ who hath said come unto me all who are heavy Laden and I will give you rest. Ask and ye shall receive. for he is a prayer hearing God and faithfull to his promises, that whosoever cometh he will in no wise cast out.

That we may be Always faithful and Ready when Our Lord shall call is the Sincere prayer of Your Affectionate

Ph.V. Cortlandt

---

1. Ann (Stevenson) Van Cortlandt, Pierre's second wife, died in Albany on February 20, 1821. Her epitaph reads in part: "Early instructed by her pious mother in the doctrines and principles of the gospel, this excellent woman became exemplary as a communicant of the church when only thirteen years old, and continuing to be a sincere and humble follower of her Saviour, even unto her life's end, was endeared to all who knew her by her Christian virtues. . . ." Bolton, I, 65.

57

Pierre, Jr. to William Terrill.[1] ALS
NYSL

Peeks Kill June 1. 1821.

Dear Sir

When I was last in New York I intended to call on you but neglected it until it was too late respecting Salisbury Island[2] —

The Vinants (or Wagoners as they are called) are all gone off & I believe you could easily obtain the possession of it if you attend to it in Person[.] I have understood there is a Man now in the possession who you could easily get to move away or take the possession under you — The Vinants are fled to Ohio, not daring to stay here for their evil Deeds. I mentioned this to Mr Diven to tell you, so that you might immediately attend to it —

I am just about leaving home for an absence of 5 or 6 weeks —

I am with respect your
Ob^{t} servant
Pierre Van Cortlandt

William Terril Esqr

[Addressed]
Mr William Terrel
Merchant
William Street
New York

[Endorsed]
June 1. 1821 from P Van Cortl.
respecting Salisbury Island

---

1. William Terrill had married into the New Jersey branch of the Van Cortlandt family in the late 1690's. The recipient of this letter may have been a descendant through that line. He was a distant relative, for Pierre referred to himself as a "kindsman." See Pierre, Jr. to William Terrill, December 4, 1822 (No. 59).

2. Salisbury Island, a small body of land in the Hudson River off Anthony's Nose, had been left to Pierre, Sr. and then to his son, Pierre, Jr., as part of the estate of Gertrude (Van Cortlandt) Beekman. See map of adjacent lands accompanying No. 13.

58

Sarah Van Wyck[1] to Philip. ALS
NYHS

New Mills November 18th 1822.

My Dear Uncle,

I fear you will think me ungrateful & forgetful of past kindness in defering writing to you to so late a period, but indeed I am not & sincerely hope this will find you in the good enjoyment of health & spirits & as happy as is consistent with the lot of humanity. I am going to solicit a favour of you for my Brother Philip Renssellear, which the philanthrophy of your nature will not permit you to refuse, which is your influence to get Phil, in as a cadet at the military Academy of West Point. I think you may do it with the greatest safety. He is of a good age & as well informed as boys of his age generally are of good natural abilities & will do credit to himself & his friends. Our highly respected friend Genl. Bloomfield[2] & some others, influential characters will give him a recommendation to Mr Calhoun Secretary of War. He is the only applicant from Burlington County which is of some trifling advantage. Genl. Bloomfield wishes you to write & has kindly offered to forward the letters to the Secretary of war. Please to present my most affectionate & dutiful Remembrance to My Dear Gramma Van Wyck. My love & best wishes to my Dear Uncle Phil, & Aunt Mary & my Dear Cousins & Rest assured I retain a most grateful sense of your kindness to me when I had the pleasure of being with you. My Dear Grandma, & mamma have been ill with the remitting fever but are at present convalescent. Grandma, mamma Aunt Eliza desire me to present their best respects & Renssellear though not the pleasure of a personal acquaintance desires his love & best Respects to you.

I have the honour to be your
affectionate & Dutiful niece
Sarah Van Wyck

Genl Philip Van Courtlandt.

[Addressed]
Genl. Philip Van Courtlandt
Courtlandt Town
New York

[Endorsed]
Letter from
Sarah Van Wyck
Nov^{r}– 1822 —

---

1. Sarah Van Wyck was the daughter of Theodorus C. and Mary (Stretch) Van Wyck. She was a member of the New Jersey branch of the Van Cortlandt–Van Wyck families. Her brother was Philip Rensselaer Van Wyck.

2. General Joseph Bloomfield of New Jersey was one of the last remaining senior officers of the Revolutionary army. In a letter written to the Marquis de Lafayette on November 20, 1822, Bloomfield remarked of Sarah's great-uncle Philip: "Philip Van Cortlandt, Col: of the 1st: New-York Reg^{t}. is now, the Senior-Officer, of the Continental Army; for no officer, is now living, who commanded him, except Major General LaFayette, and who, in fact, is the only surviving General-Officer of the Continental Army, who served under General Washington." Joseph Bloomfield to Marquis de Lafayette (November 20, 1822), SHR Collections.

59

Pierre, Jr. to William Terrill. ALS
NYSL

Peeks Kill Decr. 4. 1822.

Dear Sir.

Last Spring George Vinants who claims Salisbury Island & half of the Meadow leased to One Morris the Premisses for $100 — about One Month since Morris abandoned the premisses & since which the House &^{c} &^{c}. have been Vacant. I have understood this day that his Brother is to move on the Island next week under him I think it would be adviceable for you immediately to come Yourself or appoint an Attorney to take possession. It may save you a vast deal of trouble by this Measure If your Counsel approves of taking possession, no delay must ensue —

You might have got the possession last Spring of it, if you had taken effective measures when I wrote to you

I am with Esteem your
kindsman
Pierre Van Cortlandt

Mr William Terril

[Addressed]
To Mr William Terrel
Merchant
New York

[Endorsed]
Decr 4, 1822 P V Cortland respecting Salisbury Island

60

New York State Comptroller to Pierre, Jr. DS
SHR
March 4, 1823.

State of New-York
Comptroller's Office.

I Certify, That the Quit Rents are discharged on the following Lands in a Patent for 86,213 acres, granted on the 17th day of June, 1697, to Stephanus Van Cortland, viz.

River Lot N°	10 commonly called Anthonys Nose —	3000 a^{s}
"	9 adjoining the above, the mansion farm of Pier Van Cortland	337 "
North Lot N°	3 North half	1500 "
		4837 a^{s}.

Provided, that the owners of the said land pay to the Treasurer, for the use of the People of this State, the sum of Fourteen Dollars and 51 Cents.[1]

$14.51 Albany, 4th March 1823.

Treas$^{r's}$. Office E. Starr Dep[uty] Comp[troller]

State N.York/ Rec^{d} from P. Van Cortlandt

Fourteen 51/100 dollars in full of the above am^{t}. 4th Mar. 1823.

Ephm Starr DepComp

[Endorsed]

Quit Rent paid by Pierre Van Cortlandt

1. For previous quitrent payments made to the state, see No. 5.

61

Philip to Pierre, Jr. ALS
SHR

Cortlandt Town March. 10. 1823.

Dear Brother

I have rec^{d}. yours of the 4th. & 6th. and as you have paid half of Lot. N°. 3, Crumpond, I need not say any thing as to that Lot — then there will remain to be paid for — by me —

acres		
1255.	front lot N^{o}. one. on which I live	
3000	for Pound Ridge East of Bedford —	
4255–		
562–	N^{o}. one South of Croton —	Estate of our Dec^{d} Father
2225–	N^{o}. one South lot. —	
3168.	N^{o}. Six North lot —	

If you are in Albany when this arrives I wish you to have the Quit Rent paid and receipts agreable to the above —

Mr Verplanck is here and he wishes you to pay for him and a receipt for

932–acres front Lot N°. 2
2995–d^{o}. South lot N°. 2
2904–d^{o}. South lot N°. 3
854–d^{o}. South of Croton
915–d^{o}. Verplancks Point —
8600–

The Comptroller will make the Calculation on Each lot as the Number of Acres are Correct. I had made a Small mistake as it respects this lot in my letter to you but the above is right I believe[.]

Croton broke up last Thursday as far as the Islands. the Mills and Bridges are Safe[.]please to remember [me] to all friends

Your Affectionate brother
Ph. V Cortlandt

[Endorsed]
Memorandum of Quit Rents PVC

62

Philip to Pierre, Jr. ALS
SHR

Cortlandt Town March 17. 1823.

Dear Brother,

I have yours of the 14. and thank you for your attention to the Quit Rent there was a Small Error in my first but of Trifling consequence it was as to the Number of Acres in this lot. as you will perceive when you receive the last letter to you which I sent to Albany and which you did not receive there but I suppose will follow you. it is however of no consequence —

Cousin Stephen V Cortlandt has requested me when I pay the Quit Rent that I would also pay for him. as he knows not how to proceed — and will also pay me for his part of the Comutation which you know I paid — &c — M^r^. VerPlanck promised me to do the Same — Stephen's part is as follows —

	1447.	acres front lot N^o^. four —
in the name		or Furnace lot
of	2760.	d^o^ Great South lot N^o^. six
Stephen	2660.	d^o^ — d^o^ — d^o^ — d^o^
Van Cortlandt		N^o^. seven
	686.	d^o^. South of Croton–
		N^o^. four —
	———	
	1452.	South half of North lot
Gertruyd		N^o^. three
Beekman	2394.	Great South lot
		N^o^. Eight —
	———	

I think it will amount to for arrears about $32.21 if Int[erest] as to the Comutation he must settle with me —

If you will please to request Mr. Js. Stevensen to pay this also I will thank you. and on your Sending me word that it is agreable I will write to Stephen and Inform him as he is anxious to hear from me. Your affectionate Brother

Ph. V. Cortlandt

[Addressed]
Genl. Pierre V. Cortlandt
Peeks kill

63

Agreement between Philip and Camp Meeting Ground Petitioners. ADS
SHR

Aug. 25, 1823.

Now it is agreed between Phillip Van Courtlandt of the town of Courtlandt in the County of Westchester and State of New York of the first part, and Peter P. Sandford, Marvin Richardson, Nathan Anderson, John Fisher, William Requa, Matthias Ryder, William Morton, Andrew Wheeler, and Henry Cliff of the Second Part, and the Party of the first Part for himself and his heirs and assings [assigns] Hereby Leases to the parties of the Second part, for the terme of one Week from the twenty fifth of this Instant august all that Certain Piece of wood Land situated in the town of Courtlandtown aforesaid Commonly Called and known as the Camp meeting Ground at Croton, for the purpose of Holding a Camp meeting, on the Condition that the Said Parties of the Second Part Pays to the Party of the first part his heirs or Assings [Assigns] the Sum of one Dollar if Demanded, and the Parties of the Second Part Shall Commit now [no] wast of

Timber of any kind in the above Described Piece of wood Land, and at Experation of this Lease to make or Cause to be made up all the fences and to Cause all Persons to leave the ground in good order — and the Said Parties, of the Second Part, their heirs or assings are to make Payment for all the Damages Done on the Said Premises During thease Presants,[1] Dated this twenty fifth day of august one thousand Eight Hundred and twenty three —

in Duplicate —
Ph.V.Cortlandt
PP Sandford
Marvin Richardson
Nathan Anderson
John Fisher
Wm ReQuas
Wm Morton
And. Wheeler
Henry Clift
Matthias Ryder

Sealed and Delivered
in the Presence of
Charles Yoe

[Endorsed]
Lease given 1823 for Camp meeting

---

1. Philip Van Cortlandt had good cause for concern in regard to the use of part of his property as a Methodist camp meeting ground. The Reverend Billy Hibbard, active as an itinerant Methodist minister in the early years of the nineteenth century, left this description of camp meetings in Westchester: "I came home . . . to superintend a camp meeting at Tuckahoe, [ca. 1805–1806] and the preachers returned so as to join us in the camp meeting, after the first day. . . . Many were converted and the children of God were much quickened. . . . The meeting was large; it was supposed from twelve to fifteen thousand were present. But this was not much over half as large as one at Croton, that was supposed to consist of *twenty-four thousand.*" Hibbard then described the general atmosphere pervading such a mass gathering: "Of our camp meetings, a stranger may at first think unfavorable; for on coming upon the ground, he

first meets with groups of people around, suttlers and hucksters, wagons and tents, that crowd themselves into the roads and field, as near the camp ground as they can. . . . The people that frequent those places are such as come to camp meeting to make a frolic of it. There is swearing, gambling, and the whole vocabulary of Billingsgate language." Hibbard, pp. 293–294. See Nos. 78, 106, 124, and 138 regarding later camp meeting ground agreements.

64

Pierre, Jr. to DeWitt Clinton. ALS
HSP

Peekskill Sept 23–1823.

Dr Sir

I forgot to mention to your Excellency when I had the pleasure of seeing you to request you to issue a Brevet Commission to George Clinton Van Wart as Pay master to Leut Colonel Hammonds, Battallion of Light Infantry in the 15th Brigade[1] — If you approve of it I wish you to have it sent to the Clerks Office of this County which is held at Greenburgh (Tarry Town) —

I am with much Esteem
Your Ob Sert
Pierre Van Cortlandt

His Excellency —
Governor Clinton —

---

1. In 1822, William Hammond was promoted to a full colonel as part of a process whereby the Westchester light infantry battalion was reorganized into a regiment.

With the elimination of the civil and military councils of appointment under the revised state constitution of 1821, brigade and regimental staff officers were to be appointed by the commanding officers of such units. *Council of Appointment, Military*, III, 2394; *Niles' Weekly Register*, November 16, 1822, pp. 173–174.

65

Sarah Van Wyck[1] to Philip. ALS
NYHS

New Mills Decemb 16th. 1823.

My Dear & Venerable Uncle,

Permit me to have the pleasure of introducing to you one whom I trust will prove himself worthy your favour, it is your nephew, my Brother Abraham Van Wyck. He is now one & twenty & has supported the most unblemished reputation, He has been a respectful son & affectionate Brother. I think when you form an acquaintance with him you will be pleased with him. My Dear Gramma, mamma, Aunt Eliza, My Brother Phil, desire to be respectfully remembered to you. I hope you enjoy tolerable good health, & hope the evening of your days will be tranquil.

I have the honour to be your
affectionate & dutiful niece
Sarah Van Wyck

[Addressed]
Genl. Philip Van Cortlandt
Croton
New York

[Endorsed]
Sarah Van Wyck
Decr. 18. 1823 —

---

1. Sarah Van Wyck was the granddaughter of Catharine (Van Cortlandt) Van Wyck.

66

Philip to Pierre C. Van Wyck.[1] ALS
SHR

Decr. 31. 1823–

D^r^. Sir

Doc^r^. I. Smith the Indian Chief will call on you he wants advice relative his brother Moses Smith who served during the Revolutionary War; he Inlisted in Decr. 1776 in Capt. Israel Smiths Company Second N.Y. Reg^t^. then under my command and was discharged in June 1783[2] — He was Intitled to Land and it appears that he took out the patent himself for only 500. Acres so that the 100. Acres from the United States was not Assigned over to this state — Now the state of the Case as Represented by the Doc^r^. is that his brother Moses after taken Out his Patent went to Baltimore never Sold his land but believes some person must have obtained some fraudulent title as there is a Man Residing on the Lot who claims it as being possessed of good Title —

The Lot is Situate Near nine Mile Creek in the Township of Marcellus and is Valuable —

Moses Smith is gone to Albany, Onondaga and Cayuga Counties in Serch of records and it may be as was the case of Michael Burdge who called on me to prove My paymasters. Michael Connolly's Receipt book in which Burdge's hand writing appeared and which differed so Materially from the Name Subscribed in the Deed that the Jury gave a Virdict in favour of Burdge, Concluding the Deed forged — Where that receipt Book is I cannot say but I do think J^s^. Sacket has it — or can Inform where it is — That may be of

Service in Smiths Case if Necessary. I remain Yours with respect —

Ph.V. Cortlandt

Pierre C. Van Wyck. Esqr.

[Addressed]
Pierre C Van Wyck.Esqr.
New York

[Endorsed]
Philip Van Cortlandt
Decem^{r} 1823
Letter

---

1. Pierre Van Cortlandt Van Wyck was a practicing attorney and former Recorder of the City of New York.

2. The identity of "Doc^{r}. I. Smith the Indian Chief" remains a mystery. His brother, Moses, did serve during the Revolutionary War in the 2nd and 4th New York regiments. His immediate superior officer was Captain Israel Smith. Moses Smith enlisted in December, 1776, deserted in July, 1778, was jailed in October, 1779, and then served until being mustered out in June, 1783. Fernow, *N.Y. in Revolution,* p. 217.

67

Ann Varick to Pierre, Jr. ALS
NYPL

Utica Feb^{ry} 22nd — 1824.

Dear Friend

Your friendly and affectionate letter of the 23^{d} of January I receiv'd on the eve of my departure for Albany, where I made a visit of a fortnight and passed my time very pleasantly[.]Mr Varick and George William accompanied me down the Latter enjoy'd himself very much and has now return'd to his studies again at the academy at Lowville where he has been near three years, his Instructor give us a very good account of him that he keeps up with his Class and thinks the next fall he will be enabled to enter Colledge, he is a Large Boy of his Age.

My mother and Miss Strong are very well — Mama enjoys better health this winter than she has for several years before —

I am surprised you should let the badness of the roads prevent your going from home — I really was in hopes we should have met in Albany — I think the Country in Winter very Cheerless indeed without a Large and pleasant family to keep up ones Spirrits, should think you would almost get the *pip*[1] liveing so entirely alone — hope you certainly will be induced to visit your property in the Western part of the State in the Spring and Mr Varick and myself both hope you will make our house your home while in Utica — we talk of going to New York in the month of May or June, I assure you it would give us great pleasure to visit you at Peekskill, I have no doubt I should see very great alterations at your place I recollect many happy hours that I have passed there and the delightful fruite we have feasted upon particularly Cherries which is a favorite fruite of mine — I should be very much pleased to see your little Pierre (hope you will not spoil him) bring him with you and leave him with us untill your return —

our Children are all very well and still recollect Uncle Pierre with a great deal of pleasure — Mr Varick unites in being respectfully remembered to you

and believe me to be your old friend

Ann Varick

[Addressed]

Genl. Pierre Van Cortlandt

Peekskill

1. The "pip" was a colloquial term for a depressive state. *OED.*

68

Stephen D. Beekman[1] to Philip. ALS
NYHS

New York Feb 26th 1824.

Dear Uncle

It is with pleasure that I sit down to Informe you that my Dear Maria was safely Delivered at half past eleven o,clock on Tuesday night the 24th Instant of a remarcable fine Boy, he weighed ten & a half pounds without Cloaths. Maria had rather a tedious time of it she was thirty-seven hours in Labour. She and Child are both as well as we could possibly expect — she deserves to be affectionately remembered to you, Aunt VanWyck, and the Family.

Your affectionate Nephew
Stephen D. Beekman

1. Dr. Stephen D. Beekman, son of Cornelia (Van Cortlandt) Beekman, was married to the former Maria Clinton. For previous entries concerning Maria and Stephen, see *VCFP,* III, *passim.*

69

Philip to Philip Van Wyck.[1] ALS
SHR

Syracuse June.16.1824.

Dear Philip

I am just arrived from Clyde in Galen[2] where I went in the Packet boat in the Canal — my Journing is now compleated and I am now at Mr Mann's[3] where I am to be found Every day untill the 25th when I shall return — I have been to the Oswego falls. and to the South as far as Cincinnatus in Cortland County[.] Your letter of June 1–1824 I have rec^d^. also one from your Uncle Pierre he missed seeing me as I had not returned from Lysander when he was here. I Expect to have much business every day while I remain, as this is the time I made mention of in my tour Round to be steady to do business, there has already this afternoon been 3.Men here to talk but not to pay as much as Expected however I get some say enough to bear my Expences —

The Weather has been very changably last week on Tuesday was the warmest day I think for the last 12 Months no day last Summer like it, and on Wednesday very cold frost Thursday morning and continues so cold that fire is agreable the present prospect for Corn is very discouraging. but Wheat looks well and likely to be fine —

I expect your Uncle and Aunt Rensselaer are now with you as your letter seem'd to promise. Make my best Love and Remembrances to them and all others deserving attention and remain your

Affec^t^ Uncle
Philip

My health continues
well and hope it will
continue —

[Endorsed]
PVCortlandt June 16th 1824

1. Philip Van Wyck (–1842) was the son of Philip G. and Mary (Gardiner) Van Wyck. He was Philip Van Cortlandt's grandnephew and godson.

2. Infrequently, Philip Van Cortlandt journeyed westward to visit the lands he had acquired in the Military Tracts resulting from his years of service and rank in the Continental Army. Galen was a region originally part of an area called Junius in Seneca County. Clyde was a tiny enclave within Galen. All originally had been part of Township Number 27 of the Military Tract.

3. Philip made use of the Erie Canal in his westward travels. Slowly, section by section, the canal was opened to traffic after 1820. The small community of Syracuse blossomed as a direct result. The Syracuse House, under the proprietorship of James Mann, was a central hotel for the region. It was said to have entertained every major political figure of the day, including "Gen. Van Cortlandt . . . and many others who formed an interesting galaxy of kindred souls who discussed the affairs of the state and nation. . . ." Carroll E. Smith, *Pioneer Times in the Onondaga County* (Syracuse, N.Y., 1904), pp. 287–293; French, p. 691.

70

Philip: Notes Appended to the *State of New York Agricultural Almanack For The Year of Our Lord 1824.;* Packard & Van Benthuysen, Printers.

NYPL

July 2, 1824–January 26, 1825.

[July]
2d left.. Albany in the Richmond[1]
3.. Arrived in N.York at P.C.V.W.[2]
4. Went with Mrs.Van Wyck to
Church to hear Mr. Cummins[3]

5. Dined with the Cincinnati
at Washington Hall[4]

[August]
16th. I left Croton about 4 O.C.
& arrived in N.Y. 10m. after 9.
Saw Gen. La Fayette at Staten
Island[5] & came up with him
to Dinner at his Quarters in
the City Hotel provided for him
by the Corporation of N York
20th. Genl. La Fayette left N.York for
Boston & I left it for Croton

[September]
Left home on Sunday
5th. went to Peekskill —
Sent John Back and went
with Brother Pierre to [Colonels?]
got on Board the Steamboat
6. Dined with the Cincinn
in company of Genl. La Fayette.
7. went to see do. & requested a meeting &
8. Introduced to Navy Yard. Dinner, &c
9. at Historical society
10. Dined with Colo. Fish with GLF
fire works at Columbia Garden
14th. Castle Garden
15. West Point & NewBurg
16. Poughkeepsie & Clearmont
I left it and arrived
home the 17 in the morning
21. Went with the Somers Stage
& called at Mrs. Millers who
told me Brother Rensselaer was
gone the Day before to albany
22. arrived in alby. at 9. AM —

23. & 24 attending at Brother Rensselars
25. about half past 3 in the morning
he Departed —
28. the corps was Intered in a Vault
29. Sister Beekman arrived —

[October]
1. I left albany & Lodged at.
2. arrived Home at Croton from
Peekskill —
14. Sent the Sloop Belinda
to N. York with W^{m}. B. Lent
16. went to N. York in So^{r} Stage
21. Sold the Sloop for $1500 —
23. Came home

[November]
1st. Went with Joanna to
Peekskill and on Tuesday then
2. to albany — arrived on the
3. went to sister Rensselaers
17. left Joanna and I went
to N. York arrived on Thursday
18. and was lectured on account of Dancing
19. Stayed all night at Sister Beekmans
20. Came home —

[December]
from the 20th it has
been moderate
to the End of the Year
The River was in part
froze over about the
middle of the month
for one or two Days
went away —

1825
It froze for 2.or 3
days about — 6. or 7.

---

16. Rained —
17. all the river open'd
21. continued open
22. this morning the River
frose over Wind N. Eeast
& Very Cold like for snow
24- all frose fast
and Clear Sun
26. Clear. Wind N.W
good Roads & Dry —

[included in Almanac notes]

Pierre C Van Wyck
born 14 Sep[r]. 1778
Died 4th April 1827

Dewitt Clinton Died
11 February 1828 aged
58 years & 11 Months

Catharine Van Wyck
Died 24 Feb 1829 Aged
78 years 2 Months
and 9 Days

David Merrit loan
1 Day $1. —

W[m]. B Lent Junr
Timber $9.12½
Paid 2 April 1829

Andrew Purdy
24 Sheep Skins
27 d[o] Paid
had in the year 1826.

Daniel Acker d[o]
Sen[r] 1828
to move $3.12½
scow — 1.50
$4.62½

April 3rd 1829
CVWCv — $302. —
Paid by PVC Paid to
his note — CVW
gave a receipt

---

1. Philip had journeyed to visit his ailing brother-in-law, Philip S. Van Rensselaer, the long-time mayor of Albany. Van Rensselaer died on September 25, 1824.

2. Philip stayed with his nephew, Pierre Cortlandt Van Wyck, while visiting New York City.

3. Philip may be referring either to Pierre Cortlandt Van Wyck's wife or mother as the person he accompanied to a church service.

4. The main reason for the New York visit probably concerned advance preparations for the impending visit to these shores of General Lafayette, the Revolutionary War hero.

5. When the aging Marquis de Lafayette returned to America almost forty-three years after the decisive victory at Yorktown, the nation sought to bestow as many honors as possible on the distinguished Frenchman. He disembarked at Staten Island on August 15, 1824, in preparation for a glorious entry into New York City the following day. From the manuscript notes inserted in the *Almanack* we learn that Philip met Lafayette at Staten Island and accompanied him to the city as part of the official entourage provided by the Society of the Cincinnati. Philip remained with Lafayette until the 20th, when Lafayette traveled to Boston and Philip returned to Croton.

The wartime companions met again on September 6, when the Society of Cincinnati served as host for Lafayette's sixty-seventh birthday party. Philip remained with the group as it journeyed north on the Hudson River aboard the steamboat *James Kent.* At Claverack Philip left the *Kent* and returned to Croton by stagecoach.

Lafayette, meanwhile, continued his journey through the United States and did not return to New York State until June 4, 1825. He reached New York City on July 1, in time for a full-scale celebration of the Fourth. Philip once again joined his Cincinnati companions in the feasts and parades marking Lafayette's presence.

It is unfortunate that Philip did not leave a first-hand account of these 1825 festivities. From the printed records we know that as part of the thirteen toasts offered to Lafayette at the Fourth of July banquet, Philip rose to toast "The memory of John Hancock." New York State Department of Commerce, *Itinerary of General Lafayette's Triumphal Tour of New York State, 1824–1825* (Albany, 1957); [Anon.], *The Pamphlet, Containing A Description Of The Grateful Manner In Which The Whole Population Of The City Of New York Voluntarily With Open Arms Received General LaFayette On The 16th August 1824, And The Very Affectionate Manner In Which They Expressed Their Farewell On The Memorable 14th July 1825 . . .* (New York, 1825); Marian Klamkin, *The Return of Lafayette 1824–1825* (New York, 1975).

71

Volkert P. Douw[1] to Pierre, Jr. ALS
SHR

August 7, 1824.

Dr Sir

The important crisis which collected so many persons at the seats of government and among others your good self, created so much excitement and so completely engaged the attention and engrossed the conversation of every leisure moment, the Committee of the Hon^l Schemil Socy^t was prevented reporting the occurrence of events within the sphere of their Observation since their last communication and interchange of civilities at the Dunderbergh —

Your Committee had a partial opportunity during a few days of viewing life and manners of those fashionable resorts Balston & Saratoga where as usual was found visitors from all parts of the Union and here where all might be supposed to meet as members of one great family and act in concert; here We found an unusual share of reserve and local jealosies and distinctions prevaling.

The night of our arrival we stood silent spectators of the movement in what we shall call the saloon, here the party collected in groups which upon enquiry we found composed of visitors from Baltimore Phila & Boston and when the Hop commenced the Setts with a few exceptions formed in the same manner, And group seemed snering at group, with looks indicating conscious superiority, and each appeared to be scrutinizing and criticising the saying and doings of his neighbour; such was the inference drawn and impression made on your Committee and such they pronounce as their opinion —

Your Committee regretted extremely the absence of our Ladies but found it as pleasent as could be expected under such circumstances. The Committee however with their associates [illegible] and Spruce Dick whom they accidentally met recognized many person & renewed their acquaintance which enable them (independent of their own good Company & spirits[)] to pass the time agreably. Your Committee could not number among former acquaintances the grand trio Mrs. H. Rolla & Frisbie and more particularly the badge of our society the Ladies shadow. Here too, in beauty and appearence our ladies we are proud to add would have eclipsed the combined exhibition of the whole concern, and we are pleased to communicate the anxious enquiries & many regrets expressed at the absence of the Ladies —

Receive the assurance of our respects which you will please extend to your pleasant circle and believe me in haste your friend & Huml Servt.

V.P. Douw
In behalf of the Comm.

Calendar of Correspondence

Aug[t]. 7 1824

[Addressed]
Gen[l] Pierre Van Cortlandt
Peeks Kill
Westchester County

---

1. Volkert P. Douw may have been a relative on the maternal side of Ann (Stevenson) Van Cortlandt's family.
This is obviously a facetious rendering of high society's doings at the exclusive New York spas of Ballston and Saratoga. According to an 1837 eyewitness account, the major distinction between a ball and a hop was that "the ladies do not dress as well" at a hop. *American Heritage,* XVIII, no. 4 (June, 1967), p. 107.

72

Jacob G. Dyckman to Pierre, Jr. ALS
SHR

Albany 10th Nov. 1824.

Dear Sir

With this you will receive two copies of my manual[1] one of which I request you will accept for yourself, and the other you will please when convenient present to M Clinton together with the note addressed to him, and at the same time I will esteem it a favour if you will inform that gentleman (to whom I am a stranger) what you know respecting my standing in society particularily as a military man

I am Sir

Yours respectfully
J. G. Dyckman
No 5 Nassau Street
N. York

I shall be happy (when you can make i[t] convenient) to receive a communication from you expressive of your opinion respecting the work

[Addressed]
Major Genl. Pierre Van Cortlandt
Albany

---

1. Jacob G. Dyckman was the author of a military manual titled, *The American Militia Officer's Manual, Being a Plain and Concise System of Instruction for Infantry, Field and Horse Artillery, Cavalry, and Rifleman. . . .*

Joanna Van Wyck[1] to Philip. ALS
SHR

Albany Jany. 6th 1825[6].

Dear Uncle

I have received your letter and was very happy to here that you was all well.

Last weak we had three days rain and on Sunday it turned to snow and we have now pretty good sleighing. Mr Stevenson was made mair on Monday and saw a great deal of company.[2]

Tell Catharine and Cortlandt that I should be very much pleased to have a letter from them and Gardiner that I was very glad to here that he is a good boy.[3]

Aunt has been quite unwell she says that she has not been so unwell in two years but she says this morning she feels better that she has done in six weaks. I am very well Aunt joins with me in love to you all and wishing you all a happy New Year

I am your affectionate Niece
Joanna Van Wyck

P.S. Aunt expects her two sons Philip and Cortlandt from New Havan next weak.

---

1. Joanna Van Wyck was a daughter of Philip G. and Mary (Gardiner) Van Wyck.

2. James Stevenson assumed the office of mayor of Albany in January, 1826. Werner, p. 441.

3. Joanna referred to three of her siblings.

74

Joanna Van Wyck to Philip. ALS
SHR

Albany March 22nd. 1826.

My Dear Uncle

I have received your letter of the 8th inst and be assured that it is not out of neglect that I have not written to you before for I have been so engaged in drawing[.] Aunt says she thinks that you will be pleased with my performances when you see them.

In your last letter to me you said that you had been confined to your room with a cold but was better I hope by this time you have quite recovered and hope we shal soon have the pleasure of seeing you here.

I was very much pleased to here that the children was so much improved I have received a letter from Mama[.]give my love to her and tell her I will answer her letter soon

We are both well and unite in love to you all.

I remain your affectionate neice
Joanna Van Wyck

75

John H. Hobart[1] to Pierre, Jr. ALS
NYPL

New-York
May–22–1826.

Dr Sir,

Allow me to introduce to you the Rev: Mr Ives who is exceedingly will recommended to me from Connecticut, & whom I have desired to visit Peekskill & Philipstown in the hope that the Vestry of those Churches to whom I have given him letters may make some arrangement for securing his services.[2] May I ask your influence to affect that object.

I am with great respect
yr very obed^t^ f^d^ & serv^t^
J.H. Hobart

[Addressed]
Gen Van Cortlandt
Peekskill
Rev Edward J. Ives

---

1. John H. Hobart (1775–1830), author, teacher, and administrator, rose to become Protestant Episcopal Bishop of New York. *Appleton's Cyclopaedia,* III, 221–222.

2. Edward J. Ives became the rector of St. Peter's Church in Peekskill, New York, in 1826. He remained in that post until December, 1832. Robert Bolton, *History of the Protestant Episcopal Church, in the County of Westchester, From its Foundation, A.D. 1693, to A.D. 1853* (New York, 1855), p. 604.

76

Pierre A. Barker[1] to Pierre, Jr. ALS
SHR

Waterloo June 11th 1826.

Dear Sir

Yours of the 5th Inst was yesterday received. I hasten to inform you that the Box containing the likeness of General Andrew Jackson was received together with your letter accompanying the same, which agreeable to your request in a previous communication was published together with my answer in the Waterloo Gazette of the 31st May last —

This corespondence has roused the feelings of the political opponents of General Jackson in this county, in the Seneca Farmer of the 7th Inst much scurrility and abuse is aimed at me together with the grosest charges of corruption as an elector, and in every manner attempted to blast my reputation their attempts will wither into obscurity and pass unnoticed like the fleeting Cloud —

Sarcasm and ridicule when aimed at a public officer for conscientiousley performing a sacred duty to himself and fellow citizens will eventually mark the perpetrators rather than the object of their scandle with contempt. They will be noticed in the Gazette of this week

I am sir with great respect your obediant servant
Pierre A. Barker

Gen Pierre Van Cortlandt

[Addressed]
Genl. Pierre Van Cortlandt
Cortlandt
Westchester County

---

1. Pierre A. Barker was a local politician from Seneca County in western New York. Although appointed as a Jacksonian presidential elector in 1824, he did not attend the meeting of elec-

tors. He was rewarded for his political activities in support of Jackson by being named as the collector for the port of Buffalo in 1829.

The Van Cortlandts were enthusiastic supporters of Andrew Jackson, and Pierre actively campaigned in Westchester for the general. Werner, p. 470; Reed, II, 138.

Unfortunately, the newspapers mentioned in this letter have vanished.

77

Ann Van Rensselaer to Pierre, Jr. ALS
NYPL

Albany September 1st 1826 —

My Dear Brother

I have Recived your Letter of August the 2d and was happy to hear Mary had a son and that Sister is better. A most blessed Lord who never failest to help those that Love him — on wednesday morning — I Leave this for New york[,]middletown and New haven with Brother Stephen and my nices Miss Van Rensselaer and then to north hampton to see Alexander and then home — I then hope you will be at Albany when I Return as I have promised to go and pay you all a Visit this fall.

Please to remember my Best Love to all the family

Your affectionate Sister
Ann Van Rensselaer

78

Agreement between Philip and Camp Meeting Ground Petitioners.[1] ADS

SHR

September 4, 1826.

It is agreed between Philip Van Cortlandt of the Town of Cortlandt of the first part and Laban Cleark[,] Horris Bartlet[,] Joseph Smith[,] Peter D. Noyelles[,] John Leveridge[,] William Requa[,] James Fish[,] Jonathan Hall and Nathan Anderson of the Second part — Witnesseth that the said party of the first part hereby Leases to the parties of the Second part for the Term of one week from the 4th to the 11th both Days included of this month of Sepr. all that Certain peice of Wood Land Situate in the Town of Cortlandt commonly known as the Camp Meeting ground at Croton for the purpose of holding a Camp Meeting, and the parties of the Second part jointly and severally hereby bind themselves to pay the said party of the first part One Dollar if Demanded and to Commit no Waste of Timber of any kind on the Above premisses and leave the Same or Cause it to be done in good Order having the finces gates Or well Secured and all persons to withdraw from the same leaving the [straw] on the ground and to be accountable for all Damages that may be sustained in Consequence whereof the parties have hereunto set their hands and Seals the 4th of Sepr 1826 —

Witness — as to the
Signatures of
Ph Van Cortlandt
Laban Clark
Horace Bartlett &
Nathan Anderson by
Pierre Van Cortlandt

Ph. V Cortlandt
Laban Clark
Horace Bartlett
Nathan Anderson
Joseph Smith
John Fisher

[reverse side]

It is Said that no person Sold priviledges to Persons to Erect places to Sell in Crot. Doc^r. Lyman Cook & John Conklin. suffering their Fences to be taken down to Erect their Huts or Tents — to Foroners.

[Endorsed]
Camp Meeting Lease –1826–

---

1. See No. 63 for an earlier agreement for the use of Philip's lands as a Methodist camp meeting ground, and Nos. 106, 124 and 138 regarding later agreements.

79

Pierre, Jr. to William Miller. ALS
SHR

New York October 5–1826.

Thursday
Mr William Miller

I sent word by Lewis Constant[1] [torn] day that I would not return home until Saturday with the Govr Wolcott[2] — and that you would order Abram to come to the Landing to be there about two OClock, with the Waggon, Gig & little Waggon to bring up the Baggage — Major Van Cortlandt Lady and our young Ladies come with me — Order a good roast piece of Beef & 4 or 5 Cents of Stakes from the Butcher

I did not ask Lewis Constant for any money — you will settle with him —

Yours &c
PVC

I will write also by mail. —

[Addressed]
Mr William Miller

at Gen Van Cortlandts
Peekskill
Capt Hitchcock will please to forward this
PVC

---

1. Lewis Constant was a resident of the town of Cortlandt in 1820. "Fourth Census of the U.S. (1820)," National Archives.

2. The steamboat *Governor Wolcott* was named after Governor Oliver Wolcott, Jr. (1760–1833) of Connecticut.

80

Peter Townsend[1] to Philip. ALS
NYPL

New York 22d April 1827.

Dear Sir

presumeing that your recent afflictions in the death of your nephew & my much respected friend Pierre. C. Van Wyck Esqr.,[2] have diverted your mind from the enquiry I made of you when last at your house I would not now press the subject upon you but for reasons which require my prompt determination in regard to the establishment of my son whome I expect here, in a few weeks from Canandaigua[.]moreover should the power of that stream, on further examination be thot equal to the business which I suggested to you, I should persue there, — and should your estimate of its value not exceed my expectations in this case — I might think it expedient to commence building a Smiths Shop, a Forge and a temporary Dwelling or two the ensueing season

You will please therefore as early as possable after the receipt of this Letter to give me your Views on the subject, your Estimate of the Value of the property alluded to embraseing 100 or 200 Acres of land with all the prevelidges of flowing and all the Controle of the Stream, Dam Mills, &c — which you possess also the lowest prise at which you will sell this interest and the terms of payment which you will require[3]

Please to address me at New York to the care of Josiah L. James 109 Beekman Street

Yours Verry respectfully
Peter Townsend

[Endorsed]
Peter Townsend & answer
Apl. 22.1827

---

1. Peter Townsend, formerly of Orange County, then resided at 44 Beekman Street in New York City. He had represented Orange County in the New York Constitutional Convention of 1801. Werner, pp. 125, 322; *Longworth's Directory* (1828), pp. 337, 577.

2. Pierre Cortlandt Van Wyck died on April 4, 1827, as noted in Philip Van Cortlandt's entry in his *Almanack* (No. 70).

3. Townsend apparently sought to acquire milling rights on the Croton River; see the following two letters. The family did not agree to sell such property rights.

81

Philip to Peter Townsend. ADfs
NYPL

May–1–1827.

Dear Sir

It would give me great satisfaction if I could at this time communicate an answer to your Request as I percieve it is of the first importance to your pressing Arangements for the coming Season for business is fast approaching —

Myself, Brother, and three Sisters being all Concerned more or less and all at a distance from Each Other prevents my given you at present a Satisfactory answer

If a fortunate meeting should shortly take place and which I expect will of our Meeting together at this place a Consultation can take place and if it can be accompanied with your Estimate of Value and other propositions it will in my opinion lead to Amicable results — I Expect to be in New York the last of this week at N°. 16. Broad Street and will be glad to meet you before I return if you will send me word where to find you I will call and see you and am

&c
Ph VCortlandt

82

Peter Townsend to Philip. ALS
NYPL

Southfield Furnace[1] 9th May 1827.

Genl. Ph.V Cortlandt
Dear Sir

Your letter of the 1st Inst came to hand at this plase on the 6th from which I learn that the property I wish to purchase of you has many owners & that it will require some time before it is possable they all can be convened. It is desireable for me to obtain the Views of the parties owning the property with as much dispatch as will meet your conveniance

It will not be in my power to be in New York at the time you mention which I much regret. I have therefore requested my friend Mr James to confer freely with you on the subject as he is acquainted with my object which I think I explained to you at your House

DeWitt Clinton (1769–1828) oil on canvas, by Charles C. Ingham (1796–1863). Acclaimed as "The Father of the Erie Canal," DeWitt Clinton was one of the most influential politicians of New York in the early 19th century. His rise in politics was aided by his influential uncle, George Clinton, longtime Governor of New York and Vice-President of the United States. Upon George Clinton's death, the Van Cortlandts placed their political allegiance behind the nephew. He served as Mayor of New York City, Governor of New York, and as a U.S. Senator. A campaign to make him a presidential candidate was thwarted by his sudden death. (illustration: courtesy of The Long Island Historical Society).

I hope shortly you & your friends will meet and be able to arive at a Conclusion that will induce me to close a bargin with you

Respectfully yours
Peter Townsend

[Endorsed]
Peter Townsend — 9th of May. 1827 — Respecting Mill Seat & Water —

---

1. Most likely this is a reference to an ironworks which existed near the town of Monroe in Orange County. French, p. 508.

83

DeWitt Clinton to Pierre, Jr. ADf
Columbia University Special Collections

Albany 8 June 1827.

My dear Sir

I have this moment received your letter and I have to regret that I will not be able to accede to your intimation. Owing to my Southern and Eastern jaunts and one more that I have in view I will not have a moment's time to devote to concerns that are not implicated with my public duties.[1]

I assure you that the proposal you make would be considered an honor conferred on me not a condescension indicated by me, did the state of my engagements authorize a complience.

Accept the assurance of the high respect of

Your friend and obed^{t}. serv^{t}.

General Pierre Van Cortlandt
Peekskill
West Chester County

---

1. Pierre may have been soliciting DeWitt Clinton's appearance as the featured speaker at the dedicatory service for John Paulding's monument. See the following letter.

84

Pierre, Jr. to John Townsend.[1] ALS
NYSL

PeeksKill June 18, 1827.

Dear Sir

Yesterday I addressed a Letter to you and sent it across the River to be put on board the Steam Boat Albany but for fear you may not have received it I again write by mail It is to request you to consult Judge Spencer[2] whether he will be pleased to make an Address at the erection of a Monument over the remains of John Paulding One of the Patriots who captured Major Andre which the Corporation of the City of New York have ordered to be made & erected in the Episcopal Church Yard near my residence. And as soon as you write to me his Consent, the Committee of the Town of Cortlandt (who are authorised) will immediately address him on the Subject & solicit him to honor the Occasion and make the Address — There will be no doubt a great Concourse of People besides a number of Uniform Companies from New York which will attend the Ceremony — The Committee of the Corporation feel much pride to make it as splendid as possible, and for which reson our Committee wish to have One of our most distinguished Citizens to make the Address & no One more worthy & proper than the late Chief Justice. It will be a grand Subject to display his splendid Oratorial Talents & it will be highly gratifying to every Body that our Committee have selected a Gentleman of his high standing & Abilities. If the Judge should consent, Be pleased to present my best respects to him & that he will do me much pleasure of coming directly to my house & remaining with me while he stays in the Neighbourhood —

With much Esteem I have the
honor to be y[r] Ob[t] Ser[t]
Pierre Van Cortlandt

John Townsend Esq[r] —

[Addressed]
John Townsend Esq[r]
Albany

[Endorsed]
P. Van Cortlandt Letter
June 18 1827

---

1. New York's politics occasionally presented an incestual aura. John Townsend, "a rich manufacturer," was Judge Ambrose Spencer's son-in-law. And, as it happened, Spencer was DeWitt Clinton's brother-in-law. John C. Fitzpatrick, ed., *The Autobiography of Martin Van Buren* in *Annual Report of the American Historical Association* (Washington, D.C., 1920), II, 170.

2. Ambrose Spencer (1765–1848) served with distinction as New York's Chief Justice from 1819 to 1823. He was well known for his oratorical abilities. *DAB*, XVII, 444–445.

85

Hiram Paulding[1] to Pierre, Jr. ALS
NYPL

New.York July 6th 1827.

Sir,

As the time is approaching when it was supposed the monument would be erected over the remains of my Father, I take the liberty of requesting that you will have the kindness to inform me when it will probably take place and what arrangements, if any, have been made. And whether it is the intention of the committee to remove the remains from whence they now lie, previous to the day on which the foundation of the monument will be laid? I have taken this liberty of addressing you sir, believing it would be the most certain way of obtaining correct information, and because of the kind and obliging disposition you have ever shewn towards me. For your favours sir, allow me again to proffer my unfeigned thanks, and believe me with very great respect,

your obliged & Hbl. servt.
H. Paulding

Genl. Pierre Van Cortlandt
Peekskill

---

1. Hiram Paulding, son of Major André's captor, John Paulding, began an illustrious naval career in 1811 with strong recommendations from Vice President George Clinton and Pierre. See *VCFP,* III, 554–556.

86

Abraham Van Wyck[1] to Philip. ALS
NYHS

Phil[a]. July 13, 1827.

Dear uncle General —

In February last I had the honor & good fortune to be appointed to a Situation as clerk in the United States Bank of this place and have since received an offer from the Board of Directors to go to Nashville Tennessee, as teller for the Branch about to be established there, at a Salary (for the present) of $1000 per annum — I Shall leave this place in the course of a week at furthest & Want a letter of introduction to General Jackson — I Shall get two or three letters to him from gentlemen Who reside here, but one from yourself as a

Veteran of the Revolution & the friend and companion in arms of Washington and Lafayette, Will be an honor, of which, although I feel I am Scarce worthy, I am induced to Solicit from Your Kindness and generosity alone — If you feel disposed to confer So great a favor upon me I can only Say that I Will endeavor Never to disgrace it — Be So good as to enclose by mail, Such a letter as you may be pleased to give, addressed to me at the United States Bank — With the greatest respect

I am your obt. Servt. & nephew
A Van Wyck

Genl. Van Cortlandt at Croton —

[Addressed]
Genl. Philip Van Cortlandt
Croton
State of New York

[Endorsed]
Ab^{m} Van Wyck
Nashville —
Tennessee 1827
Octr. 8

---

1. Abraham Van Wyck (1801–1853) was the son of Theodorus C. and Mary (Stretch) Van Wyck. His grandmother, Catharine, was Philip's sister. With this letter a correspondence began between Philip and his grandnephew, who sought to join the Jackson presidential bandwagon in 1827. Ironically, it was Jackson who, as President, "killed" the Second Bank of the United States.

87

Morgan Lewis[1] to Pierre, Jr. ALS
SHR

Staatsburgh 8th August 27 [1827]

My dear Sir,

I yesterday received your very flattering favour of the preceding day, and would with the greatest pleasure accept the honor intended me, was I twenty years younger. Time, that destroyer of all Things, has completely prostrated the few rhetorical Powers I ever possessed, and has totally incapacitated me for doing merited justice to a subject, which must arouse feelings, that three score and thirteen would be very unlikely to give due expression to. I must therefore beg of you to excuse me, and to select some younger Orator who has not outlived the requisite qualifications. I do not think it very important that he should be a revolutionary Character.

When you pay your intended visit to your Son, I shall be very happy, if your convenience will permit, to see you at my house; and you will add to the obligation by dining and passing a night with me.

most respectfully
your Obt. & hble. Servt.
Morgan Lewis

Gen: Van Cortlandt

---

1. Morgan Lewis (1754–1844), former Attorney General and Governor of New York, had not always been a political ally of the Van Cortlandts. Apparently old political wounds had been healed. Pierre was still having difficulty obtaining speakers for the Paulding monument dedication. For discussions of the earlier political clashes between Lewis and the adherents of the Clintonians, see *VCFP,* III, 141, 142, 159–161, 214–215.

Pierre Van Cortlandt. Plaster bust by William J. Coffee after an oil portrait by John Wesley Jarvis. Philip Van Cortlandt presented this plaster bust of his father to the City of New York in August, 1827. This gift was the result of Philip's visit to the City Hall where he viewed busts of George Washington and George Clinton. Philip felt that his father had been slighted and that he, too, should be represented in such august company. The plaster bust is currently in very poor condition. (illustration: courtesy of The Museum of the City of New York).

88

Philip to Richard Riker.
Minutes of the Common Council of the City of New York.
(New York, 1917), XVI, 489–91.

New York August 27th 1827.

My Dear Sir

Having recently seen the Busts of General Washington and Governor Clinton in the City Hall of the City of New York it brought to my recollection the evacuation of this city by the British in 1783 at the close of the Revolutionary War At that happy event the City was taken possession of by General Washington accompanied by Governor Clinton Pierre Van Courtlandt then Lieutenant Governor many of the members of the Senate and House of Assembly and an immense concourse of our fellow Citizens — The Procession moved through Pearl street to the Battery where the American Standard was hoisted amidst the exulting shouts of thousands — As my father Lieutenant Governor Van Courtlandt was united with those Patriots in an event so interesting to our City, it has suggested a wish in me that his Bust might be honored with a station in the Common Council Hall along with them. And for that purpose I beg you will make Communication to the Common Council and tender to them a Bust of my father which is now in my possession[1]

I remain with all Respect yours
most sincerely

Ph V Cortlandt

Honbl Richard Riker

---

1. Philip offered a plaster bust of his father rendered by the artist William J. Coffee after an oil portrait by John Wesley Jarvis. The Jarvis portrait of Pierre Van Cortlandt (SHR Collections) is the frontispiece of *VCFP,* II. The Corporation of the City of New York accepted the gift on September 10, declaring, "That

cherishing as the City of New York does the memory of all those Statesmen and Heroes, who, defended the Republic by their Councils or their Valour in the time that tried mens souls the offering made to the City of the Likeness of the second Magistrate who acted in those days of danger is received with the deepest public sensibility."

The ravages of time have taken their toll on the plaster bust and it now resides all but forgotten in a storage space in the Museum of the City of New York.

Philip to Pierre, Jr. ALS
SHR

Croton Octr. 1.1827 —

Dear Brother —

I have been looking Over the Will Codicil and Surveys of Our Dec^{d}. Father and find there was Only. 1200 Acres left of South lot N°. 1 — Unsold which he Bequeath to his three Daughters as follows — to be Drawn for &cr

The Outhouse Farm to Contain	360 Acres
Knapp. d^{o}———d^{o}	340–d^{o}
And all the Remaining land in this lott. Lying Northerly of the Outhouse farm and the great Swamp by the Road and the possession of Tunis Cronkheit with the Land Adjoining S.E. containing about 500. Acres — the 1200.Acres more or less I give and Bequeath to my Three Daughters —	500
	1200.Acres

The above was Released by my Sisters to Each Other in the Words of the Will — therefore Cornelia and Ann have given to Catherine the Deed which has been proved and

Recorded — for the Whole[1] —

The Old Gentleman when he made the Codicil must have thought that the Ask farm was Exclusive of the 1200.Acres at any Rate Cornelia & Ann Cannot have any Right as they have given a Release to Catherine — I will not Consent to Sell it to any One nor have any other a Right to it but Sister Catherine — I wish to See you as Soon as Convenient. I fell Out of the Gig the Morning Coming from Sister Beekmans and hurt my Breast — I am in haste Your Affectionate Brother

Ph V Cortlandt

[Addressed]
Gen[l] Pierre Van Cortlandt
PeeksKill

Cortlandt Town
October 1

---

1. The recent death of his nephew, Pierre Cortlandt Van Wyck, may have precipitated Philip's re-examination of property rights left to his sisters, and, in particular, to Pierre Cortlandt Van Wyck's mother, Catharine. Whether Pierre Van Cortlandt had approached the relatives with specific proposals for the sale of some land remains unclear.

Abraham Van Wyck to Philip. ALS
NYHS

Nashville Oct 8 1827.

Dear Uncle General

Your kind & acceptable favor of 10 Aug last reached me at this place in due course — enclosing a letter of introduction to Gen[l]. Jackson — for which be pleased to Accept my Sincere thanks I accompanied a friend to the residence of the General, immediately on receiving your letter & Spent a most agreeable Visit from Saturday Evening until the Monday following — He lives on an excellent & Well cultivated farm about 13 miles from this place & about a mile from the Cumberland River — in a acomodious two story Brick dwelling — four rooms on the floor Large hall in the center and all handsomely furnished. Our reception was most polite & hospitable — the Gen[l]. & family Were in good health & we accompanied them to a camp Meeting on Sunday held about Seven Miles off by the Methodists — the general Was much gratified to hear from You — He reminded me Very much of you — & resembles you in his manners & address — I had no idea I should feel So much at home in his presence as I did in the course of a half hour — I have been in his company Several times Since in this place & like him more the more I See him[1] —

I am much pleased With my Situation & With Nashville — I had a Safe & agreeable ride from Phil[a]. Via wheeling — Saw many Scenes of Varied beauty, & here there is much to admire & little to condemn — the inhabitants are exceedingly hospitable but quite as extravagant — they have no system or even ideas of economy — I presume the slave holding States are mostly so — But here we have such facilities to make money — Being Surrounded With a country as luxuriant as Eden when young — that Economy Seems unnecessary — the Society is excellent whether male or female & as I am of much More consequence here than in Phil[a]. have the Same comforts & greater prospects & advantages I am rather glad of the change — I do not Know whether you are for or against the administration but presume the latter — At any rate I should be much gratified to hear from you on politics or any other Subject — You can no doubt give me Correct information respecting the probable Vote of New York — I have always regretted I did not propose to be honored as your Amanuensis to record Some of those interesting adventures of the Revolution that you Were engaged in — I Remember most that you told me but am Sorry I did not write them down — Hoping this may find you in good health I am

With great respect your

Ob^{t}. & Dutifull Nephew

A Van Wyck

Love to Grandma Vanwyck
Uncle Phil, Aunt & the Children —
Genl. Van Cortlandt

[Addressed]

Genl. Philip Van Cortlandt
Cortlandt Town
West chester
State of New York

---

1. Andrew Jackson's home, the Hermitage, so lovingly described here by Abraham Van Wyck, burned in 1834 and was later rebuilt. The future President was noted for his hospitality. A neighbor was said to have remarked that "the General was the prince of hospitality; not only because he entertained a great many people but because the poor, belated peddler was as welcome at the Hermitage as the President of the United States and made so much at ease that he felt as though he had got home." Editors of American Heritage, *The American Heritage Book of Great Historic Places* (New York, 1957), p. 151.

91

Catharine Van Wyck[1] to Philip. ALS
SHR

[December, 1827.]

My dear Uncle

I now have an opportunity of writing to you to let you know that I am much better than when Mama was down here and that we enjoy ourselves very much at school[.] I study

Geography Grammar History Arithmetic and Writing and I should like to know very much when Papa Mama and Joanna are comeing down to see me I am very glad to hear that my brother David talks French I send my love to Papa Mama GrandMama and all the children the Misses Delavans and all the young ladies are very well[.] I am very much pleased with my Geography and if my dear Uncle will let me have a paint Box I should like to begin to draw maps next quarter almost all the young Ladies attend to this branch and Miss Mary thinks it is very improving to them I will try before Spring to draw you the Map of the state of New York and put in the canal[.] Miss Mary has some paint Boxes and if you like I will get one of her[.] Give my love to all at home and if my dear Uncle would write to me it would much gratify his affectionate Neice

Catharine Van Wyck

[Endorsed]
Catharine Van Wyck
Decr. 1827 —

---

1. Catharine Van Wyck was the daughter of Philip G. and Mary (Gardiner) Van Wyck. She later married the Reverend Stephen H. Battin and settled in Cooperstown.

92

Horatio Gates Spafford to Pierre, Jr. ALS
SHR

Lansingburgh, N.Y., 1 Mo.14, 1828–72.
[January 14, 1828.]

General —

I am very glad to perceive, that, at last, some portion of the people of the Counties bordering on the Hudson, are roused from their lethargy, & beginning to think about a

Road, such as there ought to be, between NewYork & Albany. That I was aware of the importance of this measure, may be seen in my Gazetteer, particularly that of 1824, page 605, 606, article *Roads, Bridges,* &c. — I hope you will proceed, & shall be most happy to contribute by any means in my power, toward such success.[1]

Perhaps it might be desirable, in order to come imposingly before the Legislature, to get as many of the Counties as may be, to unite in the application: If on both sides of the River, no matter, for but one Road would be made, & there can be little doubt on which side it ought to be. That decision, I think, should be left to Commissioners, named in the Act for making a Road, & be kept quite out of discussion, when applying for it. I may be mistaken, however. If the People, on each side make application for a Road, none would be granted, of course, because, the Members, in voting for one side, would be sure to make about as many enemies as friends, by which they would lose votes at the next Election.

I am glad to see thy name among those of the applicants, for the object ought to be attained. Very respectfully, thy friend,

Horatio Gates Spafford

Gen. Pierre Van Cortlandt.

[Addressed]

Gen. Pierre Van Cortlandt, at Albany, N.Y.

---

1. Horatio Gates Spafford, editor of the *Montgomery Monitor* in Johnstown, New York, was best known for his *A Gazetteer of the State of New York,* published originally in 1813, with a second edition issued in 1824. In the latter edition he declared, "There ought to be, I think, as well as for the convenience as the credit of the State, a direct, well constructed road, between Albany and the City of New York. . . . There are roads, already, but there is no highway, such as there ought to be, between the metropolis and the capital of the State of New-York." Spafford, *Gazetteer,* pp. 605–606.

93

Pierre, Jr. to Joseph Howland.[1] ALS
J.L.M. Curry Autograph Collection, LC

PeeksKill Jany. 18th 1828.

Dear Sir

The Turnpike road near the Gate at Annsville requires to be filled up with Gravel and raised. As every high tide over flows it; And as I fill up the Marsh opposite to it the Water remains on the Road and becomes a muddy hole — I saw David McCoy[2] this morning who says he can do it very conveniently as he has no work for his Oxen — I wish you to write to him to do it immediately as it was not done as it should have been in The first Instance — It will require about One foot to be raised to make it good —

Yours respectfully
Pierre Van Cortlandt

Joseph Howland Esqr.

---

1. Joseph Howland had served as president of the Highland Turnpike Company at a time when the Clinton and Van Cortlandt families were heavy investors. Apparently both Pierre and Howland were still financially concerned in turnpikes. See *VCFP,* III, 228–229, 301–303, 330–333, 423–425.
   Annsville was a hamlet about one mile north of Peekskill. Pierre had inherited this land from his deceased brother, Gilbert.

2. David McCoy was a resident of Peekskill as of 1820. In 1839 he purchased a 200-acre glebe farm from St. Philips Chapel at the Highlands. Fox, p. 121.

94

Joanna Van Wyck to Philip. ALS
SHR

NewYork Feby 6 1828.

Dear Uncle

It is with pleasure I imbrace this opportunity of writing to you I intended writing you before and I hope you will excuse my not doing it. Papas last letter said you had been unwell for some days I hope by this time you have quite recovered your health again. — We have very good sleighing and the streets are full of sleighs which makes it very lively we were all out rideing yesterday. —

I wrote to Papa the other day I presume he received my letter.

I have nothing particular to communicate at present except our good health and so must finish my letter with love to your self, Grandmama, Papa Mama and Brothers tell Cortlandt I should be much pleased to receive a letter from him —

Your Affectionate Niece
Joanna Van Wyck

95

Abraham Van Wyck to Philip. ALS
NYHS

Nashville Feby 11th. 1828.

Dear Uncle General

Your highly gratifying letter of 8th. Novr last reached me on the first of the following Month — The infamous Hammond of Cincinnati has published a pamphlet recently repeating the charges against Mr. Jackson[1] — It is ushered forth with the Sanction of his Name and is filled with Certificates & documents purporting to be transcripts from the public records — I have Not read it Nor Will I. I will not contaminate my fingers With it — The annals of electioneering afford No parallel to the efforts of the infamous Hammond — But he is I am happy to say it, helping the cause he Wishes to injure & disgracing the one he Wishes to help[.]It is Yet uncertain Whether the electoral law in Kentucky Will be changed from the district Mode to the general Ticket — Should it be, the contest will be a Severe one but I am afraid the Administration Will Succeed — I judge from this that the most populous districts are favorable to M^r^. Clay and although a majority of the friends of Jackson were elected to Congress many thousand more Votes Were polled on the opposite Side — My information induces me to fear the General Will not Succeed in Louisiana[2] — The opposition to him there is Strong, and intolerant to an unaccountable degree — But all accounts (worthy of belief) concur in stating his reception in New Orleans on the 8th. to have been cordial and Splendid in the extreme — The Kentucky Legislature are making Some highly important disclosures respecting the Votes of the members from that State in Congress at the last election — What I have Seen of the testimony (before the Bar of the Senate on oath) is heavy against Mr. Clay — The result Will powerfully affect the Contest — especially as Mr. Clays recent pamphlet is alleged to be working wonders[3] — not in this State to be Sure — nor in Alabama nor in Mississippi nor even in Kentucky — but in Virginia & New Jersey — I have always Calculated on the latter State and my last accounts by no means Shake the idea that She will give Jackson a majority[4] — But New York I am Satisfied to be the arbitress in the contest[5] — And as my feelings are and have ever been Strongly enlisted, having been a Jackson-man from the beginning — I will esteem it a great favor if you inform me,

1st. whether Jackson has really and indisputably a majority in both houses of the Legislature in Your State & if so the number —

2nd Whether General Root is or is not favorable to the Election of Gen: Jackson —
3d. Whether the Republican party are united in Support of Jackson — if not whether he Will get a majority of that party —
4 — Whether it is Still probable the mode of Choosing electors will be changed as Suggested in Your last —
5 If the present mode is preserved what Number of electoral Votes I may Set down as Sure for Jackson at all events —
I am giving you Some trouble but I hope you Will excuse it — I can elect Jackson Without requiring a Vote in New Jersey, Delaware, Indiana Missouri, Illinois, Ohio or Kentucky or Louisiana & But two in Maryland, but I must have 24 in New York — Pennia. is as sure for Jackson as the bases of the Allegheny — this I Know — North Carolina also[6] — So Says a recent letter from Gov Branch to a friend of mine in this place — I spent an afternoon in the presence of Genl. Jackson a day or two after his arrival from New Orleans[7] — He, with his Lady, Were and are Still in excellent health I have read Dewitt Clintons Splendid Message,[8] and also his gratifying & beautiful toast on the 8th. I Shall Vote for him for the Next President after Jackson — but that is indulging a thought too far "infuturo" — Recent letters inform Me my friends in New Jersey are Well — & hoping the Same may be the case With those on the Hudson

I am With the greatest respect
your obt. Nephew
A VanWyck

Nashville Feby 11th. 1828

[Addressed]
Genl. Philip Van Cortlandt   Cortlandt Town
West Chester
State of New York

Calendar of Correspondence

1. The immediate circumstances surrounding the marriage of Andrew Jackson and Mrs. Lewis Robards still remain shrouded in mystery. Exactly when a divorce became effective between Lewis Robards and his wife, Rachel, in relation to the frontier marriage of Jackson and Rachel is the nub of the issue. Jackson's recent biographer, Robert V. Remini, after speculating upon several possibilities, concludes that "One thing is certain. Whatever Rachel and Andrew did, and whenever they did it, their actions did not outrage the community." For, as Remini asserts, "Community acceptance of their behavior is proven in the fact that within the next few years the people of the state conferred a number of honors on Jackson that they would never have given had they believed him guilty of acting improperly."

   The mystery surrounding the actual date of the divorce provided salacious material for such an arch political rival of Jackson's as the publisher of the Cincinnati *Gazette,* Charles Hammond. In the midst of the presidential campaign Hammond asked his readers: "Ought a convicted adulteress and her paramour husband be placed in the highest offices in this free and Christian land?" Charles Hammond, *A View of General Jackson's Domestic Relations* (Cincinnati, 1828); Remini, pp. 57–67.

2. Jackson received Louisiana's five electoral-college votes in 1828. Abraham Van Wyck was not an astute political seer.

3. Henry Clay sought to defend himself from charges hurled against him and John Quincy Adams concerning the so-called "Corrupt Bargain" surrounding disputed electoral votes in 1824. Clay's pamphlet was titled, *An address of Henry Clay, to the Public; Containing Certain Testimony in Refutation of the Charges Against Him Made by Gen. Andrew Jackson, Touching the Last Presidential Election,* published in the District of Columbia in 1827.

4. New Jersey's eight electoral votes went to Adams.

5. New York retained the district system in choosing presidential electors. John Quincy Adams captured the older Federalist strongholds in the Hudson Valley districts, while Jackson carried the rest.

6. Jackson carried Pennsylvania, Maryland, Virginia, North and South Carolina, Kentucky, Tennessee, Ohio, Louisiana, Indiana, Missouri, Mississippi, Alabama, and Illinois, and split the electoral vote in New York, 20 to 16.

7. Jackson was invited to attend the anniversary celebration of the Battle of New Orleans held in that city on February 8–12, 1828. He returned triumphantly to the battlefield where his rise to national prominence began. Isabel T. Kelsay, "The Presidential Campaign of 1828," *The East Tennessee Historical Society Publication No. 5* (January, 1933), pp. 71–72.

8. On the same day that this letter was written, DeWitt Clinton suffered a fatal coronary attack. In what became his last message to the New York legislature, he denounced the slander aimed at Mrs. Jackson. Hammond, II, 264–265.

96

Pierre, III[1] to Philip. ALS
SHR

Hyde Park Febuary 13th. 1828.

Dear Uncle.

As this is the first time that I have written to you, however I hope you will not be displeased to receive a few lines from me; The weather is very pleasant here now, it is almost like Spring — the steam boats go to Albany daily — they pass here every day. My Father is very well — I had a letter from him last thursday — Give my love to Aunt Van Wyck, and all the family. Dr. and Mrs. Allen[2] send their respects to you. I have no more to write at present.

I remain your Affectionate Nephew
Pierre Van Cortlandt.

[Endorsed]
Pierre V.Cortlandt Jun.
Feby. 13. 1828 —
answered

---

1. Pierre, III (1815–1884) was the son of Pierre, Jr. He was soon to be thirteen years old.

2. Dr. Benjamin Allen founded the private academy named the Hyde Park Classical Institution. It prepared young men for college and business careers. Edwin Williams, *The New York Annual Register for the Year of Our Lord 1834* (New York, 1834), p. 226.

97

Pierre, Jr. to William Miller. ALS
SHR

Albany Feb 16, 1828.

Mr. Wm Miller

I did not arrive here until ¼ past two OClock on Thursday when the procession for the funeral of Genr. Clinton began to move —, I regretted it extremely — I send you the Signs of the Times containing all the particulars, This Country could not have lost so great a Man[1] —

Mr. Stevenson will take Red Gauntlet, and I have promised to send him up the last of March so that it will be necessary to put him in Order by that time —

If my Brother sends up for the [torn] Waggon, You must let the Person [torn]

[torn]

[Addressed] Mr. William Miller
at Genl. Van Cortlandts
PeeksKill
N.Y.

---

1. DeWitt Clinton was buried amid appropriate pomp on February 15.

98

Catharine Van Wyck to Philip. ALS
SHR

Sing Sing March. 1st 1828.

Dear Uncle,

I have received your kind letter, and I am very glad to hear that you say that I can have a Paint Box, and I believe that I have got perfectly well. Papa come down here on Thursday, and he said that they were all well at home but Grand Mama; and I wish that you would please to tell my Sister Joanna to write to me. I should like to know how my Uncle Theadore is. Miss Dawson and the Misses Delavans, and all the young ladies are very well. I send my love to Papa, Mama, Grand Mama, and all the children. I remain your affectionate Neice

Catharine Van Wyck
Saturday Morning March 9th

I was very happy to see Papa and Sister Joanna here yesterday. Miss Margaret wished them to stay in the evening, for we had a concert. It was Hannah's birthday, and we boil'd molasses candy, and had a little party. Mrs. Voris, and Mrs. Carpenter and Mr. Miller were here in the Evening, and Hannah introduced all the young Ladies to them, so I hope we shall learn among other things, to enter a room full of company, and to make a graceful curtsey. We are obliged to enter the room so, every friday, and be introduced to Miss Mary, just as if she was a stranger. I hope to receive a letter from you soon, my dear Uncle, and it will much gratify your affectionate Neice,

Catharine Van Wyck

99

Ebenezer Baldwin[1] to Pierre, Jr. ALS
Pickering Papers, MHS

Albany, March 21 1828.

Gen. P. Van Cortlandt
Dear Sir,

An accordance in sentiment with regard to political matters will I trust be deemed a sufficient apology in soliciting your attention to certain movements now making with regard to the Presidential candidates. You are familiar with all the facts relating to the anti-masonic excitement in the western part of this state,[2] but are probably not aware that the cabinet at Washington are endeavoring to bring that feeling (disreputably) in aid of M^{r}. Adams's re-election. M^{r}. Southard[3] and M^{r}. Clay have repeatedly stated that M^{r}. Adams is not a mason, and party zealots go further and alledge that M^{r}. Adams himself has disclaimed any connexion with this institution. Why is this zeal manifested? Can it be from a laudible desire to suppress a dangerous society? — The fact that M^{r}. Clay himself is a mason disposes such a supposition. The truth is that probably ten or twelve Electoral Districts in this state will be deeply affected by such a statement, and as the friends of General Jackson admit that he is a mason, the gain will be altogether on the side of M^{r}. Adams.

A gentleman in this vicinity informed a friend of mine, that he knew M^{r}. A was a mason and that he had met with him in a lodge at Boston.

A gentleman from Boston has stated to me, that Major Benj^{m} Russel[4] Editor of the Centinel declared that M^{r}. A was a mason and that he saw him initiated at St. John's Lodge Concert Hall Boston.

Another gentleman states, that he has seen M^{r}. A's name in the Masonic Register as an officer of the lodge.

Can all these statements be incorrect? Are they not rather strengthened by the strong probability that a gentleman whose life has been chiefly spent in foreign countries and in diplomatic stations, would avail himself of the benefits of friendships with so extensive an order?

The importance of obtaining accurate and positive testimony on this subject is becoming daily more manifest. In the result this single matter may decide the Presidential question. I am informed that at a local election at Quincy, the family residence of Mr Adams, which took place on the first Monday of the present month, every masonic incumbent was removed on the sole ground that Gen. Jackson was a mason, and therefore masons should not be kept in office.

Although there is no positive proof that this course was adopted under the dictation or influence of the President, it is certainly very extraordinary that the first breakings-out of an anti-masonic spirit — in Massachusetts would occur in that particular town.

Our leading politicians are looking to the result of this matter with great anxiety, and I trust that you will not deem it unworthy your attention to use your best efforts to ascertain the truth. Probably you have friends at Boston who may procure the proof that M^{r}. A is a mason. It is said that during several years no records were kept in St. Johns Lodge, or if they were that they are now missing.

Very respectfully,
Your friend
E. Baldwin

Gen. Pierre Van Cortlandt

---

1. Ebenezer Baldwin had been a leading Federalist who served as the Recorder for the city of Albany. He was an ardent Jacksonian in 1828. Kass, pp. 124–125; Hough, p. 414.

2. Western New York demonstrated a fervor for causes in the ante-bellum decades of the nineteenth century. The region was immersed in religious movements or in social and political re-

forms. One such activity involved a mass disapproval of the Order of Masons. With the disappearance under mysterious circumstances of a disillusioned Mason, William Morgan, in September, 1826, the story rapidly spread that he had been murdered by his former lodge brothers in order to preserve the Society's secrets, which he had threatened to expose. Public opinion in the region rapidly turned against the Masons, and against anyone even suspected of membership in that organization.

Andrew Jackson openly admitted being a Mason. If John Quincy Adams proved to be a nonmember, it was obvious that he would win political support in this rabid anti-Masonic region. In a famous letter datelined Washington, April, 19, 1828, Adams categorically declared: "I state that I am not, never was, and never shall be a free mason." He then added, "I request you not to give publicity to this letter." Of course, it was almost immediately made public and Adams was well on the way to an election sweep of western New York. Henry Brown, *A Narrative of the Anti-Masonick Excitement, in the Western Part of the State of New-York* (Batavia, N.Y., 1829), pp. 232–233; W. Freeman Galpin, "Reform Movements," in Flick, VI, 274–275.

3. Samuel L. Southard (1787–1842), from Basking Ridge, New Jersey, was then Secretary of the Navy in the Adams cabinet.

4. Benjamin Russell was a Boston newspaper publisher and a local political figure.

100

Pierre, Jr. to Joseph Howland. **ALS**
SHR

Peeks Kills April 1st–1828.

Dear Sir

I have understood that the Law creating the Highland Turnpike Company or by some subsequent Amendments to the said Law, those Persons whose farms adjoin the Turnpike have the priviledge of working that Road the Number of Days they may be assessed to work in the Town — If so — I beg you will write to me particularly what is necessary for me to do to have my wishes accomplished to work that Road[1] — I would not trouble you with this Letter if I had the Law but I have never seen it —

Yours with much respect
Pierre Van Cortlandt

Joseph Howland Esqr —

[Post marked]
1 April 1828
3^{d} —

1. The Van Cortlandts and the Clintons had invested in the Highland Turnpike Company since its inception. The road ran between Hudson, New York, and Manhattan Island. Even though it was on a heavily traveled route it never paid dividends. See VCFP, III, 228–229, 330–333; Flick, V, 269.

101

Philip to Timothy Pickering. ALS
MHS

Cortlandt Town April. 1st. 1828.

Dear Sir

Presuming that our former friendships and politacal Sentiments continue the Same, I am in hopes, that the trouble I am about to Solicit will not be disagreable. It is for you to peruse the inclosed[1] which was put into my hands by my Brother requesting me to forward it to Some particular friend in the City of Boston or its Vicinity, "where he was Unacquainted" —

The subject treated of in the inclosed we think of great importance and should you concur in Sentiment with us and have leasure time to make inquiry and with the Assistance of your friends Obtain the proof necessary to Establish the fact

that J.Q. Adams is a Mason and transmit the Same to me it may be of Essential Service if Obtained in Season —
Most respectfully I remain

Your Old revolutionary
Friend —
Ph. V.Cortlandt
Timothy Pickering Esqr.

P.S. ad^{s}. to Genl Philip Van Cortlandt, Cortlandt Town in the County of Westchester, State of New York —

---

1. Ebenezer Baldwin to Pierre, Jr., March 21, 1828 (No. 99).

102

Timothy Pickering to Philip. ADfs
MHS

To General Philip Van Cortlandt
of Cortlandt Town, in the County of Westchester,
State of New York

Salem April 18, 1828.

Dear Sir,

Your letter of the first instant, I received on the seventh, and on the same day wrote to a friend in Boston, to inquire into the fact, whether John Q. Adams was a free-mason; mentioning what your friend at Albany stated on the subject. To this inquiry I have just received an answer — that his name is not found in the books of the lodges which have been examined. — From another gentleman to whom I also wrote on the same day I am in daily expectation of receiving authentic information. He is a highly valued friend, a most worthy man, and a mason. He interested himself at once, to obtain a satisfactory answer to my inquiry.[1]

But how disgraceful it is for the friends of M^{r}. Adams to resort to the pitiful means mentioned by your Albany friend, to promote his election to the Presidency, in preference to General Jackson, because the latter is a mason? Suppose it true — an ascertained fact, that Morgan (himself a free mason, I presume) had, for having betrayed the secrets of the institution, been murdered by a little knot of wretches, admitted masons, but utterly unworthy of the name; — what man of sense, what person having any pretensions to a reputable character, would have attempted, for that cause, to brand the whole brotherhood with reproach? a brotherhood which comprehends a multitude of very respectable citizens — respectable for talents, integrity, and patriotism? — I am not a mason; but I have known some distinguished men who were masons. Let it suffice for me to mention two. General Warren, so eminent for talents, for patriotism, for zeal, for heorism, at the commencement of our revolution, and who fell at the battle of Bunker Hill, was a mason — and a mason of the highest rank, a "Most Worshipful Grand-Master". And General Washington was a mason. My masonic friend, to whom I mentioned the latter as a received fact, — in acknowledging the receipt of my letter, asserts its truth; and adds "that the correspondence of Washington with the Grand Lodge is now on the files of that lodge." — And now what further evidence can be wanted of at least the innocence of the institution of freemasonry? Who will believe that the pure mind of Washington would have given countenance to an institution pregnant with evil, or that was not founded in benevolence and good will? — And shall a very numerous society be condemned because there have crept into it some unworthy members? — On this principle, what society or class of citizens can escape? Take the learned professions. That of medicine has its quacks, passing themselves off among the poorest and most ignorant portion of the people, as skillful physicians. Among lawyers there are are pettifogers, stirrers-up of strife; and among the Reverend clergy are there no hypocrites? Among merchants are there no fraudulent dealers? Among manufacturers and mechanics no unfaithful workmen? And among the most numerous class in society, the cultivators of the soil, the farmers, whom Mr. Jefferson once called "God's chosen people" — are there none of these who play dishonest tricks with the consumers of their production? — Away, then, with the revilers of the free mason! — especially away with the miserable demagogues, political imposters, who, when among their less informed fellow-citizens, would hold up General Jackson as disqualified for the Presidency, because he is a free-mason. Were Washington now alive, and a candidate for office, the same political imposters to be consistent, must pronounce him alike disqualified. — When your fellow citizens in the West, whose animosities have been excited against free-masonry, by insidious deceivers, shall give themselves time to reflect, they will repel with disdain the imposition which has been practiced on them.

I had written thus far, when the expected letter from my very worthy masonic friend arrived; and it gives the following answer to my inquiry: —

"The present Grand-Master of the Grand Lodge, who has been a mason forty years, and all the permanent members of the Grand Lodge, have no recollection of ever hearing J.Q. Adams called a mason. We have no records certifying it; and it is our firm belief that he is not one."

This information I think should be frankly published, and if its publication be accompanied with observations of the kind herein before expressed, — instead of injuring General Jackson, will bring contempt on the wretches who are using his masonry as a weapon to destroy him. Knaves only, and fools, their miserable dupes, can think, or affect to think, the worse of General Jackson because he is a mason.

I am, my dear sir,
Your respectful friend,
and humble servant,
Timothy Pickering

1. An old-line Massachusetts Federalist, Timothy Pickering (1745–1829) had been a Hamiltonian stalwart. He served in both the Washington and John Adams cabinets, and while he respected the former, he plotted politically against the latter President. His antagonism against the Adams family was a deep and long-lasting one that continued into his waning days. While Jackson did not have much of a chance in Massachusetts against a native son in the election of 1828, the Van Cortlandt brothers knew to whom they could turn for the information they sought.

Pickering was a principled politician, and he deplored the guilt-by-association brush being used against all Masons and, in particular, against Andrew Jackson, because of William Morgan's disappearance and rumored murder at the hands of New York Masons.

Philip had forwarded to Pickering Ebenezer Baldwin's letter to Pierre, Jr. (No. 99), which raised the question as to whether John Quincy Adams was a Mason. Baldwin was the "Albany friend" referred to by Pickering. *DAB,* XIV, 565–568; McCormick, pp. 41–44.

103

Timothy Pickering to Philip. ADfs
MHS

Salem April 18.1828.

Dear Sir,

Since closing my letter about the free-masons, I have thought it might not be unacceptable to you, to have a short account of the defence of New-Orleans, derived from a source which you may not have seen.

All admit that General Jackson deserved well of his country for that defence. I have read the details of it, as given by an English officer, who served with the British army there, and witnessed all that passed.[1]

The first body of British troops, sixteen hundred strong, advanced, and rested some miles below the city.

There were two American armed vessels on the river, at General Jackson's command. One of these took a station on the opposite side of the Mississippi, and with her shot raking the position of the British troops, soon caused them to flee to the bank (called by the French the Levee) raised on the brink of the river, to prevent an inundation, which, in time of freshets, would otherwise deluge the flat, or intervale land on its border. Jackson marched down and attacked the enemy, in the evening of the same day; and after several hours of hard fighting returned to the city. The officer states, that in this action, five hundred of the British troops had fallen. The first battle, on the 23th or 24th of December, was a movement to check the enemy; and in my view, laid the foundation of the final victory of the eight of January. — Jackson, without delay, began to throw up a breast-work across the whole flat, or intervale, from the river to an impassable swamp erecting, at the same time, one or two batteries for cannon. On these, in their unfinished state, the British made an attack, and were repulsed.

About this time arrived General Packenham, and one or two other British Generals, with the remainder of the troops composing the British army. The breast-work, with the ditch in its front, appeared so formidable, that Packenham judged it necessary to make a breach in it, before he should attempt to surmount it. Accordingly, in one night he raised six batteries, mounted with heavy cannon, to batter in breach. But Jackson had erected a battery on the other side of the river, the shot from which, enfilading those batteries, rendered that project of the enemy unavailing. Thus disappointed, the British General, with great labor and some days' delay, essayed other means to attack his enemy to advantage. At length he made his last gallant but desperate effort to pass over Jackson's lines. In this fruitless attempt he perservered, until he was slain — until the second in command had received a mortal wound, — and about a thousand of their troops had fallen. This is the number stated in the narrative of the British officer. — The remainder of the army then withdrew; and after obtaining a truce, to enable them to bury their dead, they departed, and re-imbarked on board their ships.[2]

You; my friend, are an old soldier of the revolution; and if you place any value on my opinion, as a fellow soldier, you will permit me to express it in relation to General Jackson. And after an attentive examination of his measures, as they appear in the British officers' narrative, I assure you, that they exhibit, to my mind, that quick discernment — prompt decision — and energetic execution, which characterise a man fitted to command an army. — And is a man thus endowed, incompetent to discern and adopt the measures calculated to promote the welfare of his country in its civil administration? The idea is absurd. A strong mind will soon grasp a new subject to which it turns its attention. But Politics, the most common subject of conversation and reading among the mass of American citizens, cannot be new to General Jackson. He has lived, I suppose, sixty years or more — was (as I have understood) attorney-general of Tennessee, and assisted in forming its constitution — was a judge of its Supreme Court — a member of the house of representatives when congress sat in Philadelphia — and of late a senator in congress at Washington. With these advantages, and all the additional light and information which he will derive from the heads of departments whom he will select for these offices — I entertain not a shadow of doubt, that under his Presidency, the Government would be wisely and faithfully administered.

But I have heard it said that General Jackson is an illiterate man; and in evidence of it, a short letter or note, to a printer in Washington, is adduced, in which there are two or three letters of the alphabet misplaced or superfluous. Of what moment is this? The Earl of Chesterfield, an English nobleman, eminently distinguished for his talents, and employed in some of the highest offices of government in Great Britain, took occasion (in the 136th letter to his son), to speak of the Great Duke of Marlborough, who, in the reign of

Queen Anne, gained so many battles over the French armies; for which he was celebrated throughout Europe; as Duke Wellington has been in our day, for his victories over the same enemies of Great Britain. — Of this Great Duke of Marlborough, Lord Chesterfield says — "I knew him extremely well" — "He was eminently illiterate; wrote bad English, and spelled it [still] worse."[3] Deep reading and scholarship, it is well known in the United States, are not essential in the head of our government, to insure faithful administration. An immense quantity of learning may be acquired, much to the pleasure of the individual; but to little purpose as respects the public. The elder Adams, in his learned defense of the American Constitutions, long since avowed a truth, — alas but too well known — that KNOWLEDGE is by no means necessarily connected with WISDOM or VIRTUE.[4]

M^{r}. Clay called General Jackson a "Military Chieftain". But with what view? Did M^{r}. Clay believe that the Liberties of our country would be endangered, if this military chieftain were raised to the Presidency? Not at all. If ever so ambitious of military glory, how would he raise an army? and how obtain revenue to support it? Both these would depend on Congress. And where would he find a sufficiently numerous band of officers to become traitors, to destroy the public liberty? M^{r}. Clay perfectly well knew, that neither General Jackson, nor any other American citizen, could effect such wild projects. Why, then, did he so emphatically call General Jackson a "Military Chieftain"? Obviously, to excite the fears of the uninformed and unreflecting portion of our citizens, for their liberties, — and to rouse and inflame the prejudices of others. General Jackson is a citizen of the West. Had he been chosen president instead of M^{r}. Adams, the political pendulum, in its next vibration, would probably swing to the East or South; and thus deprive M^{r}. Clay of the chance of rising to the Chair of State, — the object of his supreme ambition. In voting himself, therefore, and persuading his friends to vote for M^{r}. Adams, of the remote

East, he was preparing the way for his own elevation, when M^r. Adams term should expire; in effect, voting for himself. Especially may his management be so viewed; since, by securing M^r. Adams' election, he must have confidently expected to be appointed secretary of state; an office which three successive Presidential elections had shown to be the stepping stone to the presidency.

Pardon me, my good sir, one word more. I do not know that in a single act of my public life, I have ever considered, before-hand whether any advantage would result to myself. Adverse results I have repeatedly contemplated; and was willing to encounter them. I am now almost eighty-three years old; and I have nothing to fear or to hope, "at aught this world can threaten or indulge". If you, or your friend at Albany, shall think this letter and my other of the same date may contribute to the removal of prejudices and errors, they are at your and your friend's disposal,[5] for you called on me for information which had relation to General Jackson, as a candidate for the Presidency; and to remove groundless objections, I was willing to lend my aid. I do not know that gentleman; nor is it at all probable that I shall ever see him. But I have no apprehension for the safety of my own rights, for the few years I may yet live, nor for those of my children and grand-children — all of which, indeed, are involved in the rights of our country; and I shall consider them perfectly secure should General Jackson be raised to the presidency. With pleasure and respect I return your salutation,

"your old revolutionary friend"
Timothy Pickering.

---

1. Pickering's English source may have been George R. Gleig, who was the author of *A Narrative of the Campaigns of the British Army at Washington and New Orleans*. First published in London in 1821, it appeared in an American edition in 1826 under a modified title. According to Jackson's recent biographer, Robert V. Remini, the concerted American naval and land at-

tack against the British forces on December 23, 1814, did much to establish the groundwork for the subsequent great victory of January 8. As Remini states: "Always aggressive, Jackson brought the invasion to an abrupt halt. Indeed his action saved New Orleans; for had he not attacked so quickly and with such 'impetuosity', the British would have immediately marched against the city after the arrival of reinforcements and undoubtedly taken it." Remini, pp. 264–265. Gleig's study in its American edition bore the title, *A Subaltern in America, Comprising His Narratives of the Campaigns* (Philadelphia, 1826).

2. The British admitted to the death of 291 men, 1,262 wounded, and 484 captured. On the American side, 13 were killed, 39 wounded, and 19 were reported missing in action. Jackson described the British loss as "immense," whereas the American loss was "inconsiderable." Remini, p. 285.

3. Pickering may have had Lord Chesterfield's letter to his son, dated November 18 O.S., 1748, before him. He made a slight error in its transcription. Philip Stanhope, ed., *Letters Written By the Late Right Honourable Philip Dormer Stanhope, Earl of Chesterfield, To His Son Philip Stanhope* (London, 1774), I, 359–365.

4. John Adams wrote in his *Defence of the Constitutions of Government of the United States of America* (1787–1788) that "I rank knowledge among the goods of fortune, because it is the effect of education, study, and travel which are either accidental, or usual effects of riches or birth, and is by no means necessarily connected with wisdom or virtue."

5. This letter appeared in print almost verbatim in the Albany newspaper *Signs of the Times* on May 24, 1828.

104

Pierre, Jr. to William Miller. ALS
SHR

Albany May 17, 1828.

M^r W^m. Miller

After I arrived here I concluded to go no farther, I expect to return home on Wenesday, that is leave here on Wenesday & be home on Thursday — Charles Rundle did not take the Boards, altho he promised Mr Hart to do it. He has disappointed me twice, & I find there is no dependance on him — Old Waters will come up at any time when he is at home I wish you would see him & get him to come up He must enquire for Mr Herman V. Hart who has my Letter what to send — He will know where to find Mr Hart by enquiring of Godfrey & Walsh in State Street, he had better not to come to the Dock until he knows where to take in his Load —

Charles Walsh is going to New York & has promised to send this Letter on Shore at Caldwells —

Y^r friend
PVC

[Addressed]
Mr William Miller
at Genl. Van Cortlandts
PeeksKill

105

Pierre, Jr. to Philip. ALS
NYHS

Albany May 22–1828.

Dear Brother

The Rainy Weather has prevented my returning home, I now propose leaving here tomorrow take Pierre to his School[1] and get home on Saturday. On Wednesday next I have engaged to be in New York. — I hope you had a pleasant time on the Canal,[2] I would have accompanied you but perhaps after I had seen the Horses at Skeneatales, that I might not have liked them or the Man might have valued them higher than I would give him & as I have seen Mr Ellis here who says he will see the Horses on his return & write me particularly all about them, I think I have taken the most prudent course, particularly as I will be obliged to go to Bath during the summer. —

The Second Letter from Col. Pickering to you (that is the last) will be published in the Signs of the Times on Saturday with some most excellent remarks complimentary to you and Col. Pickering.[3] (His first letter about Masonry will not be published). — I will direct the Editor to send you the paper containing it, which the Printer at Syracuse may republish.

Your Affectionate Brother,
Pierre

---

1. Pierre III was attending the Hyde Park Classical Institution.

2. Philip had apparently taken a trip on the Erie Canal.

3. For the Timothy Pickering correspondence, see Nos. 102 and 103.

106

Philip: Statement Concerning Camp Meeting Ground Lease.[1] ADS
SHR

[September, 1828].

This is to Certify to all whom it may Concern that I Philip Van Cortlandt did on the application of the Reverend Mr: White one of the Methodist Preachers of the Croton Circuit consent that a Camp meeting might be held on my Ground in the Woods where it had formerly been held taken care on their part that no Injury should be done &c &c —

The Law in their favour respecting Selling Spiritous Liquours Without Licence I expected would be attended to but I was surprised when Informed that my Neighbours was forbid to dispose of the produce of their farms and Gardens or selling provision to those who was in need thereof In a peacible manner — and what Created my Surpise was that Tents was Erected on the Camp Ground for the purpose of Selling as grocers thereby ingrossing to a few favorites a monopoly to the injury of the few neighbouring Inhabitants of the Vicinity —

I remember when I was a Soldier in Command & obliged to Incamp in and among the farmers that I had Sentinels placed so that no injury should be done to any part of their property — but it appears that nothing of that kind has been attended to — but on the Contrary fences have been thrown down fields run over and injury the Consequence — but as the Law of our Ligeslature in their favour would or could be const[r]ucted the utmout [utmost] rigour was Extended, Even to fine a person — 11/. for peacebly offering a few cakes to be Sold within the Distance which the Law had proscribed and another for offering to Sell the water Mellons & apples rased on his or his neighbours farm.

Further I am informed that one Man with a load of Watermellons Sold to some of the Influential members of the

Camp his whole load and for the purpose of being disposed of by one of the Suttlers in the Camp but that was prevented by the person In[s]tructed to make reprisals and in Consequence lost all — I will not mention any Injury I have Sustained notwithstanding I gave them the priviledge of Incamping without asking of them One Cent

I make no declaration as to any future Camp Meeting only that I am determined not to suffer any to be held Without an agreement and Lease made under hand and Seal. The Conditions of which to be Subject to further Consideration

---

1. For Philip's earlier agreements (1823 and 1826) with the Methodist camp meeting petitioners, see Nos. 63 and 78. The concerns he expressed here were reflected in the 1829 agreement on the use of the camp meeting ground (No. 124).

107

Philip to Nathan Anderson.[1] ADS
SHR

Sepr 21. 1828.

Copy —

Nathan Anderson Esq

Sir Please to pay M^r. Silvanus Tomkins the usual price for hiring Planks for Camp Meeting which was customary heretofore as his misfortune by Sickness and Death in his Family prevented his receiving the Three Dollars for pulling up the fence which you told me was allowed — Therefore I have thought proper to make the Charge for the planks which I do hereby bestow on the said Henry Tompkins

And am your Humble
Servant — Ph. V.Cortlandt

Sent by M^r. G. Tomkins

[Endorsed]
Order on Nathan
Anderson to pay
Silvanus Tompkins
for the Planks
1828

---

1. Nathan Anderson was a local Methodist who had helped organize camp meetings on Philip Van Cortlandt's lands for several years.

108

Catharine Van Wyck to Philip. ALS
SHR

Novr. 30, 1828.

[fragment]

With pleasure I sit down this evening to write to you to inform you that I have got the Geography Medal every week this term. Ann is very much pleased with her situation and school. Ann has had a Medal for her improvement in reading. Pa and Ma were down here on Friday and they told me that Pierre went to Peekskill to vote for General Jackson and he had a hand full of tickets and threw them in the Jackson box. I have had a bad cold also Ann and Eliza but have got better. I want to know very much how Grandma is and also should like to know how the boys come on with their studies.

I send my love to all the family. I remain your affectionate Neice

Catharine Van Wyck

[Endorsed]
Catharine V.Wyck
Novr. 30–1828

109

Aaron Ward[1] to Philip. ALS
SHR

Washington Jany. 16th 1829.

My Dear Genl.

your several Letters with their enclosures have been duly rec^d^. And it gives me great pleasure to state that I have this instant returned from the office of Sec^y^ of State — where I have been to ascertain the place where those Gn^t^. reside. Co^l^ Buford resides in George Town Kentucky Col Taylor in Louisville of the same state and Co^l^ North in Philadelphia[2] — I have franked the Letter address^d^ to them & sent them by this days mail.

You may have observed that the list of the Field Officers of the Revolution a copy of which I sent to you has been published in the Spectator — It is proper that I should state that after I had sent the list to you — I thought it would be well to send one to Co^l^. Stone to be publish^d^.

I have the honor to be
dear Genl with great respect
Your obt Servt.
A. Ward

P.S. The list of all the officers & soldiers will be published in a few days. you may expect to receive a copy from me.

[Endorsed]
A. Ward
Washington D.C.
Jany. 16. 1829 —

---

1. See Aaron Ward to Pierre, Jr., January 22, 1819 (No. 46).

2. Philip sought the addresses of surviving Revolutionary War veterans for he, as a founding member of the Society of the

Cincinnati, was promoting greater pension rights for war veterans from the federal government. See the two following letters.

110

Henry Dearborn to Philip. ALS
NYPL

Boston January 17th 1829.

Dear Sir,

Your letter of the 8th has been duly received and I imbrace the earliest hour to reply to it — I can have no possible objection to your propositions and of course you have my full consent to place my name with your own and others to the statement of facts which you propose presenting to Congress.[1] the numbers of Cols. & Lieut Cols are so very small that by rendering to us eaqual Justice the sum would be no object of consideration with Congress or the Nation, especially as we can (I presume) on an average count at least eighty winters that have pass'd over us, and of course shall not remain here many years longer.[2] — Be assured my Dear Genl. that a communication from one of my old and highly respected companions in Armes in the most trying and interesting period of the history of our Country has afforded me peculier pleasure. I very frequently look around our Country to find the few survivers of my old Revolutionery companions and among them you stand conspicuous. —

with sentiments of sincere and
unabating friendship I am
Dear Sir your Humbl Servt
Henry Dearborn

Genl Philip Van Courtlandt

[Endorsed]
Lt Col H. Dearborn

---

1. In May, 1828, the Twentieth Congress passed a measure for the "relief of certain surviving officers and soldiers of the army of the revolution," under which surviving commissioned officers were to receive full pay dating back to March, 1826, at the rate of a captain. Under these terms Philip was entitled to receive a pension of $40 a month, or a sum of $960 to cover the increased pension from March, 1826. It is to be recalled that he served in the Continental Army at the rank of lieutenant colonel and was breveted out of the army as a brigadier general. No wonder, then, that he and the other survivors above the rank of captain were upset over this congressional act. It was reported that as of January, 1829, there were twenty-six remaining officers. "Of that number, there are but 5 colonels, 3 lieutenant colonels, and 18 majors." *Niles' Weekly Register,* May 31, 1828, pp. 218–219; June 7, 1828, pp. 239–240; January 31, 1829, p. 366.

2. Henry Dearborn (1751–1829) was prophetic in his remark that the ranking Revolutionary War surviving officers "shall not remain here many years longer." Dearborn himself was to die in June, 1829, while Philip remained "on this mortal soil" until 1831. The two comrades-in-arms had served together at Ticonderoga, Valley Forge, in the Clinton–Sullivan campaign, and at Yorktown. Dearborn was Jefferson's Secretary of War in the period when Philip served in Congress. *DAB,* V, 174–175.

111

Caleb North to Philip. ALS
NYPL

Philadelphia Jany 19th. 1829.

Dear Sir

Yours of the 8th Instant is Just come to hand. and hasten to Answer it. and am of Opinion that had Congress known, that there was so few surviving officers above the Rank of Captain the distinction would have been made; under this impression I will Join you in making the Application you propose, how this will be Accomplished is the Question, perhaps some member of Congress could be prevaild on, to bring the subject before the House to Obtain the signatures of all the Applicants in their scattered situations would be difficult, if practicable, altho their number is small. you have no doubt heard of the Death of General T. Pinkney of S. Carolina; and Major William Jackson of Our City — the number is now small indeed

With an Old Soldiers best Respects
I am
Yours sincerely
Caleb North

Col^{o}. Ph. V. Cortlandt

[Addressed]
Col: Ph-V-Cortlandt
Cortlandt-town
Westchester County
New York

[Endorsed]
Col^{o} Caleb North

112

Aaron Ward to Philip. ALS
SHR

Washington Jany. 28th 1829.

Dear Genl.

The Honorable Mr Magee[1] of the House of Representatives from NY. is desireous of obtaining some information with respect to the length of time that an old soldier served in your Reg^{t}. as you will perceive by his Letter enclosed. If you can furnish him the information he requires & will send it to me in the shape of a certificate you will much oblidge

Sir your sincere friend
and obt Servt
A. Ward[2]

P.S. I am in hopes of getting the Bill in favour of the Highland Compy. before the house in a few days[3]

[Endorsed]
A. Ward & Mr Magees letters — 1829 —

---

1. John Magee (1794–1868), originally from Pennsylvania, moved to Steuben County, New York, in 1812. He sat in Congress from 1827 to 1831. *Biographical Directory American Congress,* p. 1326.

2. Aaron Ward was then in Congress representing Philip's district.

3. Such a bill was not presented to the House.

113

William O'Neale to Pierre, Jr. ALS
NYPL

City of Washington Feby 9th 1829.

DSir,

yours of the 18 Decr 28. was recd. this Jany., Just at the time of the marriage of my Daughter to the Honble. John H. Eaton, I left the City with my soninlaw Dr. Randolph[1] for Virginia and just returned last week, I have called to see Col. Ward[2] three times & failed, I now write you, and have reserved two rooms for you and your two friends[3] —

Genl. Jackson is well and will be in the City on the 12 Inst. three of his servants is at my House; this day, the Genl. will be in Frederick Town M.D. preparations has been made for him at Mr. Gadsbys Hotel Mrs. ONeale sends her compliments to you, with respects to all our old friends wishing you a safe passage to the city and a hearty wellcom, with a good shake hands with the Old Genl.[4] Mr. J.M. Mayer[5] of the post office New York will be on with some of the Genls. friends —

I am DSir your Most
obt. Servt. Wm. O Neale

Genl. Piere Van Cortlandt
Peeks Kill N York

---

1. The Van Cortlandt and Clinton families had long been on friendly terms with William O'Neale, the famed Washington innkeeper. His daughter, the vivacious "Sweet Peggy" O'Neale, was the bride of Senator John H. Eaton, soon to become President Jackson's Secretary of War. The marriage scandalized the doyenne of Washington's high society, Mrs. John C. Calhoun. Dr. Philip Grymes Randolph (1801–1836) was married to Mary, Peggy's sister. *DAB*, XIV, 41; *VCFP,* III, 347, 441.

2. A reference to Aaron Ward.

3. Pierre was making preparations to attend Andrew Jackson's inauguration, to be held on March 4.

4. The "Old Genl." is a reference to Philip Van Cortlandt.

5. James Mayer, a native of Albany, had been associated with the post office since 1815. Amasa J. Parker, ed., *Landmarks of Albany County New York* (Syracuse, N.Y., 1897), p. 273.

114

Philip to Joanna Van Wyck. ALS
NYPL

Cortlandt Town Feby. 12. 1829.

My dear Joanna

I have received your Esteemed Letter of the 6th and am happy to hear that you and your friends are all well, and that you Enjoy yourselves so agreably with riding about the

Streets in fine Sledges which must be fine amusement as long as it continues, we have some snow here but it has made but little Sleighing —

I received a letter yesterday from Eliza they were all well there Except Miss Mary Delavan who was so much indisposed as to be removed to the Doctors House who lives 5. or 6. miles off in the Town of New Castle I sent my Carriage to remove her Yesterday, I hope she may recover for She is a great friend of Your Sisters and her loss will be a grief to them —

I have been Unwell, but am gitting better but slowly all the rest of the Family are Well, Your Grandmama is better this Winter than she has been for a long time and Your Aunt Van Rensselaer is so well that she has [gone] Out Sleighing as far as Troy so Genl. Pierre your Uncle writes he is now in Albany — Y^{r} Aunt Beekman is also pretty well so Much for News, I shall now Conclude with respects to Your friends

Am your Affectionate Uncle
Ph. V. Cortlandt

115

Solomon Van Rensselaer[1] to Philip. ALS
NYPL

Albany February 16th 1829.

My dear Sir

Will you give me a letter of Introduction to Genl. Jackson, [2] I too, as you, and him, have fought and bleed — your brother will write from here, and I leave this on Wednesday morning, your letter will find me at the Post office at Croton or you may if you please inclose it to me at Washington —

I am very Respectfully
Your Ob^{t}. Servt.
Sol. Van Rensselaer

Gen[l]. Van Cortlandt

[Endorsed]
from Gen[l]. Sol. Van Rensselaer
recommendation to
the President
Feb[y] 20. 1829

---

1. Solomon Van Rensselaer (1774–1852) was a son of Major General Hendrick Van Rensselaer. At the age of seventeen he joined General Anthony Wayne's expedition to the Maumee, and before the age of twenty he was in command of his own volunteer unit. He was elevated to the rank of captain of the Light Dragoons, and served in the War of 1812. In 1822 he became the postmaster in Albany, and later was a member of Congress. Van Rensselaer was suspected of having been an Adams supporter in the election of 1828, and there were demands for his removal as postmaster. In May, 1829, a number of distinguished Albany citizens submitted a petition in his behalf to Postmaster General William T. Barry. It read in part, "Since General Van Rensselaer has held the appointment of Post Master, the duties of the office have been discharged with ability, and with a constant regard to the public convenience." It also asserted that he "was friendly to the election of our present distinguished Chief Magistrate." Pierre Van Cortlandt submitted a postscript to the petition declaring that "He most fully accords in the sentiments and views of the signers. . . ." Catherine M. Cuyler Hardie, *Hardie's Series of Genealogical Families No. Five: Van Rensselaer* (New York, 1922–1923), p. 144; Bonney, I, 486–487.

2. See the following letter.

116

Philip to Andrew Jackson. ADfs
NYPL

Cortlandt Town Feby 20–1829.

Dear Sir

The bearor hereof Genl. Solomon Van Rensselaer of the City of Albany who like Our Selves has seen Severe Service and has Fought and bled in the cause of Our Country and who is my esteem'd Friend and as Such please to permit me to Introduce him to your Acquaintance

and am very Respectfully
Your Humble
Servant
Ph V. Cortlandt

His Excellency
Andrew Jackson
President of the U.S.
City of Washington. D.C.

117

Joanna Van Wyck to Philip. ALS
SHR

[Feb. 24, 1829.]

Dear Uncle

I have received your letter of the 12th inst and was happy to here you was getting better of your illness and I hope by this time you have quite recovered your health again.

I was sorry to here the ill health of Miss DeLavan I heard from Aunt Rensselaer a few days since she was then very well. —

We had a violent snow storm friday and the wether still continues very cold and the sleighing is very good[.] I received a letter from Pappa yesterday I have no news to write you and so must finish my letter We are all here very well Give my love to Grand-Mama, Mama Pappa and my brothers[.] I hope you will excuse my short letter

Your affectionate Neice
Joanna Van Wyck

[Endorsed]
Joanna Van Wyck
Feby 24. 1829 —

118

John L. Graham[1] to Philip. ALS
SHR

New York. March 28th. 1829.

Respected Sir

I received Your favour of the 10th instant in answer mine, soliciting information from You, in relation to the title of Some property on the corner of North & Chrystie Streets — In Your letter, you stated that Your father derived his title to this property by will from his aunt, Mrs Ann Depeyster, about the Year 1774[2] — Since the receipt of Your letter I have examined the will, and am Sorry to say, that it does not afford me all the information I desire on the subject, in as much as, I am again compelled to trouble You —

By the will, it appears that M^{rs}. Depeyster devised the one third part of her Real Estate to Your late Honoured Father, without designating, in particular, what Real Estate it was — The question was therefore very naturally presented; Of what Real Estate did She die S[e]ized and how was the partition of the same made between the devisees under her will — For my own Satisfaction, on these points I Examined, in the Registers office, but did not find upon record any conveyance to M^{rs}. Depeyster of the property in question.

Neither could I find any Deed of partition on record dividing the property between her heirs or devisees — This, no doubt, was all done but the deeds have been omitted to be recorded, which causes the present embarrasment —

I called up[on] Doct. Beekman[3] in Cortlandt Street, in hopes, he might be able to give me some information on the Subject, as he was the gentleman who originally negotiated the sale of the lots, but he could not — he, however, Suggested to me the probability of Your having among Your old title papers the deeds relating to the property — and recommended my writing You, in order to get You to make a Scout for them —

I am really very sorry to be so troublesome, and I can assure You, that nothing but absolute inability to derive the information from any other quarter, induces me to call upon you —

If you will, therefore, have the goodness to examine among Your papers — 1st for the deed of the property in question to Mrs Depeyster — 2nd for the deed of partition thereof between her heirs or devisees and Should You find them to apprys me of the fact so that I may have the opportunity of seeing them, You will confer a very particular [favor] upon him who has the honor of subscribing himself

Your obdt Serv.
J. L. Graham
New York

Genl. Van Cortlandt

[Addressed]
Genl. Philip Van Cortlandt
Cortlandt Town
New York

[Endorsed]
J. L. Graham
March 26.1829
about the lots in the Bowery

1. John Lorimer Graham (1797–1876) was a prominent and successful New York attorney. He later held a position with the U.S. Treasury. McAdam, I, 338.

2. Pierre Van Cortlandt, Sr. had owned four lots on the Bowery in New York. They were located at the corner of North (Houston) and Chrystie streets. He obtained part of the land by inheritance from an aunt and, apparently, by purchase. See *VCFP*, III, 706–707.

3. Dr. Stephen D. Beekman, son of Gerard G., Jr. and Cornelia (Van Cortlandt) Beekman, was Philip's nephew,

119

John H. Eaton to Pierre, Jr. ALS
NYPL

War Department
Washington May 20 1829.

Sir

I have the honor to inform you that, you are appointed to Preside at the Board of Visiters, invited to attend the examination of the Cadets, at the United States Military Academy, on the first Monday in the ensuing Month.[1]

Respectfully.
Your Obt. Servt.
Eaton

Genl Pierre Van Cortland
Peeks Kill
New York

1. The West Point Board of Visitors consisted of "five gentlemen versed in military and other science" who were to consult with

the academic board, attend graduation ceremonies, and make recommendations to the Secretary of War. Stephen Ambrose, *Duty, Honor, Country: A History of West Point* (Baltimore, 1966), p. 56.

120

Nicholas Fish[1] to Pierre, Jr. ALS
SHR

New York June 8.th 1829 —

My dear Sir —

Permit me to introduce & particularly recommend to you two Spanish Patriots Don Joseph & Don Carlos Rabadan, who were friends and associates of the illustrious and unfortunate Riego,[2] and distinguished themselves in the cause of their Country; they are warmly recommended to me by General Lafayette who takes a deep interest in their behalf. Don Joseph proposes to establish himself in Georgia for the purpose of cultivating the Olive and the Vine and his brother Don Carlos wishes employment in one of our literary Institutions as Professor or Teacher of Mathematics, Spanish &c^{r}. for which he is admirably well qualified[3] —

Should it be in your power from the situation in which you are now placed[4] to afford him any facility towards obtaining his favorite object you will do an act of great benevolence and confer a particular favor on

your old friend
and Humble Servant
Nich^{s}: Fish

[Addressed]
To General P. Van Courtlandt
West Point

By Don Joseph & Don Carlos Rabadan

---

1. Nicholas Fish (1758–1833) became Adjutant General of New York in 1786 and President Washington appointed him a supervisor of the revenue in 1794. He was the father of the famed nineteenth-century statesman Hamilton Fish. *Appleton's Cyclopaedia,* II, 463.

2. Rafael del Riego was the hero of an uprising against Ferdinand VII of Spain in 1820. *Encyclopaedia Britannica,* XXI, 129.

3. The munificent sum of $50 per month plus food was provided for a professor of mathematics at West Point. Languages fared poorly, with a language professor receiving only $40 per month plus food. Peter Force, ed., *The National Calendar and Annals of the United States 1828* (Washington, D.C., 1828), p. 188.

4. Fish referred to Pierre's recent appointment to the West Point Board of Visitors.

121

Pierre, Jr. to Solomon Van Rensselaer
Catharina V.R. Bonney, *A Legacy of Historical Gleanings* (Albany, 1875), I, 487.

New York, June 25, 1829.

Dear Sir,

Mr. Moore the Embassador to South America arrived here yesterday, he sails from this port in a few days. I think it would be well for you to come down immediately if you wish to see him before his departure.[1] He has put up at Mrs. Southards in Broad Way, just below Grace Church.

Yours truly
Pierre Van Cortlandt

Solomon Van Rensselaer, Esqr., P.M. Albany

---

1. Solomon Van Rensselaer's son, Rensselaer, was then in Bogota, Colombia. The father was attempting to place him as the private secretary to Thomas P. Moore, recently appointed minister to Colombia. Solomon also sought to obtain the latest information from Moore, an active Jacksonian, as to whether he was really in danger of losing his Albany postmaster's position. Bonney, I, 487, 507.

122

William T. Barry[1] to Pierre, Jr. ALS
NYPL

Washington 6. July 1829.

Dear Sir

I have the honour to acknowledge the receipt of your favour of the 2. Inst. & to state that the book & letter to our friend Capt. Davis[2] have come safe to hand. He has not yet arrived in the City but we expect him daily, your request shall be attended to

very respectfully
your Ob. St.
W. T. Barry

Honble. Pierre Van Cortland
Peeks Kill
N.Y.

---

1. Pierre had begun a correspondence with William T. Barry (1784–1835), Postmaster General under Andrew Jackson, for the purpose of supporting Solomon Van Rensselaer's efforts in remaining in office as the Albany postmaster. Barry had been an early Jackson supporter in Kentucky who served as governor prior to his federal appointment. McCormick, p. 214.

2. "Capt. Davis" may have been William A. Davis, a native Kentuckian, who owned a Washington, D.C., printing establish-

ment. Davis had recently visited New York and corresponded with Solomon Van Rensselaer. Bonney, I, 507; William Ames, *A History of the National Intelligencer* (Chapel Hill, N.C., 1972), p. 33.

123

Pierre, Jr. to Solomon Van Rensselaer.
Catharina V.R. Bonney, *A Legacy of Historical Gleanings* (Albany, 1875), I, 506.

Peekskill July 13, 1829.

Dear Sir,

By the last mail I received a letter from my friend Dr. Davis whom you saw at Albany, and he writes to me from the City of Washington dated the 6th instant: "Tell Genl. Solomon Van Rensselaer he has nothing to fear." When I see you I will tell you more. But my present Advice is, to take no Notice in your behaviour of anything that has taken place, to any one, and let your friends be prudent and say nothing.[1]

Yours assuredly

Pierre Van Cortlandt

Genl. Solomon Van Rensselaer Albany, New York

---

1. Solomon Van Rensselaer weathered the political storm and remained in office into the 1840's.

124

Agreement between Philip and Camp Meeting Ground Petitioners. ADS

SHR

July 28, 1829.

Articles of agrements made between Philip Van Cortlandt of the Town of Cortlandt Esqr. of the first part and the Rev^{d}: Aaron G. Brewer and Thomas Blakeney of Cortlandt Town parties. of the second part. Witnesseth that the said party of the first hereby Leases unto the said parties of the Second part for the purpose of holding a Camp Meeting and for no other purpose whatsoever all that inclosure of Wood land where former Camp Meetings have been held, Bounded Southerly by the highway leading from Croton Bridge to Peeks Kill. northerly by the landing Road Easterly and Westerly by Fences now standing inclosing the same from Monday the 17th: to Friday the 21st: day of August next both days included. when the fences are to be will made good and put up in as good order as when received and the incampment to be Cleared of all Persons, Waggons, Carriages Horses Cattle Sheep Hogs, Boards plank &c leaving the Straw on the ground. And the said parties of the second part are not to suffer any Timber-Trees or or Saplins to be cut or injured or any other Injury to be done — and not to Suffer and permit any Tent to be Erected for Victualling as Sutlers Selling anything whatsoever within the Incampment or premises or Trading of any discreption — as the Law of the State is their guid and protection to keep order Especially as to Selling ardent Sperits. however they are not to prevent any of the peasible Inhabitants in the Neighbourhood of the Incampment from selling any kind of provisions, Bread Cake pies Butter Cheese Milk Fruit or Vegatables of any descriptions in their Dwelling Houses or Inclosed Buildings in their possission[1] and further to pay as a Consideration to the said party of the first part one Dollar when demanded and also to

him or his order whatsoever Damage he may Sustain relative to the above premices — and the said parties of the Second part do hereby bind themselves Jointly and severally to perform all the Contracts above mentioned — given under our hands and Seals the 28th day of July in the Year. 1829
Sealed and Delivered in duplicate —
in Presence of

Ph. G Van Wyck

Ph. V. Cortlandt
Aaron G. Brewer
Thomas Blakney

---

1. This stipulation was inserted into the agreement as a result of Philip's concern over the banning of his neighbors as provisioners for the previous year's camp meeting. See No. 106.

125

Richard D. Davis[1] to Pierre, Jr. ALS
SHR

Poughkeepsie August 17, 1829.

Dr Sir

The approach of the election requires from political friends an interchange of sentiment and I avail myself of our similar feelings to invite your attention to a subject not a little interesting to me.

The Senator comes this fall from this County. I am not solicitous who he shall be — but am anxious that he shall not be N.P. Tallmadge Esqr. of this place — a relative of the Genl. and a man of the same political stamp & currency — Without further description you will know enough of him[2] —

He and his friends are making great efforts to get him nominated not only in this County but all over the District — We shall do all we can to get a Delegation to the

Senatorial Convention from Dutchess hostile to him & have great & strong hopes of success. Should we fail in that we should like still to defeat him if possible — & if we do not it may be adviseable to have some pains taken to get right Delegates from the other Counties — to prevent his friends obtaining them by their secret and industrious exertions to secure them in his favour. I hope it will be in your power to fix your County — on this subject — and would advise an early attention —

The term of four years is wholly too long, for any man who changes his politics every two years — & I deem him politically ineligible, as a party man.[3] He would be against us before his time would be out — Can you do any thing in relation to this in Putnam — Rockland — or any other County of the District? — A few letters from you about the District might be of excellent service

We shall do all we can to put him down at home — & I hope to effect it — But too sure we cannot be —

Accept assurances of my respect and of the consideration with which I am

Your obedt servt
Richard D Davis
Poughkeepsie 17 Aug 1829

Gen Pierre Van Courtlandt —

---

1. Richard D. Davis (1799–1871) was a noted orator who exhibited "great skill and ability as a forensic debater" and who possessed a "style of eloquence scarcely if ever before surpassed by any orator in the state." Prior to his election to Congress in 1840, he filled various minor local positions. His particular area of activity centered in and around Dutchess County. Hammond, II, 527; Werner, pp. 483–484.

2. Nathaniel P. Tallmadge (1795–1864) was a practicing attorney who rose rapidly in the political world. He began as a state assemblyman, successfully won election as a state senator in 1829, and then moved into the national arena in 1833 as a U.S.

Senator. He remained in that office until 1844, when he resigned to become governor of the Wisconsin Territory. *Biographical Directory American Congress,* p. 1595; Hasbrouck, pp. 219–220, 502.

3. Davis proved correct in his appraisal of Tallmadge, for he became an outspoken leader of a New York group who opposed Jackson's bank policies and gradually moved into the Henry Clay camp. Nathaniel was related to James Tallmadge (1778–1853) of Missouri Compromise fame.

126

Richard D. Davis to Pierre, Jr. ALS
SHR

Pokeepsie 5 Oct 1829.

Dear Sir

Yours of the 2d I got as I was starting on Saturday morning for our Co. Convention — and in the words of Perry, I might almost say that in that Convention we met the enemy & made them ours — but that we did not quite effect — We have however divided the Delegation — they have two Messrs. Hooker & Bockee — and we two, Haight and DeLamatter — They were cocksure of success until we took the first round in the Convention when they found our strength — and after that they went to work to bargain & buy off or we should have beaten them out of the field — They had old John Radcliff, of lobby fame, in the Convention, & but for his intrigues and bargains, we should have swept the board — All things considered we reckon & so do all our friends that the result is a victory — and we look with confidence to beat them on Thursday at New Burgh — It now stands — your County 3. Ulster 2 & Dutchess 2 — in all 7 — who we sense to be against Tallmadge. We want two more to have the majority — & that we must have without doubt.

I shall be at NewBurgh if alive & able to get there —

on Wednesday evening — & will rejoice to meet you — Come on with your Delegates & size them up against Tallmadge —

Our County meeting was the most awful contest I have ever seen — and every body says that we have flogged them — They are evidently thunderstruck at the ressult — for they were perfectly confident of carrying all before them — The victory is ours in the County — let us make it ours in the District —

Mr Hooker is Tallmadge partner. & is the man who is to be made Circuit Judge after Emott if Tallmadge gets the nomination — & was an old federalist before he turned Bucktail[1]

Mr Bockee was an old federalist — & the only man in this town who refused to illuminate for Perrys victory[2] —

These are the men who are Tallmadges Delegates — Ours are democrats from the cradle — & Jackson to the core — As to the Nelson intrigue & agreement — I do not doubt it — myself — but such things are incapable of positive proof —

We feel confident of beating Tallmadge & shall give the Convention all Dutchess Co. to choose from besides him — if they want it — Our language is any body but him —

I am with great esteem & respect. Your

Obedt & humble Servt
Richard D Davis

Gen Van Courtlandt

[Addressed]
Gen. Pierre Van Cortlandt
Peekskill
West Chester County

---

1. James Hooker of Poughkeepsie then served as a Dutchess County surrogate judge. He did not succeed James Emott as a circuit court judge. Werner, pp. 250, 396.

2. Abraham Bockee (1784–1865) graduated from Union College and practiced law in Poughkeepsie. He was elected to Congress as a Jacksonian Democrat in 1828 and remained in that office until 1837, when he returned to state office as a senator and later served as a judge of the court of errors. *Biographical Directory American Congress,* p. 606.

127

Catharine Van Wyck to Philip. ALS
SHR

November 14th 1829.

My dear Uncle

I have been very well since I left you[.]I have found the medal that I thought was lost and I am very glad that I have found it[.]we took a very beautiful walk yesterday which was the thirteenth of November and it was all around by Mr Mecknights and we went into the garden where we had a very beautiful prospect of Mr Fields house[.]I want to know very much how Brother Pierres health is now and if he coughs any more How is Brother David and all the rest of the family at home[.]please dear Uncle to tell Sister Joanna and Brother Cortlandt that I intend to write to them in a few weeks and I shall expect an answer from them. Eliza and Ann are very well. I send my love to all the family — I am your

ever affectionate Niece
Catharine Van Wyck

128

Eli S. Davis[1] to Pierre, Jr. ALS
SHR

AbbeVille So Ca Nov. 14. 1829.

My dear Sir,

I acknowledge with much pleasure the receit of your kind letter of the 28 of Octr. Such is the increased facility now given to the transportation of the Mail that your letter was Rec^{d}. in ten days from Peeks Kill a distance of nine hundred Miles. Twenty years ago it Required three Months for a letter to go from here to N.York & back. Thus we see exemplified the enterprise & industry of our people.

This is one among the Various improvements which originated from the Exertions of that man, whose untiring zeal in the promotion of the best interests of his country led to the most splendid results. I mean De Wit Clinton, for whose Memory I shall always cheerish the most affectionate recollection. I thank you for the information in relation to the venerable Gen. Philip Van Cortlandt, your brother. As one of the relicks of the Revolution he is pointed to [as?] a monument bearing all the inscriptions of the glory and achievements of that eventful period. I am happy to learn that he enjoys good health. My devotion to such men knows no limits. Have you Gardens Anecdotes of the Revolution? If you have not, pray buy it. In it you will find a Resolution introduced by me into the Legislature of this State commemorating the death of Col. John E. Howard of Maryland.[2]

I shall look with no little solicitude for my young friend Pierre' letter. I am glad M^{r}. Ross has become Reconciled to the marriage of his daughter, And I should be equally proud to learn that he had become a member of the Temperance Society.[3]

like yourself I have Rec^{d}. no letter from Old Kentuckey.[4] I am fearful he has fallen a victim to some beautiful widow whose charmes, and Smiles have entirely diverted him from us. I am glad that you intend to pay the President a visit he will meet you with much cordiality. I expect to [go?] on to

Washington with M^r^. Calhoun[5] to whom I have repeatedly spoken of you. He will be glad to see you. We must try and meet again next summer at West Point. We can do so if we should desire it. Be pleased to remember me most kindly to Pierre. Tell him I should be glad that he would spend one year at least in the University of Virginia. Accept my dear Sir, the Renewed assurances of my first and best wishes.

E.S. Davis.

Gen: Van Cortlandt.

[Addressed]
Gen: Pierre Van Cortlandt
Peeks Kill
New York.

---

1. Eli S. Davis was a resident of Abbeville County, South Carolina. He sat in that state's General Assembly from 1822 to 1828, and again from 1830 to 1831. He was a member of the West Point Board of Visitors in 1829. Walter B. Edgar, ed., *Biographical Directory of the South Carolina House of Representatives* (Columbia, S.C., 1974), I, 306, 310, 314; *Niles' Weekly Register,* June 20, 1829, p. 269.

2. Alexander Garden in *Anecdotes of the American Revolution* . . . (Charleston, 1828) included a resolution adopted by the South Carolina legislature which asserted that they could "never forget the distinguished services of the deceased." Davis, apparently, was the author of the resolution.

3. Another member of the 1829 West Point Board of Visitors was William Ross, from Newburgh in Orange County, New York. A practicing attorney, he served as a state senator from 1815 to 1822, and prior to that time as an assemblyman from 1808 to 1813. Ross had a choice of three temperance societies to which he could belong within the Newburgh area. Ruttenber, pp. 149, 321, 352, 415.

4. Still another member of the West Point Board was Major

William M. Davis of Kentucky. *Niles' Weekly Register,* June 20, 1829, p. 269.

5. John C. Calhoun was then Vice President.

129

Jacob Burnet[1] to Pierre, Jr. ALS
SHR

Washington City Feby 14–1830.

My dear Sir,

Your friendly and very acceptable letter, was handed by your kinsman Mr Stevenson; and I regret to say that being located at a distance from each other; in this extensive wilderness of a city, I have not had the pleasure of as much of his company as I could have desired.

He has been, however, surrounded with friends and attentive acquaintances, who have occupied all the time which he has been able to spare from the object of his visit to this city. I was introduced to him in the lobby of the Senate; when he handed your letter. I gave him a pressing invitation to call at my quarters, but from the cause to you stated, I presume, it has not been in his power to do so.

Since the opportunity we had, at the Point, of reviving and strengthening our juvenile friendship, I have frequently turned back to the ocurrences with great satisfaction, and among all the pleasant, interesting incidents of the meeting, that one has been uppermost, on my memory. It carries me back to by gone days, and to scenes, the most sincerely interesting of my life, when the world lay before us, holding up its honors, distinctions and wealth, and inviting to the pursuit, and we were anxiously adjusting the arrangements, necessary to commence it. Many of those who started with us, and had our warmest wishes for their success, have fallen by the way, and are almost forgotten, while we have been spared to continue the voyage and, it would be ungrateful not to add, with as liberal a share of success, as we have a right to claim. Whatever may have been the fate of some of our companions on the same pursuits, we have no cause to complain, and it may be said truly, that we do not. By this impression I do not mean, however, to say that my philosophy is sufficient to neutralize all the incidents that befall me. This you will conclude, is not the case, from the past, that yourself, with a larger share of it, than I can boast of, are sometimes disappointed, and driven to complain; but the idea that I wish to convey is, that our calculations and hopes, have been so far influenced by prudence, that the general result of our course, has been satisfactory.

I need not, and trust you will not, say how much you would have gratified me by executing your purpose of visiting the seat of government —

With very great esteem I am
your friend
J. Burnet

General VanCortlandt

[Addressed]
General Pierre VanCortlandt
Peeks Kill
New York

---

1. Jacob Burnet (1770–1853), a native of New Jersey, spent most of his life in Ohio. He held many elected positions in that state's legislative and judicial branches. He was appointed to the unexpired senatorial seat of William Henry Harrison in 1828. Burnet had met Pierre most recently when the latter served as president of the Board of Visitors at West Point in June, 1829. They both had attended colleges in New Jersey, Pierre at Queen's (Rutgers) and Burnet at the College of New Jersey (Princeton). They seem to have shared common experiences at that point in their careers. *Biographical Directory American Congress,* p. 673; *Niles' Weekly Register,* June 20, 1829, p. 269.

130

Catharine Van Wyck to Philip. ALS
SHR

Sing Sing Feb 19th 1830.

My dear Uncle

I have not written to you in a great while. and I could not employ my time any better than in writing to you. we were all very glad to see Pa down here. and the letter that Eliza received from Ma which told us of our coming home and we were all rejoiced to hear of it for we want to see all the family very much. Miss Fish is very well and also the Misses Delavans and my Teachers[.] Dear Uncle will you please to ask Ma to send me some fine thread and floss cotton
Eliza Ann and myself Join in love to you all
This from your ever affectionate Niece

C. Van Wyck

[Endorsed]
Catharine Van Wyck
Feby–19–1830 —

131

Pierre, Jr. to William Miller. ALS
SHR

Albany Feb. 28th. 1830.

Mr William Miller

I am very Anxious to be at home, and if the River does not open by the middle of this week, I will take passage in the Stage & come down — So that you may expect me the last of this week — One of those Horses of William Walsh is lame in his hind foot which I suppose will always be so — I did not know this when I wrote you I then thought it was only swooln [swollen] —

I believe I mentioned to you that Harrington has sold

Eclipse Colt, for $250 — He is about five miles from here but so wicked they cannot do any thing with him, which was the reason Harrington sold him —

I hope Bob behaves himself —

Your freind

Pierre Van Cortlandt

132

William M. Davis[1] to Pierre, Jr. ALS
SHR

Hartford Kentucky. 30 March 1830.

My Dear General

yours dated in November last I received. and it afforded me great pleasure to hear from you; particularly that you were in the enjoyment of good health and spirits. I spent the greater part of the past winter in Frankfort during the Session of our Legislature, where I found it some what disagreeable in consequence of the prevalence of a violent party spirit which was caused by the violence of the Clay party who has the ascendancy in our Legislature.

The Republican party who were the supporters of the present Administration, although in the minority maintained their cause well and measurably defeated them in their plans of proscription, and turning out of office, the friends of General Jackson, you no doubt have seen the extraordinary Resolutions in answer to those of South Carolina upon the subject of the Tariff, in which they gave Mr. Clay a whitewashing these proceedings have created a considerable excitement in Kentucky. and I have no doubt will bring about a reaction against him in our elections to the Legislature the present year. We shall have a violent struggle in our elections to the Legislature, it will devolve upon them to elect a successor to Mr Rowan in the Senate of the United States and a violent effort will be made by both parties for the majority; I entertain no doubt of our success, we have made all of our arrangements and stand prepared for action when the day of battle arrives.[2] We have but a bare majority in the U.S. Senate the loss of one Senator may change that majority and place our worthy President in a very unpleasant predicament, and may deprive us of all we gained in the late struggle, We shall therefore be at our posts, and fight a funeral, and be assured, we shall give a good account of the enemy on the day of battle. Mr Clays influence in Ky is yet very great. we shall have a difficult task to keep him down.

I should be happy to visit N.Yorke the ensuing summer, and have the ineffable pleasure of seeing you once more and my friends in your quarter; it will be out of my power to attend the Board of Visiters in June, my public duties here will not permit me, But in August I may have time, and if so, I shall visit Washington and the Saratoga Springs, when I shall certainly do myself the pleasure to see you. Maj. Shannon of Lexington Ky. will be appointed from Ky., as one of the Board of Visiters at West point. he is a very fine fellow, I recommended him myself to the Secretary of War, he married a relation of mine a daughter of Gov. Shelby of [torn][3] his lady will accompany him and I expect Mrs Sharp[4] also, when you will have the pleasure of seeing her, whilst at Frankfort Mrs Sharp showed me a small painting she had prepared for you and told me she should transmit it to you in a letter by mail; the Book I mentioned she told me was sent by Kendall[5] if you have not received it yet. you can get your Representative in Congress to bring one to you by writing to him, I saw at Frankfort Dr. Clelland. he was well & told me he should write to you

God bless you
William M Davis

P.S. Dont fail to remember me particularly to your son Pierre and tell him I shall expect to hear of his rapid advancement in his studies remember me also to Mr Stevenson and Mr. John Walsh of Albany —

W.M.D.

[Addressed]
Genl. Pierre Van Cortlandt
Peekskill
New York

---

1. William M. Davis of Hartford, Kentucky, saw army service during the War of 1812. He was appointed to the West Point Board of Visitors in 1829. Heitman (1903), I, 360; *Niles' Weekly Register,* June 20, 1829, p. 269.

2. Andrew Jackson was not an overwhelming favorite in Kentucky, where the hearts of many voters belonged to Henry Clay. After the election of 1828, when it became obvious that John Quincy Adams had been eliminated as a serious future presidential candidate, a group of Kentuckians began to press for Clay's nomination in opposition to Jackson. As part of this local effort, the state legislature incorporated a ringing endorsement of Clay within a series of resolutions supporting a protective tariff policy. The Kentucky General Assembly declared that Congress had the power "to encourage and protect the manufacturers of the United States, by imports and restrictions on the goods, wares and merchandise of foreign nations. . . ." The majority then added the statement that it was an opportune occasion "to call to its aid the oft repeated sentiments of that most distinguished fellow citizen, *Henry Clay,* whose zealous and able exertions . . . have been only equalled by his *ardent patriotism and unbending integrity.*" *Niles' Weekly Register,* February 20, 1830, p. 428.

3. James Shannon, along with John Rowan of Kentucky, was appointed to the West Point Board of Visitors in 1830. *Niles' Weekly Register,* May 29, 1830, p. 256.
   Isaac Shelby (1750–1826) was the first governor of Kentucky. He had a long and illustrious military career in the Revolution, against the Indians, and in the War of 1812 before entering politics. *DAB,* XVII, 60–62.

4. For a discussion of Eliza T. Sharp, see the letter that follows.

5. Amos Kendall (1789–1869), the famous editor of the Kentucky newspaper *The Argus of Western America,* was a staunch supporter of Andrew Jackson. After Jackson's victory, Kendall journeyed to Washington where he officially filled a minor Treasury post, but served most prominently as a member of Jackson's famous "Kitchen Cabinet." *DAB,* X, 325–326.

133

Eliza T. Sharp[1] to Pierre, Jr. ALS
NYPL

Frankfort May 3rd 1830 —

Honored Sir,

The orders of my brother John M. Scott to repair to West Point, afford me an opportunity of performing a duty which my heart has often upbraided me for neglecting so long: that is to acknowledge the gratitude I feel, for the kind expression of your regard contained in the little volume handed me some time ago by our mutual friend Majr. W. M. Davis.

So severely have I suffered from the malignity of Party misrepresentation that it is truly solacing to find that the good and virtuous have not been thereby deceived — Never was a familly more unjustly treated than we have been, the dearest object of my heart torn from my arms by the murderous blade of a midnight assassin in my presence, my heart sickens at the relation — O: twas a scene would chill joys rosy cheek forever And strew the snows of age on youths Auburn ringlets

and yet the monsters instead of receiving the Anathema of every being in human shape was even lauded by some; and his crime extenuated by others, under the false plea of personal wrongs, a baser charge than which they well knew ever existed, and yet with a knowledge of its falsity and the uniform rectitude of my dear husband's moral deportment did this Political Party disseminate their scandal against him whom they had by their dagger laid low. this was too harrowing to my already lacerated heart. I would have sacrificed my life to vindicate his injured honor — I therefore made an appeal to Public Justice by a publication of facts with a hope of irradicating false impressions; but political animosities had so far got the better of every enobling feeling of the human heart that I myself become the subject of their most bitter imprecations and they infused into distant prints a portion of their venom which was abundantly manifested by the cruel animadversions on myself and family by the Editor of the Cadet (a paper printed in one of the New England States which I presume you have seen) I however thank Providence for having sustained me thro' these accumulated wrongs & I cannot but hope that "Truth is Omnipotent and will Prevail"

I will not attempt an apology for having wearied your patience by the above recital the well known benevolence of your heart will I trust plead for any weakness of mine.

Will you please accept the enclosed watch paper as a memento of my high esteem — Believe me Respectfully your grateful Friend

Eliza T. Sharp

Gen[l]. Pierre Van Cortlandt

N.B. I sent you (via Washington City) a Publication made by my brother in law Doctr. L.J. Sharp entitled a "Vindication of the late Col. S.P. Sharp" have you received it?

E.T.S.

[Addressed]
Gen[l]. Pierre Van Cortlandt
Peeks kill
New York
John. M. Scott

1. Eliza T. Sharp was the widow of Kentucky Congressman Solomon P. Sharp. Her husband had been murdered in their home on the night of November 7, 1825. The alleged murderer was soon apprehended, brought to trial, and sentenced to death. During the trial it came out that while the assailant did not know Sharp, he was familiar with Sharp's wife. The trial and its implications of marital infidelity were reported across the country. To add drama to the situation, the assailant's wife committed suicide while visiting her husband in prison just prior to his execution. *Niles' Weekly Register,* June 10, 1826, p. 267; July 29, 1826, pp. 382–383; August 26, 1826, p. 443.

134

Peter Augustus Jay[1] to Philip. **ALS**
NYPL

New York 29 Sept 1830.

Dear Sir

Mr John Peterson has applied to me for a loan of $1600 to be secured by mortgage on 330 acres of land conveyed to him by your Sister M^rs. V Rensselaer & at present mortgaged to her for $1000 — & he proposes to take up her mortgage with part of the money to be borrowed. I have agreed to lend him the $1600 out of moneys in my hand of the Corporation for the relief of widows & of Clergymen of the episcopal Church, provided the first mortgage is taken up or assigned & provided this arrangement is agreeable to M^rs. V Rensselaer. If she will assign the mortgage to me & acknowledge & Send it to me at any time within a fortnight I will pay to her order the principal & interest due upon it. I understand that interest is due from the 29 March 1829 —

Pardon me for troubling you in this business — M^r. Peterson tells me that you act as your Sisters agent —

I am Dr Sir with great respect
Your very Ob Sert
Peter Augustus Jay

Genl. Ph. V. Cortlandt

---

1. Peter Augustus Jay (1776–1843) was the son of the distinguished diplomat John Jay. Educated at Columbia College, he became one of the most eminent lawyers in New York City. He devoted much attention to his alma mater and to the New-York Historical Society. Upon his death, a close friend, the diarist Philip Hone, remarked, "Few more learned and accomplished men, and none more upright and honourable, are to be found in this city. . . . He was a gentleman of the old school; he adorned society by his deportment and manners, by his strict integrity he rebuked the corruption of the times. . . ." Reynolds; II, 767–768; Tuckerman, II, 173.

135

Philip to Thomas Wintringham. ALS
NYHS

Cortlandt — Novr 23^d 1830.

M^r: Wintringham

Please to send me one Doz — bottles of Cider and one Doz — bottles of Porter,[1] I have Sent the Box to put the Cider in and a Basket for the Porter you will find them on board of Capt^t. Farrington you had best send for them and the Captain will inform you when to send the things, and am your

Hum^ble Servt
Ph. V.Cortlandt

[Addressed]
Mr Thomas Wintringham
N° 5 Nassau Corner Pine Street
New York
Per Capt^t D Farrington
Sloop Parris

---

1. Thomas Wintringham operated a cider vault on Nassau Street. It is interesting to note that as of 1830, cider was apparently not being produced on the Manor. Porter was a type of malt brew, sweetened with a low alcoholic content. *Longworth's Directory* (1831), p. 647.

136

John M. Baker[1] to Philip. ALS
NYPL

Washington City
26–March 1831.

General Philip Van Cortlandt.
Sir,

I received the Letter which you had the goodness to promise me when I had the honor to pay you a visit; I have to regret that my stay was only a few minutes, in consequence of having an engagement at New York, which compelled me to return by the same Boat — but on my re-visiting that City, I will have the pleasing satisfaction to call upon you & avail myself of your goodness to pass a few hours and recount to you, Sir, my Services, perils at Sea and difficulties during the many years I served abroad as Consul of the United States. —

I reiterate to you, Sir, my thanks for the Letter referred to, but permit me, Sir, to observe that as my sole object is to promote the advancement of my Son, now eighteen years old — and the only Son living; named Louis Jean Marie Baker, for whom, tho' well educated it is the greatest difficulty for me to obtain him any decent competent situation to settle him in Life — I will now beg of you, Sir, to state upon paper in a Letter to me, your knowledge of his Grand Father, the late L^{t}. Colonel Commander Frederick H. Weissenfels of the Revolutionary Army of the U.S.[2] —

who was your Colonel during the arduous struggle of the Revolutionary War; his merits and his Services, these facts under your hand, as the General, when Baron Weissenfels was your Colonel, will bear testimony and avail in the heart of the Soldier & Warrier and every honorable honest Man, to have a feeling and consideration for his offspring — and may afford my Son Louis the means of exercising his talents and diligence for his honest support and consolation for his dear Mother and three good sisters — Your goodness of heart will pardon an anxious Father's solicitude for the Welfare of his son, and the happiness of the whole Family in which all are so nearly and dearly connected.

Praying you to be pleased to oblige me with my request as soon as conveniently possible, I remain with Respect and consideration, Sir, Your Oblig^{d}: h. Servant

John M. Baker

M^{rs}. Baker (daughter of the late Col. Frederick H. Weissenfels) and my three Daughters & my Son Louis, pray you, Sir, to accept their respectful remembrance.

P.S. Our much respected Friend Gov. Troup of Georgia,[3] Senator — passed last winter here, he left this on the 6th ins^{t}. — We frequently, sir, had the pleasure to speak of you.

Yrs Respectfully
JM Baker

I pray you to write me by Mail —
Please address —
John M. Baker
Dep^{t}. of State
Washington D.C.

---

1. John M. Baker, a career officer, ranked as the seventh highest official in the State Department during the secretaryship of Henry Clay. He later served as U.S. consul in Brazil. Peter Force, ed., *The National Calendar and Annals of the United States*

1828 (Washington, D.C., 1828), p. 34; *The American Almanac and Repository of Useful Knowledge for the Year 1834* (Boston, 1834), p. 134.

2. For Frederick Weissenfels, see *VCFP*, I and II, *passim.* Philip's reply to this request follows.

3. George M. Troup (1780–1856), a former governor of Georgia, was then serving in the Senate. As a strong states' rights advocate he would be nominated as a presidential candidate on the Southern Rights ticket in 1852. *DAB, XVIII,* 650.

137

Philip to John M. Baker. ADfs
NYSL

Cortlandt Town [April 26] 1831.

John M. Baker Esqr

Dear Sir

I have had the Pleasure to Receive yours of the 26th March last, and pleased to find that your good Family, who are decended from my old much Esteemed Friend the late Lieut Colonel Frederick H. Weisenfels who together with my self Entred the army in the beginning of the Revolutionary War and Served to the End thereof are in good Health and that your self are Retained in the Service of the United States, which is a proof that there yet remains some remembrance of the Old Soldiers ardent services: Yes Sir your Children's Grand Father was a good Soldier and faithful in the interest of the United States & that he was highly Esteemed by his Excellency General Washington and others all which was to me well known and that we both of us Experienced the hardships and Severe Conflicts in the early part of the War, and on the Debarcation of Rudolphus Ritsma who was the Col^o^. of the Second New York Regiment, Lieut Col^o^. Weisenfels at the Battle of White Plains Commanded that Reg^t^ and bravely Faught the Enemy, after which he accompanied Genl Washington with the army across the Hudson and through the State of New Jersey to the State of Pensylvania and assisted in the Capture of the Heshens at Trentown, and as the Regt was much reduced by Desertion and treachrous Discharges given by Ritsema before he went to the Enemy, Genl Washington Order' Colo Weissenfels to take the Regt to Fishkill in the State of N. York to be Reunited and the next day I arrived and took the Command as Colonel having been appointed by Genl Washington's Order who had Blank Commissions for the purpose Sign'd John Hancock's Pret. of Congress which he sent to me by Express to Lake Champlain as soon as he found that Ritsman had Deserted to the Enemy and when the Regiment Was reunited in 1777, I was Sent to Command a Detachment on the frontier at White Plains & was ordered from that place with the Regt. to Join the Army under Genl. Gates and Assisted in the Capture of Genl. Burgoiyn and all his army and Saw them ground and Surrended their arms as prisoners to the United States

Imediately after this the Brigade to which I was Attached was Orderd to March from Saratoga to Join the Grand Army under the Command of his Excellency Genl. Washington then in the State of Pensylvania, I being the Senior in Command Marched the Brigade untill we came near the grand Army in the State of Pensylvania where we was Joined by Genl. Poor after his Recovery from Sickness and then Received orders from the Commander in Chief to make ready & to Winter in thru at Valley forge but being ordered myself by Genl. Washington' to take Command of a Selected detachment to Radner on the Frontier 24 Miles advanced from the army only Nine Miles from the City of Philadelphia and Continued there a long time Untill Genl. Washington Recalled me and gave me the Command of Superintending the Incampment he left at Valley Forge When he move'd off with such as was able to make an attack on the British army which he did at Monmouth Court House and Colo. Weisenfel's was so fortunate to be ingaged —

Successfully to make a Charge with the Bayonnet to the honor of himself and Credit of the Second N.Y. Regt. After my Superintending and Recall from Valley Forge I Join'd the army and took the Command of the Regt. which I found Incamped at the White Plains — & after the army moved to Winter Quarters I was ordered on the frontier of the State of New York to appose the Indians under capt. Brant and in the Spring of the Year 1779 Genl. Washington Sent Express orders for me to proceed to the state of Pennsyla and Receive orders from Major Genl. Sullivan and Under his Command to drive off and destroy the Indians which was done as far as the Genesea River, and had a very Severe Battle with them at New Town on the Tioga River where I Charged them with Bayonets and by that means a Victory was obtained —

The New Orgination of the Army takes place the 5 New York Regt. being Reduced to Two. Colo Weissenfels was obliged to leave me but Retained his Rank in the army of the United States as long as he lived and after he left me he was in the Service of the State of N. York on Several Commands — I was Continued as Colo. of the Second New York Regt. and ordered to Commd. Fort Stanwix on the Mohawk River, and after distroying it I was Ordered to The State of Virginia and Assisted in the Capture of all the British Army under the Commd. of that very Famous General Lord Cornwallis and had the pleasure to See them Surrender not only their arms by [making] also themselves prisoners of War &c &c Some of The army Returned of Which my Commd. Was part made Hutts & Wintered at Pumpton in the State of New Jersey and Where His Excellency Genl. Washington with his Lady came to Visit and Remain'd with me from the Evening Untill the Second Morning — pertaking of such as I could provide in a Humble Cottage and which I then did and Ever Shall Esteem the greatest Honor I Ever Received for the Comr. in Chief of all the United States Forces to pass from Morris Town with his Lady to Pumpton passing the Residence of Gentlemen well known to him Who lived in affluence To Visit a Tryed and faithful Servant of the army over which he Commanded is to say I Esteem him Worthy and now make it Evident —

Dear Sir The above being a Short Statement made from memory of some of the Joint and Separate Services of Col^{o}. Weisenfels and myself during the arduous and most trying periods of the Revolu^{r}. War,[1] is Intended that the Relatives of the Colonel may know and Venorate his Virtuous Endeavours to promote the Interest of the People of the United States of America and in a speachel maner by Your Son Louis that he may appresiate the Virtues of his Predicessor —

I am Yours most Respectfully &c
Ph. V. Cortlandt

P.S. I should have answered your letter Sooner but have been afflicted with Severe Sore Eyes so that I could not write with Ease — Ever since Rec'd. your letter and am not yet Recovered.

[Endorsed]
John M. Baker; Dept. of State Washington D.C.
& answered 26 Apr. 1831

---

1. This outline of Philip's Revolutionary War career probably came directly from his *Memoir.* See *VCFP,* I.

138

Agreement between Philip and Camp Meeting Ground Petitioners. ADS

SHR

July 27, 1831.

This Indenture made Between Philip Van Cortlandt of the Town of Cortlandt in the County of Westchester Esquire of the First part, and Joseph Smith — Andrew C. Wheeler[,] John Fisher[,] Andrew Hanford and William Requau[1] of the Second part. Witnesseth that the said party of the first part for and in Consideration of one dollar and the covenants here in after contained on the part and in Behalf of the parties of the Second to be paid and performed. Hath demised Granted and Leased, and by these presents doth demise Grant and Lease unto the s^{d}. parties of the second part all that Certain Inclosed piece of Wood land in the town of Cortlandt aforesaid as the fences now stands known as the Camp Meeting Ground at Croton In Trust for the Ministers and people of the Methodist Episcopal Church to hold a camp meeting to commence the 5th day of September next and to Continue Untill the 13th both days Included, and the said Meeting Shall be Conducted and regulated according to Law. And they are not to commit waste or Suffer it to be done by Others and to Close up and leave the premises in as Good Order as they found, it, and to pay the aforesaid rent of one dollar to the party of the first part if demanded.

Given under our hands and seals this

27 day of July 1831.

Ph. V. Cortlandt

Witness: —

Noble W. Thomas

Joseph Smith
And. Wheeler
John Fisher
Andrew Hanford

1. An amanuensis prepared the body of the document, while Philip wrote in the names of the individuals involved in the lease. For earlier camp meeting ground agreements, see Nos. 63, 78, 106, and 124.

139

West Point Military Cadets to Philip. ADS
NYPL

August 18, 1831.

The first class U.S. Corps of Cadets request the honor of Gen. Philip Van Courtlandt's company at a Ball to be given on the 26th inst. at Mr. Cozzens' Assembly-room.

Managers[1]

P. St. Geor. Cocke	J.C. Vance
R. G. Fain	George Willard
G. H. Griffin	D.P. Whiting
H. Swartwourt	F.F.J. Wilkinson

West Point NY
18th August 1831

1. Philip St. George Cocke graduated from West Point on July 1, 1832, as did all the cadets listed. He resigned from the army in 1834. Although Richard G. Fain resigned in 1832, he later served in the Tennessee militia from 1836 to 1844, and was a merchant in that state from 1866 to 1878. George H. Griffin served in the Florida wars in 1838 and 1839, dying in the latter year. Henry Swartwourt received a second lieutenant's commission in 1832, and later achieved the rank of captain. Joseph C. Vance resigned from the service in 1835 and became a farmer in Virginia. George Willard remains unidentified. Daniel P. Whiting served in the Florida wars from 1839 to 1842 and in the Mexican War; he retired in 1863 with the rank of

lieutenant colonel. Frederick Wilkinson resigned in 1835 to become an engineer, and died six years later in New Orleans. U.S. Military Academy, West Point, New York, West Point Alumni Foundation, *Register of Graduates* (1970), p. 222; Heitman (1903), I, 939.

140

George William Clinton to Pierre, Jr. ADS
NYPL

August 26, 1831.

To all to whom these presents shall come, Whereas Pierre Van Cortlandt of Peeks kill one of the Executors of the last will & Testament of my Father George Washington Clinton[1] has fully accounted with me for all monies which came to his hands as such executor & for all acts done by him under virtue of said will now therefore I do by these presents fully release and discharge said Pierre Van Cortlandt from all claims & demands against him as such executor as aforesaid. In witness whereof I have hereto set my hand & seal this twenty sixth day of August 1831.
In presence of
D. Wager
Ab^{m}. Varick George W. Clinton
State of New York

Oneida County. On this 26th day of August 1831 personally appeared before me George W. Clinton to me well known to be the person described in & who executed the within deeds, who acknowledged that he executed the same freely for the uses and purposes therein expressed.

D. Wager Supreme Court Com^{r}.

---

1. The late Vice President George Clinton had one male heir, George Washington Clinton. He was Pierre's brother-in-law

through Pierre's first wife, Catharine. The son had given the father cause for concern on a number of occasions. After a lifetime of sporadic illness, George Washington Clinton died on March 27, 1813. George William was his only child. See *VCFP, III, passim.*

141

Philip G. Van Wyck to [Philip Cortlandt?] Van Wyck. ALS NYPL

Croton November 5th 1831.

Dear Son

The evening after I parted with you in Newyork I received a Letter from your Mama that Uncle Philip was something better but shortly after she had sent it he had a bad turn since which he has rapidly declined untill this evening at 8 oclock when he departed this life without a struggle or a groan.[1] —

The Funeral will take place on Tuesday next. —

I sent your Apples & a bundle containing your blue Vest by the Sloop Regulator bound to Sag harbour the day after you left New York

May this find you well is the will of us all who join me in Love

your affectionate father
Ph G Van Wyck

---

1. Philip G. Van Wyck herein announced the death of Philip Van Cortlandt. The *Westchester Herald* and the New York *Commercial Advertiser* carried the same obituary notice, in which it was reported that "at the time of his decease, [Philip was] the senior surviving officer in the country of the army of the Revolution." It also declared Philip to have been "remarkable for his personal dignity — and [he] combined two traits of character seldom united in the same person, loftiness of manner with urbanity of disposition." New York *Commercial Advertiser,* November 10, 1831.

⁂ 142 ⁂

Will and Codicil of Philip. AD [Copy]
SHR

[March 9, 1824]

In the Name of God Amen, I Philip Van Cortlandt of the Town of Cortlandt being in sound mind and memory do Make this my last will and testament hereby revoking all former wills in manner and form following —

And first it is my will that my Earthly Body be buried at the discretion of my Executors hereafter to be named and all my debts paid soon after my decease —

And whereas it may appear by the last will and testament of my deceased Grand Father Philip Van Cortlandt that the Lot of Land whereon I now Reside at the Mouth of Croton River being known as front Lot Number One" of the Manor of Cortlandt was devised and left to my Father Pierre Van Cortlandt with Intail to his Eldest Son and as the Laws of the State of New York have abolished all Intails and my Right established both by Law and the decease of my Father I am authorised to dispose of the same —

And Whereas at my decease it may be probable that a Ballance of Monies may be due from me to the Estate of my deceased Father and in order to discharge the same without disagreement among my Relations and to promote harmony and prevent Law Suits. I do hereby direct and it is my will that the said Lot of Land on which I live the same being amply sufficient shall be accountable for the extinguishment thereof, And as my Brother & Sisters will be entitled to an Equal part of the Ballance which may be due from me to the Estate And as the Land I shall give to Each will be of more value than their Individual share of said ballance it is my will that no Account be made thereof this being a Settlement —

Therefore in Consideration of the above I do in the first place give and bequeath unto my Brother Pierre Van Cortlandt and to his heirs and Assigns for Ever All that part of said front Lot Number One of the Manor of Cortlandt. Beginning at the North West Corner thereof where it joins the Land of John Conklin and Runs with the Line of said Lot North Easterly to the Landing Road then following the said Road to a Run of Water, then down the said Run of Water to Croton River then to the middle thereof Then down the said River keeping the Middle thereof passing the Deep hole to the Island called Deer Island then to the tree standing on the South Side of said Croton River and is the Corner of the Town of Greensburgh and of the Town of New Castle then down Croton River on the South Side thereof to Hudson River then Northerly and as it may Run with the waters of the said Croton to the Meadow Creek then up the same to the Neck of Land then following the said Neck of Land and Meadow Creek until it comes to Dike made by Robert Underhill then a West Line to Hudsons River then Northerly along the said Hudson River to the place of Beginning Containing about Six hundrd Acres of Land Subject to the discharging the aforesaid Ballance and also the payment of five hundred Dollars "when necessary" as stipulated to be paid to the Underhills on the lease given them for the Mill seat to be paid for buildings exclusive of Mills which said buildings was erected on the Land hereby bequeathed —

Item — I give and bequeath unto my Sister Catharine during her natural life All that part of said Lot Number One Beginning at the Line of John Conklins Land on the North Easterly Side of the Landing Road and Runs with said Road Easterly to a Run of water then down the same to Croton River then to the Middle thereof then up the same to the Brook North Easterly to the House where David Ford now lives then following up the Brook to where the Rock was blown to drean [drain] the Swamp, Thence North Westerly course to the Line of said Lot Number One in the South Westerly End of said Swamp then following the Line of said Lot to the Place of Beginning Containing about two hundred Acres and after the decease of my said Sister Catharine I give and bequeath the same to her Son Philip G Van Wyck his

Heirs and Assigns for ever Subject nevertheless to the discharging the aforesaid ballance —

Item — I give and bequeath unto my Sister Cornelia and to her heirs and Assigns for ever Subject to the proportion of the aforesaid Ballance The North Easterly End of said Lot Number One. Beginning at the Mouth of Pond brook and Runs to the Lot leased to Jeremiah Pugsley for the Still House then following on the East Side thereof leaving Garret Williams possession of House Stable and Garden on the Corner to the East until it comes to the Road, then up the Road as runs to the North Westerly Line of said Lot Number One, then North Easterly along the said Line to the North East Corner thereof then South Easterly along the Line to Croton River to the place of Beginning Containing Two hundred Acres more or less Reserving thereout for the Use of the part to be bequeathed to my Sister Ann that piece of Ground lying before the house where Jeremiah Pugsley lives containing about One Acre to extend far enough so as to include a Spring of Water which may be brought to the House — Also Reserving One Acre Northerly thereof to place a Barn or Stable leaving a Lane between the two Lots from the Road Eastward

Item I give and bequeath unto my Sister Ann and to her heirs and Assigns for Ever All that part of said Lot situate between the part bequeathed to my Sister Catharine and the part bequeathed to my Sister Cornelia containing about Two hundred Acres including the Two Acre pieces in front of the House Jeremiah Pugsley lives. Subject Nevertheless to the discharging the before mentioned Ballance

And Whereas I am indebted to my Sister Catharine as may appear from Settlement, to be made and in Order to secure the pay ment thereof I do hereby direct that my part of the Mills South of Croton River and the House and Land in the possession of John T Hollman be accountable And I do hereby give and bequeath the said House Land and my part of the said mills and every thing oppurtaining thereunto together with what the said John T Hollman is or may be in my debt on Account thereof unto my Nephew Pierre C Van Wyck and to his heirs and Assigns for Ever Subject to an equitable discharge of the Debt hereafter to be found due to my said Sister Catharine as aforesaid —

And Whereas I have Received Money from Walter Fowler which arose from his being miller and superintending the mills left by the Underhills and have also Received some profits from the Lands belonging to the Estate of my deceased Father South of Croton River and South and East of John T Hollman and whereas I have paid the Taxes and for Improvements made thereon but perhaps not equivalent and as my deceased Father by his last will did give and bequeath to me a part thereof therefore wishing that full compensation be made I do give and bequeath the said part which in my Opinion is of more value than the Equivalent unto my Brother Pierre and my Sisters Catharine Cornelia and Ann and to their Heirs and Assigns for Ever

Having thus far arranged and disposed of the Estate which was derived from my Grand Father and Father in the Most equitable manner that my Understanding could devise in order to prevent discord and promote happiness, good will and affection among all concerned which I hope and most sincerely pray may be the Result —

I shall now proceed to dispose of what it has pleased my heavenly Father and God to bless me with in Addition And in Order to prevent difficulties in the distribution of Articles of Trifling amount and to place in One Confidential Person property sufficient to discharge all my Debts I do give and bequeath unto my Nephew Philip G Van Wyck and to his heirs and Assigns for ever All the Residue of my Estate both Real and personal Excepting such parts thereof as I may particularly designate give and bequeath by a Codicil or Codicils hereafter to be made and added to this my last will with full power to sell and convey Real Estate foreclose Mortgages fulfill Contracts collect Debts and pay all what is due from me to the People of the State of New York and all other Demands against me except such as is Already provided for by this my last will —

And I do hereby direct and appoint my Brother Pierre Van Cortlandt my Nephew Pierre C Van Wyck my Nephew Philip G. Van Wyck Executors and my Sisters Cornelia Beekman and my Sister Ann Van Rensselaer Executrix's to this my last will

Signed sealed published and declared to be my last will and Testament the Ninth day of March In the year One thousand Eight and Twenty four —

In the Presence of
Robert Acker
Rachel Tompkins — Ph V Cortlandt (L.S.)
John Guild —

[January 18, 1831.]

— Codicil[1] —

To All to whom these presents shall come send Greeting Whereas I Philip Van Cortlandt of the Town of Cortlandt on the Ninth day of March in the Year One thousand Eight hundred and Twenty four did execute an Indenture purporting to be my last Will with a Reservation therein expressed to make a Codicil thereunto if I should conceive it proper and therefore on Reflection being of sound Mind and Memory for which the Lord be praised. I do make this a Codicil to my said last Will with amendments and alterations as follows

Whereas I did in my said last will bequeath to my much lamented and deceased Nephew Pierre C Van Wyck my Mills South of Croton River now in the possession of John T Hollman together with Land and Premisses All which Bequest with the Conditions annexed in the Clause as the same is expressed is hereby made void and Revoked to all Intents and purposes. And Whereas I have discovered a Mistake in my said last Will in the fifth line from the bottom of the first page or Sheet of the Word "Greensburgh" which should be "Mount Pleasant" Therefore hereby direct the Alteration —

And Whereas I have directed by my said last Will in order to discharge what I had Received from Walter Fowler and Others given to my Brothers & Sisters my part of the Lands South of Croton River as payment and whereas I have purchased most of that Land from my said Brother and Sisters. And I being also chargeable with all the Debts due from me to the Estate of my deceased Father conceive the whole of that Clause Useless And do hereby direct the said Clause be Revoked and made void to all Intents & purposes —

And Whereas I have in this Codicil made void the Clause in my Will which gave to my deceased Nephew Pierre C Van Wyck my Mills South of Croton River &c&c and whereas I have paid One thousand Dollars for Law Books which I left in his possession And also paid several hundred Dollars to purchase up his Notes at his Request to relieve him from Debt. It is therefore my Will And I do by this Codicil bequeath the said Law Books for his Sons benifit and that no charge be made for the said Notes And whereas I have been informed that there is found among my said Nephews papers a promisory Note for several hundred Dollars due from me to him which might have been made to obtain Money for me from some of the Banks in New York and Neglected. However for certainly I do here-by make it payable for his Son's benefit —

I give and bequeath all that piece or parcel of Land as the same is now in fence and which joins the Highway and the Land of John Conklin whereas the Methodist Meeting House now stands Containing about Two Acres be the same more or less and to be used for a burying place for the Inhabitants of the Neighbourhood, And the Meeting House for a Place of Public Worship under the direction of the Methodist Congregation. They always conforming to the Laws and Constitution of the State of New York as long as the said Meeting House and the Fences are kept in good Order and Repair. The same to be used for a place of Worship and burying ground and for no other purpose whatsoever —

I give and bequeath unto Philip Cortlandt Van Wyck my Godson the Son of my Nephew Philip G Van Wyck, The Salt Meadow at the South West part of this farm now in my possession called the Round Island Meadow being bounded by the Meadow Creek, the Upland and the Ditch heretofore made by my Fathers Order sometime before his Death. And on the West by Hudson River Containing about twelve Acres including the Round Island be the same More or less to him and his Heirs and Assigns for Ever

I give and Bequeath unto my Nephew Pierre Van Cortlandt, Son of my Brother Pierre All that piece or parcel of Land and Tenements situate on the South Easterly Side of Croton River in the Town of Mount Pleasant being bounded on the South Easter Side by the Highway and the Land now in the Occupation of Samuel C Merrit Containing about five Acres be the same more or less including the Brook of Water Running from the highway into Croton River which I give to my said Nephew Pierre Van Cortlandt and to his Heirs and Assigns for Ever

And it is my Will and I do hereby direct that my Nephew Philip G Van Wyck and his Family keep the possession and occupation of my House and farm whereon I now Reside and Receive the Profits thereof until the Year of our Lord One thousand Eight hundred and Thirty Six that being the Year my Brothers Son Pierre becomes of Age —

And with Resarving if I should think of it and proper to make an Additional Codicil or Codicils, I hereby declare this to be a Codicil to my last will & which I sign in the presents of Three Witnesses the Eighteenth day of January In the Year of our Lord One thousand Eight hundred and Thirty One

Signed sealed and
declared to Codicil

to my last Will in the presence of

Ph V Cortlandt (L.S.)

Robert Acker — Town of Cortland
John D Ludlum — Town of Cortland
Jacob Acker — Cortlandt Town

---

1. Philip Van Cortlandt's will and codicil posed some interesting legal questions. His estate consisted, in part, of inherited property derived from his father Pierre, and from his grandfather Philip. The inherited estate had descended to Philip in entail under the then-existing laws of colonial New York. In addition, over the years Philip acquired property by purchase, either from other members of the Van Cortlandt family or from the state while serving in a post-Revolutionary capacity as a Commissioner of Forfeiture (see No. 300).

Philip remained a bachelor and therefore had no legal direct heirs to whom he could pass on the estate. He was surrounded by family members, however. Soon after moving back into the Manor house upon the dissolution of the Continental Army in 1783, he was joined by his recently widowed sister, Catharine Van Wyck, and her young children. Philip grew to love the two boys almost as his own and sought to provide for them after his death. Pierre C. Van Wyck was to inherit Philip's interest in a mill complex on the Croton River operated by John T. Hollman, along with other lands. To Philip's great distress, Pierre C. Van Wyck died at a relatively early age, thus compelling Philip to negate the original bequest. The other nephew, Philip G. Van Wyck, was to receive different benefits.

As part of the Revolutionary upheaval, New York moved to eliminate entail from its laws. Philip acted according to his conception of this revision in that he assumed the right to determine the distribution of his estate without being confined by the process of entail. Under colonial laws, Philip would have been compelled to transmit his properties directly to his surviving brother, Pierre, Jr., or in case of Pierre's demise, to Pierre's oldest surviving male descendant. Philip hit upon a variation which, he thought, would be acceptable to all. He provided that his surviving nephew, Philip G. Van Wyck, was to receive the right to reside and enjoy the Manor house and its adjacent lands until 1836, the year when Pierre's son, Pierre III, would turn twenty-one. Hopefully, Philip must have thought, this would offer his nephew the opportunity to establish himself before being compelled to withdraw from the Manor lands. This also had the effect of denying Philip's brother, Pierre, the use of the Manor house and lands.

Another devise pertained to lands acquired by Philip which he came to regard as part of his estate along the Croton River. He originally divided those holdings among his relations, including the deceased nephew, Pierre C. Van Wyck, along with Philip's surviving siblings and their children. When Philip revised this portion of his will in the codicil dated January 18, 1831, the permanent disposition of this portion of the estate was left unclear.

Almost immediately, lawsuits were commenced by Pierre in order to vacate several portions of Philip's will. These suits tended to alienate the surviving Van Cortlandts from the Van Wycks, and brought handsome fees to a multitude of attorneys. The legal questions may be cited in the following manner.

First: Did Philip have the right to break the Van Cortlandt line of possession of the Manor house and its lands? That property had been inherited from his grandfather's estate by way of his father. Under the terms of both the grandfather's and father's wills, the property was to descend to the next surviving male sibling or descendant. Regardless of entail, had Philip violated the clear stipulations made in the two previous wills by not turning over the properties to his surviving brother?

Second: If Philip G. Van Wyck was upheld in his right to reside and use the estate, who would be liable for any debts or repairs incurred during his years of occupancy, Philip G. Van Wyck or Pierre?

Third: Did nephew Philip G. have any right to remove any household or farm possessions from the estate?

Fourth: With the abrogation of the original bequest of lands south of the Croton River to Pierre C. Van Wyck, who had the right to such properties — Philip G. or the surviving Van Cortlandt siblings?

Philip G. Van Wyck remained in the Manor house through 1835 and then vacated it in favor of his uncle, Pierre. Pierre, in turn, immediately provided his son, Pierre III, with a five-year lease on the property.

In particular, see the following legal opinions of Abraham Van Vechten dated February 16, 1832 (No. 144), and that of Ambrose Spencer, April 5, 1832 (No. 147).

143

Cornelia Beekman to Pierre, Jr. ALS
SHR

Jany 20–1832.

My Dearest Brother

I could have wished to have seen you before this relative to the Propperty left me by our father, and that left me by Brother Philip — While Philip was living he had the Estate all in his hands, and we all Looked up to him to Settle the Estate, but he did not, and so it remained till his Death unsettled — to Delay now it will not do any longer — Consider I am Old, Life is unsertain, therefore, I am come to this conclusion, I now must look up to you My Dear Brother — Must beg you will take Charge of all my Propperty Left me South of Croton River (untill I Shall Direct you Other wise) to do the best you can for my Intrust [interest] and I will be Sàttisfyed Confiding in you to do for Me as you would for your self[1] — Sister Rensselear has frequently told me to do for her intrust, as I did for myself, in settling any part of the Estate that she was intitled to, and she would ratify it — therefore I am Confident that Sister will be Sattisfyed, for you to act for her as you doe for me — but you must write her, what I have concluded on, — and have her answer also.

I wish to consult you relative to the Propperty Left me North of Croton River, I feel very Anxious to have things brought to a conclusion, your undertaking for me will Greatly Oblige your affectionate Sister

Cornelia

[Addressed]
Gen[l]. Pierre Van Cortlandt
Peeks Kill
Cortlandt town

---

1. Cornelia (Van Cortlandt) Beekman was then in her seventy-ninth year. Although she turned to Pierre, in this instance, to assume charge of her family legacy, she was a shrewd real estate speculator in her own right. She was primarily responsible for the opening and development of Beekmantown (North Tarrytown) in the nineteenth century.

144

Abraham Van Vechten's Legal Opinion. ADS
SHR

February 16, 1832.

Case.

L[t]. Governor Pierre Van Cortlandt under the Will of his Father Van Cortlandt was prior to and until the year one thousand seven hundred and eighty two seized in tail of certain lands in the County of West Chester. By the Acts passed in 1782 and 1787 to abolish entails his estate in the said lands was converted into a fee simple absolute. The Lt Governor by his Will dated 5th December 1805 disposed of the said lands in the manner therein expressed to his Sons Philip and Pierre and his three daughters after the death of their Mother, but on the 12th day of March 1811. he by a Codicil to his Will devised the lands therein for that purpose particularly described to his Son Pierre in fee simple. Both the Lt. Governor and his wife are dead. The latter survived his wife and died in May 1814. His Son Philip entered into possession of the lands so as above devised to his Brother Pierre at his Fathers death and held the same until he died in the year 1831. when he devised the use and income thereof until the year 1836. to his nephew Philip G. Van Wyck and family. —

> The only material question which arises on the above case is whether Pierre Van Cortlandt the Son of the Lt Governor is entitled to the premises devised to him under the Codicil to the Will of his Father? —

Answer.

The Codicil is plain and explicit. It gives the property in fee simple to the Testators Son Pierre. The enjoyment of it by Philip since his Fathers death in the year 1814. being less than 20. years does not bar Pierres right as devisee of his father, who by our Statute was the owner in fee when he made his will and Codicil; nor can the devise by the Will of his Brother Philip in any manner impair the title of Pierre under the Codicil of his Father.

February 16. 1832. Ab. Van Vechten

145

Inventory of Philip's Estate.[1] ADS
NYHS

[April 2, 1832.]

A TRUE and perfect Inventory of all the Goods, Chattels, and Credits of Philip Van Cortlandt late of the County of West Chester deceased, taken by the Executor of the said deceased, with the aid of the subscribers, sworn Appraisers, duly appointed for such purposes, by the Surrogate of the County of Westchester. Dated this 2nd day of April 1832.

I, Robert Acker, do solemnly swear and declare, that I will truly, honestly, and impartially appraise the personal property of Philip Van Cortlandt deceased, which shall be exhibited to me according to the best of my knowledge and ability.

Sworn before me, the 23rd day
of January 1832 Robert Acker
Jonathan Ward, Surrogate

I, Simmons Purdy, do solemnly declare that I will truly, honestly, and impartially appraise the personal property of Philip Van Cortlandt deceased, which shall be exhibited to me, according to the best of my knowledge and ability.

Sworn before me, the 28th day
of February 1832 Simmons Purdy
Daniel Hains, Com. of Deeds

	Estimate $	Cts
Money belonging to Testator in the hands of Philip Van Wyck at the time of the decease of Testator	416	37
Specie found in the desk of the Testator	22	07
One Bank Note for One Dollar on the Commercial Bank of New Jersey	1	
Cash received of Henry Hutchins for rent $4.86	4	86
Cash received of Samuel Kipp for rent $12.15	12	15
Cash received for an ox sold S. Kipp $50	50	
Cash received Jany. 24th 1832 of Manhattan Bank $551.36	551.	36
Cash received for four pigs sold	7	30
Cash received for nine small hogs	35	86
Cash received 14th March 1832 for Dividend on the Seneca Turnpike Company on Thos Rockwell's Draft dated Utica October 27th 1831	138	
Cash received for one fat Hog	19	64
Cash received for Turnips	4	34

Cash received for Potatoes	21	33
Cash received for parsnips 7/		87
One fat cow value	15	
1 fat cow	20	14
1 fat cow	19	60
1 fat cow	21	09
1 Steer (fat) Value killed	18	12
1 Steer (fat)	20	12
1 fat Ox	40	22
1 fat Hog killed	13	50
1 fat Hog	3	75
1 Do Do Do		
	13	25
1 Do Do Do	10	50
1 Do Do Do	8	65
(Amount carried over)		
one fat hog killed	8	
Do Do Do	14	50
Do Do Do	9	
Do Do Do	10	50
Do Do Do	7	
Do Do Do	8	25
Do Do Do	11	25
Do Do Do	11	
Do Do Do	11	
Do Do Do	14	
Do Do Do	10	
Do Do Do	13	40
2 small fat hogs killed	4	75
Wheat 181 Bushls	181	
Rye 83 Bushls	51	87
Buckwheat 116 Bushls	58	
Turnips 16½ Bushls	1	65
Parsnips 1½ Barrels	1	25

Potatoes 68½ Bushls	25	68
Potatoes Small 120 Bushls	19	20
Potatoes (Black) ten Bushls	3	13
Fifty lbs. Flax	5	
Hay 2880 lb	14	35
Corn 306 Bushls	153	
4 Barrels of Apples	6	
1 live pig	2	50
1 Do Do	2	50
1 Do Do	1	50
1 Do Do	1	01
1 Do Do		85
1 ox Cart	10	
1 ox Cart	20	
1 ox Cart	20	
1 Wintered Sow	7	50
1 Do Do	6	50
1 Do. Seed hay	4	
1 Wintered Sow	5	50
1 Do Do	5	50
8 Shoats at 20/each	20	
3 Shoats at 16/each	6	
1 Shoat	4	
9 Shoats at 24/each	27	
1 small fish Sean [Seine]	10	
125 lb. Wool		50
1 Lot old fish net	1	
8 pair Sheep Shears at 2/each	2	
7 ox Chains 12/each	10	50
One Gold Watch with Chain and Seals	40	
2 Canal Medals	2	
13 Silver Table Spoons	29	20
1 Silver Sugar Dish	9	60
1 Silver Sugar Tongs		85

1 Silver Wafer Box	8	40
1 pair small Scales		50
1 pair Spectacles	1	
1 pocket compass		50
1 Gold Sleve Button	2	
1 Miniature	2	
1 Locket	3	
1 Magnifying Glass		25
1 pair of Dividers		50
1 Pocket Book		50
1 pair small steelyards		13
1 port folio		50
3 Raisors and Strop		50
2 Crow Bars 8/each	2	
(Amount carried over)		
22 oak plank at 2/each	5	50
35 Dock fenders 1/each	4	37
1 Grind Stone & Crank	1	
2 Cart Hooks 4/each	1	
2 boat hooks at 3/each		75
2 Blocks and tackle	2	50
1 Ton Coarse Hay	5	
1½ tons good hay	11	25
1 stack hay	7	50
1 stack hay	7	50
1 stack hay	15	
1 stack hay	22	50
1 Barrack hay	20	
12 Acres wheat growing (old orchard)	96	
7 D° D° D° on shares ⅔ to estate	18	66
13 D° Rye growing on shares of ⅔ to estate	26	
4½ acres wheat growing	27	
½ an acre wheat growing	4	

8 Acres Rye growing on shares of one half to Estate	12	
3 Mare Blankets 4/each	1	50
1 Thermometer		75
12 Chairs at 3/each	4	50
1 Feather Bed	10	
4 flannel sheets	1	
1 Bolster		75
2 pillows at 4/each	1	
3 small blankets 2/each		
3 more blankets 3/each	3	75
1 Set Bed Curtains	5	
1 Down Bed	2	
1 half Bushl measure		50
1 Drawing Knife		50
1 Hay knife		1
(Amount brought over)		
Stephanis Naritive 1 vol.		10
Anual register 1 vol.		10
Court of st. cloud 1 vol.		10
Causes evils & cures 1 vol.		06
Gustavis Vassa 1 vol.		20
1 Map State New York		25
Tourist 1 vol.		12
History United States 1 vol.		13
True godliness 1 vol.		13
Rowlands Husbandry 1 vol.		12
Monument to Paulding 1 vol.		06
Notes on Revised Statutes 1 vol.		25
Agriculture 1 vol.		04
Watson on Canals 1 vol.		12
Mineral Waters 1 vol.		13
Directory of Rochester 1 vol.		12
21 pamphlets		25

Algernon Sidney 3 vol.		30
Nature Displayed 7 vol.	1	75
Life of Washington 1 vol.		25
History of the War 2 vol.		25
Ladies Museum 9 vol. (odd)	2	25
Tom Jones 3 vol.		75
Pitts Virgil 2 vol. (odd)		75
Roberts Sermons 1 vol. (odd)		25
Ten Virgins 1 vol.		13
Animal economy 1 vol.		10
Fovery 1 vol.		10
Blackstone 1 vol. (odd)		13
American Gazetteer 1 vol.		12
Reformer 1 vol.		25
Dyckmans manual 1 vol.		12
Hopkinsionism 1 vol.		12
(Amount brought over)		
1 Hogshead of Cider	8	
3 Hogsheads Casks at 6/	2	25
1 Barrel		37
1 Windfan	15	
1 Lot old Iron	1	25
1 Do Do Do	2	
1 Do Do Do	1	75
6 ox yokes at 8/each	6	
3 Scythes	2	25
1 Scythe & Sheath	1	
1 Spade		25
1 old Wind Fan	3	
1 Scoop		50
1 Beetle		25
4 Iron Wedges at 2/each	1	
1 Auger (2 inch)		31
1 Do (1 inch)		25

1 Scow	5	
1 undivided half part of a Scow	10	
1 Barrack Hay	15	
Hay in sheep house	11	25
Part of a barrack of hay	8	
2 Grain Cradles at 12/each	3	
1 Tared Rope & Hook	1	
2 Barrels of Vinegar at 16/each	4	
2 Vinegar Hogsheads at 6/each	1	50
9 Old Casks at 1/each	1	12
1 Book essay on sheep		12
Brook's Gazetteer 1 vol.		25
World Displayed 6 Vols.–odd	1	50
Felton Sermons 1 vol.		25
Philanthropist 1 vol.		18
Dutch Bible 1 Vol.		25
(Amount carried over)		
Shakespear–8 vol.	2	
Universal Gazettere 1 vol.		06
Sherbourn 1 vol.		18
2 pamphlets agriculture		12
Masonry 1 vol.		10
oration 1 vl.		13
Memoirs Boar Agriculture 1 vol.		10
Coxes View US 1 Vol.		25
Federalist 2 Vol.		12
Cooks life of Charles 1 vol.		25
Foresythe on fruittrees 1 vol.		18
History of the War 1 Vol. (odd)		12
View of Commerce 1 Vol.		12
Journals of Congress 13 Vols.	1	63
Journals house of the representatives 15 vols.	1	87
Journals of the Senate 3 vols.		38

Acts of Congress 1 vol.		06
Laws 6th congress 1 vol.		13
Eddies Map of New York		50
Examiner 4 vol. (odd)		24
Hatchers Journal 1 vol.		25
Calders Memoirs 1 vol.	1	
Laws New York (old) 5 vol. (odd)	1	25
Laws New York 4 vols. (odd)	1	
Laws U.S.A. 4 vols.		50
Laws Congress 5 vol.		50
Agricultural Transactions 3 vols odd		37
Debate on treaty 2 vols.		25
AristiDies 1 vol.		13
Memoirs of Lafayette 1 vol.		37
Wallers Lafayette 1 vol.	1	75
Hools Tasso 2 vols.	1	
Spy unmasked 1 vol.		25
(Amount carried over)		
1 old Dutch Bible	1	
Laws New York 1st & 2nd vol.		25
One Blacksmith Bellows	8	
One Do Anvil	8	
One Do Vice	3	
One Do Bickhorn	3	

One Bill of the Bank of Niagara for three dollars dated 1st Dec. 1826 Letter A.

One Bill of the Eagle Bank of New Haven for one Dollar dated 4th Feby 1824.

One Bill of the Eagle Bank of New Haven for five dollars dated 4th November 1823

One Bill of the Middle District Bank for three dollars dated october 1st 1826.

One bill of the Green County Bank for five dollars dated 27 Sept. 1820.

On a promise in writing against Peter Balen for $74.60 dated 11 Jany 1810.		
On a promise in writing against Anthony Conklin for fifty two shillings dated 11 April 1791.		
On a promise in writing against John French for Four pounds dated 3rd day March 1787.		
on a sealed note against John Simpson for nine pounds dated 8th August 1796. Endorsed thereon recd. 8th August 1801 two pounds nineteen shillings and eightpence.		
On a ballance of Pension due to Testator pensioner of the United States	100	
One Portrait	2	
One Do	2	
One Do	1	
one carpet	5	
one Rug		25
one looking-glass	10	
one writing Desk	3	
one Do Do	2	
one sand box		12
Three Window Blinds at 4/each	1	50
one Mahogany Table	5	
one small carpet		50
one pair shovel & tongs	1	
one valice	1	
one leather trunk	1	50
one chest	1	50
one book-case desk	4	
one Surveyors Compass & staff	3	
one Do chain	1	50
one Do and half-chain	1	

3 Vests at 2/each		75
4 yards Nankeen		50
2 pair Drawers at 4/each	1	
3 flannel Waistcoats at 2/8.	1	
one flannel Night Gown	1	50
one pair Silk Britches		25
one flannel Coat	1	
one Cotton Jane Coat	2	
one Woolen Vest	2	
one blue cloth surtout	6	
one D° D° D°	2	
one Camblet over coat	4	
one Pair Woolen pantaloons	1	
one old Map United States		50
One D° D° Washington City		25
(Amount carried over)		
4 pair shoes at $-.37 each	1	50
one D° over shoes		75
Two pair Boots	2	50
2 pair black pantaloons at $2 each	4	
one Tight body coat	2	
2 pair Britches at $.50 each	1	
1 small map of France		12
1 Umbrella	1	
one old Bombazine Coat		50
3½ yards Muslin		44
1 Bombazine Coat	4	
1 D° Pantaloons	2	
2 Vests at $.50 each	1	
2 Buckskin Waist Coats at $1 each	2	
2 Hats at $2.37½ each	4	75
1 pair Gloves		25
1 tight bodied Coat	10	

1 D^{o} D^{o} D^{o}	3	
6 Shirts at .37½ each	2	25
6 old shirts at .50 each	3	
6 Cravats at .12½ each		75
2 Coarse shirts at .75 each	1	50
one Stock		25
one muslin waist coat		13
1 Vest		25
1 pair Drawers		25
3 Napkins at $.12½ each		37
2 pair socks at $.12½ each		25
3 D^{o} D^{o} at .12½ each		38
2 Silk Handkerchiefs		50
2 pair pantaloons at $1 each	2	
3 Vests at $.50 each	1	50
3 pair Drawers at $.33⅓ each	1	
4 Waist Coats at $.37½ each	1	50
1 Calico Morning gown	1	
5 pair Socks $.25. each	1	25
4 D^{o} Drawers $.54¼ each	2	25
1 flannel Waistcoat		50
1 picture		25
10 Chairs at $.25 each	2	50
2 Wicker Baskets at $.25 each		50
1 pair shovel & tongs	1	50
1 pair Andirons	2	
1 Carpet	3	
1 D^{o} in hall	2	
1 Glass lamp	2	
1 Map City of New York	1	
1 Portrait	1	
1 Maple Bedstead	3	
2 small pictures at $.50 each	1	
1 Large Picture	10	

1 Mahogany side board	10	
1 Picture	1	
2 Mahogany Tables $5 each	10	
1 Dozen Champain Glases at $.12½ each	1	50
1 pair decanters		75
1 pair Glass flasks		50
3 Glass Dishes at $.12½ each		38
1 Dozen Large Plates	1	
1½ Ditto Small plates	1	12
3 wooden window blinds at $1 each	3	
1 pair window blinds	1	
1 small round Table	1	50
1 stove	5	
2 Window blinds		75
3 D° D° at $.37½ each	1	12
1 Bedstead	1	
1 Cot frame		50
124 Bottles at $.03 each	3	72
(Amount carried over)		
Eleven Demijohns at $.62½ each	6	88
Eleven Gallons wine	11	
5 bottles Champain at $1 each	5	
3 Gallons cider spirits	1	50
6 wine flasks at $.25 each	1	50
1 Barrel		75
12 Gallons wine in Barrel	15	
1 Lot old Harness & piece Leather	3	
34 volumes Congress Journals and state papers	8	50
3 volumes American Senator		75
2 D° Debates on Treaty		50
1 D° Martins law of Nations		25
1 D° Scetches on American History		25
7 Vol. Congress Papers	1	75

1 Large Jug		25
1 Tent Cloth	5	
13 Milk pans at $.25 each	3	25
1 picture old Brant		50
1 Cloak woolen old blue		50
1 pair steelyards	2	
4 old tables at $.37½	1	50
1 Kitchen cupboard		50
1 Lot old milk pans		75
2 Iron pots cracked at $.50 each	1	
1 Pie pan		50
1 Griddle		75
2 Cloths frames at $.25 each		50
1 Cherry Bureau	2	
2 pair Andirons	1	
1 shovel & tongs		50
2 Meat Casks at $.50 each	1	
8 D° D° $.43¾ each	3	50
7 Meat Barrels at $.37½ each	2	63
12 Barrels of Apples at $1.50 each	18	
1 Sorrel Mare	50	
1 Bay Horse	65	
1 Bay Horse	20	
1 pair Carriage Horses	250	
12 yearling cattle at $5 each	60	
8 Cows at $18 each	144	
16 three-year old heffers at $14 each	224	
8 three-year old steers at $13 each	104	
7 two-year old heffers at $8 each	56	
5 two-year old steers at $8 each	40	
13 cows at $20 each	260	
2 two-year old Bulls at $10 each	20	
61 Head of sheep at $2 each	122	
2 Brindle oxen at $30 each	60	

2 Steers at $27.50 each	55	
2 oxen hided & Red at $35 each	70	
2 red Stags at $25 each	50	
2 oxen George & Mary at $35 each	70	
3 Large pattent ploughs at $4 each	12	
2 Corn ploughs at $3 each	6	
3 old pattent ploughs at $1 each	3	
8 stone boat planks at 2/each	2	
9 White oak planks at 2/each	2	25
1 Grindstone and crank	1	
1 Gig & harness	35	
1 one Horse waggan	12	
1 Set of one horse harness	5	
1 Carriage	100	
11 white oak joice at 1/6 each	2	06
1 Lot Carriage Harness	20	
1 Lot Cooper stuff	2	
9 old wheeles at 4/each	4	50
1 Horse rake	5	
1 Log sled	1	
(Amount carried over)		
3 Wood Sleds at $2.50 each	7	50
2 old wood sleds at $1 each	2	
1 Wooden Harrow	1	
1 Iron Tooth Harrow	5	
1 Two Horse Waggon	10	
6 Black Oak plank at 2/each	1	50
2 old cart wheeles at 6/each	2	
2 Cart wheeles double Tire	10	
2 Wheele Barrows at 12/each	3	
87 Long plank at 3/	32	62
14 short plank at 2/	3	50
2 Mens Riding saddles at $3 each	6	
1 Set of Wiffletrees traces & Collars	1	

1 Double and two single wiffletrees		50
1 Corn Sheller	5	
4 Iron Crobars at $1 each	4	
4 Shovels	1	50
3 Shades at 4/each	1	50
6 Hoes at 2/each	1	50
1 Garden Rake		50
7 Rakes at 6d each		44
2 four tine forks at 3/each	50	
1 Stubbing hoe		25
1 Sledge hammer		50
4 Axes at 4/each	2	
1 Stone Drill	1	
1 Bushhook		50
2 pair Horse Hobbles at 2/each		50
12 Bags at 1/each	1	50
1 Lot of Broom Corn	1	
1 Garden Seed Chest	1	
1 Copper kettle	2	
Agreement under Seal to convey Land to Thomas J. Vinton for the sum of $828.45 on condition Dated 2nd June 1830.	934	76
Agreement under Seal to Convey Land to Levi Ellis for the Sum of $731. on condition Dated 5th June 1830.	825	05
Agreement under seal to convey land to Hazard Browning for the sum of $1360. on Condition Dated 24th June 1828 Endorsed thereon Recd 4th June 1828 fifty Dollars Recd 27th May 1829 one hundred and forty seven dollars Recd 5th June 1829 Thirty Six dollars Recd 16th November 1830 one hundred and forty one dollars	1317	28
On agreement under Seal to convey		

Land to Elias Whitmore for the sum of $300 on the Condition. Dated 4th June 1829	358	72
On agreement under Seal to Convey Land to Charles Keyes for the sum of four hundred dollars, on condition dated 6th June 1826 Endorsed thereon Recd 14th June 1827–$27	535	46
On an agreement under Seal to Convey Land to William Jenkins for the sum of Four hundred Dollars on Condition. Dated 31 May 1830.	470	
On an Agreement under Seal to Convey Land to John Terpenny for the sum of Seven hundred and forty one Dollars on Condition Dated 4th June 1829 Endorsed thereon Recd June 2nd 1830 $37 Recd 14th October 1831 $654	74	71
On an agreement under seal to Convey Land to Enos Smith for the sum of three hundred and twenty dollars on condition Dated 31 May 1830 Endorsed thereon Recd 3rd October 1831–$22.40	338	66
(Amount Carried over)		
On an agreement under seal to Convey land to Abraham Reynolds for the sum of Two hundred and seventy-five dollars. On condition. Dated 14th June 1827.	389	84
On an agreement under Seal to convey land to William Heath for the sum of three hundred and thirty two dollars, on condition, dated 31st day of May 1830.	374	60
On an agreement under Seal to convey Land to Orry Phelps dated 31st day of		

May 1830 for three hundred and twenty dollars on condition.	360	95
On an agreement under seal to convey land to Laurin J. Austin dated 1st June 1830 for the sum of Three Hundred and fifty dollars on condition.	394	91
On an agreement under seal to convey land to Martin Barber dated June 1st 1831 for the sum of one hundred dollars on Condition Endorsed thereon recd present pay $25.	78	36
On an agreement under seal to Convey land to Enock G. Kenyon and Satrip Kenyon Dated 3rd day of June 1828 for one hundred and fifty dollars on Condition. Endorsed thereon Recd 31st May 1830–$40.	147	71
On an agreement under seal to convey land to Royal Horton Dated 22nd day of June 1818 for six dollars per acre for about thirty seven acres. Endorsed thereon, I have agreed the 21st day of June 1824 that ten acres be taken off this and added to Jedediah Sewards as to leave about twenty seven acres to this. Solomon Polly has recd of Horton and paid him for betterments and will pay all the Interest due the first week in may 1826 and as much of the principal as he can. Recd 12th June 1827 of Solomon Polly one hundred dollars and I promise that if the interest is paid yearly he shall have two years to pay the remainder.	217	22
On an agreement under Seal to Convey land to John Bellows Dated 4th Day of June 1829 for four Hundred and Six dollars on condition.	486	12
On an agreement under seal to Convey		

Land to Moses Bailey Dated 4th June 1829 for the sum of Three hundred and sixty-three dollars on condition. 434 62

On an agreement under Seal to convey land to Edward Giles Clark dated 1st June 1829 for two hundred and fifty six dollars, on condition. 306 77

On an agreement under Seal to convey land to James Marshal Dated 30th May 1823 for Five Hundred dollars on Condition.
Endorsed thereon
Recd 30th May 1823 fifty dollars present pay
Recd 14th May 1825 of James Marshal forty five dollars and gaine or lose Recpt.
Recd 3rd June 1828 of James Marshal twenty eight dollars. 615 67

On an agreement under seal to Convey land to Bernard Barrel and Elizabeth Barrel dated 1st of June 1829 for Three hundred dollars, on condition.
Endorsed thereon
Recd 1st June 1829 fifty dollars of Elizabeth Barrel
Recd the 26th day of June 1831 of Elisha Jenning by the hands of Horatio N. Wood ninety eight dollars for Interest and part principal of within agreement 198 28

On an agreement under seal to convey land to Shepherd W. Ruggles dated 24th May 1828 for three hundred and fourteen dollars, on condition.
Endorsed thereon
Recd the 2nd day of June 1830 of Elijah Clark forty four dollars for Interest and prolong this 1832 358 72

On an agreement of lease under seal dated 1st day of June 1830 to Matthew

Sly for one year for the sum of thirty dollars on condition.	15	
On an agreement under Seal to convey land to James Healy Junior dated 13th day of June 1827 for the sum of one Hundred and twenty five dollars on condition. Endorsed thereon Recd 1st June 1829 of James Healy Seventeen dollars and fifty cents for two years interest. Recd 3rd of June 1830 of J. Healy eight dollars 75 cents.	140	76
On an agreement under seal to convey land to Asa Horton dated 2nd June 1828 for the sum of Two Thousand dollars. On condition.	2536	66
On an agreement under Seal to convey Land to William Rowel dated 2nd day of June 1829 for two hundred and ninety seven dollars 50/100 on Condition. Endorsed thereon Recd 2nd June 1830 of William Rowels son Twelve Dollars on account.	344	50
On an agreement under Seal to convey land to David Porter. Dated 4th June 1829 for Five Hundred and thirty seven dollars, on Condition.	643	90
On an agreement under seal to convey land to Menossah Calkins dated 4th June 1828 for five hundred and seventy-six dollars on condition. Endorsed thereon Recd 4th June 1828 of Menossah Calkins twenty four dollars. Recd 2nd June 1829 of Menossah Calkins eight dollars	690	78
On an agreement under seal to convey land to Elijah Hill dated 17th May 1825 for Six Hundred dollars on condition–		

Endorsed thereon Recd 17th May 1825 one hundred dollars Recd 27th May 1826 one hundred dollars. 614 40

On an agreement under seal to convey land to William Kelly dated 19th of June 1824 for Four Hundred and Eighty dollars on condition.
Endorsed thereon
Recd 19 June 1824 twenty dollars
Recd 6th April 1825 forty six dollars 50/100
Recd 6th Sept 1825 forty six dollars 50/100
Recd 15th June 1827 one Hundred and five dollars
Recd 3rd June 1829 one hundred and sixty five dollars also ten dollars
Recd 1st June 1830 forty dollars 266 34

On an agreement under seal to convey land to William Henderson dated 18th day of June 1827 for Five Hundred dollars on condition. 661 70

On an agreement under seal to convey land to Elisha Calkins dated 31st day of May 1830 for three hundred and five dollars, on condition. 344 23

On an agreement under seal to convey land to Abraham Bell, dated 5th day of May 1820 for Four Hundred Dollars, on the fulfillment of the agreement and contracts therein mentioned by said Abraham Bell–Endorsed thereon the 23rd March 1828. Ab^{m} Bell paid my Brother Pierre on account of this agreement Two Hundred Dollars.
The 16th of May 1829 Ab^{m} Bell sent me one hundred Dols. 423 88

On an agreement under seal to Lease and convey Land to John A. Williams for and during his natural Life dated 13th day of October 1828, for the yearly rent of ten dollars, said Land to be conveyed to said Williams by Deed for the sum of five hundred dollars and interest at four per cent from the date hereof on the Conditions therein contained. 30

On an agreement under seal to Lease Land to Eliphalet Glazier dated 20th day of June 1823 during his natural life and the life of Rachel his wife for the sum of Fifty Dollars paid in hand and the yearly rent of one dollar if Demanded. Endorsed thereon recd 20th June 1823 of Eliphalet Glazier the fifty dollars mentioned to be paid in hand. 8

On a Bond and Mortgage against Henry Bart Dated 23rd day of June 1817 for the sum of Five Hundred and Sixty Dollars.
Endorsed thereon
Recd in November 1818 Eighty five dollars
Recd 6th of May 1825 One hundred and thirty dollars 50/100 of Henry Bart
Recd 6 day of May 1825 of Phineas Mackeys one hundred dollars. Also received of said Mackeys one hundred and fourteen dollars by the hands of Augustus Norton paid for the eight acres Mackeys sold him being part of the land he bought of Henry Bart. On settling the above in company of Henry Bart and Phineas Mackeys there remains due on the 6th day of May 1825 Four Hundred and Twenty dollars. Received the 16th day of June 1827 of Hazard Browning one hundred dollars.

Recd 4th June 1828 of Hazard Browning twenty eight dollars on account of this Bond.
Recd 5th June 1829 Eighteen Dollars
Received June 2nd 1830 of Hazard Browning Twenty nine Dollars. 392 76

On a Bond and Mortgage against John McMillen Dated the 13th day of May 1826 for the sum of one thousand dollars.
Endorsed thereon
Recd 16th of June 1827 of John McMillen One Hundred and Seventy dollars.
Recd 13th May 1828 of John McMillen Three Hundred and Sixty three dollars.
Recd the 2nd of June 1829 of Ebenezer Bennit forty two dollars for interest.
Received the 21 of July 1830 of Ebenezer Bennet forty two dollars for interest due on the first day of May Last and I now receive of the said E. Bennet Two Hundred dollars of the Principal. 459 52

On a Bond and Mortgage against Joshua Jayne dated 6th day of July 1815 for three hundred dollars.
Endorsed thereon
Recd the 15th August 1816 twenty one dollars
Recd the 7th June 1817 twenty two dollars
Recd 19th June 1819 twenty eight dollars
Recd 22 June 1824 one hundred and eighteen dollars
Recd 11th May 1825 Twenty dollars
Recd 30th May 1826 twenty two dollars
Recd 18th June 1827 twenty one dollars

Recd 28th May 1828 twenty one dollars Recd same day one hundred and fifty dollars Recd the 31st May 1830 Twenty one dollars	163	55
On a Bond and Mortgage against Annanias Westcot and Samuel Westcot dated the 6th July 1819. Given to Jacob Ryder and assigned by him to Philip Van Cortlandt the 7th July 1819 For Three Hundred and eighty dollars and fifty cents. Endorsed thereon Recd 7th June 1819 Sixty eight dollars Recd 7th June 1822 thirty five dollars Recd 22 June 1824 of Samuel Wescott Twenty dollars Recd 11 May 1825 of Samuel Wescott one hundred dollars and sixty four dollars in Clearing Recd the 18th June 1827 of Samuel Wescott forty dollars on account of this bond Recd the 4th June 1829 of Samuel Wescott forty six dollars 57/100 in full for interest and part principal and there is now due $200. of the principal.	239	54
On a bond against Nicolas Vader and James Johnson dated 3rd day of June 1828 for two hundred and nineteen dollars Endorsed thereon Received the 3rd day of June 1829 twenty dollars on account of written Bond	260	12
On a promise in writing against Isaac Teller dated October 7th 1828 for one hundred dollars due 1st May 1830.	124	39
On a Promise under seal against P. Van		

Cortlandt dated the 17th day of September 1827 for two hundred Dollars payable the 1st May next and a promise therein contained to deliver a certain writing on account of Lot Number one hundred and seventy seven.	263	58
On a receipt against Charles A. Baker for a Note of Hand executed by Elijah Philips for twenty dollars pay first May 1827 to Collect or return.	26	87
Receipts of Henry Remsen Treasurer of the Highland Turnpike Company.		
Recd from Philip VanCortlandt Esq[r] Two hundred and fifty dollars for first installment on Fifty Shares in Highland Turnpike Company Dated 6th May 1807.		
Recd from Philip VanCortlandt Esq[r] Two hundred and fifty dollars being the second installment on fifty shares in the Highland Turnpike Company dated 6th May 1807.		
Recd from Philip Van Cortlandt Esq[r] Two hundred and fifty dollars being the Third installment on fifty shares in the Highland Turnpike Company dated May 6th 1807.		
Recd from Philip Van Cortlandt Esq[r] Two Hundred and fifty dollars being the fourth Installment of fifty shares in the Highland Turnpike Company Dated 10th July 1807.		
Recd from Philip Van Cortlandt Esq[r] two hundred and fifty dollars being the Fifth Installment on fifty shares in Highland Turnpike Company dated July 10th 1807.		
No value at present.		
Certificate of Ozias Wilcox Pres't. and the		

Secretary of the Manchester Manufacturing Company dated November 28th 1827. States Philip VanCortlandt is entitled to Two & Twenty one 36/100–shares in the Capital stock of that Company.	221	36
Certificate of Henry Guest President and P. Hochstrapser Treasurer of the Eastern Turnpike Road Company dated August 30th 1816. States that Philip VanCortlandt is entitled to Fifteen Shares in Said Company.		
BAD: On Book against Solomon Teller dated May 1st 1820 for $26.62		
On Book against Nathaniel Baremore dated 14th May 1811 for $20.62		
On Book against Gilbert Anderson dated 1st May 1819 for $67.67		
On Book against Isaac Vredenburgh dated 1st May 1814 for $29.50		
On Book against William Williams dated 1st December 1816 for $99.50		
On Book against James Manger dated Nov. 13th 1815 for $32.14		
On Book against J.F. Ryder Dated Sept. 17th 1817 for $3.50		
On Book against Joseph Babe dated Sept. 1818 for $33.91		
On Book against Erastus Marshal dated Decem. 19th 1819 for $31.94		
On Book against Pierre Van Cortlandt dated 30th Sept. 1829 for $9.31 and 7 Bushls seed wheat $10.50	19	81
On Book against the Estate of Pierre Van Cortlandt deceased dated Decem. 8th 1830 for $392.05	392	05
On Book against Pierre VanWyck dated		

Decem. 14th 1814 for $1300–This is the account mentioned in Testators will.

Account on Book against Garret Williams dated April 2nd 1831 for $31.39

On Book against Amos Gardiner dated April 1st 1824 for $5.

On a promissory Note of Hand dated May 1st 1813 Drawn by John F. Hallinan payable to Elihu Gardner or order on demand for the Sum of eleven hundred dollars and endorsed by said Elihu Gardner. Endorsed there on 1814 May 2nd–received the Interest on the within not for one year $77.

–Elihu Gardner

BAD

On Book against William Tompkins dated May 22nd 1818 for $65.83.

On Book against Nathan Anderson dated March 6th 1821 for $25.

On Book against Henry Tompkins dated Augst 8th 1823 for $118.36.

On Book against Theodorus C. VanWyck dated January 18th 1820 for £2.11.6 Also on book against him dated July 3rd 1810 for $200. Also on Book against him dated Decem. 21st 1821 for $.86.

On Book against Abraham Miller (at factory) dated Jany 5th 1821 for $14.99

On Book against Junior Vredenburgh dated Jany 22nd 1824 for $7.02

On Book against William Purdy dated Decem. 23rd 1830 for .14 14

BAD

On Book against Nehemiah Lownsberry dated March 29th 1825 for $20.

On book against Jacob Valentine Dated April 1st 1825 for $32.46.

On Book against Ruben Tucker Dated April 1st 1830 for $14.90.	14	90
On Book against against Elisha Merrit and Robert Fisher Dated March 31st 1825 for $15.75		
On Book against James Swiffin Dated April 5th 1828 for $12.59.		
On Book against Abraham Maynard Dated September 14th 1830 for $10.	10	
On Book against John Outhouse Dated 5th April 1828 for $63.		
On Book against John Peterson Dated Nov. 5th 1831 for $55.26.	55	26
On Book against Jacob Wandell Dated March 4th 1829 for $11.25	11	25
On Book against James Delaney dated May 18th 1831 for $22.	22	
On Book against David Haight Dated April 1st 1831 for $2.43. Desperate.		
On Book against Mrs. Cornelia Beekman Executor of Gerard G. Beekman, deceased. Amount not ascertained.		
On Book against Philip G. Van Wyck Dated Feby 29th 1830 for $155.16	155	16
On Book against John B. Anderson Dated 5th Novb. 1831 for $4.45.	4	45
On Book against Lyman Cook Dated 5th Novmr. 1831 for $74.29	74	29
On Book against William Dobbs Dated 5th Novemr 1831 for $14.53	14	53
On Book against Peter Luke dated 5th Novembr 1831 for $17.83	17	83
On Book against John Lawrence dated 5th November 1831 for $22.38	22	38
On Book against John Mosher dated November 1831 for $9.24	9	24

On Book against Lewis Munro dated Nov. 5th 1831 for $8.42	8	42
On Book against James McCord dated Nov. 5th 1831 for $2.97	2	97
On Book against Jessee Purdy dated Nov. 5th 1831 for $2.08	2	08
On Book against Simmons Purdy dated Nov. 5th 1831 for $32.69	32	69
On Book against Simmons Purdy dated Nov. 5th 1831 for $30.11	30	11
On Book against Abraham Williams Dated Nov. 5th 1831 for $1.53	1	53
On Book against Samuel Teller dated Nov. 5th 1831 for $41.60	41	60
On Book against William Williams (Carpenter) dated October 5th 1831 for $75.32	75	32
Certificates for twenty four shares in the stock of the Seneca Road company dated June 2nd 1810.		
Certificate for fourteen shares in the Stock of Seneca Road Company dated June 25th 1810.		
Certificates for twenty six dolls stock and one share in Seneca Road Company dated November 26th 1812.		
Certificate for forty dollars & Ten shares in Seneca Road Company dated 18th June 1814.		
Certificate for Ten Shares in Seneca Road Company dated August 26th 1816.		
Certificate for Eighty Shares in Seneca road company dated October 29th 1829. Valued at	3475	00
On a note of Hand against Jacob Ryder Dated 18th May 1819 for Thirty Dollars. (Doubtful)		
On an agreement under seal to Convey		

Land to Ralph Barber dated 1st June 1831 for Two Hundred dollars on Condition. Endorsed thereon the present pay of fifty dollars is received to my Credit in the Onondaga Bank	158	75
On an agreement under Seal to convey land to George H. Cutler dated June 1st 1831 for the sum of one hundred and fifty dollars. Endorsed thereon. The Present pay of fifty dollars is Received to my Credit in the Onondaga Bank.	105	83
On an agreement under Seal to Convey Land to Joseph Snethen Dated June 19th 1827 for one thousand and thirty four Dollars on condition. Endorsed thereon Received the 19th day of June 1827 of Joseph Snethen by the hands of Artemus Curtis Five Hundred Dollars.	712	93
On an agreement of Lease for the term of one year from the Date against Jeremiah Pugsley Dated 1st day of April 1830 for the sum of one hundred dollars. On the Back of said lease is an obligation under Seal signed by Gabriel Purdy Dated 1st April 1830 as security for the payment of such sum or sums of money as will be sufficient to satisfy the same.	40	
On an agreement of Lease for the term of five years from the date against Henry Haley for forty five dollars yearly dated 1st day of April 1827. Endorsed thereon Received 21st April 1828 of Henry Haley forty five dollars. Recd 10th Feby 1829 of D° by Ambrose Cott forty five dollars. Recd 27th Feby 1830 of D° by John Cock		

Forty five dollars. Recd 22nd March 1831 by John Cock forty five dollars	15	62
On an agreement of Lease under Seal against David Farington for the term of five years from the date for the sum of thirty five dollars a year dated 1st April 1827. Endorsed thereon Recd one years rent due 1st Apl. 1828 \$35. Recd for one years D° D° 1st Apr. 1829 \$35. Recd for one years D° 1 Apl. 1830 \$35 Recd of James McCord D° 1 Apl. 1831 \$35.	20	86
On an agreement of Lease under Seal against Nehemiah Sherwood for the term of one year from 1st April 1831 for the sum of sixty five dollars, dated 14th March 1831.	38	63
On an agreement of Lease under seal against David Farrington and Ambrose Cocks for the term of seven years from the 1st day of March 1831 dated the 9th April 1830 for the sum of one hundred and eighty dollars yearly and every year during the term of said lease.	32	50
On an agreement under seal of Lease against Henry Hutchins dated 23rd day of February 1830. For the sum of fifty dollars yearly–for the term of Seven years from the 1st of April 1830.	29	85
On an agreement of Lease for one year under Seal against Robert Fisher and John Leacock from the 1st day of April 1825 for the sum of one hundred dollars and to make 25 Rods of stave fence.	19	38
On a sealed note against Nehemiah Harris for the sum of ten dollars Dated		

26th Feby 1825.	14	96
On a sealed note against Garret Williams for the sum of thirty one dollars and seventy five cents dated 20th day of Feby 1811. (Doubtful) Endorsed thereon Recd the 6th day of January 1818 of Garret Williams fifteen dollars and fifty four cents for seven years interest.	62	97
On a sealed note against John Clark dated 27th Jany 1818 for forty seven dollars. Endorsed thereon recd 26th March 1831 for Work on my upper Dock 23 days for which I paid him except eight dollars and sixty two cents. (Doubtful)	85	02
On a sealed note against Stephen Mangham dated 28th March 1823 for seventeen dollars and ninety cents $17.90 Desperate.		
On a sealed note against Joshua Williams for Nineteen dollars fifty three cents Dated 22nd day of April 1822. Doubtful	33	04
On a sealed note against Simeon Vredenburgh dated 21st April 1823 for $30–Desperate.		
On a note of hand against Elias Smith in upper Cannada dated July 1807 for one hundred and twenty five dollars payable 1 June 1810. Desperate.		
On a sealed note against John Holmes Junior dated 22nd January 1816 for twenty dollars payable 1st March next. Endorsed thereon Recd 26th July 1822 of Mr Holmes Junior twenty dollars. Doubtful.	16	42

On an assignment of a Judgement by Gerard G. Beekman under seal to Philip Van Cortlandt against Jacob Acker dated 2nd day of August 1814 for two hundred and two dollars forty five cents.		
On an account against Orion Broad dated 4th August 1830 for $20. Paid thereon $16.		
On a sealed note against Matthias Ryder dated 7th Feby 1811 for sixty four dollars. Endorsed thereon Recd 16th Feby 1819 sixty three dollars 34/100 Recd Nov 16 1826 five dollars Recd Jany 5th 1828 Ten dollars	55	02
On a Sealed note against Amos Gardiner dated 26th Feby 1822 for fifty five dollars–Desperate		
On a Sealed Note against Jesse Barton dated March 28th 1825 for thirteen dollars.	19	38
On a sealed note against Samuel Pugsley dated 13 June 1791 for £7.16		
Note against David Fairbanks dated 29th August 1814 for seventy dollars. Endorsed on it Recd 4th Jany 1816 $63.80		
Note against James Abeel dated 8th August 1775 for £35.10		
Note against John C. Schindle dated 5 March 1804 for ten dollars.		
Sealed note against Gilbert Hoyt dated 1st May 1791 for £6.15 Endorsed thereon Recd April 1792 on this note £3.		
Sealed note against Nathaniel Hill dated 30th April 1805 for $17.50.		

Sealed note against Nehemiah Tompkins Junior and Nehemiah Tompkins dated 24th October 1792 for £14.10
Endorsed thereon Recd. October 16th 1800 6.5.0
Recd. 4.0.0
Sealed Note against Thomas Cornel dated 21 Novm. 1806 for $90.
Endorsed thereon Recd June 1st 1807 forty dollars.

Sealed Note against David Chapman dated 31 Decem. 1799 for $10.75

Note against Moses Ward dated 4th June 1793 for £3.8.11

Bond against Henry Mathews dated 12th August 1783 for £63.4

A Bond and Power to Confess Judgement against James Tuttle dated 2nd April 1785 for £20.

Bond against Oliver Bloodgood dated 13th August 1791 for £88.
Endorsed on it Recd. 9 May 1792 £20
Recd 22 Augt 1792 50.
Recd [?] 1.5.8
Recd 13 Augt 1796 8.0.0
On book against Mrs. Chard March 13th 1822 for $123.75

On Book against Robert Fisher dated April 19th 1825 for $24.

On Book against Highland Turnpike Company dated May 1815 for $368.90

On Book against Nehemiah Purdy dated May 1st 1808 for $99.99

On Book against Jacob Acker dated July 23rd 1814 for $407.57

On Book against David Dingee dated July 26th 1810 for $7.63

On Book against Gamaliel Fairbanks

dated Novm 22nd 1820 for $317.50
On Book against James Haines dated June 1814 for $27.12
On Book against Annanias Westcott dated Dec. 31st 1813 for $66.56
On Book against William Baker Jun. dated Sept. 13th 1824 for $68.86
On Book against John Hamilton dated Feby 5th 1816 for $31.71
On book against Samuel Chard dated March 16th 1816 for $1.06
On Book against Jonathan Knapp not dated for $4.
On Book against John Calligahn dated Jany 7th 1812 for $27.
On Book against James Williams dated Jany 12th 1821 for $3.20
On Book against David Peterson dated Jany. 24th 1823 for $4.22
On Book against John McCoy dated Jany 15th 1825 for $63.42
On a Bond and Mortgage against Henry Avery dated the 1st May 1815 for one thousand seven hundred and eighty four dollars. Endorsed thereon
Recd 11 day May 1816 $450.
Recd. 9th May 1817 $160.25
Recd. 25th April 1818 $56.
Recd. 5th May 1818 $80
Recd. 12 May 1821 $48
Recd. 25 Sepr 1822 $220
Recd. 8th October 1822 $55
Recd. 23rd March $428
Recd. 28th March 1823 $60
Recd 26th Feby 1825 $62
Recd 21 Sepr 1827 $40
Recd 26 Decr 1827 $135
Recd 12 Novem 1829 $140

Recd 30th Novmr 1830 $15 Recd 16th June 1831 $21	1338	47
On a Bond and Mortgage against John Holmes Dated 9th March 1831 for one Thousand Dollars. Endorsed thereon Recd 29th March 1831 of John Holmes two hundred dollars on account of this Bond.	860	61
On a Bond and Mortgage against Henry Avery Junior, dated 23rd of March 1823 for four hundred and twenty dollars. Endorsed thereon Recd 26th Feby 1825 $10 Recd 4 Novem 1826 $20 Recd March 27th 1827 $35 Recd 11 Decem 1827 $55. Recd 27th Augt $6 Recd 30 Novm 1829 $50 Recd 8th Jany 1831 $35 Recd 28th Feby 1831 $45	427	57
On a Bond and Mortgage against Robert McCord dated 27 Feby 1817 for Three Hundred and fifty three Dollars and sixty cents Endorsed thereon Recd 10th May 1820 $38.87 Recd 17th Novmr 1825 $90.92	597	46
Note of Hand against Henry Tompkins Dated 5th January 1824 for two hundred dollars.		
Note of Hand against Daniel Mosher dated 13th August 1807. for fifty dollars. Endorsed, Recd. 12 Decm 1812 $10.		
On Sealed Note against John Chatterton dated 3rd October 1799. for ninety two dollars and seventy five cents. Endorsed recd 9th July 1802–$15.		
On a sealed note against Elnathan Hitch		

dated 7th May 1800 for $7.50		
On a sealed note against Michael Eldridge dated 30th July 1801 for twenty dollars.		
On a sealed note against Abraham Depew dated March 10th 1789 for £ 10.		
On a sealed note against Andrew McCastin dated 11th May 1811, for seventeen dollars & ninety cents.		
On a note of hand against Noah H. Sutton dated 30th April 1805 for twenty two dollars and twelve cents.		
On Book against William VanWart dated Nov. 5th 1831 for $15.07	15	07
On Book against Levi Buckbee dated Nov. 5th 1831 for $36.59	36	59
On Book against William Alert dated Nov. 5th 1831 for $1.58	1	58
On Book against Elijah Dunkan dated Nov. 5th 1831 for $2.58	2	58
On Book against Edward Pitgate dated August 30th 1831	50	
On Bond against Walter.D.Sicoll dated 19th September 1799 for $100. (BAD)		
On Bond against Samuel Clark Dated January 11th 1815 for $790. (BAD)		
On an account against Cornelius Hayes Novm. 1831 for $20.	20	
On account against Timothy Almsted dated June 2nd 1831 for $3	3	

ROBERT ACKER
SIMMONS PURDY } APPRAISERS [Total 37,145.85]

1. As previously noted, Philip Van Cortlandt's estate became an immediate cause for litigation with his death. His brother, Pierre, Jr., challenged in particular Philip's right to permit a

nephew, Philip G. Van Wyck, to reside and use the estate at Croton River until 1836, when Pierre III was to come of age.

What is of particular interest in this inventory, along with the possessions commonly found on a prosperous Westchester farm, is the list of books included in Philip's library. Whether this collection signified Philip's taste alone or that of his late sister, Catharine Van Wyck, cannot be ascertained. Philip's surviving correspondence does not seem to bear the marks of a widely read individual, yet the library exhibited a catholic taste, varying from legislative journals and political pamphlets to Fielding's *Tom Jones* and John Hoole's edition of Torquato Tasso's two-volume epic, *Jerusalem Delivered; an Heroic Poem.* Much of this library collection became part of the Parke-Bernet sale in 1941, when the bulk of the Van Cortlandt manuscripts were sold.

For some reason, the appraisers did not include the individual page totals or the net value of the estate. A calculation of the appraised values produces a grand total of $37,145.85. This sum did not include land evaluations of his personally controlled real estate holdings.

146

Pierre, Jr. to Ambrose Spencer. ADf (Copy)
SHR

[1832.]

Philip Van Cortlandt (one of his Britannic Majastys Council for the Province of New York) on the 1st of August 1746 made & published his last will and testament — By which among other things he devises to his son Pierre (as by reference to the extract herewith sent) South Lot Number One of the Manor of Cortlandt — He departed this life about the year 1748 leaving his sons Stephen and Pierre surviving him — Pierre went into the possession of the Lands so devised to him —

Pierre (The late Lieutenant Governor) on the 5h day of December 1805 made and published his last will and testament in due form of Law to pass Real Estate and on the 12th day of

March 1811 he duly made and published a Codicil to his said will by which he devises to his son Pierre, all the Land and waters mentioned in the said Codicil reference to the Codicil to the will, appears — to his Son Pierre in fee Simple —

Lt Govr Pierre Van Cortlandt departed this life may 1st. 1814 leaves his Sons Philip & Pierre and Three Daughters[.]At the time of his Death his Son Philip was in possession of that part of the farm in the said Codicil mentioned and devised to his Son Pierre and continued so up to the time of his Death claiming Title thereto — and by his last will and testament devised the same to his Brother Pierre withholding from him the possession thereof untill 1836 —
1st — What Estate did L^{t}. Govr. Pierre Van Cortlandt take in the said Farm at Croton River under the will of his Father Philip Van Cortlandt after the passing the Acts abolishing Entails? Did not his Estate become a fee Simple absolute in the said premisses?
2^{d} — Does not Genl Pierre Van Cortlandt under the Codicil to his Father's will take the said Farm in fee Simple?

Genl Philip Van Cortlandt the Son of Lt Governor Pierre Van Cortlandt died the 29th Day of October 1831 — leaving no legal Issue —

If the succession by Entail under the will of Philip Van Cortlandt (the Elder) was destroyed by the Acts abolishing Entails — What Estate had the late Genl Philip Van Cortlandt in the farm at Croton River under the will of his Grand Father the Hon^{bl}. Philip Van Cortlandt or Father the late L^{t}. Govr Pierre Van Cortlandt —

If it is acceded that the Acts for abolishing Entails do not give the late Lt Govr Pierre Van Cortlandt the farm at Croton River in fee Simple — Does the Codicil to Genl Philip Van Cortlands will directing that his Nephew Philip "G Van Wyck and family keep the possession and occupation of my house and farm whereon I now reside and receive the profits thereof until the year 1836" — give Ph. G Van Wyck such right that he can use the said farm to the injury thereof by suffering it to be tilled on shares by every[one] who wishes to do it?

Is not Ph. G Van Wyck obliged to keep up the Dikes around the meadows which are a part of the said farm wherever the water makes a breach through there to the great injury and ruin of the meadows, for by suffering the River Water to remain on them destroys the fresh grass and brings them back to a state of nature & worse —

How can Gen[l] Pierre Van Cortlandt compel Philip G Van Wyck to repair the Dikes around the meadows which are already much injured & if suffered to remain in the State, from the waters lying on them, the meadows will be entirely ruined as it respects the fresh grass before the year 1836 — or whether Gen Pierre Van Cortlandt can prevint Ph G. Van Wyck allowing People to till the said farm on shares to the injury thereof under that Clause of the Codicil to the will of Gen[l] Philip Van Cortlandt directing his Nephew Ph G Van Wyck and family to have the possession and occupation thereof and receiving the profits until the year 1836 — If Gen[l] Pierre Van Cortlandt has the right of preventing the farm to be so injured & misused — What is his remedy against Ph. G. Van Wyck?

147

Ambrose Spencer's Legal Opinion. ADS (Copy)[1]
NYSHA

April 5, 1832.

Copy of Judge Spencer's Opinion

I have been asked my opinion on the Will of Philip Van Cortlandt the Elder — Leu[t] Governor Van Cortlandt & Gen[l]. Philip Van Cortlandt & without recapitul[at]ing the terms of their Wills I proceed to answer the questions propounded by Genl. Pierre Van Cortlandt —

What Estate did Lieut Governor Van Cortlandt take in the farm at Croton River under the will of his father; & as intimately connected with this question, What estate did Genl Philip Van Cortlandt take under that will, since the passage of the Statutes abolishing Entails?

These questions are by no means to be answered with entire and perfect confidence & the more they are examined the deeper will be the conviction that it is impossible to reconcile the conflicting decisions which have taken place in Westminster hall for the past two or three centuries upon the Questions propounded — After bestowing the best considiration in my power now & on former occasions, my conclusion is that the weight of Authority is, that Lieut. Governor Van Cortlandt took under the will of his Father an Estate for life Only in all the Real estate devised to him and that Genl. Philip Van Cortlandt as his eldist Son took an estate tail & consequently under the provisions of the Statutes abolishing entails — he became seised of the premises devised to his father for life in fee simple absolute[.]The premisses were devised to Lieut Govr Van Cortlandt for life with remainder to the first Son of the Body of his said Son Peirre whether then born or unborn & to the heirs male of the Body of such first Son lawfully issuing &c. &c. I am aware that the mere fact that the demise to Leut Govr Van Cortlandt for life, does not prevent his taking in tail, but there are other expressions in the will which in my Opinion do determine that point, the devise over after the termination of the life estate devised to Leut Govr Van Cortlandt to his first Son with a limitation to the Heirs male of his Body, operates as a designation of the person who was to take the Estate after the termination of the life Estate previously devised, so that the first Son of Leut Govr Van Cortlandt would take as a purchaser under the Will of his Grand Father, but in consequence of the limitation being to his Heirs male, He would take as Tenant in tail male

If Lieut. Governor Van Cortlandt took only an Estate

for life as I think he did, and was not seised in tail, when he made his will & Codicil, he had no capacity to devise any part of the Real Estate which he took under the will of his Father & consequently Genl. Pierre Van Cortlandt took nothing from him

I have perused & considered M[r] Van Vechtens opinion[2] on the effect of the revocation by the codicil of Genl Philip Van Cortlandt of the devises made by his will to his Nephew Pierre C Van Wyck & his Brother and Sisters & concur in that opinion, as regards the devise to his Nephew Pierre by his death in the lifetime of the Testator, the devise to him became lapsed. The devise of the residue of Genl Philip Van Cortlands real & personal Estate to his Nephew Philip G Van Wyck must be considered to such and real & personal Estate as he had not specifically disposed of by his will to other persons. The lapsing or revocation of any of those specific devises could not enlarge the devise of the residue, for the spesific devises did not in the intention of the testator constitute any part of that residue when the will was made and executed. When therefore the Testator revoked the devise to his Brother & Sisters he either inadvertently omitted to dispose of it or else intended as to that & also the property devised to his nephew Pierre to die intestate —

I am asked my Opinion whether the direction in the Codicil to Gen[l] Philip Van Cortlandts will "That my Nephew Philip G Van Wyck & his family keep possession & occupation of my house & farm whereon I now reside & receive the profits thereof until the year 1836 that being the year my brothers Son Pierre becomes of age" will give to P. G. Van Wyck a right to the possession of dwelling Houses & tenements owned by the Testator & included in the devise to his Brother & which were rented to other Persons by the Testator & were not in his actual possession & whether the rent of such tenements do not belong to Gen[l] Pierre Van Cortlandt & also whether the fishing place on the beach is included within the direction that Philip G. Van Wyck & his family shall keep possession &c. —

I am of opinion that this direction in the codicil is to be confined to the House & farm in the personal residence & occupation of the testator & that it does not extend to other Houses & tenements in the occupation & possession of the testators tenants, & that consequently the rents of such Houses & tenements belong to the devisee Genl Van Cortlandt I am also of Opinion that Mr Van Wyck under this direction in the Codicil has no right to the fishing place on the beach unless it forms part of the farm in the personal tenure of the testator

Signed A Spencer

Albany Ap^{r} 5. 1832.

[Marginal Note] see 1st Rev. Lawes 725. section 2d not as governing the Case, but as illustrative of the opinion of the Legislature —

---

1. This copy of Judge Ambrose Spencer's legal opinion is in the handwriting of Pierre, Jr.

2. Abraham Van Vechten's legal opinion regarding the codicil to Philip's will was written on February 16, 1832 (No. 144).

148

Pierre, Jr. to Erastus Corning.[1] ALS
HSP

Peekskill July 12–1833.

Dear Sir

Your joint Letter with Mr King I received on Tuesday morning last the Day after the Election for Cashier of the Westchester County Bank

It was the original wish of a great many of the Directors to have Mr Peck the Cashier, I have never seen Mr Peck but was informed that he would have been pleased to serve but that he afterward withdrew from being considered a Candidate for Reasons unknown to me; When the Directors met last Monday Mr Anderson who was the Director selected from the south part of the County & had not met with us before was highly in favor of Mr Seymour he knew him personally and spoke of him in high terms, other Gentlemen who also knew him spoke of him in the same manner — Mr Van Ingan had very flattering recommendations & was known personally to several of the Directors who were pleased with him; But one great object was to have an efficient Cashier and to get him elected as unanimously & harmoniously as we could. few of us knew Mr Perkins, for my part I do not recollect of seeing him but once & then in the Exchange bank it was said that he was at this place when we received Subscriptions for the Stock of the Bank, but being much engaged I had forgot it — Mr Seymour was elected very unanimously & Mr Perkins could not have been elected with such unanimity — I want the Bank to prosper & be conducted on honorable Terms, for unless that is the case we must fail in our prospects. As far as my abilities fidelity & Industry are concerned, nothing shall be wanting — I will at all times take it kind if you will write to me & suggest such Operations as you may think proper to be done to promote the Establishment.

I am with the greatest Respect
Your Ob^{t} Servt
Pierre Van Cortlandt

Erastus Corning Esqr

---

1. Erastus Corning (1794–1872) was a wealthy Albany merchant who owned one of the largest ironworks in New York. He was the master spirit behind the consolidation of small railroad lines into the New York Central Railroad, and served as president of that corporation for twelve years. Active in politics, he was a mayor of Albany, a senator in the New York legislature from 1842 until 1845, and was elected as a Democratic representative to Congress for two terms (1857–1859 and 1861–1863). *DAB*, IV, 446–447.

2. The Westchester County Bank was incorporated in May, 1833, and began its operations in September of the same year. The first president was Pierre Van Cortlandt, who continued to serve until his death. From Pierre's letter, it is learned that the election for cashier was held on July 8. The person chosen was Isaac Seymour, who succeeded Pierre as president in 1848. According to a contemporary chronicler, William J. Cumming, "This was probably the first bank instituted in Westchester County, and, during its earlier years, the greater part of the banking business of Westchester and Putnam Counties was transacted there. . . ." Scharf, II, 407.

149

Mary Van Cortlandt[1] to Pierre, Jr. ALS
SHR

F. Brewers Esqr Old Ghent Road
London
February 26th 1834.

My dear Cousin

I was glad again to receive a letter from you I began to fear you had quite forgotten me I assure you that all the relatives of my beloved husband are doubly dear to me now and nothing can exceed the kindness I have received from them all. I was obliged in consequence of indisposition to leave my once happy home the 2^{d} of December as it was considered right for me to come to Town for the advice of the first Surgeons here I have a large tumour (brought on by fatigue and anxiety) which has extended under my arm an operation was decided on and the day fixed and every thing prepared but upon inspection it was found that the inflamation was too great to admit of the operation and although I have had leaches and other things I fear that I shall never be in a state to bear it but I desire to be resigned to the Will of God in all things I am truly thankful that my beloved husband knew nothing of my illness you knew how he loved me and how deeply he would have grieved. I am much surprised to hear of your brothers having deprived you of what I considered you had an undoubted right to and I suppose had you chosen you could have disputed the Will. I daresay you have long since heard from Charlotte I do not think there is any chance of her going across the Atlantic she has such an aversion to the Sea. I have been looking over the Genealogy of the Cortlandt family I can only find Philip Van Cortlandt born the 9th of August 1683 married Catharine De Peyster but no date to that there is no Wil^{m} Rickets Van Cortlandt at all. The ages of my beloved husbands brothers & sisters are as follows[:] Mary Ricketts born the 21 June 1763 married John Anderson Esqr Maryland[.]Elizabeth born 19th of November 1764 married Wm Taylor Esqr in England[.] Catharine was a twin Sister[.]Philip and Stephen born 30 of July 1766 Stephen went to the West Indies and was never heard of supposed to have been carried off by fever[.]my beloved died Oct 1st 1833[.]Margaret hughes born Octr 29 1768 married Capt Onesiphonus Elliott Queens 57th Reg^{t} died Sep^{t} 9th 1828[.]Sarah Ogden born 13th of March 1771 died April 18[.]Gertrude born 4th of August 1772 married 15th of March 1789 Captain Buller[.]Sarah Ogden 2nd born 4 of August 1774[.]Richard Welling born 24 Sept 1775 died 16 March 78[.]Jacob Ogden born 13 of Decb 1777 killed in Portugal[.] Henry Clinton born 21st of January 1780[.]Jane born 22nd of April 1783 died 28 June 83[.]Charlotte born the same day

William born at Chester in England 12 of June 85 died 30th of Oct 85[.]Arthur Achmuty born at Madeira 9th of April 1787 died Novr 16, 29[.]Sophia Sawyer born at Halifax Jany 7 89 married Sir W Howe Mulcaster in 1817 I think but I am not quite sure. I dare say that you have heard of the sad Afflictions of the Freers at Quebec in the death of Mrs Wulff and her eldest and of dear little Gertrude Mrs Freers eldest child & of their great pecuniary losses by the failure of Augustus Freer which has involved his Father very deeply. I am glad to hear that your Neices are happily married give my kind regards to them I think your son will soon be looking out for a wife and if he takes her to your house you will not feel so dull[.]give my love to him and your Sisters I shall have much pleasure in hearing from you at all times direct to me here as I have no home at present[.]I have this moment heard from Torquay they are all well and desire their love to you when I write Accept my sincere love and Believe me your affect. Cousin Mary Van Cortlandt

[Addressed]
General Pierre Van Cortlandt
Peeks Kill
State of New York
1st Packet
Ship

---

1. This letter was written by Mary (Addison) Van Cortlandt, wife of the recently deceased Philip Van Cortlandt (1766–1833) of London. Her husband was one of seventeen children born to Philip (1739–1814) and Catharine (Ogden) Van Cortlandt. Mary's father-in-law was an eminent New Jersey Loyalist during the American Revolution. Clare Clutterbuck, "Philip Van Cortlandt: An American Loyalist" (Honors Thesis, Oxford University, 1978), pp. 47–59.

150

Daniel D. Barnard[1] to Pierre, Jr. ALS
SHR

Albany–Oct. 22.d '34 —

My dear General,

In answer to your letter (without date) recd. today, I can do little more than repeat the opinion I have before expressed to you.

Mr. Van Wyck was bound beyond all question to keep the Meadow Dykes, in the Croton Farm, in repair;

& if, in consequence of his neglect, injury has been done to the Meadow, he is liable for the waste. If the Dykes, being in ordinary repair, were demolished by a storm, he would not be liable for that injury; but if, in consequence of his neglect, to keep them in a state of ordinary repair, they were assailed by a storm & broken down, he is liable. He was bound to keep them in such good order, as they had been used to be kept in, & such as would resist not only the ordinary action of the water, but also such storms as from the very nature of their case and their position, they were liable to encounter –

Catharine is quite well again, &, with Cora, desires her love to yourself & Pierre —

Your sincere friend
D.D. Barnard

Gen[l]. Van Cortlandt

[Addressed]
Gen[l]. Pierre Van Cortlandt
Peekskill
Westchester Co.
(N. York)

---

1. Daniel D. Barnard (1797–1861) was a graduate of Williams College who then studied law. A native of Massachusetts, he moved to Rochester, New York, and opened a law office there in 1821. He served several terms in Congress, 1827 to 1845. He moved his law practice from Rochester to Albany in 1832. Barnard also became engaged in foreign affairs, receiving an appointment as minister to Prussia in 1851. He retired from that office and from his legal practice in 1853. *Biographical Directory American Congress,* p. 553.

151

Richard R. Voris[1] to Pierre, Jr. ALS
SHR

Sing Sing Nov 14. 1834.

Genl. P: Van Cortlandt

Dear Sir

For the last week & more, I have been almost laid up with the influenza, but have made out to get over to the Point, & have had an interview with Wm. Underhill. William seemed to be willing to state frankly his knowledge on the subject of inquiry; But, I must confess, I was rather disappointed in the relation he gave me, & more especially, his own views & opinions on the subject of the meadows & dykes:[2] He recollects calling on you in the winter of 1833, respecting the dykes, & informing you that they wanted repairing the next spring, and that you requested him to examine, & see to the repairing of them &c. — and he says, he tried to see Philip Van Wyck about the repairs, but he could not obtain an interview; nor did he have any communication with Van Wyck himself, on the Subject; But he says, that Jere: Lewis told him that Van Wyck was going to repair the Dykes, and upon that he wrote to you — and he thinks, he probably wrote you that Philip Van Wyck said he would repair them himself, without saying to you that he had this from Lewis. Then he goes on to say: that Philip Van Wyck did repair the dykes that Spring. but how thoroughly he does not know; but says, that Van Wyck had Lewis & other men then at work at the dykes, off & on, for several months, — & refers to Lewis, who he says, can tell more about the condition & repairs of the Dykes than any other person — But Underhill said that in the fall of that year (1833) after Philip had made the repairs, there came an unusually high tide, and rushed in upon the meadows & tore up the Dykes, & left them in a very ruinous condition & Since when, Van Wyck has done nothing to them — & he says it will cost many dear Dollars to repair — this tide he describes as very unusual one — Underhill seems to be impressed with the idea, himself, that the dykes cannot be kept up, of latter years, as formerly, he says, the Muskrats abound so much more, & so work in, & make holes continually, that it is almost impossible to guard ag^{t}. the injury they produce — I urged to him that your brother was able to keep up the dykes & protect the meadows, this he admits, with some qualification, viz. that in the latter part of his life, he says, the increased ravages of the rats, made head[way] so far ag^{t}. repairing, that the meadows in many places had considerably deteriorated.[2]

To my enquiries, distinctly made, whether Van Wyck had taken the same care — repaired the dykes to the same extent & efficiently, as your brother did in his life time — he can answer no further, he says, than that Van Wyck has worked more or less every year, till this, but how much he can't tell, & refers to Lewis — Underhill volunteerd the observation, that in his opinion Van Wyck had never received as much profit from the Meadows as he had been at expense of repairs — I have endeavored, as far as I can in this mode of Communication, to give you the substance of Underhill statement — I am afraid he w^{l} be but a poor stick of a witness, the man seems to be set against such kind of meadow say [save] his own, he can't keep up — the rats plague him and all such stuff — not that his opinions would coulor the question — But his unfavorable impression against the meadows, makes him view Philip Van Wyck's conduct in a more favorable light, I think, than he w^{d} otherwise — and induces him to attribute the disaster to the Dykes less, to Philip's neglect, than he w^{d} if he had a different opinion of the practicability of protecting the meadow by fair & proper repairs. — but when we meet I will more fully communicate — Lewis I have not be[en] able to see yet — but shall in a day or two — The Process in part: first, has been served on all here & is sent to Albany to serve on Mr. V Rensselaer &cr. —

Most respectfully yours &c
R.R. Voris

[Addressed]
Gen. Pierre Van Cortlandt
Peekskill

---

1. Richard R. Voris was an attorney practicing in Sing Sing (Ossining). He was elected in 1844 as a district attorney in Westchester County. Werner, p. 408.

2. Philip G. Van Wyck was then residing in the Van Cortlandt Manor house at Croton under the terms of his uncle Philip Van Cortlandt's will. He assumed that he also had been given the use, until 1836, of the meadows and farms associated with the estate. Part of the property consisted of meadowlands on what is now known as Croton Point, a body of land jutting out into the Hudson River. The problem noted here concerned the maintenance of a series of dikes on the Point which protected the land from washouts. Philip G. Van Wyck was accused by his uncle of neglect in maintaining these dikes during the years of his tenure at the Manor.

152

James Brooks[1] to Pierre, Jr. ALS
NYPL

Washington Dec. 30, 1834.

My dear Sir

Indeed I am glad to hear from you, after so long a silence, — and with so long and so pleasant a letter. Marcy and all has [survived?] — and today I will go out, and see if [Knowles?] has come, for I shall be happy to know him. But I doubt whether any body is alive today, for the snow is a foot–and a half deep at this moment, and yet even now it is snowing like a vengeance. You see, that we have set up an opposition winter here. We Southerners don't like your Northern monopolies.

The devil is to pay here in the way of President-manufacturing. Such a lot of great men have we, that there is no knowing what to do with them. The New Englanders are pulling lead for Webster. Clay aren't give quite up yet. Calhoun even to this hour thinks he is the most-popular man in the world. — And McLean has not a doubt, that both parties in a mass will go for him. So we go.[2]

You have mistaken my destination after the 1st of January. I have the misfortune to be a member of the Legislature "away down East, in the State of Maine", — and there I must bend my way to spend the winter, amid ice and snows, to which, however, I am quite reconciled by the appearance of things in Washington this morning, for seldom or ever has there been such a snow-storm here.[3]

I am sorry that I have not seen your article entitled "Architects of Ruin."[4] If you have a extra copy, I wish you would send it to me at Augusta, Maine.

Yours Truly
James Brooks

P.S. Wayne[5] [illegible] hard name. Here I have been spelling it Waney for months, and you have just told me! that a man with so much [illegible] in his veins should have such an [illegible] name! it is astonishing. What will you give me for mine, that will rhyme with almost any thing. — to say nothing of its being pastoral &c &c. However, you have an advantage. When any one once leaves your house, he'll never forget it. So when you get to be immortal none will ever forget your "immortality," as is the case with us men of honourable names.

---

1. James Brooks (1810–1873), a man possessed of an impossible handwriting, was born in Portland, Maine, but devoted most of his career to New York City and Washington, D.C. He served as a newspaper correspondent and editor, as well as being a congressman from New York in both Whig and Democratic capacities. In 1835 he became a member of Maine's state legislature. *Biographical Directory American Congress,* p. 643.

2. Brooks was commenting on the confused state of affairs concerning the anticipated battle for the presidential nominations at the conclusion of Andrew Jackson's second term. Among the Whig contenders, as listed by Brooks, were Daniel Webster, Henry Clay, John C. Calhoun, and U.S. Supreme Court Justice John McLean of Ohio.

3. Washington, D.C., was hit by a massive snow storm in December, 1834. While most activities ceased for a number of days, a scheduled speech by John Quincy Adams in praise of the late General Lafayette took place on the allotted day. *Niles' Weekly Register,* XLVII, 290, 313.

4. An article appeared in the Albany *Daily Advertiser* on December 18, 1834, condemning Mormonism and labeling Joseph Smith and his followers "Architects of Ruin." It is questionable whether this is the article to which Brooks referred. Although Pierre wrote occasional newspaper pieces on political themes, this one is out of keeping with his prior activities.

5. James M. Wayne (1790–1867), a congressman from Georgia, was nominated by Andrew Jackson on January 7 to fill a vacancy on the U.S. Supreme Court. *Niles' Weekly Register,* XLVII, 313.

153

Pierre, Jr. vs. Philip G. Van Wyck. AD
NYHS

April 10, 1835.

THE PEOPLE OF THE STATE OF NEW YORK, to

Philip G. Van Wyck

and to his Counsellors, Attorneys, Solicitors workers Laborers servants and Agents, and each and every of them, Greeting: WHEREAS it has been represented to us in our Court of Chancery, on the part of

Pierre Van Cortlandt

complainant that he hath lately exhibited his Bill of Complaint[1] in our said Court of Chancery, before our Chancellor, against you, the said Philip G. Van Wyck to be relieved, touching the matters therein complained of; in which Bill it is stated, amongst other things, that you are combining and confederating with others, to injure the said complainant touching the matters set forth in the said Bill, and that your actings and doings in the premises are contrary to equity and good consience: We, therefore, in consideration thereof, and of the particular matters in the said Bill set forth, do strictly command you, the said

Philip G. Van Wyck

and the persons before mentioned, and each and every of you, under the penalty of Ten Thousand Dollars, to be levied on your lands, goods, and chattels to our use, that you do absolutely desist and refrain from the commission of any further waste upon the farm of Land and premises whereon Philip Van Cortlandt late of the Town of Cortlandt in the County of Westchester deceased resided (and which said farm of land and premises you occupy and possess as tenant for years by virtue and in pursuance of a codicil made and executed by the said Philip Van Cortlandt to his last will and

testament[)] by ploughing up the meadows ground thereon situated and being; or converting such meadow into arable land; or committing any other waste whatever upon the said farm of land and premises
until the further order of our said Court of Chancery.
(Copy)
Witness, Reuben H. Walworth, Esquire, Chancellor of our said State, at the City of New-York, the tenth day of April one thousand eight hundred and thirty-five.
R.R. Voris Sol'r.

John Walworth
Assistant Register

1. The bitter legal struggle to compel Philip G. Van Wyck to leave the Van Cortlandt lands continued. Since the Van Cortlandts were stymied in their efforts to remove Van Wyck, they sought to restrain him from further land encroachments.

154

Ebenezer Baldwin[1] to Pierre, Jr. ALS
Baldwin Family Papers, Yale University Library

December, 1835.

To/The Hon Pierre C. VanCortland

My Dear Sir

If you have, or have not, got out of humor with "LaUah RoaNe," and Black Susan and other sporting tastes,[2] I may venture to command to your friendly regard, a Prospectus of an Historical Work that will accompany this note. Let me tell you in frankness, what I wish to claim from your friendship. You belong by birth and marriage—alliance, to families, best & most intimately connected with the History of the State. I trust I do not presume too much on the friendship of years to solicit the temporary loan of such papers, as may be under your control, or the Control of your brother, Gen. Philip Van Cortland, as may tend to the proper minstration of American History and the proper Vindication of patriots who have passed.

All papers noted for return will be carefully preserved & subject at all times to your order — With Sentiments of the Warmest friendship — Yours truly

Ebenezer Baldwin

New Haven
Connecticut
Dec. 1835

[Addressed]
To/Gen. Pierre C. Van Cortland
Westchester, New York

---

1. Ebenezer Baldwin had been an Albany resident and local politician in 1828. He apparently removed to New Haven in later years. See letter of Ebenezer Baldwin to Pierre, Jr. dated March 21, 1828 (No. 99).

2. A seeming reference to race horses.

155

Robert M. McLane[1] to Pierre III. ALS
SHR

West Point. March 19th–36.

Dear Pierre.

I have indulged the hope every week almost since the receipt of your letter written from Albany, to pay you a visit, but the Weather and difficulty of obtaining permission (as difficult now as it once was under the old reign of Sylvanus Le Grand)[2] have disappointed me but Col. willing — and if nothing unusual occurs I shall try and pay my respects to you and the general next Saturday. Your letter was short and not half as full of gossip, as it might have been, considering you had been spending months in Albany, all of which time too, you have no doubt [been] under the inspiring influence of Miss Euphemia. We have had as you may suppose a dull and stayed Winter, nothing to amuse, and every thing to dispare under these circumstances you must excuse me for epistlizing to any length — I write now particularly to acknowledge your letter and to say why I have not been able to pay my dearies to the General — but with such good sleighing and oceans of time you have no excuse for not having been [here] to cheer me in my solitude —

Sincerely your friend
Robt M. McLane

[Addressed]
Major Pierre Van Cortlandt
Peekskill
West chester Co.
N.Y.

---

1. A native of Wilmington, Delaware, Robert M. McLane (1815–1898) had a distinguished career as a politician. His positions included congressman from Maryland, ministerial roles in

China, Mexico, and France, and governor of Maryland. At the time of this letter, McLane, then twenty-one, was attending West Point under an appointment from President Andrew Jackson. *DAB,* XII, 115–116.

2. A reference to Sylvanus Thayer (1785–1872), superintendent of West Point from 1817 to 1833.

156

Pierre, Jr. to Pierre III. ADS
SHR

June 10, 1836.

Know all men by these presents. That whereas I am the owner & Proprietor of the Mansion House, & Farm, at Croton River, in the Town of Cortlandt, lately belonging to my late Father. I do therefore for the natural love, and affection I have for my son Pierre Van Cortlandt Jr: give it to him for the ensuing five years, to be entirely under his sole and absolute controul, and governance, he to receive all the rents, issues, and profits from it, without the let, hindrance, or molestation from me, or any person, or persons whatsoever, unless by his order or direction — The persons now residing on it to account to him in all respects whatever; and I hereby resign all my right to the said Mansion House, & Farm, to my said son Pierre for the term above mentioned[1] —

In witness whereof I have hereunto set my hand & seal this 10th day of June one thousand eight hundred & thirty six.

Sealed & delivered in presence of
Jas: Stevenson

Pierre Van Cortlandt

[Endorsed]
Pierre Van Cortlandt to Pierre Van Cortlandt Jr:
Lease for 5 years — June 10th 1836 — Lease for Croton river Farm

1. Philip G. Van Wyck's period of residency in the Croton Manor house came to an end in 1836. The property then came under the exclusive control of Pierre, Jr. under the terms of Philip's will.

157

Pierre, Jr. to Theodric R. Beck.[1] ALS
Albany Institute of History and Art

July, 1837.

My dear Sir

You ask me what I know or remember respecting the Capture of John Andre the Adjutant General of the British Army[2] — In answer to which I inform you that I was then a Student in Queens College New Brunswick in the State of New Jersey — It happened at the Commencement of the College on my way home I met Mrs Arnold in a Eton Carriage near Joshua Smiths House in Haverstraw, after passing the Carriage I met Major Franks who had been an Aid de Camp to Arnold although a Boy I was in the habits of Intimacy with Franks — I inquired of him who was in the Carriage I met he told it was Mrs Arnold, that he was directed by the Commander in Chief Genl Washington to escort her to Philadelphia to her Relations that Arnold was a Traitor & had fled to the British, that Andre met Arnold at the House of Joshua Smith near w[h]ere we then were that he had changed his clothes (his Regimentals) and had attempted to get to New York by the way of PeeksKill Crumpond Pine's Bridge over the Croton & had been captured near Tarry Town on the News of which Arnold made his escape in his Barge to the British ship which had brought up Andre — It rained very hard & he remarked you are going in the Neighbourhood of the Traison, and will soon know all the particulares — Good by — I arrived that Evening to the House I now occupy — But at that time my Brother in Law

G.G. Beekman resided here — The next morning about Ten OClock Captain Hoogland with a party of Horse having Andre a prisioner made a halt for a few minutes at a house about 200 yards from where I was on his way from Salem to take Andre to West Point from whence Andre was taken by water to Kings ferry & from there by Land to Tappan the Head Quarters of General Washington — His tryal by a Court Martial of General officers you know from history — But what you particularly wish me to communicate is the Rout of his travels from Smiths House at Haverstraw until the time of his Capture —

I was informed from the best information that he stripped himself of his Regimentals or British Uniform and put on Smiths Clothes[.] The Reason for taking a Land Rout & disguising himself in Smiths Clothes was that Col James Livingston who commanded Fort Le Fayette at Verplancks Points had sent down in the night (while Andre was at Smiths House) — a 32 Pounder to the South point of Tellers point where the Vulture was at anchor opposite, threw up a breast work which the remains of it is now visible and opend a severe firing on the vessel (Vulture) which compelled her to slip her Cable and proceed down the River some miles, The Cannon was brought back to Verplanks point when Col Livingston took the precaution be [by] sending Roe Boats & other Garde Coasters to prevent any Communication on either side of the River communicating with the Vulture, So that it was impossible for Andre to return on board of her (although at this time Col Livingston was not apprehensive of the treasonable project of Arnold nor did he know that Andre was secreted at Smiths House, He acted as a vigilant officer to protect his Command) He was compelled to disguise himself in Smiths Clothes and make his return to New York by Land — Smith not being informed of the disposition of our Troops thought it most prudent and safe without being exposed to suspicion to go across the River at Kings ferry, pass over Verplancks point (which was garrisoned by Col. Livingston, Regiments) to Peeks Kill from thence through the Interior of the Country to Crumpond and Pines Bridge — He arrived at Peeks Kill about Sunset & there took the Road to Crumpond, Three miles from Peeks Kill there was a militia Patrool stationed under the Command of Captain Boyd who would not permit to pass during the night, although they showed Gen[l]. Arnolds pass, detained them until just before day Light, they then proceeded on to Crumpond and was stopped by a Centinel in the Road who took them to his officer who was Ebenezer Foote Esq[r] assistant deputy Commisary who had a Gaurd at the place to protect many fat Cattle and Sheep belonging to our Army (This Ebenezer Foote was afterwards many years a Senator in this State & First Judge of the County of Delaware who related to me this fact) Mr Foote told me it was so early in the morning that he could not read the pass without the help of a Lamp which was burning in his Room — Smith made particular inquiry how our Troops were stationed, M[r] Foote informed them that we had no Troops on the Lines Except Col. Jamesons Cavalry and that they were stationed at Robin's mill some miles East of Pines Bridge on the Croton River. Smith wished M[r] Foote to direct him the Rout to get there[.] M[r] Foote told them that they must cross Pines Bridge, about half a mile below there were two Roads the One leading to Robin's mills the other to Sing Sing — Smith inquired (for Andre said nothing) whether if they went by the way of Sing Sing to the White Plains where they alledged they were going, whether they would meet any of our Troops, Foote told them no — That Col Jamessons detachment were the only Troops we had below the Lines and further told them that if they called on Jameson he would send an Escort with them to the White Plains — They left M[r] Foote and proceeded to Pines Bridge, where Smith parted with Andre I dont know, but after they had passed Pines Bridge Andre took the Road to Sing Sing and met no obstruction or resistance whatever until he came to the Brook about One quarter of a mile North of Tarry Town, where he was stopped by those Three patriotic young men Paulding, Van Wort and Williams — Paulding seized the

Bridle of Andre's horse, (Paulding had on a Yaker coat, (Green paced with Red) which he had procured in New York four days before when escaped over the board fence in the Rear of the North Dutch Church which was occupied as a Prison to confine the American Prisoners and by the Assistance of a friend Nathaniel Leviness who found a small skiff in the Creek near the House the late Burrage Norton built on the Bank of the Hudson three miles out of the City on which he padoled himself across the River in the night to Wehawk the next morning he found himself among friends being the Light Infantry Corps commanded by Marquiss De La Fayette — My Brother gave Paulding a pass to return to the Manor of Cortlandt and on his arrival there he went with Van Wort & Williams on a Scout and placed themselves at the Brook above mentioned they had not been long there before Andre appeared — The dress of Paulding deceived Andre, for his first inquiry was, what party they belonged to and whether they were the Lower party (meaning the British) Paulding told him look at his dress & he could not be mistaken — On this Andre replied if you belong to the Lower Party so do I. Paulding answered there are so many Rebels through the Country I must be better satisfied that you are not One — Andre anxious to proceed and not be detained, told them that he had been up in the Country & had the plan of West point fort and its dependencies, on which Paulding told him that he was now in the hands of those he stiled Rebels and they would search & detain him until they were assured that he was not a Spy — On which Andre recovering his self possession of mind, told them that he had only used that finesse, thinking perhaps they belonged to the Lower party, But that he now asured them he was a friend & going on public business of Genl Arnold whose pass he produced — Paulding told him that he supposed the pass might be from Genl Arnold, but his declaration he had been up and procured the papers he mentioned respecting West Point, if such Papers were found on him that would detain him as a spy — They took him in the woods some distance from the public Road, searched his Clothes but found nothing. Paulding told me he pulled of his Boots & discovered the Papers — On this discovery Andre attempted to bribe them — He told them if they would name the Sum for his release it should be given to them & proposed that he would remain with Two of them secreted and send the third to New York to receive the Sum of Money they would demand for his release — But those three patriotic young men, sperned at the base proposition and carried him immediately to Col. Jameson at Robin's mills, who sent him by the way of Salem to West Point under the escort of Capt. Hooglands troop of Horses — from West Point he went by water to Kings ferry & from thence by Land to Tappan as I have before mentioned —

The Story related in the small Book in a series of Letters intitled "Letters about the Hudson with respect to Two Young men Sherwood & Peterson cannot be any thing else but fabulous —

Andre's rout from Smiths house in Haverstraw wher he had an Interview with Arnold is herein truly described. I had the whole Story from the late Captain Boyd who commanded the militia Patrool & who detained Smith and Andre the night previous to his Capture and also from the late honorable Ebenezer Foote relation of his Centinel stopping them at Crumpond at break of day & his conversation with Smith about the disposition of our troops and the different Roads &c &c about Pines bridge on the Croton River which is at least ten miles from Mothers Lan so called at Tellers point — That I have no hesitation to say that the whole story as told respecting Sherwood & Peterson is without the least Shadow of truth —

---

1. Physician, philanthropist, naturalist, and administrator, Theodric Romeyn Beck (1791–1855) was also the father-in-law of Pierre III. Dr. Beck's daughter, Catharine, married Pierre III on June 14, 1836. In addition to being a practicing physi-

cian, Beck wrote on many subjects, including historical and scientific studies relating to New York. *DAB*, II, 116–117.

2. This, and the following communication to Dr. Beck, illustrate that the Van Cortlandts realized that they had been on the periphery of a major historical event. How much of what Pierre actually remembered of events that transpired some fifty-seven years earlier and had become family tradition is difficult to determine. It is amazing, for example, how much they supposedly knew — as related in the July 17 letter — of Washington's thoughts and plans while he was in Westchester those many years ago. Compare these comments to Pierre's 1817 statements in support of John Paulding (Nos. 21–23 and 26).

158

Pierre, Jr. to Theodric R. Beck. ALS
Albany Institute of History and Art

Peekskill July 17 — 1837.

Dear Sir

My communication respecting the Capture of Major Andre and his Rout from Joshua Smiths house in Haverstraw until his being taken by Paulding[,]Van Wort and Williams is not so expresed as I wish for publication. The facts stated are True — But yet I wish you not to publish it until I have a personal interview with you —

There is also another very important transaction which had slipped my memory until reminded me by my sister Beekman, at her late visit to me last week — It is this — General Washington had made an Engagement to meet the Admiral of the Franch fleet and his principal Officers then lying at New Port in the State of Rhode Island at Hartford in Connecticut — He came on with the Marquis De La Fayette and a number of others with several Aid de Camps of the General. He stopt at the Village at Peeks Kill in the afternoon late in the day made all preparation to remain there that night — The General sent his aid Col[l]. Humphreys to this House then occupied by my Brother in law Gerard G Beekman requesting a Room and Bed for the General. There was little Room in the House at that time, being only one story, a small bed room on the Garret which the General occupied for that night. De La Fayette and the Generals Suite had to sleep in the best manner they could be accommodated. As soon as it was dark the General with his Suite left the Village of Peeks Kill giving out that he intended to ride to Quaker hill that night in the County of Dutchess, a necessary precaution to delude the Tories that no One should know of his movements The General had not been long at Mr Beekmans before Arnold arrived intending to have remained there all night (He and Mr. Beekman had had mercantile transactions before the war & were intimate acquaintances) but finding the Commander in Chief here, he had to get lodgings in the Neighbourhood, But very anxious to know from the General where he was going and how long he should be engaged at Hartford and when he would be at West point to all which the General gave him evasive answers — The General pursued his Journey before sun rise the next morning. Arnold after breadfasting at the Farmer house stopt again at M[r] Beekmans & in his conversation mentioned that he was going to Haverstraw to meet a flag of truce — Arnold went to Haverstraw but on his return did not stop at Mr Beekmans.

A day or two previous to this, Captain John Webb belonging to Colonel Sheldens Regiment of Dragoons had left a valice in the particular charge of M[rs] Beekman containing a new Suit of Uniform Clothes which he enjoined on M[rs] Beekman not to deliver to any Person whatever unless a written order from him (the Reason of this caution was that Captain Webb had the year before been attached to Col[l]. Van Cortlandts command and that the Colonel had left with his sister much of his baggage & cloathing and his Servants came as if by his directions from his Colonel got the Baggage &[c] &[c]. and deserted to the British) a day or two after Arnold had seen Gen[l] Washington at M[r] Beekmans and it must have been while Andre was at Joshua Smiths House & Captain Webb had passed on a few days before to the Light Infantry Corps then stationed in the English Neighbourhood in New Jersey and on his way there had stopped at Joshua Smith & told him he had left an elegant suit of Regimentals at M[r] Beekmans. That Joshua Smith came to M[r] Beekmans to get the valise belonging to Cap[t]. Webb. M[rs] Beekman inquired of Smith whether he had a written order for it from Cap[t] Webb, if he had not he should not have it, Smith disappointed returned to Haverstraw immediately where no doubt Andre then was secreted in his house & wanted this uniform that he might make his escape as an American Officer for there is no construction to be put on this transaction except that

I am with much respect and
Esteem your Ob[t] Ser[t]
Pierre Van Cortlandt

To
Doctor T. R. Beck

159

James Faulkner to Pierre, Jr. ALS
SHR

Sing Sing Janury 7th 1838.

General Pierre Van Courtland

Dear Sir

The men that are living near the Croton on your land are making great harvests amongst your wood and as I have discharged them they are beyond my controul they have not worked for me since the first of November and they are determined to do all Damage they can Possibly do, I Cannot hinder them, all I Can do is to Report this to you I have given Mr Voorhees their Names a month ago.[1] General I feel willing to Pay to the utmost farthing for all Damages that my men do but these desperadoes I Cannot Control[.] they tell me that the wood is not mine nor any of my Buisness they will Cut as much as they please for all me So that you See what a situation I am Placed in[.] if you Cannot Come down Please Direct Mr Voorhees what to do so that there shall be a stop put to Destroying timber wantonly. I Certainly do feel it my duty to do all in my Power to Prevent Damage from being done But without your assistance I Can do Nothing with these men that Cut wood they will only laugh when I threaten them there must be prompt measures taken or they will do as they Please —

yours with Every Sentiment of Esteem
Respectfully
Jas Faulkner

To Gen. P. Vancourtland
Peekskill

---

1. The characters involved in this affair remain unidentified.

160

William C. Brownlee[1] to Pierre, Jr. ALS
NYPL

New york, May 9, 1838.

General Pierre Van Courtland
My dear Sir: — You may remember that I stated to you on a former occasion, that a select number of the Livingston family,[2] had been pleased to constitute me their almoner on behalf of an unfortunate branch of the family, namely Mr. Beekman Livingston of Salinas, N.Y., brother of the

late D^{r}. Livingston of New Brunswick. Mr Peter G. Stuyvesant, and his sisters & brothers contribute liberally.

But $10 per month is very little to make the aged couple M^{r}. Livingston, and his aged lady, comfortable; especially when we consider that they have at least one helpless widowed daughter depending on them.

I have cheerfully undertaken this service on behalf of my aged & venerable friend. He was pleased to select me for the service, because he knew the intimacy between myself & the late D^{r}. Livingston of New Brunswick. — Another circumstance which has drawn us close together is the historical & traditional remembrance in my family, & the family "forbears" of Mr Livingston. In the grand national struggle for religion & liberty in Scotland, in the days of the last of the Stuarts, — my ancestor, the "Laird of Terfoot" stood shoulder to shoulder with the famous ancestor of the Livingston family, I mean Revd John Livingston of Ancrum. And There was this difference — my ancestor, Laird Brownlee of Terfoot, was a soldier and fought gallantly untill he fell on the field of Bothwell,[3] — not killed, — but by his horse tumbling headlong in the heat of Battle, — he fell into a crowd of the foemen and was taken prisoner: Your ancestor John Livingston on the contrary, was a Minister, & sustained the cause by his eloquence, until he was taken, & banished to Holland.

The remembrance of those things has caused a close friendship between Beekman Livingston & myself & other branches of the family. —

The last sum contributed for this year is exhausted. And now I request you, on behalf of your relative, and my good friend, to send me your annual contribution of $10, that I may make his months remittance.

I am, my dear General
Your very obedient & humble servant,
W.C. Brownlee

To Genl. Pierre Van Courtland

P.S. I keep a minute account of receipts & expenditures; and at the close of the year, lay the paper before P.G. Stuyvesant Esqr.[4] &c &c, for the satisfaction of all concerned, as well as my own —

W.C.B.

---

1. The Reverend William C. Brownlee, of the Dutch Reformed Church, was the minister of the North Church on Williams Street in New York City. *Longworth's Directory* (1838), p. 124.

2. Pierre, Jr. was a Livingston relation through his mother, the late Joanna (Livingston) Van Cortlandt.

3. A decisive battle between adherents of Scottish Presbyterianism and Anglicanism was fought at Bothwell Brigg on June 22, 1679. Under the Test Act of 1681, which followed this Scottish defeat, Dr. John Livingston was banished to Holland. William L. Langer, ed., *An Encyclopedia of World History: Ancient, Medieval, and Modern, Chronologically Arranged* (Boston, 1948), p. 428.

4. An early president of The New-York Historical Society and a founder of the General Theological Seminary, Peter G. Stuyvesant was an influential businessman and socialite of New York City. Wilson, III, 416; IV, 103, 105, 600.

161

William W. Mather[1] to Pierre, Jr. ALS
NYPL

New Burgh Sept 24th 1838.

My Dear Sir

While examining the shore of West Chester Co. last summer in the discharge of my duties as geologist of the state, I had occasion to observe that there are two locations for fine quarries between your gneiss quarry & Anthony's Nose. I think the external indications of the rocks are such as to justify the opening of quarries. The material is of a strong & durable quality, & can be blocked out, I judge, in large blocks free of seams, & suitable for buildings, both where ashlar masonry[2] & heavy blocks are required. The material may be called a granite.

I have the honor to remain Sir Yr obdt Sert
W.W. Mather
Geologist 1st Dist. N.Y.

To Gen. Van Cortland
Peekskill N.Y.

P.S. I had neglected in the above to say, that they are on the waters edge, & the stone may be swung on board vessels lying along side by means of a crane.
W.W. Mather

---

1. William W. Mather (1805–1859), a native of Connecticut, was a state appointee to the U.S. Military Academy in 1823. He served as the New York State Geologist from 1836 to 1844. George W. Cullum, *Biographical Register of the Officers and Graduates of the U.S. Military Academy, at West Point, N.Y. From its Establishment, March 16, 1802 to the Army Re-Organization of 1886–87* (New York, 1868), I, 330–331.

2. Ashlar masonry is a hewn or squared stone especially used as wall facing.

Martin Van Buren (1782–1862). Oil on canvas, by an unknown artist. Known as "The Little Wizard of Kinderhook" for his political acumen, Martin Van Buren controlled New York's politics through The Albany Regency. Van Buren served as a U.S. Senator, as a Secretary of State, as Vice-President under Andrew Jackson, and was elected as the eighth President of the United States. He suffered political defeat after being held responsible for The Panic of 1837. He continued active in state politics upon his forced retirement from national office, while seeking the presidency on a number of occasions after 1840. The Van Cortlandts were not among his admirers for they held him responsible for DeWitt Clinton's inability to obtain a presidential nomination. (illustration: courtesy of The Long Island Historical Society).

162

Richard Riker[1] to Pierre, Jr. ALS
NYPL

NYork 1st Octr '38.

Dr Genl.

We made arrangements last evening to go to Syracuse to be there on the 3d Octr.[2] I have written to S. Simson.

Can you not have a meeting of a few Old Republicans & send Delegates. We can save the State & with it our Country. I conjure to meet the Convention — Get E. Lockwood[3] & others together.

Truly yours
R. Riker

Genl. Van Cortlandt

---

1. For Richard Riker, see *VCFP,* III, 97–99.

2. The New York Democrats were in political turmoil as of 1838. While their national leader was President Martin Van Buren, many had broken with him over his sub-treasury scheme. It is to be recalled that Pierre was a leading Westchester banker and, therefore, would have been unalterably opposed to Van Buren's plan to reorganize the U.S. Treasury system.

The Democrats held a convention at Syracuse on October 3, at which time they openly denounced the President and came out in support of William H. Seward as the gubernatorial candidate. Alexander, II, 24–25; Hammond, II, 486.

3. Ezra Lockwood was a surrogate justice in Westchester County. O. L. Holley, ed, *The New York State Register for 1843 . . . Also, a Full List of County Officers, Attorneys, &c.* (Albany, 1843), p. 72.

163

Caspar T. Pruyn to Pierre, Jr. ALS
SHR

Water Vliet Jan:y 28.th 1839.

Genl. Pierre Van Cortlandt
Sir,

It becomes our sad duty to apprize you of the death of Stephen Van Rensselaer the late Patroon[1] — He expired at the Manor House without a struggle or a groan on Saturday last, exemplifying in the long and painful Illness with which he was afflicted the fortitude and virtues of the Christian; his death tho' naturally expected in the course of Providence was unlooked for at the time and has caused to his immediate family the deepest distress, as one of his connections and friends it may be a gratification to be informed of the happy end of a long and useful career

At the request of the Family
respectfully yours
Caspr: T. Pruyn

[Addressed]
Genl. Pierre Van Cortlandt. —
Peekskill
Westchester Co. —

---

1. Pierre was related to the Van Rensselaers through several Van Cortlandt marriages. The closest was that of his sister, Ann, to Philip S. Van Rensselaer.

164

Cornelia Beekman to Pierre, Jr. ALS
SHR

August 23 1839.

My Dearest Brother

I wrote you on the 2d of this month, and I also received yours of the same date, I feel gratifyed with your affectionate remembrance of the day of my Birth, it may be the last time, the Lord alone knows how soon it may please to call me, from this transtory Life, to a better one, of rest I hope to find,

Sister Rensselear I hear has left Sing Sing for Albany. I have only Seen her but Once, but regard for me must be but Little.

I observe what you wrote relative to Mr Vorris and the contestors — Philip Van Wyck has receive 1000^{00} as his part, as he sais, of the Money that was paid in Court, of the Damag the Water Commishonors Valuation our Proppperty for, What intitles him to $1000–00 As his part of the Damage done, I could wish to know[1] —

Last Spring I was deprived of One of My Carriage horses by being drowned in the Mill pond — About six weeks Since Clark meet with a Good horse that was a true match for My Jackson horse a handsome good in every respect to be depended on — and so much like Jackson, they hardly could be told apart, I then had a good span of Carriage horses again to depend on — but Last week an unhappy accident happened to the horse I bought — One of my black Oxens hooked him in his body — that he dyed in ten hours after it happened — Now I am Again deprived of Carriage horses — and how to replace them I cannot I have not got the means to do it with. — I feel hurt to be destitute now when I always had them at command

am with Love your most affectionate Sister
Cornelia

---

1. The creation of the Croton water supply system for New York City caused a diversion of water from the lower Croton River. The Van Cortlandts were to be involved in extended litigation with the Croton Water Commissioners concerning the flow of the river.

165

Henry Clay to Pierre, Jr. ALS
NYPL

Ashland 25th Nov. 39.

Dear Sir

I recd. your favor of the 11th. inst. and most cordially reciprocate the congratulations which it contains on the recent glorious issue of the N.York election.[1] It has filled me with astonishment and inexpressible pleasure. Your State has now established her right to be considered the Empire State by a much nobler title than any which mere courtesy or custom could confer — by shewing that she deserves it.

May the great event lead to the revival of National prosperity and lend to the perpetuity of free institutions.

I am, with the greatest respect
Yr. faithf St.
H. Clay

Pierre Cortlandt Esqr.

[Addressed]
Free — H. Clay
Pierre Van Cortlandt Esqr.
Peekskill
New York

---

1. In the New York elections of November, 1839, the Whigs successfully won control of the state Senate and captured the

majority of Assembly seats outside of New York City. This was in striking contrast to their relatively poor showing in the 1838 elections. Pierre had gradually shifted allegiance from Jacksonian to Conservative Democrat to Whig, thus eliciting this ebullient response from the perennial Whig presidential candidate. *Niles' Weekly Register*, LVII, 166, 179, 180, 198, 243.

166

Pierre, Jr. to William H. Seward.[1] ALS
HSP

PeeksKill Decr. 5, 1839.

My dear Sir

Permit me to congratulate you most sincerely on the result of the late Election in this State. It is a victory of correct principles over the destructive measures of the General Government[.] Nothing has saved the Nation from Ruin but the Ballot Boxes —

The Whigs in this County have been defeated by the undue influence of the Office holders of New York sent through the District & County expending money freely in electioneering — The Agent of the State Prison was active using the power of his Office over the Guards and Keepers of that Institution[.] Even the Paupers in the Poor House were brought out poor and infirm as they are in a Body to give their votes against Us.

I suffered my Name to be run as a Senator in this District, not that I expected a successful Issue — for John Hunter was One of Van Buren Nominees at the Baltimore Convention & I knew full well that he would have all the Office holders of the General Government & pecuniary Aid from Washington to defeat me. Van Buren had a pride to sustain him & much money has been spent to effect it — yet notwithstanding We have reduced the Loco foco Majority in this County[2] & the next year with proper management we will obtain a victory over them — The State Prison institution requires to be reformed, It is now inhuman, tyrannical, and the Keepers and Guards are compelled to vote at the Election to please the Agent or lose their places, The present Inspectors were appointed in April 1838 for three years,[3] They have by Law the appointment of the Agent. He will not be removed by the present Inspectors, therefore the Necessity of repealing the Law and giving the appointing power to the Governor & Senate —

You will be assailed by many applicants for the Office of Surrogate of this County — My impression is that Alexander H. Wills [Wells] is the most popular Candidate[.] He is Honest, capable, Industrious & unites our Interest more than any other Candidate I have heard mentioned — I will write you more fully shortly — I have the honor to be Your Excellency Most Assured friend

Pierre Van Cortlandt

Govr. Seward

[Addressed]

To His Excellency Governor Seward

Albany

---

1. William H. Seward was one of the most conspicuous figures in the political life of nineteenth-century New York. A graduate of Union College, he was elected to the New York Senate in 1830 when only twenty-nine. He made the acquaintance of Thurlow Weed, who became his political tutor and who engineered his rapid rise in the Anti-Masonic and, later, Whig parties. In 1838 and again in 1840 he was elected governor of New York on the Whig ticket. Sent to the U.S. Senate in 1849, he became an outspoken opponent of slavery and of the Compromise of 1850. Re-elected to the Senate in 1855, Seward was an influential force in the newly founded Republican Party. Alexander, II, 281–290; Glyndon G. Van Deusen, *William Henry Seward* (New York, 1967), pp. 121–134.

2. John Hunter narrowly carried the election for state Senator in Westchester County, defeating Pierre 3,427 to 3,392. Pierre

was successful in Yorktown, Somers, South Salem, North Salem, Cortlandt, Poundridge, and Bedford.

An editorial camparison of the two candidates appeared in the New York *Times and Commercial Intelligencer* of October 21, in which the writer asserted: "General Van Cortlandt, the first elector of Jefferson, who began life within the democratic party — the friend and supporter of Madison, Monroe, and of Jackson, until Mr. Van Buren controlled his administration — yes, this 'old stager' of the democratic party is in the field in the second district, for the senate, in opposition to Hunter, an old blue light federalist — a black cockade federalist of John Adams line, the advocate of the alien, the sedition, and the bankrupt laws passed under Adams — repealed under Jefferson — the opponent of the last war — the advocate of the sub treasury; in short a genuine loco foco federalist who advocates measures for political preferment. . . ."

Locofoco, denoting radical or (to opponents) incendiary political views, derived from the name of a friction match. The term was usually applied to the New York radical wing of the Jacksonians.

3. Pierre was particularly bitter because he had been replaced as a prison inspector by a Democratic stalwart, Henry Romer, as part of a purging of Whig adherents under Democratic Governor William L. Marcy. *Hudson River Chronicle,* April 10, 1838.

167

Pierre, Jr. to William H. Seward. ALS
HSP

Peekskill January 20–1840.

My Dear Sir

I have this day left with Col. Williams at the Village to be forwarded in the Stage this Evening a very fine Bass caught in the River opposite to this place, of which I beg your acceptance and hope it may arrive safe —

I have the honor to be

Your Excellencys Ob^{t} Servt
& assured friend
Pierre Van Cortlandt

His Excellency
Governor Seward

P.S. Since writing this Letter my son took a ride up from Croton to see me[.] He desires me to say that he has left at the Stage House at Peekskill a very large Bass weighing 40 lbs which he begs your acceptance which you you will receive with the one I send

Yrs
P.V^{n}.C.

168

Pierre, Jr. to William H. Seward. ALS
HSP

Peekskill Jan^{r}. 21–1840.

My Dear Sir

Yesterday my son Col. Pierre Van Cortlandt Junr. forwarded to you by the mail Stage a very large Bass and by the same conveyance I sent you another not quite so large which we begged your acceptance — I merely write now to know whether the Mail Carrier was faithful to deliver them. As I lately sent my Sister Van Renselaer some fine Fish which she has not received.

With assurances of my high
Respect & Esteem I have the honor
to be y^{r} Exc^{l}. Ob^{t} Ser^{t}
Pierre Van Cortlandt

His Excellency
Governor Seward —

169

Pierre, Jr. to William H. Seward. ALS
HSP

PeeksKill Jany. 28. 1840.

My dear Sir

William H. Brown of Sing Sing is an applicant for the office of Clerk to the State Prison at that Place. He has recommendations from Jacob Acker the Sheriff and Joseph Hoxie the Clerk of the City of New York besides a number of other Gentlemen

I am personally and I may say intimately acquainted with him and know him to be competent to perform all the duties of the Office —

He is temperate, honest and very industrious, writes a fair hand and understands Book Keeping. He is a staunch Whig and is esteemed by all his acquaintances for his correct moral Character — He is Needy and has a wife with Children to support. He has followed House Painting but has found it injures his health —

I take much pleasure in recommending him to your Excellencys notice for that appointment to take place when the present Incumbent Hiram P Rowel's term expires,[1] who is a most violent Loco foco Partizan & has used his official Influences at every Election since his attachment to the Prison to bring up the Guards & Keepers to vote the Loco foco ticket. He obtained the appointment from Govr Marcey through the influence of John Hunter & the White Plains Regency — I only add that I will be much gratified if Mr Brown receives the appointment — for I believe it cannot be bestowed on a more worthy Character

I have the Honor to be
Your Excellencey's Ob ser^{t}
Pierre Van Cortlandt

His Excellincy
Governor Seward

---

1. Hiram P. Rowell was appointed later as a county clerk in November, 1858, and served until his death in May, 1867. Werner, p. 430.

170

Caleb Roscoe[1] to Pierre, Jr.
Westchester Herald, February 25, 1840.

Sing-Sing, February 13, 1840.

Gen. Pierre Van Cortlandt —

My dear Sir, — in view of the great interests of the county of Westchester, and the discussions now progressing in relation thereto, I am induced to ask you to favor me with an expression of your sentiments in relation to the dismemberment of Westchester County, the proposed annexation of the four northern towns to Putnam county,[2] and the other propositions which are put forth to obviate the difficulties and disadvantages bearing upon the citizens of those towns, and of which they very justly complain.

I am led to make this request, from the confidence with which I entertain the opinion, that you highly value and justly appreciate the name, character, landmarks and historical renown of Old Westchester, not only by reason of your birth, education, and long residence upon its soil, but also of your connexion with an illustrious and patriotic ancestry and kindred, who with unfaltering fidelity to our common country, hesitated not to peril their lives and fortunes in its defence, — and whose names are happily identified with the historical recollections and important events of this country in a manner that is ever grateful and refreshing to the heart of the citizen and patriot.

Accept, dear sir, the expression of my sincere respect, and best wishes for your health and happiness.

Very respectfully, your ob't serv't.
Caleb Roscoe.

---

1. Caleb Roscoe (1800–1877) resided in Westchester County his entire life. He was most noted as the publisher and editor of the *Westchester Herald,* with an office in Sing Sing (Ossining). The paper continued under his ownership from 1825 until December 6, 1856, when a disastrous fire destroyed his home, office, presses, and files. Scharf, II, 352.

2. Pierre's response to this request follows. The annexation did not take place.

171

Pierre, Jr. to Caleb Roscoe.

Westchester Herald, February 25, 1840.

Peekskill, Feb. 15, 1840.

Caleb Roscoe, Esq.

Dear Sir, — I have received your letter of the 13th instant, requesting to know my opinion of dismembering the county of Westchester, by taking the four upper towns, and annexing them to the county of Putnam, the division of the county of Westchester, or to have a Central Court House. Previous to receiving your favor, I had received a letter from Mr. Wells on the same subject, and have sent him a letter expressing my opinion. I feel somewhat delicate in intruding it upon the public, as many may say it is gratuitous and not called for. But the subject is so momentous, and having been born, and lived all my long life in this county, I have my attachments to it, which can not be eradicated: and on that account comply with your request, and send you a copy of my letter to him. You are at liberty to make such use of it as you think proper.[1]

Living as I do in the most northerly section of the county of Westchester, and in one of the towns designed to be annexed to Putnam county, I may by many be supposed to favor the project of dismemberment. This impression may also be strengthened by the fact that my property in this vicinity would be enhanced in value by the adoption of the measure. But, sir, such is not the fact; on the contrary, I am and ever have been decidedly opposed to any division or dismemberment of Westchester County, and I should deprecate the passage of any law for the consummation of either of those projects, as the greatest calamity which (in a local point of view) could befall us.

That the people of this county, or a vast majority of them, have labored and do labor under great disadvantages, and are subject to grievous inconvenininces from the injudicious and unjust location of the public buildings, I am free to admit: and will most cordially unite with my fellow citizens to correct the evil in any way which shall not be deemed prejudicial to the interest and welfare of Westchester county. In this section of the county we are compelled to travel from twenty to thirty miles to attend to the recording of a paper at the clerk's office, to transact business with the surrogate, or to attend courts as officers, jurors, witnesses, or parties. This arises not so much from the particular form of our territory, as from the location of the public offices; the jail and the principal Court House being located at a place some miles south of the geographical centre and the centre of population, and at the same time on the eastern border of the county. The present location was designated at a time when that portion of our county which now contains the great body of our population, was very limitedly settled. But it is evident to the most casual observer, that it would be difficult to select any location more inconvenient and difficult to arrive at for the present dense and wide-spread population.

The people of my section of the county are not desirous of leaving it, if they can obtain a location of the public buildings which shall afford them equal facilities and conveniences with those in other parts of the county; and in this I cannot believe they ask for any thing improper, unfair, or unjust. In view therefore, of the heavy grievances under which the people of the northern and western sections of the county labor would it not be much better for the honor and credit of the county if all were to unite in urging upon the Legislature the passing of an act abolishing the half-shire system, and adopting a central Court House at such point as disinterested Commissioners taken from remote counties, shall select? It appears to me this plan would have the merit of distributing equal justice, equal convenience, and equal privilege to all; and I believe it is the only plan that can be adopted which will effectually heal the dissensions, remove the prejudices, and allay the unpleasant and sectional feelings which have originated in this long agitated question.

As to the value of the present buildings I conceive that is a question which should operate in favor of new and central Buildings. They are small and inconvenient, and fall very far short of answering fully the purpose for which they were intended. I am told, that grand juries are compelled to hold their sessions in small and unpleasant houses of the village, taverns, or private dwellings, and that the room allotted to petit juries is by no means adequate to their accomodation.

The Building at the Whiteplains is old, and it is known the county is annually taxed for repairs upon the dilapidated edifices which are by no means a credit or ornament to the county. The cost for the erection of a new, commodious and convenient Edifice, would be trifling to each taxable inhabitant, and the sale of the old buildings for private purposes would aid in defraying a portion of that. If the County, containing as it does nearly forty thousand inhabitants, and ranking as it does in point of wealth and intelligence among the first in the State, is, indeed, too poor to provide itself with respectable and commodious Public Buildings, I presume there would be found within its borders public spirited individuals who could contribute the cost of their erection, rather than see the county become still poorer by thrusting one third of its territory into the county of Putnam.

I have drawn much longer on your patience than I at first intended, but the importance of the subject, and my great desire to see it amicably adjusted, must plead my apology. And in conclusion I would again repeat my decided opposition to any division or dismemberment of the county, and my earnest desire that the present Legislature will put the question for ever at rest by the passage of a law appointing Commissioners to locate a central Court House and Public Buildings.

With much respect, I am your obt. servant,

Pierre Van Cortlandt.

---

1. Pierre's reply to Alexander H. Wells, identical to this letter printed in the *Westchester Herald*, appeared in the *Hudson River Chronicle*, also on February 25, 1840. Wells, of Sing Sing (Ossining), was a local politician who became a justice of the surrogate court in February, 1840. Werner, p. 400.

172

Robert M. McLane[1] to Catharine (Beck) Van Cortlandt. ALS

NYPL

Macinaw Island. At the Head of Lake Huron.

July 20th 1840.

My Dear Madam — the rememberance of your sweet reproaches, for my breach of promise in not writing last Fall from Sacketts Harbor, has been, odd as it may seem, a constant source of agreable thought when every thing has had a tendency to change all that ought to be 'Couleur de Rose' to the most sombre of hues — the result of this agreable reflection on my part has been a determination to inflict upon you a history of all my adventures on the upper Lakes for the rest of the summer and I open from this place where I arrived this morning, because it is the point from which our wild life of adventure commences — here we abandon Steam Boats and take to our Canoes & Mackinaw Boats — and here we have met the wild men of the North West — their being at this moment encamped on the Island more than a thousand Indians stopping here on their way from the Lake Superior settlements to the English posts on Lake Huron where they go every year to receive presents and make speeches, not so long but a great deal better than most of those, we would hear in Washington; The Indian is seen here to great advantage, they live in a beautiful hunting Country to which they are very much attached, and are caressed by both the English & American Group, they thus feel all their importance, and having as much self esteem as the best of us, they cherish this consideration they enjoy beyond every thing else, tho' the women like the dear creatures every where else, are very fond of trinkets, and very fond of their own bright eyes. I have been all the afternoon engaged in decking the prettiest of them with beads & ribbons, in return they have piously promised to tell their great Father of my goodness, and obtain for me a place in the Hunting Grounds of the Moon — and as I am very fond of the Moon, (you recolect I hope who is my moon) I am very happy and very much interested in the success of their prayers. The day after I left you, I dined in Albany with Brt. Temple, and talked of you with M^rs^. T. but had no time to see any of your other friends, as I was "en route" to Utica by the first train of Cars the next morning, and had a rather uninteresting ride as far as Niagara tho' John V.R. was our Companion 'de voyage' part of the route and talked very much of every thing & every body — Fancy Balls however he avoided — you have doubtless both seen Niagara yourself, and read more than one Travellers account of it — I am sorry I can not add to these another, which would give you pleasure — The truth is however Niagara should never be described — it is like nothing in Nature or Art — hence you can have neither comparison or analogy to aid in the description, without one or both of these, description must be very lame — the grand and sublime wonder of the Falls, can only be felt, it will be felt by all, in their different degrees of feeling & imaginations — I was very much disappointed in my own feelings, they were of a totally different order, than what I had prepared myself for, but far deeper — more lasting & more agreeable — I am sorry to find, I have scribbled on to the close of my sheet, without talking at all of yourself, and yet I wished to talk of nothing else — but I pray you to forgive what must be the result of mans natural egotism — for instead of my own travels I prefer pic-nics on paradise Island — but tho' [three words obliterated], and I shall wait with anxious hope to see if I am to be allowed the happiness of telling you what I see up in Lake Superior — my post office is Fort Brady — Michigan — best regards to Pierre — and with great Respect & regard

Your very humble servant
R.M. McLane

[Addressed]
Mrs Pierre Van Cortlandt Colonel Pierre Van Cortlandt
Sing-Sing West Chester Co. New York —

---

1. Robert M. McLane befriended Pierre III when he was a cadet at West Point. See No. 155. Catharine Beck had married Pierre III in 1836.

173

Richard Riker to Pierre, Jr. ALS
SHR

New-York Nov. 28th 1840.

My dear General,

I have the pleasure to introduce to you my good cousin John L. Lawrence Esqr, one of your Co-Electors of President and Vice President of the U. States.[1]

Mr. Lawrence like myself is a nephew of that brave man, Captain Riker,[2] who under your gallant brother Colonel Van Cortlandt aided in the capture of Gen. Burgoyne and his army. It affords me unspeakable pleasure to See you and him after a lapse of more than Sixty years acting together to preserve those principles which they So gloriously contributed to acquire.

I most solemnly declare, my Dear General that our political institutions have at no time in my opinion been so much in danger as under this profligate, bold and wicked administration of Martin Van Buren. Thank God it has received its deserts from a most deeply insulted and injured people.

Wishing you and my good Cousin may long enjoy those blessings which you are now about to give to our common Country I remain

Most Sincerely and truly
Your old friend
R Riker

P.S. Excuse my employing an Amanuensis. My hand is lame.
Gen. Pierre Van Cortlandt.

---

1. Pierre served as a Whig presidential elector in 1840 pledged to support William Henry Harrison. The Albany *Evening Journal* of August 26, 1840, had declared, "The honorable James Burt, the name that heads the list of electors, and Pierre Van Cortlandt, were Jefferson electors. The whole electoral ticket is composed of the staunch supporters of Democracy, and will rally to its support all the old Jefferson Democrats, and all who approve of their principles. . . ."

2. For the Revolutionary services of Abraham Riker, see *VCFP,* I, *passim.*

174

John Bell[1] to Pierre, Jr. ALS
NYPL

Genl. P. Van Cortland
West Chester
N York

War Department
April 30,1841.

Sir

I have the honor to invite you to attend the approaching general examination of the Cadets of the Military Academy, as a Member of the Board of Visitors,[2] in whose presence the regulations of the Academy require that the examination take place.

It is desired that, in conjunction with the other Members of the Board, your enquiries may be directed to a full and free investigation of the Military and scientific instruction of the Cadets, and to the internal police, discipline, and fiscal concerns of the Institution, for which purpose every facility will be afforded by the Superintendent.

The result of your observations, with any suggestions for the improvement of the Academy, will be communicated to this Department.

The examination will commence on the first Monday in June next.

Your transportation, going and returning by the most direct mail route, at the rate of four cents a mile (provided it does not exceed One hundred dollars) and your expenses while at the Academy, will be paid by the Government.

I shall be pleased to learn whether it will be in your power to accept this invitation.

I have the honor to be sir
Your obt Servant
Jno:Bell

---

1. John Bell (1797–1869) was then Secretary of War in Harrison's cabinet.

2. Pierre received his political reward for supporting William Henry Harrison in 1840 by being appointed a member of the Board of Visitors to the U.S. Military Academy. He had served in a similar capacity on a number of occasions in the past.

175

Gerard Troost[1] to Pierre, Jr. ALS
NYPL

Nashville Tenn. October 13 1841.

My dear Sir

Since we parted at Peekskill on the Hudson River, I have spend about 14 days in Philadelphia, as long in Washington and a few weeks in Newhaven, New York and Baltimore, So that I arrived home late in the Summer, where I found all my family in a good State of Health. But I found also an accumulation of professional labor — Nevertheless remembering always with pleasure the agreable moments I have spend in your company during our stay at West Point. I should have written to you sooner, were it not that I had promissed you that I would see whether the name of any of your Holland Ancestors were mentioned in the historical works of Holland in my library, as these are numerous, and as I could only peruse them during my leisure moments, and as these moments were partly taken up with the preparation of my report to our legislature, it has taken a great while to accomplish this investigation. — These labors have been as yet fruitless. — If I recollect well, you mentioned to me that the name of Your family has been not always Cortlandt; that it was changed by the Prince of Orange to that what it is now? If you could ascertain when this change has taken place or by whom of the princes it was done, I could perhaps find something of it.

The session of our University terminated last Week — I am now preparing for an excursion which will take from 5 to 6 weeks; when I return I shall have more leisure time, and can then investigate this matter more fully.

I shall be glad, on my return home, to find a few lines noticing the good state of health and contentment of my friend Van Cortlandt

Very respectfully, My dear Sir, Your obd. Servt. and friend

G. Troost

[Addressed] General Pierre Van Cortlandt Peekskill on the Hudson River N.Y.

---

1. Gerard Troost (1776–1850) was born in Holland and died in Nashville, Tennessee. Educated in Dutch universities, he was a noted mineralogist. After coming to the United States he was appointed, in 1821, as a professor of mineralogy in the Philadelphia Museum and in 1822 was made professor of geology and mineralogy at the University of Nashville, a chair he held until his death in 1850. His collection of geological specimens was considered to be the largest in the United States at that time. Troost apparently met Pierre at West Point when the latter was serving on the Board of Visitors. *Appleton's Cyclopaedia,* VI, 162.

176

Pierre, Jr. to Jabez D. Hammond.[1] ALS
NYSL

PeeksKill May 23^{d}. 1842.

Jabez D. Hammond Esqr
Sir

I observe in the 1st. volume Page 423 in your political history of New York speaking of Pierre C Van Wyck you mention that among the friends of Governor Clinton "Those in New York with the exception of Thomas Addis Emmitt, who really could not be said to be a party politician, and Sylvanus Miller and Pierre C. Van Wyck, who though irregular in his habits and stricken with poverty, was a Man of Talents, were Men either of broken down fortunes or profligate habits and who appeared to know or do little else politically than laud Mr Clinton." —

The Historian, Biographer or Author ought always to be well informed of Facts, before he attempted to make strictures or sully the Characters of honorable Individuals, and then only when it cannot be avoided, when the Author fails of doing this his work will not or ought it to command that respect he anticipated — I am led to these remarks by the Quotation from your history mentioned above repecting the Character of my Pater Nephew Pierre C Van Wyck (formerly Recorder of the City of New York and afterwards District Attorny of that City) and I think it my duty to his memory to rebut the slander. It is not true that he was irregular in his habits. He was not Rich, but that was no disgrace — He was unfortunate in a speculation which rendered him embarrassed. But notwithstanding he was esteemed by All who knew him that he was correct in his habits. A high minded talented and honorable Man. Even his political Enemies (for he had none other) although they feared to combat with him in argument.[,] Yet respected and acknowledged him as a Man of honor and his strict propriety of Conduct — He opposed the Bucktails party from principle As he would now if he was living oppose the Loco foco's as Agrarian and disorganizers —

He was removed as Recorder of the City of New York by the Bucktail party As he also was as district Attorney on political motives. At his death he was a Member of the Corporation of the City of New York and was esteemed the most effecient talented Member of the Board — The great Improvements which then took place in the City originated with him. And if I have been rightfully informed.[,] It was owing to his sagacity that the Corporation purchased Blackwells Island —

You have done his memory great injustice by your publication and which as a true historian it is your Duty to correct[2]

I am respectfully
your Obt Servt

Pierre Van Cortlandt

[Addressed]
The Honble. Jabez D. Hammond Esqr
Coopers Town
Otsego County N.Y.

[Endorsed]
Peir Van Cortland's
letter
Recd. May 27 1842

---

1. Jabez Delano Hammond (1778–1855), historian and politician, was born in New Bedford, Massachusetts. After practicing medicine for a short period, he opened a law office in Cherry Valley, New York, in 1805. He began a public career with his election in 1815 to the Fourteenth Congress. He later served as a judge in Otsego County and as a regent of the University of the State of New York. He is better known as a historian, particularly for his two-volume study *The History of Political Parties in the State of New York,* originally published in 1842. *DAB,* IV, 205–206.

2. The text of Hammond's subsequent editions read: "With the exception of T. A. Emmett, who really could not be said to be a party politician, and S. Miller, of whom I have before spoken, and P.C. Van Wyck, who was a man of fine talents. . . .*"

Hammond then added the footnote: "A few words contained in the first edition are here omitted, as they have been supposed to imply an imputation against Mr. Van Wyck, not intended by the author." Jabez D. Hammond, *The History of Political Parties in the State of New York* (Cooperstown, N.Y., 1844), I, 423.

177

Clarkson Crolius[1] to Pierre, Jr. ALS
NYPL

New York July 13.1842.

Respected Sir

On the 2^{d} of July intended for the 4.th I published some revolutionary reminisce[nce]s, addressed to the surviving patriots of that day. I would have handed you the paper containing them, but was not apprised of the place you put up at the time. I now forward it to you.

I am Sir. Yours.
with high consideration of respect
Clarkson Crolius

1. Clarkson Crolius was the Grand Sachem of the Tammany Society. Stokes, V, 1533.

178

Pierre, Jr. to Thurlow Weed.[1] ALS
Morristown National Historic Park Library

PeeksKill July 21st 1842.

Confidential
Thurlow Weed Esqr
Dear Sir,

I observe by the Notification of the State Central Committee — That a State Convention of Whig Delegates from the different Counties in the State is to held at Syracuse on Wenesday, the 7^{h} day of September next — I would suggest the propriety of our friends in the different Districts to choose as many of the late Electors for General Harrison & Tyler too — as will conveniently attend — It will shew the public Opinion of the Empire State against the Acts and doings and the course taken by the Accidental President to break down the Whig Party — If this County should select me as a Delegate I will chearfully attend —

I write this in Confidence to You to mention to our friends that they may address Letters to influential Gentlemen in different Counties, that they make choice as Delegates the men who were Electors in 1840 —

I am with much Respect
Your Ob serv[t]
[torn]

[Addressed]
Thurlow Weed Esq[r]
Albany

[Endorsed]
Pierre Van Cortlandt
PeeksKill
July 21. 1842

---

1. Thurlow Weed was a self-educated man of humble background. In 1821, at the age of twenty-five, he began the publication of the Manlius *Republican*, and later became manager of the Clintonian newspaper, the Rochester *Telegraph*. His popularity with Rochester businessmen resulted in his being sent to Albany to secure a charter for a bank. A tireless worker and gifted organizer, he made many friends in high places and was largely responsible for swinging New York's electoral vote to John Quincy Adams in 1824. In 1828 he became the leader of the Anti-Masonic movement in western New York using, after 1830, his newly founded Albany *Evening Journal* as a mouthpiece for this political and quasi-religious movement. He later hired Horace Greeley to edit the New York *Jeffersonian*, which became the organ of the New York Whig party. Weed was virtual dictator of the state's Whig organization during the late 1830's, and his support of William H. Seward made possible the latter's gubernatorial victory over William L. Marcy. Throughout the 1840's Weed and Seward controlled

the Whig machine in New York. Under Tyler — the "Accidental President" — the alliance of former Jacksonian Democrats and Whigs began to fall apart in New York. After 1855 Weed supported the Republicans and was a major backer of Seward at the party's presidential convention in 1860. Alexander, I, 294, 317–319, 324, 338, 374, 394–401; II, 200, 229–232.

179

R.G. Thompson to Pierre, Jr. ALS
SHR

Yorktown Aug. 15th 1843.

Gen. Van Cortlandt.

Dear Sir.

I received your note accompanying the Pamphlets of Dr. Pusey, and a bundle of Papers; for which, and the numerous others which you have sent me, you will permit me most heartily to tender my acknowledgements. In the fears which you express in reference to the spread of Popery I fully participate.[1] The followers of the Pope are making gigantic efforts to obtain the ascendancy; and they are assisted by Catholics throughout Europe. The great, if not the only object, of the Leopold Foundation in Austria, at the head of which is Prince Metternich is to sow the seeds of Popery in the United States. Our country is considered in Catholic Europe as missionary ground, and hence they are pouring into it, (1) their friends, (2) their priests, (3) their private church members: and these are becoming so numerous as to sway, in some sections of the country, all the elections. I am told that in the city of Pittsburgh it is never known how an election will result, until the Catholic organ, a paper entirely under the control of the Catholic priest, has taken its side: and the Catholics of the city vote to a man as their priest directs.

Another ground of fear is found in the efforts which are making to exclude the Bible from our system of education.[2] In some school districts in the city of N.Y. it seems the Bible is a sectarian book — a Protestant affair, which must be excluded from the schools, with all others which contain any selections from its sacred pages: and all this is demanded as a sacrifice to the tender consciences of a portion of our fellow citizens. And what gives to this fact its greatest importance is, that it seems not only to excite no alarm in the public mind, but to receive to some extent public approbation.

The Bible, Dr Sir, as you well know, was considered by the fathers of this nation as the great charter of human rights — the only correct standard of morals, — and the only adiquate source of all moral and religious knowledge. When they received the elementary principles of their education it was almost the only class-book. From it they derived those pure, enobling, and patriotic sentiments, and it inspired them with that noble daring in defence of the rights of their country and of mankind, which have made them the admiration of the world. What a different set of men would they have been, if they had been educated under the teachings of the Pope, or in the doctrines of a Voltaire, or a Robespierre? What our country owes to Protestantism and a so called sectarian Bible, may be ascertained from a comparison of our own country with Austria, Spain, Portugal, and France in the days of her revolution — countries in which the Bible has been proscribed for ages by the Pope, and its reading prohibited. Who that loves his country would wish to see her peaceful, upright, intelligent, and industrious citizens converted into the slaves of a ghostly superstition, or the victims of priestly domination, such as may be seen in most papal countries; or into the frantic and blood-thirsty demons of a Paresian mob, activated by the principles of a French philosophy? And does not, my Dear Sir, the history of the world teach, that where the Bible does not exert its appropriate influence upon the mass, and especially in training of the young in the virtue and admonition of the Lord, such is the tendency and fate of human affairs.

I regard then the introduction of the anti-protestant

principle of excluding the Bible from our common schools as an alarming feature of the present times. Our country was organized as a Protestant nation, and not as Roman Catholic, and the principles on which it was founded and rose to eminence should never be abandoned.

Excuse Dear Sir the lenth of this rambling letter. It is a subject in which I feel deeply. May the Lord long preserve to you the blessings of health, and to us all, the great principles in which you were educated, and which were those of your fathers.

I remain Dear Sir, yours affectionately
R.G. Thompson

[Addressed]
Gen. Pierre Van Cortlandt
Peekskill NY.

---

1. This correspondent evidently shared Pierre's convictions regarding the growing "menace" of Catholicism. It is not too surprising to find Pierre among the ranks of those, like Samuel F. B. Morse, who feared the influx of Catholics in New York. The so-called nativist movement first appeared in the 1830's in New York and enthusiastically endorsed the incorporation of its anti-foreigner stance into the local political platforms of the Whigs during the following decade.

   Pierre apparently had read and then sent Thompson pamphlets by the Reverend Edward B. Pusey (1800–1882), a leading Anglican fundamentalist.

2. New York City Catholics, under the leadership of the dynamic Bishop John Hughes, sought to eliminate the use of the Protestant version of the Bible as a text in the city's common schools. The issue soon became politically involved, especially when the local Whig press launched nativist attacks against Hughes, his Catholic adherents, and all foreign newcomers. John W. Pratt, *Religion, Politics,* and *Diversity: The Church-State Theme in New York History* (Ithaca, N.Y., 1967), pp. 164–192.

180

Pierre, Jr. to Richard R. Voris. ALS
SHR

Confidential

Peeks Kill March 16, 1844.

R.R. Vorhis Esqr
Dear Sir,

My Father in the year 1776, retired from his Estate at Croton River. The British Army had taken the possession of the City of New York — In the Spring of 1777 he rented the Old Domain of Col. Henry Beekman at Rhinebeck Landing my Aunt Gertruydt Beekman was then Alive — She died that Spring — My father and his family occupied that Domain until The Spring of 1780 when he removed his Family to Amelia Town, in the Interior of Dutchess County — He remained there until the Spring of 1783. when he removed his Family to this House I now reside at — the reason he stopt here was that the Old Manor House at Croton was not in a situation to take My mother & family there — As the House had been occupied by our Army as an Out post — The Tories having taken away every door and window & he could not move there until it was made tenetable & comfortable — He immediately sent Carpenters to put the House in repair — The Farm was in good Order & the fences had not been destroyed, (The Odell farm of which you enquired about was in compleat Order) Every thing was in good Order except the House — I mentioned that he stopt here because this House although then Only One Story appeared to him an eligible stopping place until he could repair the Old Manor House — This farm at that time had no fence on it whatever[.] It had all been destroying by our Army and the whole of it was a perfect Common — While my Father was making his Arrangements in putting the Old Manor House in order for him to go & reside there — The American Army was discharged — My Brother came here & asked my Father whether he could go & remain at Croton until he placed himself in business — My Father told him he might — But as soon as the House was repaired & which he had employed Carpenters to do it. — He would move his family down As this property was ruined by the Army — He could not remain here & must go home

My Brother did not say anything at that time adverse — But as soon Doors Windows &c. were made to the House and my Father telling him that he intended to remove from here to Croton — My Brother behaved very improper & told my Father to remain where he was — that he had permitted him to go to Croton & that he would occupy it — My Mother who was a pious religious woman, but it appeared She loved my Brother more than Other Children & could not see Nor beleive any improper act of him — My Father remained here under every privation, while my Brother enjoyed all his Estate about Croton River from 1783 until the Death of my Father May 1, 1814[.] In the year 1801 — I married — The next year I raised the Second Story to my House in the Year (I think) of 1805 or 1806[.] My Father & mother left me & went to Croton[.] All this time from 1783 — until the time of my Fathers death My Brother had all his Estate under his Controul & management & receiving all the profits as well on the North Side of Croton as the South — My Father had the Controul of not any thing My Brother had it all —

Now in regard to the Underhill Lease I remember very distinctly — The Legislature were then in Session in 1792 in New York My Father — Brother & myself (I was a Member of assembly — my Brother a Senator & my Father Lt Govr.) lodged at Verdine Elsworth, in Maiden Lane — I saw my Brother in close confab with Robert Underhill and after their Confab he related to my Father the Object[.] Robt. Underhill had in view to get a Lease for the waters of Croton River &c. &c. My Father was very Adverse to it & would not consent to it But through the persuasions of my Brother & his accustomed perseverance would not hear to any thing my Father said in opposition Underhill must have a Lease — at an ill judge Moment my Father at length acquiesced — This is the Truth of that transaction & which I could attest to — I was opposed to it But my Brother replied it was none of my business as I had nothing to do with it — I was therefore compelled to be passive[.] How was this? My Father sold a Piece of Land the n^{o}. of Acres I dont know to Mattocks My Father gave Mattocks a Deed for it — he could not pay for it and transferred it to my Brother — He could not pay for it & my Brother accepted a Deed from Mattocks but my Father never received a Cent for it, This is now a part of the Kipp farm —

With respect to the mill my Brother built (Jesse Fields Mill) the Timber was all cut on the South Side of Croton[.] My Fathers Oxen were sent from here to draw it out they were there a long time & one night the Oxen left the place where they were fed — came down to Croton a[t] the ferry & were nearly been drowned — from that Circumstance I know the Timber was got for the mill on the South Side of Croton —

As a farther proof that my Brother took all the management & profits of my Fathers property — I will rilate this circumstance — It was at the time the Yellow fever was raged in New York & Every Person wished to get a retreat in the Country — I rode to Croton very Early in the morning from this place I arrived at Croton about half past Eight OClock in the morning met Abraham Underhill at the Ferry House passed him without speaking — I rode up to the House at Croton left my Horse standing, found my Brother walking on the Piazza in deep thought. I addressed him good morning my Brother he continued walking in a great thought — I repeated cannot you find leisu[r]e to speak to me — At last he replied — Have you seen Ab^{m} Underhill I answered Yes what of that — He has been here & wants me to purchase all the Surplus water of Croton River which he holds by his Lease & what do you think he asks for it? I answered all your Property here farm & all — He became Outrageous said I meant to insult him as a fool & treated me so unbecoming that I was on the departure[.] He then became a little Cold &

asked me whether I intended to insult him — I told him not — Then he related that Ab^{m} Underhill would give him all the Surplus water of Croton River — If he would obligate himself to pay for the Buildings they would put up — I laughed most heartily That my prediction was right — They would put up so many buildings for a Summer Residence for his freinds that he never would be able to pay for — So I told him that my first prediction was right — At last when he came to reflect — He said Brother you have saved me from ruin — Forgive my petulance and stay the Day with me, how fortunate you have been here this morning or perhaps before to morrow I would have agreed with his Proposals — This transaction must have been before my Marriage in 1801 — & this is another proof that he took all my Fathers property in his direction —

Now in respect of the lease given by H. Beekman and his wife Gertruydt to my Father for lives &^{c} &^{c}. &^{c}. you have it with the Assignment to my Brother Gilbert & his devise to me — That speaks for itself — Only that I have paid in 1823 — $3000 — ignorantly & innocently as the Lease was always kept from my Inspection untill I had paid the money — But I presume My Sisters Beekman and Van Rensselaer will do me justice when the Appraisement is made for the waters of Croton River — The whole of that transaction — about the Lease & my Fathers will is a very delicate Subject — I therefore refrain any thing about it — My Brother was the Chief Negociater respecting my paying so much money promising me whatever I allowed there he would pay — But it was as all his promisses to me he never performed that or any Other he engaged to do for me[1] — I have written this for your Own Eye — It would not do to make a publick Exposure — You may Argue it from these facts — But this Letter must be seen by no other Person than yourself — which you will hand me hereafter —

Yours respectfully

P. V^{n}. Cortlandt

I wrote this some time since but neglected sending it to you

---

1. The bitter family feud between Pierre Van Cortlandt and his nephew Philip G. Van Wyck continued long after the nephew vacated the Manor house at Croton in 1836. As the years progressed, Pierre seemed to become obsessed with the notion that he and his father had been used by his domineering older brother, Philip; that, at least, is the theme of this letter to his lawyer, Richard Voris. It was Philip, according to Pierre, who cajoled the father into permitting Philip to occupy the Manor house at Croton and, at the same time, forced their father and mother to reside elsewhere after the Revolutionary War; furthermore, for a number of years Philip had tricked both Pierre and his son, Pierre III, out of their rightful heritage, the house and estates at Croton.

   The lawsuit against the Underhills stemmed from the action of Pierre, Sr. and Philip in leasing Croton River water rights to them for milling activities. The Underhills, particularly Abraham and Joshua, who had acquired Robert Underhill's share, were given exclusive use of Croton River water for a period of twenty years. During that time they could build whatever buildings were necessary for dwelling and milling purposes. At the conclusion of the twenty years, independent appraisers were to evaluate the buildings, and the concerned parties were to arrange an amicable financial settlement based on assessed valuations. Of course, such amicability never occurred. Suits and countersuits began in 1813 and dragged on through the years. The appraisers evaluated the mill properties at $18,000, a sum which was supposed to be paid to the Underhills by Pierre, Sr. and Philip. Philip then claimed that he was not a party to the agreement and that any final settlement must come from his father's holdings. Furthermore, it was charged that the assessors had overrated the value of the property. When Pierre, Sr. died in 1814, the suits were renewed, now naming Philip and the other heirs to the father's estate. Philip G. Van Wyck became a party to the suits, and so did his uncle, Pierre, Jr. Then each began to sue the other. *Cases in the Court of Errors of the State of New York,* Johnson, XVII, *New York Reports* pp. 405–436; "Philip Van Cortlandt and Others vs. Abraham Underhill and Others, January 23, 1815," Chancery Court Records, NYSL; New York Chancery Reports, Annotated 2 Johnson, p. 339. See also No. 182.

181

Anthony Lamb to Pierre, Jr. ALS
SHR

New York April 11.1844.

General Van Cortlandt
Dear Sir

I have received your favor the Books of the Society are in the hands of E.P. Manellin on which the Accounts and transactions with your brother are Recorded. I spoke to Mr Manellin and he said he would get the Books from Charles Chulor the former Secretary and I will then examine them and do what is necessary as far as in my power. I will call on M^rs. Jordan & see what is wanted.[1] We yesterday buried Genl. Lewis President of the Society[2] I was in hopes to have met you at the Funeral.

Sincerely yours,
Anthony Lamb

[Addressed]
Genl. Pierre V. Cortlandt
Peekskill
New York

---

1. In a quest for information regarding his brother Philip's accounts with the Society of the Cincinnati, Pierre wrote to Anthony Lamb, son of the Revolutionary War hero John Lamb, and asked him to check the Society's records. The individuals named in this letter were second generation or collateral members of the Society. Pierre belonged because Philip had been a founding member but had left no direct heirs to continue the membership.

2. General Morgan Lewis (1754–1844) followed a distinguished military career by active participation in New York politics in both legislative and executive capacities. A former governor of New York, he was inducted as president of the Society of the Cincinnati in 1839 and remained in that office until his death. Schuyler, pp. 248–249.

182

Pierre, Jr. to Cornelia Beekman. ADf
SHR

Peeks kill April 24, 1844 —

My dear Sister

I wrote to you in a great hurry on monday as I had many Letters to write about the Underhill judgment against us — I will now be more particular & state all the facts respecting the Property I possess here —
Viz — On the 27 September 1773 Henry Beekman & his Wife Gertruydt gave a Lease to my Father to River Lot N° 10 in the manor of Cortlandt — called Anthonys nose Lot and 347 acres of Land which is the farm I reside on, for the lives of Joanna Van Cortlandt & her Two Sons Stephen and Pierre, for a Stipulated Rent or rather a nominal Rent[.] By the Last Will & Testament of Gertruydt Beekman She devised this Property to my Father during his natural life, & after his discease to his Son Gilbert — By the Law abolishing Entails the demise to Gilbert was vested in him in Fee — On the 2d Day of January 1784 My Father assigned the Said Lease to his son Gilbert reserving the Rents to my Mother during her life — On the 17th September 1784 Gilbert Van Cortlandt made his last will & testament and devised all this Property mentioned in the said Lease so assigned to him by his Father to me — By the Assignment of the Lease to his son Gilbert by my Father, my Father had Only his life Estate in the Land mentioned in the Leases & I by my Brother Gilbert last will & testament devising the whole property to me — I was Bona fide the whole owner & possessor of this property, No Person could claim the least right, or Title to it whatever — The Lease given by Henry Beekman & his wife Gertruydt My Father had assigned over to his Son Gilbert and could not have any Controul over the property only during his Life which he claimed his Life Estate in it by virtue of the last Will and testament of Gertruydt Beekman, as for the Lease he had no Interest for that he had

assigned to his son Gilbert — I always understood my Father had got just a Lease and I also knew from hearsay that my Life was Mentioned in it — But I never saw the Lease & the assignment When I paid the three thousand Dollars to my Sisters nor had I ever saw it before, I took everything for granted paid the money & Ph G. Van Wyck me the Lease — My Sisters Quit Claim on this property (by virtue as was said of the Lease) I took all the Papers packed them in my Desk & did not look at them — I felt hurt that I had paid so large a sum of money for Property which did not rent for $200 — in rents — Nor perhaps would I have ever looked at them again — Until I was informed by Mr Vorhis that Van Wyck's Counsel OConner had intimated to him — that Van Wyck intended to make me the Chief Debtor to the Underhills because I possessed great property from my Father at this place with GREAT VALUABLE LEASES & wished me to inform him (Vorhis) how it was — Then for the first time since 1823 I looked at the Lease & discovered the Assignments of the Lease by my Father to my Brother Gilbert — The next day I met Mr Vorhis at my Sons — handed him the Lease with my Brother Gilberts Will — which Mr Vorhis has left with the Master in Chancery in New York who is appointed to investigate the whole Concern on the exhibiting the Lease & my Brother Gilberts Will — OConner (Van Wyck's Counsel) said he must adjourn the Investigation until next Saturday, for he found by the Assignments of the Lease & my Brother Gilberts will I inherited no Part of this Estate from my Father — But on the Contrary had paid $3000 — for property which then belonged to Me —

I now intend to get Proof that my Father sold the Bowery estate to pay my Brothers indebtedness to the Society of Cincinnati[.] If I can make that out — PhVanWyck will have to pay the whole of the Underhill judgment Mr Jordan told me that would exert himself to saddle the whole Debt on Van Wyck —

I have written to you thus fully to let you know all the

Concerns & what I have done — I exhibited the Lease to save myself from Van Wycks Information from my Fathers Will that there was a vast deal of property left me by my Father in valuable rents at this place, When it appears my Father had no right whatever to the least particle of it after my mothers life & could not dispose any part of it as it belonged to me — When I lately discovered the assignment of the Lease I was astonished that my Father should have made such a devise in his will — He must have forgot that he had assigned it Or he could not have done such injustice to me — Had the Lease with the Assignments been shewn to me before I paid the money I should most certainly never have paid it, Because It was My Property uncontrovertible — But through ignorance I did it — & the Money I paid — and which was done through the absolute persuasion and promise of my Brother that he would immediately reimburse me and repay it to me again — But so it is I paid in the year 1783 Three Thousand Dollars — My Brother has not paid me a Cent on his promise — He had all my Fathers property & I spent the most valuable part of my life to assist my Father & Mother at this place when at the same time I had the assurance & promise of General Hamilton to take me in his Office as a Partner to do the Attorney's business with an adequate compensation But I choose to be here & assist my Parents rather than accept this great offer — I did it & do not Repent that I obeyed the Commandment — What may be the ulterior destiny of my life I cannot tell but I trust that I have always lived in high respect & esteemed by my Conduct[.] So it will end[1]

[Endorsed]
Copy of a Letter
to Sister Beekman

---

1. It is difficult to accept, at face value, Pierre's statement that he had paid $3,000 in order to obtain the release of property which he already legally owned, especially when one remem-

bers that he was a trained attorney. While it is dangerous to read psychological motivations and values into such historical material, note Pierre's whining comment, written at the age of eighty-two, that his mother "loved my Brother more than Other Children & could not see Nor beleive any *improper act* of him" (No. 180). And when commenting upon Philip's activities, Pierre seemed to border on paranoia.

His memory also began to recall only those stories it desired to retain. Pierre recounts, for example, that he remained in Peekskill looking after his parents at a point in time when "I had the assurance & promise of General Hamilton to take me in his Office as a Partner to do the Attorney's business with an adequate compensation." There is no evidence supporting such a statement. It is known that Pierre, Sr. paid Alexander Hamilton the sum of £ 150 to train his son in the law. Hamilton made no reference to Pierre, Jr. during his apprenticeship years, and Pierre, Jr. certainly never distinguished himself in the law. See *VCFP,* III, xxxviii–xxxix.

The statement concerning the sale of Bowery properties so that Philip's outstanding debts to the Society of the Cincinnati could be discharged calls for some explanation. Philip was the first treasurer of the New York division of the Society at the close of the Revolution. He held various state and national certificates in the name of the Society just prior to the time of Alexander Hamilton's funding and assumption schemes. Philip apparently invested some of the monies in his charge, for which he became personally obligated. By 1799–1800 there was an outstanding sum of over $3,500 due the Society. Philip was sued for this sum and he subsequently reimbursed the Society for the amount plus court costs. Philip Van Cortlandt to the Society of the Cincinnati, April 11, 1795; Leonard Bleecker to Philip, December 18, 1798; Leonard Bleecker to Philip, March 30, 1798; Jacob Reed, Jr., Matthew Clarkson, and Brockholst Livingston vs. Philip, April 10, 1800; all manuscripts in NYHS.

183

James Burt[1] to Pierre, Jr. ALS
SHR

Warwick Orange County June the 13th 1844.

Honorable Sir

I have received your friendly letter of the 8th instant whitch seemed to renew my reflections on our long acquaintanc in publick life . . and altho I am permited to breath the air to 4 ckore & 4 yeares I Still feel very desirus that the princeples that moved to action in 1776 might prevail in this republick and ther is no man — tolked of for Chief Magistrate that comes so near the likeness of 1776 as Henry Clay — and I am very sorry that Martin Van Buren was not nominated by the Lowcoos [Locofocos] had that been done I should have been assured of Clys victory but if our opponents in those North and Middle States is going to swllow John the traitor and texes and the ante Tarrif princeples and swllow Polk our hopes of success seemes to vanish but I hope the god of providence will stimelate the Whigs of 1840 to come forth with their 225.989 votes for Electors as in 1840

my respected friend you express a Desire to Come and visit the old wore out farmer and wish to be informed whare to holt on the rale road[.] I expect you would wish to start either from New York or Peirmont and if from either the boat from the foot of Duanes Street starts at 7 oclock A M you will then step on board the passage Carr and arive at the depo at Chester at 12 or one oclock and if you Come up on Monday or Wednesday you will find a stage standing ready to bring you to Warwick the distance to my dwelling is 9 Miles from the Chester depo[.] should you resolve to coll as you propose will you please to informe me by letter the day you intend to Come so that I may be at home if spared in life for it might be if you Came unawars that I might be absent whitch could be a disappointment to us both — please to excuse my bad writeing & spelling my old trembling renders me incapeable of making a good pen or useing well when made

my best respects to you
James Burt

the Honorabe
Peire V Cortland

[Addressed]
The Honororable
Peire Van Courtland
Peekskill
Westchester County

---

1. James Burt, the president of the Electoral College in 1840, was an old-time New York politician. He began his long career in 1798 as an assemblyman, was a state senator, and served with Pierre as a presidential elector in 1800 and again in 1840. Burt obviously was an ardent Whig who could not continue supporting John "the traitor" Tyler, and who pinned all his hopes on Henry Clay. Werner, pp. 273, 281, 284, 321, 470–471; Richard Riker to Pierre, Jr., November 28, 1840 (No. 173).

184

James Burt to Pierre, Jr. ALS
NYPL

Warwick the 17th of August 1844.

Honble Sir

I have this day received your favor of the 15th instant and was Glad to learn that you was yet liveing and in helth I had been expecting to hear from you for many weeks and not only to hear from you but to see you at my house but have been dissappointed — but I do not bring any Charge of fault against you, I am sorry for the sufferings of your much respected Sister[1] and I hope you will pay all attention to her that you may be Capeable of rendering. the political tideings from the south & west is Cheering and if New york Ohio and pensulvania will give Clay their vote and he should be spared in life I expect he will take a seat in the White house may the god of providence speed his way thither.[2]

I should be pleased to meet you and many other friends at Albany on the 27th but my privious engagements are such that I cannot meet my friends as I could wish if it should be convenient for you to give me Call at the old farm house please to give me notice in due time

James Burt

Honble Piere Vancourtland

---

1. It is unclear which sister had become ill. Cornelia (Van Cortlandt) Beekman died three years later, in 1847, and Ann (Van Cortlandt) Van Rensselaer survived until 1855.

2. Henry Clay came very close to winning the presidential prize in 1844. James K. Polk carried the Electoral College by 170 to 105, but his popular vote margin was much narrower — 1,337,000 to 1,299,000. In New York, Clay lost out to the abolitionist candidate James G. Birney.

185

Hamilton Fish[1] to Pierre, Jr. **ALS**
NYPL

Washington January 27.1845.

My Dear Sir

I owe you very many apologies for the length of time which has elapsed without an answer to your two esteemed favors of 21:Dec & 1st. inst — I have not had an opportunity, since their receipt, to make a personal examination as to whether my Father ever received the commutation[2] to which he was entitled under the act of the Continental Congress — I have made the enquiry & been informed that it was paid, but I intend before leaving this place to make an examination to satisfy myself as to the evidence of the payment — for I have no recollection of having ever heard him say any thing about it. & while engaged in making this Examination as to his pay, with your permission I will do the same in your behalf. (as also I am requested to do for our friend Major Popham)[3] & will advise you of the result.

You will observe from the Papers, that the Texas scheme[4] has passed the House by a large majority — but I have strong faith in the integrity of the Senate for the preservation of our Country, at least for a time — how long that time will be God in his Wisdom only knows — to me the prospect of the future looks gloomy. the old adage that "extremes often meet" cannot be applied to the territorial extent of your Country — that very extent constitutes our weakness — & yet blind to this fact we are our national & hereditary love of territorial aggrandisement, & are encouraging the natural disposition of our mind (the love of conquest) although the object of which we are in pursuit may produce the entire destruction of our present institution.

Are we prepared to admit Florida, & some four or five other Slave-States to be carved out of Texas, with their Slave Representation in Congress, to bear down, to over-ride the wishes & the interests of the free population of the North? And yet what is the North about? quiet under this effort to subjugate them? nay worse than quiet. It is the North which has effected their own degradation — on the villainous Texas vote there were seven votes in its favor from New England — nine from New York — three from New Jersey — & the whole of the Loco-focoism of Pennsylvania. when National interests are committed to such hands, need we wonder that both northern & national interests are sacrificed — the race of "dough-faces" is not yet extinct —

But I will not weary you, my Dear Sir, on this

subject — it was not my intention to have introduced it, but it has unconsciously forced itself here, & there is nothing left for me but to crave your pardon for my tedious letter, & to close it with my best wishes for your continued health & happiness, & to add the assurances of the sincere Esteem & Respect of

Your friend & Obed^{t} Servt
Hamilton Fish

Genl. Van Cortlandt

---

1. Hamilton Fish (1808–1893) was a distinguished politician and statesman from New York. At the time of this letter, Fish was completing a term in office as a Whig congressman. Unsuccessful in a bid for re-election on the Whig ticket, he returned to New York to practice law. He soon went on to serve as a U.S. Senator and as governor of New York. Possibly his most lasting fame came from his activities as Secretary of State during the Grant administration. Fish had joined the majority in the House in defeating a Texas annexation measure on January 25. *DAB,* IV, 397; *Biographical Directory American Congress,* p. 943; *Niles' Weekly Register,* February 1, 1845, p. 350.

2. Pierre had apparently requested information pertaining to Revolutionary War veterans' claims still outstanding against the federal government.

3. Major William Popham, a relict of the American Revolution, survived until 1847. Heitman (1914), p. 446; *VCFP,* II, 462–463.

4. The absorption of the Lone Star Republic into the Union became a major issue in the presidential campaign of 1844. If Texas became a part of the United States, there was a good chance that it would be divided into five units, with all or most eventually becoming slave states. President Tyler, a Southern Whig, desperately sought to bring Texas into the Union during his term. His political stance, particularly the possibility of providing increased slave state representation in Congress, alien-

ated his Whig supporters in the middle states. Those New Yorkers who had originally supported Henry Clay's bid for the presidency were also dismayed at the breach that had occurred between Tyler and Clay over internal improvements, the tariff, and banking issues. Fish was numbered among the disillusioned and disenchanted Whigs of New York.

186

Obituary Notice for Pierre, Jr.
Westchester Herald, June, 1848.

[ca. June 16, 1848].

Died, at his residence Near Peekskill on Tuesday the 13th Inst. Genl. Pierre Van Cortlandt in the 86th year of his age —

Such is the announcement of the death of one of the oldest and most famous of the citizens of our County — Genl. Van Cortlandt was born at Croton River on the 29th of August, 1762; & he was the son of Pierre Van Cortlandt (late Lieutenant Governor of this state) — and Joanna Livingston — at an Early age he entered Queens College — and at the time of his death was the oldest living Graduate — His Alma Mater had conferred upon him the degree of L.L.D. He was one of the Jefferson Electors. and was the last surviving elector from this State — He represented this District two years in the Congress of the United States, and was subsequently one of the Electoral College which voted for Genl. Harrison. At the time of his decease he was President of the Westchester County Bank — An Elder Sister, Mrs Beekman, died March 14th 1847 — And the only survivor of the family is the aged widow of the late Philip S. Van Rensselaer Esqr of Albany.

Genl. Van Cortlandt held a high place in the esteem of all who knew him — he was buried in the family burying grounds at Croton Manor on thursday — and a large concourse followed him to his tomb. His memory will long live in the hearts of all who knew him.

187

Last Will and Testament of Pierre, Jr. ADS [Copy]
SHR

February 11, 1848.

The last Will & testament of Pierre Van Cortlandt the Elder of Cortlandt near Peeks kill.

I the said Pierre Van Cortlandt being of Sound and disposing mind & memery do make this my last will & testament in manner following:

First I direct and order all my just debts and funeral Charges & Expenses to be paid by my Executors herein after named out of my personal Estate as soon as conveniently may be after my decease.

Second. I give & devise unto My Son Pierre Van Cortlandt Junr. all my farm house & Buildings thereon Whereon I now reside; and all my farms & Lands Lying above & northerly of Peekskill; and also all the farm Called the Mannor farm at the Mouth of Croton River where my said son now resides together with all the Land adjoining the farm which was devised to me by the last will & testament of my late Brother General Philip Van Cortlandt deceased, being part of front Lot number One & particularly described in the said devise in my said Brother's will and Containing about Six hundred acres all which said several farms & Lands I give & devise to my said son for & during his natural life, and at his death the farm and all & Every part thereof to be divided between and among all the lawful children of my said son Pierre who shall be then living & the descendants of such of them (if any) as may have died in Equal parts or portions Except that I give & devise to my Grandson Pierre the Eldest son of My Son Pierre the Manor House at Croton wherein My Son now resides with forty acres of Land round about the same to be located by him my said Grandson but not to Extend further East than the East line of the Garden which I devise to him in fee. All of which I give & devise to them my said grandchildren in manner & proportions aforesaid and to their respective heirs & assigns forever in fee. Subject nevertheless to the following provisions And grants, that is to say; In case my daughter in Law Catherine wife of my said Son should outlive & survive her said husband, and any of their said Children shall at my Son's death be under age then I give & grant to her the said Catherine the use of all the above mentioned farms & lands during the minority of my said Grand children or any of them, And after they shall attain their full age, or, after the death of my Son in case my Grandchildren shall all then be of age, in either case, thence there after I give & grant to my said daughter in Law the use & benefits of the one equal third part of all the aforesaid farms of Land & real estate during her natural life.

Third. I give & bequeath unto my colored Servant John Jackson commonly called Jack the sum of two hundred Dollars to be paid him by my Executors out of my personal estate.

And all the rest & residue of my Estate real & personal I give bequeath & devise to my said son Pierre Van Cortlandt Junr. forever and I hereby Appoint D^r^ J Romeyn Beck[,] James Stevenson[,] Richard R Voris & my Son Pierre Executors of this my said will & testament

In Witness whereof I have hereunto set my hand & seal this Eleventh day of February in the year of our Lord One Thousand Eight hundred & forty eight.

Pierre Van Cortlandt

Signed Sealed published &
declared by the testator as & for
his last Will & testament in
the presence of us who have here
unto at his request & in his presence

& the presence of Each other Subscribed
our names as Witnesses Hereto

Sigby B Milton[?]	New Brunswick N Jersey
John B Holmes	Cortlandt Westchester C°

Westchester County Is., Be it Remembered, that on the day of the date hereof, the last Will and Testament of Pierre Van Courtlandt, late of the County of Westchester deceased (being the foregoing written instrument), and duly proved before Lewis C. Platt, Surrogate of the said County, According to law, as and for the last will and testament of the real and personal estate of said deceased; which said last will and Testament and the proofs and examinations therein are recorded in this Office.

In testimony Whereof the Surrogate of the said County has herewith set his hand and offered his seal of office, this thirty first day of July Annodomini eight hundred and forty eight.

Lewis C. Platt
Surrogate

Additional Correspondence

Editor's Note

WHENEVER THE ASSUMPTION is made that the extant manuscripts relating to a particular historical publications project have been gathered and collated, invariably, additional materials emerge. Such is the case with the Van Cortlandt Family Papers. Some manuscripts previously held in private hands were subsequently donated to Sleepy Hollow Restorations or noted in dealers catalogs, while others were found in an abandoned trunk within a home scheduled for remodeling. In addition to those items which suddenly came to our attention, further materials are herein included at the discretion of the editor with the expectation that they will enhance our knowledge concerning this significant family.

These four volumes by no means contain all known manuscripts relating to the Van Cortlandts of Cortlandt Manor. Their business records and land papers could comprise another set of publications. Furthermore, it should be kept in mind that the Cortlandt Manor branch of the family remained distinct from the Van Cortlandts of New York City, Yonkers, and New Jersey.

Perhaps, if sufficient support could be obtained, the papers of those Van Cortlandts would be subsequently published. In this telephone age it is hard for us to realize that the only means of communication other than oral contact which existed at an earlier day remained the written word. Some families realized the significance of such materials and preserved them for posterity. We are fortunate that this abundance of historical riches remain for the Van Cortlandt family.

188

Peter Stuyvesant[1] to Pierre. ALS
SHR

[February 12, 1766.]

New York 31st Januy. 1761.

I have left a picture at my Lodging & if I Should not return I Desire it may be Sent to My Worthy friend Don Phillip Ferrigan at Pensacola

Corn: Livingston[2]

Dear Brother

the above is a Coppy of an order found amoungst Mr: Corn: Livingston Papers a Coppy of which you Can Send to Mrs: Ransaler if you think Proper. I have Just Now Recd: yours by G: Briggs[3] & am Very Glad to find that you are all well. I note you say that you intend to be Down next week. I Don't know how to Credt: that part of yr: Letter if you are here by ye 20th of March I shall think you have gest pretty well. we are all in Health thank God. My Father was here Just now & Desires his Love to you, Sister, & ye Children, we are all going to Dine with him, My Rib Joines with Me with assurance of best Respects to you & yours & am

yr Loving Brother
Pr: Stuyvesant

Petersfield ye 12 Feby: 1766

---

1. The son of Gerardus Stuyvesant, Peter Stuyvesant (1727–1805) was a New York businessman who lived at the family estate known as Petersfield, located approximately two miles from the hub of the city. Often away on business, Stuyvesant leased the residence on a number of occasions. Stokes, V, 1208.

2. The twelfth child of Gilbert and Cornelia (Beekman) Livingston, Cornelius Livingston died unmarried on September 3, 1750, at the age of eighteen. William W. Reese, "Family Bible of Joanna Livingston Wife of Pierre Van Cortlandt,"

Dutchess County Historical Society *Yearbook* (1942), XXVII, 72.

3. George Briggs of Westchester was charged with "treasonable practices" by the British in September of 1783, and was confined to the New York City jail for the remaining few months of the British occupation. He later served as a captain of militia until his resignation in 1797. *Manual of the Corporation of the City of New York, 1870* (New York, 1870), p. 906; *Council of Appointment, Military,* I, 77, 365.

189

Pierre to [?] Travis[1]. ALS
SHR

Manor of Cortlandt Aprill 22. 1766.

M^r: Traviss

I Should take it Kind of you if you Could Send Joseph Dean word from me That he Can send my Young horse if he Cannot Keep him to M^r: Bryants.[2] Or to Keep him till I Come up,

Yesterday I heard Some News from the Citty. Send you the Inclosed. Capt: Bishop[3] had Like to have fainted when he was Called before the Court which was Then Sitting. hope now That affairs may be In a better Situation. I Remain Your Friend to Serve —

Pierre Van Cortlandt

---

1. A number of Travis family members resided on the Manor. This letter could have been addressed to Hezekiah, Elijah, Absalom, Robert, or Joseph Travis. *Heads of Families 1790*, p. 197.

2. Joseph Dean and John Bryant were tenants of the Manor. *Ibid.*

3. "Capt. Bishop" is a reference to Joshua Bishop, who participated in the tenant uprising against John Van Cortlandt. See the following letter.

190

Pierre to [unknown]. ADfs
SHR

[April, 1766].
Wednesday Evening

Honored–S^{r}

I Receved the Inclosed by Express from B^{r}: James Livinston,[1] which I now send to you by my Son Philip, Express. from which you will be better Inform'd

The Last Mob or Ryot here In the manor was when, Pendegrass. &. Bishop. Took out of possession, One Brady. on Cossin Cortlandts Land & put in Isaac Wrigh, Since which have heard nothing from the East ward only am Credibly Inform'd that Pendigrass publickly Said by way of proclamation, that he bid Diffiance to any officer or person that should molest or Disturb any of his Men at their perril & that he wod Vindicate them at all Events. and belive his Interests here in this Manor More than is generally Expected; as a great many such Turbulent fellows Only want oppertunity, Either to be screan'd from paying any Rents at all (or Such as they say shall be Reasonable) or from paying thier Just Debts — and do wish that Law never Should take place[2] —
Am Dr Sir with the greatest Respect
to you Cousen Livingston & family
Your affectionate kindsman &

Very Hum^{l}. Ser^{t} —
PVC

---

1. James Livingston (1728–1790) was the son of Gilbert and Cornelia (Beekman) Livingston and the grandson of the first lord of Livingston Manor. He married Judith Newcomb (1733–1808), the daughter of Thomas and Judith (Woodworth) Newcomb. Residing in Poughkeepsie, he served as a captain of militia and as the sheriff of Dutchess County prior to the Revolution. In 1776 Livingston was a member of the Provincial

Congress, and in the following year he acted as chairman of the Committee of Safety. J.W. Poucher, "Dutchess County Men of the Revolutionary Period: James Livingston, and Some of His Descendants," Dutchess County Historical Society *Yearbook* (1943), XXVIII, 67.

2. Discontent between the manor lords and their tenants exploded in a series of so-called "land riots" in the 1760's. What began in the eastern counties of the province, especially in Dutchess County, with the Daniel Nimham countroversy in 1765, had spread to Westchester County by March of the following year. A small group of yeomen from Cortlandt Manor gathered at the home of Daniel Brundage on February 28, 1766, presumably to plan the strategy for their actions. They were, in addition to Brundage, Joshua Bishop (whom Pierre referred to as "Capt: Bishop"), Daniel Chapman, Daniel and Richard Cornell, Joseph Tidd, and Isaac Wright. Contemptuously called "levellers" by their detractors, these farmers sought to alter the landlord–tenant relationships which had been operating under a system of life estates and term leases. In the interest of greater independence and security, they sought a system of absolute fees.

On April 10, 1766, Joseph Golding was removed from his house and property on Cortlandt Manor. This was accomplished, according to Attorney General John Tabor Kempe's charges, with "force and arms." In the process of ejecting Golding, the armed group apparently assaulted him as well, "so that of his life it was greatly dispaired." On a second occasion, one week later on April 17, the rioters, joined by other tenants, removed Simon Brady from his property in an attempt to install one of their own, Isaac Wright, in his place. Not until April 19 was any legal action taken, at which time twenty-one of the yeomen were "brought into the Supreme Court *en banc* by the sheriff of Westchester in virtue of Mr. Chief Justice's warrant."

Joining the Westchester yeomen for the ejectment of Brady were several Dutchess County men, among them William Pendergast (Prendergast), who would later be charged with high treason for his role in the Dutchess County disturbances in May and June. That trial, which began on August 6, 1766, ended with his being declared guilty. The verdict was delivered despite the brave efforts of his wife, who served as his attorney and who so ably defended him that she drew the admiration of all who witnessed her efforts. After the verdict was announced, she immediately rushed to Governor Henry Moore, who offered a reprieve from the death sentence which had been imposed. King George III granted a pardon in December.

The Westchester case was not as celebrated or as extensive as that of Pendergast. No trials for treason resulted. After posting rather sizable bonds — "a recognizance of £200 with two sureties of £100 each" — only small fines were actually imposed. The most stringent sentence was that upon Joshua Bishop, who was ordered to post bond of £100 New York money "to keep the peace for five years."

For the legal procedures relating to these cases, see: "A list of the persons concerned in the riots in Cortlandt Manor taken from four informations," *John Tabor Kempe Papers,* Lawsuits C-F, *sub. nom.* Joshua Bishop *et. al.*, NYHS; "Draft of an information for a riot — The King ag^{t}. Daniel Cornell and others," *Ibid.;* Julius Goebel, Jr. and T. Raymond Naughton, *Law Enforcement in Colonial New York* (New York, 1944), p. 203. For a recent interpretation of these events, consult Sung Bok Kim, *Landlord and Tenant in Colonial New York Manorial Society 1664–1775* (Chapel Hill, N.C., 1978), pp. 346–415.

191

Gertrude (Van Cortlandt) Beekman to "Cousin." ALS
Clermont State Historical Park

Rhine beck June th25 1771.

Dear Couzen

I received your letter by Mr Livingston with pleasure I Congratulate you on the birth of your Grand Son May he live to be a blessing & honor to his family[.]I am happy to hear you intend soon to pay me a visit I must trouble you to get twenty pounds for me of Thompson the Barber & give him receipt Keating also owes me Fiffteen pounds you can desire him to send me in part of pay two pound Congo or Green tea and a Ream of paper[.]All here desire to be remembered to yourself & family I remain with affection —

Dear Couzen
Your Aunt
Gertruyd Beekman

192

Pierre to Robert R. Livingston, Jr.[1] ALS
Swann Galleries Inc. Auction Sale 1052:
February 10, 1977

New York, January 11, 1776.

[In reference to the domestic manufacture of saltpeter, which Congress is expected][2] to give all due Encouragement . . . in this view, it is probable that there will be full employ for Powder Mills; and for this reason we beg leave to recommend the reErection of the Patriotic Work of the late Mr. Justice Livingston[3] to your immediate attention.

Pierre Van Cortlandt

[Addressed]
Robert R. Livingston, Jr.
Claremont
Dutchess County

---

1. Statesman, farmer, diplomat, and juror, Robert R. Livingston (1746–1813) graduated from King's College in 1765 and began a law practice in New York City prior to the Revolution. Elected to the Continental Congress during the war, he served as Secretary of Foreign Affairs in 1783 and as minister to France from 1801 to 1804. Upon his retirement from public office, Livingston pioneered experiments with merino sheep and played a vital role in the work of Robert Fulton of *Clermont* fame. *DAB,* XI, 320–325; George Dangerfield, *Chancellor Robert R. Livingston of New York 1746–1813* (New York, 1960).

2. Agreeable to the recommendation of the Continental Congress dated February 23, 1776, the New York Committee of Safety voted "to errect Works for the manufacturing of Salt-Petre, in every considerable Town or Village in the several Counties." In addition to this ambitious aim, the Committee sponsored a newspaper series as early as January which detailed the making of saltpetre and gunpowder. New York *Mercury*, April 22, 1776; Stokes, IV, 911.

3. A member of the famed Livingston clan, Robert R., Sr. (1718–1775) first served on the Admiralty bench and later as puisne judge of the Supreme Court of New York. As father-in-law of General Richard Montgomery, Livingston was rumored to have died of grief upon hearing of Montgomery's death before the gates of Quebec on December 31, 1775. In fact, however, Livingston died on December 9. *Pennsylvania Gazette*, December 20, 1775; *DAB*, XI, 319–320.

193

Alexander McDougall[1] to Pierre. ADS
SHR

July 6, 1784.

This shall certify that the Honorable Pierre Van Cortlandt Esquire, was duly elected an honorary Member of the Society of the Cincinnati this day.

Given under my hand at the
annual meeting held at New
York this Sixth day of July.1784[2]
Alex.McDougall
President

Attest

J.W.Fairlie Secy —[3]

---

1. A native of Scotland, Major General Alexander McDougall (1732–1786) was a prominent New York businessman and

political activist prior to the Revolution. During the war McDougall was in charge of the Highlands and later replaced Benedict Arnold as commander at West Point. As founder and first president of the Bank of New York, McDougall turned conservative and spent much of his leisure time fulfilling his responsibilities as president of the New York branch of the Society of the Cincinnati. *DAB,* XII, 21–22.

2. The annual meeting of the Society of the Cincinnati for 1784 was held at Cape's Tavern on July 5. The officers elected for the year ensuing were Alexander McDougall, president; Governor George Clinton, vice president; Philip Van Cortlandt, treasurer; Nicholas Fish, assistant treasurer; and James W. Fairlie, secretary. New York *Packet* July 8, 1784.

3. A New York City businessman and financier, James W. Fairlie acted as aide-de-camp to General von Steuben throughout most of the Revolution. In addition to his position in the Cincinnati, Fairlie served on the board of New York Fortifications in 1807, and as a negotiating commissioner for the exchange of property between the federal government and New York in 1814. Heitman (1914), p. 221.

194

Gilbert to Pierre. ALS
NYHS

N. York Decr 19, 1785.

Dr Papa

I now send you as many News Papers of the Different Printers as I could collect, among those now sent you will find all the Letters that have pass'd between Mr. Jay & Mr. Little Page.[1] Mrs. VanWyck[2] is pritty well, her Husband, in my oppinion, is going to the Shades. — Philip this morning leaves Town, has been here One Day. —

I have bot Goods at Vendue to Amo^t of £ 160 Ad. in our way Cheap. And now stand in want of money, if convenient, please to send the balance of the within Act[t] for I was oblig'ed to take the Company's Money.[3] —

My love to Mamma, Nancy, &c.
Your Son, Gilbert V. Cortlandt

---

1. John Jay first met Lewis Littlepage when the young Virginian came to reside with the Jay family in Spain. This arrangement was prompted by a request from Thomas Adams, a friend of Jay's, and by the uncle and guardian of Littlepage, Benjamin Littlepage. During his residence with the family, which lasted several years, Jay assumed payment for Littlepage's expenses with the expectation of reimbursement by his guardian. The relationship between Jay and his charge became strained on several occasions. Against Jay's advice, Littlepage joined a Spanish military expedition to Cadiz. Despite his disapproval, Jay underwrote his expenses and paid his salary as a captain for six months. Littlepage eventually was introduced to higher circles of acquaintances and to loftier styles of life. In 1784 he met Stanislaus, King of Poland, who offered him a permanent position at court. Littlepage then obtained a one-year leave of absence in order to return to the United States to seek permission of Congress to enter the Polish service.

Littlepage returned to Virginia to settle his affairs and found that his uncle and guardian had died some time before. The governor of Virginia, Patrick Henry, entrusted him with a sum of money with which to pay the French sculptor Houdon for his completed statue of George Washington. Littlepage took this money with him to New York, where he presented petitions and letters on his own behalf to Jay so as to be introduced to Congress. At this time, Jay requested payment of the long-standing Spanish debt. Meeting resistance, Jay pressed a suit through Alexander Hamilton and Robert Morris and served Littlepage who was about to embark for France, with a writ. Littlepage retaliated by publishing accusations against Jay in the *Daily Advertiser* of December 6, 1785. He asserted that Jay should have sued him upon his arrival in the United States, that Jay ignored his letters on the matter, and — more seriously — that Jay had delayed in presenting his petitions to Congress. Jay took the unusual step of replying in print in the next day's issue of the newspaper. Soon the dispute took on political overtones, as enemies of Jay conspired with Littlepage to bring more public attention to the accusations. Brockholst Livingston and Barbé-Marbois, the French charge d'affaires, were two who sought to humiliate Jay. Littlepage subsequently settled the debt, which some have asserted was accomplished with the funds entrusted to him by Patrick Henry. In January, 1787, Jay published a pamphlet containing the correspondence which had passed between the two men. Six months later Francis Childs, publisher of the *Daily Advertiser,* printed Littlepage's responses. Supposedly spent by a dissolute life, Littlepage died at the age of forty in 1802. William Jay, *The Life of John Jay* (New York, 1833), I, 204–229, Monaghan, pp. 235–243.

2. Gilbert made reference to his younger sister, Catharine (1751–1829), the wife of the ailing Abraham Van Wyck.

3. In mentioning the "Company's Money," Gilbert was no doubt indicating that he withdrew funds used by G. Cortlandt Company, ironmongers, located at 42 Dock Street, New York City. *Polk's Directory* (1786), p. 24.

195

Gilbert to Joanna (Livingston) Van Cortlandt. ALS NYHS

New York March 25th 1786.

Dear Mamma,

Papa just now received your Letter wherein you mention the receiving of the bundle Hannah Mangle[1] is to make up for me. I have wrote you another Letter on that subject by Mr Ferris[2] — Papa will write to Justis Waistcoat[3] concerning his work — The Carpenters Tools he desired me to get for him I sent to Mr Beekmans. Six Weeks since I told Tite[4] of this when he was in Town.

— Please to inform James Spock[5] not to forget the

Promise he made me to trim my Apple Trees — Tell Martin my Colt must not be neglected — Remember my Love to little Nancy. I am Dear Mamma
your Dutifull Son &c &c

Gilbert

---

1. Hannah Mangle was a widow with two young daughters, who in 1790 lived in Philipstown, Dutchess County. *Heads of Families 1790*, p. 89.

2. The first Ferris in America was John, who initially settled in Fairfield, but soon after relocated in the town of Westchester, where he was an original patentee in 1667. The Ferris mentioned here may have been one of three living in Cortlandt: David, the town constable in 1788; Jonathan; or John. Bolton, I, 517–519.

3. Probably Justus Wescott, whose business account with Pierre appears as No. 284.

4. "Tite" was a family nickname for Titus, a Van Cortlandt slave.

5. James Spock was a Cortlandt resident in 1790. *Heads of Families 1790*, p. 197.

196

Pierre to Philip. ALS
SHR

Sunday Morning June 4, 1786.

Dear Son Philip

Your Sister Catharine was Through the goodness of the Lord Safely Delivered of a fine boy and seems to be well as Can be Expected Tho verry week[.][1] She was put to bed about 11 O'clock Last Evening. mama and Cornelia with all of us are Exceeding happy that the Child is as it is. The Lords name be Praised who is able to Raise the week and make them Strong. You can make your Brother & Sister aquainted here with [the news?] if you have an oppertunity. with our Love

am your affectionate Father

Pierre Van Cortlandt

[endorsed]
Pierre V. Cortlandt Esq
Informing of the
Birth of Caty's Son
Philip G. Van Wyck
4 June, 1786

---

1. Pierre, Sr. was announcing that his daughter, Catharine (Van Cortlandt) Van Wyck, had given birth to a son, Philip G. Van Wyck.

197

Gilbert to Philip. ALS
NYPL

[ca. 1786.]
Tuesday Morning 6.OClock.

Dr Brother

I forgot to mention last Night for you to go to Doctor Goodwin,[1] near the Fly Market and let him prepare some more Gum Guranum & Flour of Brimstone for me & send it by the first Boat that comes to this Landing

My arm is much better this morning — In haste I am

your Brother
Gilbert

[Endorsed]
Gilbt. Van Cortlandt

1. Dr. John Goodwin of New York City was a close friend of the Beekman family and often acted as their business agent. Gilbert most likely was introduced to the doctor through his brother-in-law, Gerard G. Beekman, Jr. Philip L. White., ed., *The Beekman Mercantile Papers 1746–1799* (New York, 1956), pp. 1156, 1286, 1389.

198

Robert Harpur[1] to Pierre. ALS
SHR

(ca. 1785–87).

Dear Sir,

I am Informed by Coll Hamilton[2] that it is [the] wish of several of the Regents of the University[3] that there should be a meeting appointed on some business of Importance. You therefore will please to give the necessary notice by publishing an advertisement according to the mode prescribed in the act. That I have appointed the Last munday In August to be the day of said meeting at 3 Oclock In the afternoon at the Exchange in the City of New York but should this not come timely to your hands then said meeting to be on the munday following.

Robert Harpur Esqr
Secretary to the University

[addressed]
His Excellency
Pierre V Cortlandt Esqr
Leutenant Governor

[endorsed]
Coll Hamilton
on a meeting

Additional Correspondence

of the Regents to
be on the last
Munday in August

---

1. Robert Harpur is identified in *VCFP,* II, 167–168, 264–265.

2. "Coll Hamilton" is, of course, Alexander Hamilton.

3. Pierre served as an *ex officio* member of the Board of Regents from 1784 until 1795. *VCFP,* II, li.

199

Pierre to Joanna (Livingston) Van Cortlandt. ALS
SHR

January 27, 1787.

My Dear, Yesterday I Sent a Letter by Conklyn[1] Who Came to Me to hire the Ridge farm Adjoyning the Paper Mill Farm. To his Brother Joseph Conklyn[2] that he might have it With paying me Eight pounds a Year one days Riding[3] and two fouls. to pay Eight pound this next April and Eight pounds Every April after as Long as the Lease Last. Which Is to be for his Life Or fourteen years. Wee have been Loosing the Rent of that farm Ever Since the year 1775 by John Keatons not taken it According to Agreement,[4] I think Conklyn Will make a better Tenant than Nehimiah Horton,[5] I believe you think So Also. he is One of the Widow Conklyns Sons & Lives Now in Dutches County.[6] And has Way Withal to Improve the farm; he is to make an Orchard of 150 trees. to be planted within four years. You will Keep this Letter As it is a Coppy Sent Conklyn, I have Not as Yet Receive'd One Line from you. My Love to all with you and am your Ever Loving Husband

Senate Room
Jany. 27. 1787

Pierre Van Cortlandt

[Endorsed] Letter Respecting Jacob Conklyns Farm
Dated Jany. 27 1787

---

1. Pierre was referring to one of two contemporary Jacob Conklins (Conklyn) living in Cortlandt at this time. *Heads of Families 1790*, pp. 196, 197.

2. There was a Joseph Conklyn residing in Frederickstown as of 1790. *Ibid.*, p. 85.

3. "One days Riding" referred to a day's labor on horseback.

4. Although John Keaton remains unidentified, he apparently refused to pay his rent to the Van Cortlandts. See *VCFP*, II, 520–521.

5. Nehemiah Horton was a Cortlandt resident in 1790, along with his wife, two sons, and two daughters. *Heads of Families 1790*, p. 197.

6. As of 1790, there were two Conklin widows residing in Cortlandt, Abigail and Mary. Both women were listed as heads of a household, each with four children. *Ibid.*, p. 197.

200

Robert Pemberton[1] to Philip. DS
SHR

New-York, March 17, 1787.

Sir,

It not being convenient to assemble the Members of the Cincinnati before the time advertised for the general meeting on the 27th instant, Major-General Baron Steuben,[2] as President of the Society, begs leave to inform you of the death of Captain-Lieutenant Clinton,[3] and to request you will, in common with the rest of our Brethren, wear a Mourning Crape on the left arm for the space of twenty-one days from the 20th instant.

I have the honor to be,
With the highest respect,
Sir,
Your most obedient Servant,
Robert Pemberton Secy

Genl Cortlandt

---

1. A captain in Colonel Oliver Spencer's New Jersey regiment during the Revolution, Robert Pemberton (–1788) served as secretary of the New York Cincinnati from 1785 until his death. Schuyler, p. 271.

2. Fredrick William Augustus (Baron) Von Steuben (1730–1795) was a veteran of the Prussian army who volunteered his services to America in 1777. Within a year, Congress appointed him inspector-general of the army at the rank of major general. Best known for the organization he brought to the Continental service, Von Steuben was awarded 16,000 acres in New York in recognition of his services. In 1785 he was elected vice president of the Cincinnati, and he became president the following year. He died a bachelor in 1795 and was buried in an unmarked grave as was his last request. *Ibid.,* p. 298.

3. The eldest son of General James Clinton and the nephew of Governor George Clinton, Alexander Clinton (1765–1787)

served as a lieutenant of New York artillery as well as private secretary for his uncle during the Revolution. He was drowned while crossing the Hudson River at Bull's Ferry on March 15, 1787. *Ibid.*, p. 177.

201

Pierre to Philip. ALS
SHR

[1787.]

Dr Son Philip

I Agree that Hendrick Davids[1] May Stay On the farm this year without paying any Rent (and if the Place Should not be Sold) he may have it on the Same lay that merrit[2] has the other farm or on any other Terms that you may agree with him[.]you Can also Desire Mr. Hammond[3] to make the distress and In order to Secure the property Every farthing of Rent that is Due on the Said farm Aught to be Included. Which will Alway Shew that the Rent due amounted to a Large Sum.

I dont Know that Charlis Davids had any Right to the Improvement. As his Father Hendrick Davids had it at first Seven years free Rent and the Verry Little Rent that has Ever been paid will Amount In the Whole to a Verry Small Sum. They all Realy have had the farm As if it was their Own. However you Must do the best you Can With him. I want nothing more than my Just Right. Am With Respect your Loving Father Pierre Van Cortlandt

[Addressed] Philip Van Cortlandt Esqr
@ Crotons River

[Marginal Note] NB the Distress Should be Made
for at least 70 Or £80

---

1. Members of the Davids family remain unidentified.

2. Possibly David Merritt, a Cortlandt resident in 1800 with a family of three. *VCFP,* III, 45.

3. Elisha Hammond of Cortlandt served as quartermaster in Lieutenant Colonel John Hyatt's militia regiment in 1786, and later became a captain in the same outfit. *Council of Appointment, Military,* I, 79, 127, 144, 604.

202

Stephen DeLancey[1] to Pierre, Jr. ALS
NYPL

Fredericksburgh[2] precinct Febry ye 2
1788.

Dear Cousin

I am Return'd from poughkeepsie very much fatigued: & should undertake to Come to your fathers, to meet you, but at present it is out of my power, I hope however to see you as soon as there falls a snow sufficient to carry me so far: at present there is no snow here: but I hope it wont be many days before there falls one as I want much to see you, but Cant come on account of my Arm: it fatigues it so much, but I must see you, or hear from you soon if there dont fall a snow this week or by Monday, I must send to you, as I must set of for Dover[3], the first Day of March: if it is good slaying: as I have made an Appointment then, & then shall go over to Beekmans precinct: I will meet you at Mr Verplanck's mills[4], if I knew when you wou'd be in that Quarter: I saw Mr Bailey[5] at poughkeepsie, & he has Undertaken for me. he Desired me to inform you that all you have to do is to Come up, & take out a license: as he has done every thing Else Requisite for you I wish you to Inform me by a line sent to Captn. Elvin Purdys at Crompond[6], what is done about the land belonging to the Cortlandt family at or near Wapping Creek[7]: Do let me know also what Money you sent to Billy Walton[8], & what Riker pay'd you, & how you settled with him, & Strong: you must let me know as above, (which will be a Safe Conveyance) when you will be at your fathers & if you will be there the first snow I also want to Consult you about Laying a petition before the Legislature, about my Mothers Dower, due from my Brother Jameses Estate[9]: as it is high time it was pay'd me: I also wish you to speak to your father about it: I wish your papa to Interest himself about the Affair so far as Respects Susan[10], & me: I am very much fatigued with writing: my love to friends at peecks Kill. Adieu my

Dear Cousin
Yours
Stephen DeLancey

pierre Van Cortlandt Junr. Esqr.

---

1. Stephen DeLancey was the son of Chief Justice James DeLancey and Anne Heathcote. On his paternal side, he was an heir to Cortlandt Manor lands, through his grandmother, Ann Van Cortlandt. He controlled the Great Lot, Numbers 9 and 10, of the Manor. Bolton, I, 486, 735–736.

2. Fredricksburgh, New York, was located in Putnam County and is now called Patterson. William J. Blake, *The History of Putnam County, New York* (New York, 1849), pp. 341–342.

3. Dover, New York, located on the Ten Mile River, was known chiefly for its iron mines, loam deposits, and marble quarries. French, pp. 270–271.

4. A reference to the mill works of Philip Verplanck (1768–1828), whose father, Philip (1736–1777), established the mill near Sprout Creek in the Rombout Precinct prior to the Revolution. VerPlanck, pp. 178–179, 210–214.

5. Theodorus Bailey was a Poughkeepsie resident who served in the state Assembly in 1802, and who was elected to both the U.S. House of Representatives and the Senate. Werner, pp. 418, 598, 603. See also No. 243.

6. Elvan Purdy of Westchester served as a second lieutenant of militia in 1778. Bolton, I, xxiv. Crompond, New York, is better known as Yorktown.

7. Wapping, or Wappinger's Creek, is located near Fishkill in Dutchess County, New York. French, p. 271; Edward M. Ruttenber, "Indian Geographical Names," New York Historical Association *Proceedings* (Newburgh, N.Y., 1906), VI, 39–40.

8. A New York merchant with a home in Montgomery Ward, William Walton (1731–1796) acted as a trustee of the New York City Library in 1754, held every major office in the city's Chamber of Commerce, and served as a member of the Committee of 100 in 1775. A Loyalist during the Revolution, Walton vacated his New Jersey property for the safety of New York, and thereby lost it through confiscation. In 1779 he was appointed to care for American prisoners of war as a member of the vestry under British supervision. He married Anne DeLancey, the daughter of James and Anne (Heathcote) DeLancey, and later acted as the family's executor upon his father-in-law's death. VerPlanck, p. 191; *Heads of Families 1790*, p. 122.

9. James DeLancey, Sr. had property in New York valued at £56,781. 17s and his son, James, had an estate worth £3,009. Both applied for compensation as Loyalists, the father receiving £29,848. 12s, the son £2,300, from the Claims Commissioners. Yoshpe, p. 193.

10. Susan DeLancey was the daughter of James and Anne (Heathcote) DeLancey. She, too, was a Van Cortlandt heiress through her paternal grandmother. Bolton, I, 486.

203

Henry Adams[1] to Pierre. ADS
SHR

[April 17, 1788.]

Dr: The Hon: Pierre V: Cortlandt, Esqr:
To Henry Adams
For Innoculating, & Attending four
Children, during the Small Pox £3.4.5
April 17th: 1788[2] —

Recd: Payment.
H Adams

[Endorsed]
Docr: Adams
Rect: In full
for Enoculation

---

1. Dr. Henry Adams was a Cortlandt resident in 1790. He was called upon in his professional capacity by the Van Cortlandts on a number of occasions. *Heads of Families 1790,* p. 197.

2. Prior to the introduction of a smallpox vaccination in this country by Dr. Benjamin Waterhouse in 1800, the only preventive measure against the disease was by inoculation. Used effectively for centuries in the Far East, the process of actually infecting patients with a mild case of smallpox was first undertaken in America by Dr. Zabdiel Boylston of Boston in 1721. Public reaction against the procedure was immediate, and officials throughout the colonies prohibited inoculation on moral, religious, and medical grounds. The high incidence of smallpox during the Revolution modified public opinion on the process, and Pierre, Sr. no doubt saw its benefits for his household. Usually conducted in the spring or fall, as cooler weather was thought to hasten recovery, the infectious state lasted about two weeks, with two or three days actually spent in bed. Howard Haggard, *Devils, Drugs and Doctors* (New York, 1940), pp. 232–240; *VCFP,* II, 199.

204

Pierre to Philip. ADf
SHR

[ca. January, 1789.][1]

Son Philip

Last Winter When I was at Albany there Came to me two men, Abraham Pelts and Jacobus Van dyke[2] Who Informed me that they had discovered a Valuable Mine On Anthonys Nose that they would take and Work it provided I gave them a Lease for the Same[3] they Insisted On having the Lease for Ten Years and promissed to give One Sixth part of the profits Arising therefrom Without any deduction[.] after a great deal of Conversation I Consented to give them a Lease for a Term Not Less then Seven years for the Same, thinking it would be An Advantage for my Self and the family to have the discovered made, they have been to me Several times for the Lease and I have as often put them Of Untill the Last time that Abram. Pelts was here when I promissed him I wod do it[.]I therefore Now am Ready to give them a Lease for my part of the Mine with given me One Sixth part As the Lease Shall Express under Certain Restrictions[.]Now if Couzn. Philip V Cortlandt and his Couzns. Stepn. & John[4] with the family Will Consent to take the Same Lay as I have done and will give you or your brother Pierre a Lease as Above then there is the Greatest Likelyhood that the Mine Will be Worked on As I Will Engage for the Part of Couz Philip And William[5] Who are also Entitled to One Quarter between them As Tennants in Common And I think they Can have No Objection to the proposall above; And it will be Using me hard for My Kindnisses if Not Acceeded to. As I did it for the best of the Whole family According to my Judgment you Can Communicate this to Our Couzs. And advise them to it As they Will Run No Risque at all[.]And the Mine Reverts to them again In the time above Specified And if they Will not Join me It must Lay as it is, for Inspection

[on a separate sheet]

I Write this Last of all[.]Since the Other part Enoch Billingham[6] has brought me a piece of Silver which he Refined in his forge from a Small piece of Oar Suppose 2 Ozs. Worth 9^{d}. or there Abouts[.]It is No[w] Ablase all Over. I Make no doubt but it is as Rich a Mine as Ever Was Discover. And Should Not the Greatest deligence be Used In Order to Secure an Equal part to my Self who is the Only promoter of it And that with his Own Right for the benifits of the family[.]Therefore Use Your Utmost Endeavors to git the Cortlandts if On No other Term than that Each of us Shall have an Equal part with paying Equal Cost[.]200 £ Will gain perhaps: 2. with as many o^{s} as you May add, there is No Knowing the Value of it. And Should I have Our Couz^{n}. part on the Same Lay as I have put Out Mine, Gratitude Could Always hereafter Make Compensation[.]All that I want is to Secure my Own Rights, press hard for it So that the Work May not Stop, it it does Confusion and Disagreement fallow. I wod Come down to you but have No Saddle and Cannot Hardly Leave home. Think Seariously of What I have Now Wrote in this packet. and do as your Judgment Shall direct, a deligent hand maketh Rich

---

1. From January, 1789, through the summer of that year, Pierre Van Cortlandt was seized with "silver fever." He was convinced that he sat astride a vast reservoir of silver ore that represented a source of substantial wealth. He went to great pains in these months to arrange for the working of mines and to obtain legal clearances from the Van Cortlandt relations who shared inheritance rights to minerals found on the estate.

The ensuing correspondence and documents which passed between Pierre and his son, Philip, demonstrate that Philip dutifully carried out his father's wishes. It is interesting to note that Pierre rose to a high fever pitch of excitement regarding such potential wealth, and then suddenly dropped every reference to this venture from his correspondence. Van Cortlandt lands did have traces of silver, but at no time did they reach commercial proportions.

2. Abraham Pelts was a Poughkeepsie resident with a family of nine in 1790. Jacobus Van Dyke was possibly the son of Jacobus, sheriff of Westchester from 1727 to 1730. *Heads of Families 1790,* p. 91; Werner, p. 741.

3. Only abandoned shafts remain as testimony to the lost dreams of instant fortune through the mining of precious metals in Westchester County. Would-be miners such as the Van Cortlandts were soon disappointed with the digs at Anthony's Nose, Continentalville, Philipse Mills, and Canaan, New York. What silver they found, if any, ran in shallow veins that were soon exhausted. Despite reality, local legends about such mines were widely circulated. Upon investigating reports of active mines, the state geologist, William Mather, found no evidence in the 1840's to support the long-standing legendary claims. Of all the supposed locations, Mather stated that only the Ossining site could be mined productively. As that property was in the possession of the state, Mather concluded his report with the rather novel suggestion that the Sing Sing prison inmates be used as miners. Shonnard and Spooner, p. 16; Fox, pp. 106–108. See also William Mather, *Geology of New York, Part I, Comprising the Geology of the First Geological District* (Albany, 1843), pp. 117–118, 501, 506–507; and Irene D. Neu, "Hudson Valley Extractive Industries Before 1815," in Joseph R. Frese and Jacob Judd, eds., *Business Enterprise in Early New York* (Tarrytown, N.Y. 1979).

4. This Colonel Philip Van Cortlandt (1725–1800) was a veteran of the Revolution and a resident of Belleville, New Jersey. His kinsmen, John, Jr. and Stephen Van Cortlandt, were the sons of John and Hester (Bayard) Van Cortlandt of New York City. *VCFP,* II, 615, 616; Yoshpe, p. 167.

5. The Loyalist Philip Van Cortlandt (1739–1814) was the son of Stephen and Mary (Ricketts) Van Cortlandt. As of 1789 he was a resident of King's County, Nova Scotia. His younger brother, William Ricketts (1742–), the husband of Elizabeth Kortwright, had been an importer of dry goods prior to the Revolution. By this time, however, he was a patient in an insane asylum. Roebling, pp. 431–432; New York *Gazette* and *New York Weekly Mercury,* April 12, 1773. See also Arthur Eaton, *The History of King's County, Nova Scotia, Heart of the Acadian Land 1604–1910* (Salem, Mass., 1910), pp. 105–106.

6. Enoch Billingham was a Cortlandt resident with a wife and three sons in 1790. *Heads of Families 1790*, p. 197.

205

Pierre: Mining Lease. AD (Copy)
SHR

January 24, 1789.

To all to whom these Presents may Come Greeting Know ye that I Pierre Van Cortlandt have this day given my Consent That Abraham Pelts of Dutchess County and Jacobus Van Dyke of the Same place and their associates to Say these are the Names of the Leases. Abraham Pelts. Daniel Lefferts. Richard Cantillon[,] Jacob Maraquat and Nicholas E Gabriel[1] May go to work On any part of my Land on the Noose Lott in the Manor of Cortlandt and open any mines or mines at their Own Proper Cost and Charge with paying or Delivering one full Sixth part of all the profits Arising thereon without any Deduction thereof whatsoever Unto the Said Pierre Van Cortlandt his heirs or assigns Which Said Sixth part is to be Appropriated according to the direction given in the Will of the Late M^rs. Gertruyd Beekman and the Said Pierre Van Cortlandt is to give to the Said Abraham Pelts. Daniel Leffers. Richard Cantillon, Jacob Maraquat and Nicholas E. Gabriel a proper Lease for the Same for a Term of years not Less than Seven. Provided that the Said Abraham Pelts, Daniel Lefferts, Richard Cantillon Jacob Maraquat apply Unto the Said Pierre Van Cortlandt for the Same any time before the first day of May Next Who are Actually to Continue and Work the Said Mine or Mines from time to time from and after the first day of June Next and Not to Leave of Working Said Mine or Mines for any Longer time than two Months Under forfiture of the Said Lease.

NB they may begin to work the Mine or mines As Soon as they please, In Witness hereof the Parties have hereunto Set their hands this 24th. day of January 1789

PVC
JVD
&cr

No One of the Parties to Whom the Lease is given to Sell or dispose of his Share or any part thereof Without the Consent of the Said P V Cortlandt In writing Under his hand and Seal Nor to Remove the Oar from the Premisses. but all the Smelting And Refining the Same is to be on the Premisses. the Lessees are to have Liberty to Cut Wood for Coal and Timber for building, And may take of what buildings they put on at the Expiration of the Term Unless otherwise Agreed On, NB Should there not be a further forfiture for none performance

[Endorsed] Copy of the Writing
given at Albany by
P.V.C. Esqr. Relative
Leasing Out the Mine
— 1789 —

---

1. Daniel Lefferts of Clinton, New York, served as a tax assessor and overseer of highways on a number of occasions throughout the 1780's and 1790's. A fellow resident of Clinton, Richard Cantillon also served as an overseer of highways in 1779 and 1781. In addition, he acted as a road commissioner in 1786, 1787, and 1789, and as town supervisor in 1788. Jacob Maraquat and Nicholas E. Gabriel remain unidentified. Franklin D. Roosevelt, ed., *Records of Crum Elbow Precinct Dutchess County New York 1738–1761 Together with Records of Charlotte Precinct 1762–1785, Records of Clinton Precinct 1786–1788, and Records of the Town of Clinton 1789–1799*, Dutchess County Historical Society *Collections* (Poughkeepsie, N.Y., 1940), VII, 93, 95, 97, 99, 112, 120, 124, 128, 129, 136, 139.

206

Pierre to Philip. ALS
SHR

May 12, 1789.

Dear Son Philip

I have had John Grist the Refiner[1], Who has in my presents Refined some of the Oar to my Surprise And Satisfaction It is Exceeding Rich and Verry Valuable and great Plenty of it[.] It has been tryed by Several who Can make Nothing of it and Say it is Iron Let that be as it Will I am Convinced, I have Wrote for Pierre for his Advice and Assistance, Captn. Platt was here and has Seen the Silver that I had had Refined Should you See him Speak to him the Refiner is Suspected of putting Silver in With the Oar.

I have here with Sent you a piece of the Oar[.] Speak to Stephen and John Cortlandt as they Are proprietors of all the mines in Aunt Beekmans Right And try and git them to Let you have their part With given them 1/6th of the profits of One half Clear of Charge that is One twelft of the Whole do it at all Counts, or If they Will Join in Working the mine In partner Ship do that also. however you Can use your prudence in Acting, You Know how farr I have Consented that Pelts and Van dyke and their associates have my permission to work and open Mines on my Right on the Nose Lot, that perhaps may opperate against me therefore wee must Join with Our Couz^{ns}. Cortlandt Apprise them So far of it as Not at any Rate to Consent that Any person Whatsoever Shall have their permission to Work in any Mine that they have a Claim on. I Must In Some measure fullfill my promice for the Discovery of the Mine but Can do no more than My part of the Mine which is Only 1/4 thereof, the Oar I am told is Stolen away by Night[.] I Shall want the Petiager to Attend me at the Mine for first if our Couz^{ns}. part Can be Secured So that No Stranger git their Right

You Must be Verry Causious how you Act but above All that they do not put their part out of the family without privious Consulting me[.] I have Sent a Sample Couz^{n}. Stephen and John With yourself Can have it tryed in New york if they please[.] The persons Who have discovered the mine are to have a Share which I am In duty bound to perform if No otherwise than it Must Come out of my part which would be Most unjust and Unreasonable. I hope there may be no dispute About it and that the family may be profitted by it the Sooner you Can Come up the better as it now Is Spread abroad that the mine In Some peoples Oppinion Is as Rich as possible Am with

Respect your Loving father.

Pierre Van Cortlandt

P.S.

I Shall want 40 boards for the Above Uses to Cover a house at the Mine as a Gaurd house

I Expect there Will be Immeadiately Repeated applycations to Mess^{r}. Cortlandt as Soon as it is Known that I Cannot give a Lease for the Whole

May 12–1789

---

1. John Grist was a resident of Dutchess County as of 1789. See the Indenture Concerning Mines dated May 19, 1789 (No. 211).

207

Pierre to Philip. AL
SHR

[May, 1789.]

Dr Son Philip

I have given Pierre the piece of Silver that I have had Refined under my Inspection for your Satisfaction

I Sent with Conklyn a piece of the Oar and a Letter to you at New York with Orders if you was not in town to bring it back to me again you Make No Mention of it

the Purport was to Secure the family of Cortlandts. Their Interest in the Mine So that No person whatsoever Should do it, Either to give them a part or that they Should undertake with me in Working the Mine in Common. I wod give Unkle Cortlandts family 1 Twelft Clear. of all Expences[.]you may depend on it as Soon as it is Known that Judge Morris will apply. and Some others from Poghkeepsie[.]They are full of it and it must Soon be blazed about which will create troble[.] you must Send me the Petiager Immeadiately if you dont take her to New york She may Lay at the Mine while wee biuld the block house and take in Oar. I wod advise you Not to Loose One hour if you have Not Seen the Letter I Sent by Conklyn to Set of with the Petiager for New York And do What Ever you Can prudently Do with our Couz^ns. it Is in my Oppinion of the Greatest Moment As I have promiced those people a Lease who have discovered it to me, And must give them One; for one Quarter, So that I Shall be Cut out of it for 7 years if Not otherwise Secured, the Mine is the Same Oar that was Carried in the 1745. and 46. to the furnace of unkle Cortlandt Same place. HDP told me

[the rest is torn]

208

Pierre to Philip. ALS
SHR

Saterday May 16, 1789.

Dr Son Philip

I have Rec^d. your favor by Mr Shoup,[1] Since Which have Sent you One by Pierre with an Essay of the mine hope you have not been too free in Exposing of it: It is Out of the mine where Unkle Cortlandts people used to git Iron Oar out of for the furnace

Wee Shall want the Petiager here to Attend when She Comes up you Can Send one or two bus^ls of Potatoes for to help out the Provisions for the Workmen at the Mine, if there is any plank on the farm fit to make the Cause way from the Mine to the River Send What you have, I have had made two Wheelbarrows for the Purpose[.] What is to be done must be done Immediately as wee dont Know how far or how deep the Vein Runs therefore the Sooner wee begin the better[.] I am told the oar is Carried away In the night The Cont-hookers are on the Coast and are apprised of it by appearance a Great deal of oar is already Carried away. I Long to hear from you how you have Made out with Our Couz^ns. I am Determined to git out of it as Much as I possibly Can at all Events Let the Matter turn out as it will, I make Lite of it here as it now is in the mouths of Every One and have not heard any thing further from Pelts and his associates. Shall do Nothing with them Untill I Consult you. There will be Wanting for the Air furnace at Least 5 thousand brick and two hun^d: w^t: of Iron. Which wee Can git hereafter the first work is to Secure the Oar And Wee must bend Our bussiness Wholy to it at first, all well here with our Love &c^r.

your Loving father
Pierre Van Cortlandt

[Marginal notes]
to Come up With the Petiager

Mamas hat and band box it is in Catys Room
Sent the Key of the door with the Stage yesterday
Potatoes
plank if any

[Endorsed]
Pierre V. Cortlandt. Esqr
May 16, 1789
Relative Mine on
Anthonys Nose —

---

1. Possibly Lodowick Shoup of Cortlandt, who was a Westchester mine operator. *Heads of Families 1790,* p. 196; *VCFP,* III, 210.

209

Philip to Pierre. ALS
SHR

Croton Sunday Afternoon —
[May 17, 1789.]

Hond. Sir.

Agreable to your Request I have been to New York and Second River[1] and am Just Arrived Somewhat Fatigued or should have Came up to See you and let you know in person the result of My Negotiation but at present perhaps this method will answer the purpose —

I arrived Thursday Evening in town but too late to wait on Our Cousins the Next morning I went to See them And had Some Conversation the Result was that they were disposed provided it was Agreable to Couz^{n}. Philip their Unkle to leave the whole Affair Intirely to you to do as you thought best[.]I then Resolved to go to Coll^{o} Ph. V. Cortlandt which I did and told him you was about turning Miner and Asked him what he thought of it he said he would Come up and See to it himself and that I Should go with him I was fearful to let him know Every thing Only told him that You was determined to go to Work at any Rate and Either that he Should agree to be his part of the Expence or you would give him 1/12 Clear he Said he would think of it this was all I could git from him only his promice not to Sell or be Concerned with any one but Our Family[.]I Came to New York again Yesterday Morning and went to See Stephen and John[.]Stephen Said as before he would lieve it all to you but upon pressing the Matter with John about the Immediate Necessaty of going to work and my wish for him to declare wether they chose to be their part of Expence or take up with 1/12 he Chose the latter and Said he was Shure it would be the Wish of his Family upon which I told him that I believed you would proceed and depend upon giving 1/12 of the Whole and further as I had Reason to believe you was much Ingaged that I should See him again on the Subject so as to Compleat the Matter before much Expence Arrived I then left him — I now think it will be best to have an Instrument of writing drawn by way of Agreement between your Self and all the parties of that Family and have it Signed by them or as Many as will Immidiately and then when you give Your lease to Pelts and his Associates let it be Expenesed for the Wright You hold as yor. Aunt Beekmans Will and not further then you will afterwards Come in for Your Right as p^{r}. Contract with Our Couzens — I Send this wishing Your Answer the Boat is Ready to go up but will it not be best to have the Affair with Our Couzins first Settled but you know best if you think She had best go up I will go myself and Can take what you write for and Can Call at Mathews where I have a number of Boards Sawed and will take them with me or if you want further to Consult. I will Come up tommorrow Afternoon by land You will please to write to me what is to be done —

M^{r}. Isaac Odel[2] Sampsons Dyckmans Brother in Law wants your 3.Year old Steer to Return when 5.years Old I am to determine him tomorrow by Y^{r}. Answer —

This is all from Your Dutifull
Son — Ph.V.Cortlandt

---

1. The New Jersey branch of the Van Cortlandts settled around the Second River in Belleville.

2. Isaac Odell was a Westchester dock owner and resident of Cortlandt Town in 1790. *Heads of Families 1790,* p. 196.

Pierre to Philip. ALS
SHR

Munday Noon. May 18, 1789.

Dr Philip

In Answer to yours of Yesterday afternoon I Should think it best (from What Couzn Stephen And John Gave for answer) to proceed and git out what Oar wee Can, and Should Couzn. Philip Chuse to Come to Any Agreement, or Leave it as Stephen and John will do for a 1/12 part free, Well, if not Wee Shall have the first part of the Oar Which is Easiest got Secure, Therefore Let the Petiager Come up and bring as many plank as Will make about 200 feet for the gang way. Wee Can go to work Verry Strong if we Chuse however that Can be better Regulated When on the Spot,

If you Can Spare One barral of fish Send one and a few buss of potatoes for Provisions

I Want my Stears and Shall Send for them Soon And the Cow; Charls brings this Pierre Says he must bring up Little black to morrow morning Early. Our Love to you &cr am Yours &cr

Pierre Van Cortlandt

211

Pierre: Indenture Concerning Mines. ADS
SHR

May 19, 1789.

This Indenture made the Nineteenth Day of May in the Year of our Lord One thousand seven hundred and Eighty Nine Between Pierre Van Cortlandt of the County of West Chester Esquire of the first Part and Abraham Pelts, Richard D Cantillon, Daniel Lafferts[,] Nicholas E. Gaberell, Jacob Marquat and John Grist and their heirs All of the County of Dutchess in the State of New York of the second Part. Witnesseth that the said Party of the first part for and in Consideration of the Rents and Covenants hereinafter mentioned doth grant bargain and Lease unto the said Parties of the second Part All the Right Title Interest Property Claim and demand of him the said Party of the first part of in or to any Silver mine or Silver mines heretofore discovered by the said parties of the second part or any One of them situate lying and being on the Nose Lot in the Manor of Cortlandt for the term of Seven Years from the Date of these presents to open and work the same at the proper Cost charge and Expence of them the said Parties of the second Part Yielding and delivering to the said Party of the first part his heirs or Assigns at the expiration of every two months or oftener if thereto required by the said Party of the first Part his heirs or Assigns One equal sixth part without any deduction of the produce thereof either in Oar or Metal refined as the Party of the first part may from time to time prefer, the whole to be brought and refined near the mill at Peekskill belonging to the said Party of the first part and at no other place whatsoever. And the said Party of the first Part doth further Covenant and agree that such wood and Timber as may be necessary to carry the same into Execution may be procured by the said Parties of the second Part on the unappropriated Land West of the Paper Mill Creek on the said Nose Lot. And it is further Covenanted and agreed by and between the said Parties that the said Parties of the second part or any One of them shall not assign or transfer his right or a part thereof in the said premisses herein before expressed without the approbation of the said Party of the first part first had and obtained in writing Nor shall the said parties of the second part neglect working the same for two months together And it is further convenanted and agreed that the said Parties of the second part may after the expiration of the term aforesaid remove any Buildings that the said Parties of the Second part may have erected at the place aforesaid for the smelting or refining the Oar aforesaid. And it is further Covenanted and agreed by and between the said Parties that if at any time the said Parties of the second Part or any one of them shall not comply with the Covenants herein expressed and every Matter article and thing therein that then in such Case this Lease shall be void and of no effect and that the said Party of the first part may re-enter and take possession of all and singular the premisses herein before expressed without any Let hindrance or interruption from the said Parties of the second part or any one of them. In witness whereof the Parties to these presents have hereunto set their hands and seals and have also interchangeably set their hands and seals to a Counter part of these presents for the faithful performance thereof the Day and Year being first above written.

Sealed & delivered
In the presence of

It is also further Covenanted and Agreed by all the Parties aforesaid before the Signing and Sealing hereof That John Grist above named Shall be Intitled to An Equal Share for his Services with the parties of the Second part without any Cost and Charge In Smelting and Refining the Oar Either in a forge or furnace he the said John Grist faithfully performing his part of the business afores^{d} With out any fraud Or Coven whatsoever during this Lease

Sealed & delivered	Pierre Van Cortlandt
In the Presents of	Abraham Pelts
Henry A Cooper	
Jarvis Dusenbery	Dan[l]. Lefferts
	Nich[s]. E. Gaberell —
	John Grist

[Endorsed]
Pierre Van Cortlandt
to Abraham Pelts — Lease
Richard D Cantilhon — for
Daniel Lafferts — 7 Years
Nicholas E Gaberill
Jacob Marquat — 1789
John Grist

Lease for Silver Mine

212

Pierre to Philip. ALS
SHR

[May 1789.]

D[r] Son Philip

I Now Send Ismael down to you With a Coppy of the Lease I gave the Company for your Perusal and Guide in Writing One from the family to me I hope you will proceed as Soon as possible and Urge them to it all in your power. I am Apprehensive if it is Not Now done, that there Will be Confusion. there has been Several Strangers to View the mine James Conklyn told me, who Said the mine was worth ten Miles Square with all the buildings and Improvements About Peeks Kill And more, Tell the family that I got the Old Lady to make her Will as it is, that it was in My power to have had the Whole if I wod have Acted otherwise than upright, that the mines were given to the Whole family; Delancey &[r].

Included, as all her undivided Right, that I got Aunt to Insert Couz^{n}. Renssalaer and Couz^{n}. Hannah Cortlandt In the will[.] Aunt first Intended that part of the Estate for her Niecees by her Own Sisters that Coz^{n}. John Cortlandts daughters And Mine Were taken in, As the Bayards and Delanceys Were disaffected,[1] That I Leased my part of the Mine in Order to get the discovery, And that the mine is on My Land, and Wod do Every thing to Serve them, that there Must be great Cost before Any profit Can Arise, And any other Argument that you Can Use to Induce them So that I may be On An Equal footing with the Rest of the family for my goodness to them that I appeal to them All for what I have done In their faver I believe I have Said Enough[.] You Will please to bring a hat for me from Mr Bicker, a Little Tobacco, and Anest of Crusables Am your Loving father

Pierre Van Cortlandt

Aunt Beekman gave a Lease for four hundred Acres On the Nose to Stoutenburgh, Corolins, Adam Miller, And others for twenty One Years. for a Tenth, free from All Charges.[2] I have had the Lease [*marginal note cut off*]

[Added note]
Fruess [?] Wortle it grows in low ground
Something like Skunk weed — good
to Soak Corn in — 1789 — 3

---

1. In mentioning the "disaffected" members of the Bayard and DeLancey families who were related to the Van Cortlandts, Pierre was speaking of Stephen DeLancey and Samuel Bayard. DeLancey was married to Anne Van Cortlandt and had served as a lieutenant colonel of the Loyalist 1st battalion of New Jersey Volunteers. Samuel Bayard was the husband of Margaret Van Cortlandt and had acted as a major of the King's Orange Rangers during the Revolution. Scharf, II, 427; Lorenzo Sabine, *The American Loyalists or Biographical Sketches of Adherents to the British Crown in the War of the Revolution* (Boston, 1847), pp. 149–150, 245–255.

2. William Stoutenburgh was a large landowner in Westchester in the 1750's. Adam Miller was a resident of Cortlandt Manor in 1768. *VCFP,* II, 5, 596.

3. This marginal note appears to be in the handwriting of Philip. Which particular weed he had in mind is hard to discern. The term "wortle" or whortle was sometimes used in designating a vine-like plant.

213

Pierre to Philip. ADS
SHR

May 23, 1789.

Know all men by these Presents that I Pierre Van Cortlandt of the Manor of Cortlandt Esquire have Assigned Ordained and made and in my Stead and place by these presents put and Constituted my trusty and Well beloved Son Philip Van Cortlandt of the Manor of Cortlandt to be my true and lawful Attorney for me and in my Name and to my Use to Agree with Philip Van Cortlandt of the State of New Jersey Esquire and also with the Heirs of John Van Cortlandt late of the City of New York Deceased Relative to the Share or Shares they have in the Mines already Discovered or to be Discovered on the lot of Land Situate in the Said Manor of Cortlandt Called the Anthonys Noes Lot and what Ever agreement my Said Attorney Shall make and whatsoever Instrument of Writing he Shall Execute Respecting the premisses Shall be binding on me and my heirs in Witness whereof I have hereunto Set my hand and Seal this Twenty third day of May One thousand Seven Hundred and Eighty Nine

Sealed and Delivered
in the presence of Pierre Van Cortlandt

Henry A Cooper
his
Martin M.H. Hillicor —
mark

[Endorsed]
Power of attorney from
Pierre Van Cortlandt Esqr to Ph.V.C. 1789

214

Pierre to Philip. ALS
SHR

Saterday May ye 23, 1789.

Son Philip

Mr Gabriel has wrote to Abraham Pelts that he had hear me Say I Wondered that he had Not Come for the Lease as the Season was favorable Now to go to work and Advised him to Come down Soon, as I proposed going from home for a Time therefore the Sooner he Came the better as he Mr Gabriel was on Unnessarary Expences here this was with the Last Stage So that Expect them here Every day. Gabriel has Seen the Lease and Says it will be Joyfull new to them, that they will or Can Expect it No Stronger[.]Now I wod Advise you to go to our Couz^{s}. and do the best with them you Can for I am determined as Soon as I have given the Lease to go to Work on the part of Philip and William Cortlandt if no further. And Will take away As much of the Oar as I Can With my Own Strenght. You Can think of this and Let me Know you Oppinion Am

Yours &c^{r}. Pierre Van Cortlandt

Grist is Come and Says the Company are Coming in a barge So that I must Stay for them, Grist has Made an Essay of the Oar in the presents of two Gentlemin from New york

— Lately at Poghkeepsie[.]It will Now Run Like Wild fire as A Number Want to be Concerned There; dont Neglect One moment to git it One way or the Other Secured by the Cortlandt family Write a Similar Lease Ready. if Not for 7 years than 5. or 3 So that a fair tryal may be Made if the family dont Come into it than it must Lay as it is And the Oar will be daily more proved Which Will Make it More dificult dalay is dangerous

Since I Wrote what goes before Abram Pelts has been with me And he Mr Gabriel & Grist have Executed the Leases and Deposited them in to Docr. Coopers hands Untill the other Persons Conserned Come down With a promice that Lafferts who is Comming down Next Saterday Shall bring the Paper I Signd at Albany with him Or they are not to proceed[.]I Expect they will bring Every thing Wanting with them they were Exceedingly well pleased with the Lease And Confessed Everything Was done to bargain[.]Pelts was Sorry that Lafferts was not here to give me up the paper it was put in his hand that Van Dyke Should have No Claim, I told them that I wod not Stand to the Lease Unless that paper was here however I hope All for the best. Now it Only Remains With You to Secure Me And As I wrote to you before Must Urge it Again to do it And if the Couzs. dont Agree the Work must Stop which will be great dammage to those that are Concerned And Will be hurting My Interest As I did it to git a discovery for the benifit of the family this Mine was Knowing in the Year 1758, git a Lease for it if One for 3 years Only

Am yours &c Pierre Van Cortlandt

[Addressed]
General Cortlandt
Crotons

215

Philip Van Cortlandt [of New Jersey] to Pierre. ADS
SHR

May 30, 1789.

This Indenture made the thirtieth day of may One thousand Seven Hundred and Eighty Nine Between Philip Van Cortlandt of the County of Essex and State of New Jersey Esquire of the first part and Pierre Van Cortlandt of the Manor of Cortlandt County of WestChester and State of New York Esquire by his Attorney Philip Van Cortlandt of the Said Manor of Cortlandt Esquire of the Second part, Witnesseth that the said party of the first part for and in Consederation of the Rents and Covenants herein after Mentioned — doth grant bargain and Lease unto him the said party of the second part his Heirs and Assigns all the Right title Share Interest property Claim and Demand of him the Said party of the first part of in or to any Copper Silver or Gold mine or Mines heretofore discovered or to be discovered Situate lying and being on the Lot of Land Commonly Called the Nose Lot in the Said Manor of Cortlandt for and during the full Term of Seven Years from the date of these presents at any time during the said Term to Open and Work in the said premisses in Such manner as the said party of the Second part his Heirs or Assigns Shall from time to time direct or think proper yeilding and Delivering to the Said party of the first part of the Yearly Rent of One Shilling and at the Expiration of Every Six Months if thereunto Required One Sixth part of the Said Share or Right of him the Said party of the first part free from any Expense whatsoever. In Witness whereof the parties to these presents have hereunto Interchangably Set their hands and Seals and have also Interchangably set their hands and Seals to a counterpart of these presents for a faithful performance thereof the day and Year first above Written — *[see over]*

Sealed and Delivered in the presents of Elisha Hammond George Harrison	Philip V. Cortlandt Ph. V. Cortlandt attorney to Pierre Van Cortlandt

216

Stephen DeLancey to Pierre, Jr. ALS
SHR

March ye 4th: 1789.

Sir/

On my Arrival at New York, I wrote to you, & let you know, that the Intricacy of my Affairs had made it Necessary, for me: to put Every thing belonging to me, Into the hands of Mr John Watts: Attorney at Law: New York:[1] I then Requested you to send to him, that bond Jonathan Bayles,[2] had given me: & also to let him know what Money you had Received of Samuel Baker: & also to send the lease of Thomas Nicols & Abigail his Wife, also your Account against me, I now once more make the same Request to you: & that you will also let him know soon as I want my Affairs to be Setled: I beg therefore, on the Receipt of this you will Comply with the Above Request: & either send them to my sister, or Mr. J. Watts Imediately: & let him know what sort of A Receipt you gave Baker, & what moneys you Received of him, & how apply'd: as I long to have my Affairs once more in a good way: you will also send him, the bond Against Judge Purdy, & Abraham Knoxes[3] order of £ 9 I hope you wont fail to do it: as I cannot get my matters Regulated: Untill Mr John Watts, has them before him: I hear you was Afronted at my Desiring Coll Burr:[4] to Assist you, in my suit with Bayles: but surely it cou'd not give you offence, to Employ A man of Judgment, to Assist you in so very Intricate A matter: I am with Respects to your papa & mama, brother, & Mrs B. & VanWyck[5]

Your affectionate Cousin
Stephen DeLancey

[*see over*]

pierre Van Cortlandt Junr. Esq[r] —

[Addressed] Pierre Van Cortlandt Jun[r]: Esquire
Croton River or Peecks Kill

Miss DeLancey

---

1. Son of the Loyalist John Watts, John Watts, Jr. (1749–1836) was a lawyer, speaker of the state Assembly, and a New York congressman from 1793 to 1796. A member of the politically active Tontine Coffee House, Watts was successful in regaining his father's forfeited estate and went on to become one of the city's leading lights. Removing to New Rochelle in 1802, he served as a county judge until 1807. *Appleton's Cyclopaedia,* VI, 395; Wilson, III, 29, 75, 80, 81, 93, 97, 104, 150.

2. Jonathan Bayles of Westchester served as a captain of militia in Lieutenant Colonel Thomas's command until 1793. *Council of Appointment, Military,* I, 77, 273.

3. Ebenezer Purdy is identified in *VCFP,* II, 546, 582. Abraham Knox was a North Salem resident with a family consisting of his wife, two sons, two daughters, and one slave. *Heads of Families 1790,* p. 203.

4. Prior to his emergence as a national figure, Aaron Burr (1756–1836) was already compiling a brilliant record in the legal profession. After graduating from the College of New Jersey with honors, Burr began to study for the ministry, but by 1774 abandoned it for the law. The Revolution interrupted his studies while he served with distinction on Washington's staff. He then returned to his law books and was admitted to the New York bar in 1782. For the next seven years Burr enjoyed a high reputation as a lawyer. He soon launched his political career in the U.S. Senate.

5. "Mrs. B." was, no doubt, Cornelia Beekman (1753–1847), the wife of Gerard G. Beekman, Jr. and the third child of Pierre, Sr. Her sister, Catharine (1751–1829), was married to Abraham Van Wyck. *VCFP,* II, 14.

217

Pierre to Philip. ALS
SHR

Apl^l:2–<u>1789.</u>

Dr Son Philip

I Received your Letter Inclosing M^rs: Parents.[1] I told the Bearor I wo'd give him an answer to morrow, I shall send him to you and you may do with the farm as you think best, And if Rented it should fetch fifteen pounds a year Or as you Can Agree I leave it to you to Act for me take Security for the Rent. Let who will take it if you think proper.

If I had a Saddle I would go down to you, So As to Consult about the Committee business, I Observe there were but 6 present all the Eastern Gentlemen and Cap Hunter[2] were not there, I propose to send as an answer the Coppy I Sent to Coll. Hamilton,[3] people only act In a great measure to Serve their own Interest and I am determined not to be made their tool this I Send with Philip Ver Planck In haste

am &c:
Pierre Van Cortlandt

[Endorsed]
P.V.C. Esqr
Subject — Parents plan. & the Committee Business —
Apl. 1789

---

1. Possibly a reference to Mrs. Levi Parent, whose husband purchased a large farm in Stephenstown (now Somers) from the Van Cortlandts. Levi Parent later served as the town's overseer of highways in 1788. Scharf, II, 474, 484.

2. It is likely that "Cap Hunter" was James Hunter of Cortlandt. *VCFP,* II, 7.

3. Pierre sought the Federalist nomination as their candidate for New York's gubernatorial seat. Alexander Hamilton had in-

formed Pierre in February, 1789, that the Federalists could not endorse him. This may be a reference to that affair. See *VCFP*, II, 514–515.

218

Stephen and John Van Cortlandt to Philip. LBC NYPL

New York 10th July 1789.

Dear Sir

Inclosed is a Petition to the Legislature for a Compensation from the Estate of John Tabor Kemp[1] for possessing the Dwelling house of our fathers during the War:[2] we shall esteem it a favour if any Petitions are presented this Session if you will be so kind as to present it if not keep it untill the next Sessions[.] the Peculiar Circumstances of this Case prevented us from getting a Certificate from [illegible] our only resource was to Petition the Legislature your attention to this Business will much Oblidge your

Very Humble Servts
Stephn & Jno V Cortlandt

Genl. Philip VCortlandt

---

1. John Tabor Kempe served as the last royal Attorney General of New York, 1759–1783. Through his marriage to Grace Coxe of New Jersey he inherited a vast fortune, which he lost as a result of his loyalty to the crown. In compensation, Parliament granted him the fourth largest sum awarded to a New York Loyalist. Catherine S. Crary, "The American Dream: John Tabor Kempe's Rise from Poverty to Riches," *William and Mary Quarterly*, 3rd Ser., XIV (April, 1957), pp. 176–195.

2. Although entrusted to the care of Philip, it was Pierre, Jr. who finally submitted this petition to the New York legislature on January 24, 1791. It was not until 1795, however, that the peti-

tion was reviewed and then denied by a vote of 33–20, with Pierre, Jr. abstaining. In its final form the document read:

> A petition of Hester Van Cortlandt, widow of John Van Cortlandt, Esq. of the city of New York, deceased, stating that her said husband on the approach of the British army in 1776, left his property in the city of New York, and retired to the country; that John Tabor Kemp occupied a large dwelling house of the said John Van Cortlandt's during the greater part of the war; that said John Tabor Kemp at the evacuation of the British army left this country; and that his estate has been confiscated and the proceeds thereof are now in the public treasury — praying that a sum equal to that which the said John Van Cortlandt was justly entitled to for the use and occupation of the said house, may be paid out of the proceeds of the estate of the said John Tabor Kemp, was read.

New York (State) Assembly, *Journal of the Assembly of the State of New York, At Their Eighteenth Session, Begun At the Town of Poughkeepsie, in the County of Dutchess on Tuesday, the Sixth of January, 1795* (New York, 1795), p. 117.

219

Philip Verplanck to Philip. ADS
SHR

[November 10, 1789.]

I do hereby certify that as one of the heirs of the Cortlandt family, I was entitled to one full equal tenth part of all the undivided Land in the Mannor of Cortlandt that on the 18th day of Novr. in the Year 1789 I sold the same to Philip Van Cortlandt Esqr. his heirs and assigns and received from his a Valuable Consideration for the same, for his own Use in which was included all my Right to Montross^{s}. Point[1]

Philip Verplanck

---

1. Montrose Point lies directly south of Verplanck's Point and derives its name from its original settlers, the Montrose family.

During the Revolution it was also known as Parson's Point, as the pastor of the Reformed Dutch Church had his farm located there. Scharf, II, 416.

220

Randall, Son & Stewart[1] to Pierre. ALS
SHR

N:Yk 13th May 1790.

Dear Sir —

Mr Green[2] has called here in behalf of John Drake[3] & Wishes us to join in some plan of taking his effects & giving term for the Ball". We have informed him that we are willing to take Stock of any sort at an Honest and fair price and we beg of you to take such articles for us as will be usefull on the Farm and have them placed thereon n^{t}. Drake falls Short in himself — he may Assign over good Notes he has against the Farmers in this Country & you can take from them Oxen . . Cows Sheep Horses &c in such proportion as you think will be proper to Stock the Farm at Pecks Kill Open we conceive to Answer best as we can fatten them & kill them off in the Fall — would not wish too many Horses — he has some handy Slaves that would be useful — Teams & waggons &c. we commit the whole to your prudent management and beg of you to take such Steps for our Security as you would if the property was your own. We wish you to send Sheriff DeWitt the boundaries of the Fulling Mill Farm & the 500 Acres in Dutchess County — DeWitt wants them to make out the Deeds and we beg you to have all the Deeds Made out in the Name of Robert Richard Randall instead of to the Firm of Randall Son Stewart to avoid the inconvenience of Dower when we dispose of the Farms — please to let Sheriff Thomas[4] know this to be our wish — M^{r}

Stewart gave all our Separate Names — but he did not advert to this inconvenience at that time

We are with Great Esteem

Dr Sir

Your Assured Friends
Randall Son & Stewart

[Addressed] Pierre Van Cortlandt Esqr
Croton
pr Mr Green

---

1. In 1790 Randall, Son and Stewart were merchants located at 211 Water Street, New York City. In that same year, Robert R. Randall purchased from Baron de Polinitz the property of former Lieutenant Governor Andrew Eliot, situated on the Bowery. Acting on Alexander Hamilton's suggestion, Randall stipulated in his will that the location was to serve as a home for old and disabled sailors. In fulfilling Randall's wishes, DeWitt Clinton pressed the state legislature for the establishment of the Sailor's Snug Harbor. Duncan (1790), p. 81; Alvin F. Harlow, *Old Bowery Days: The Chronicles of a Famous Street* (New York, 1931), p. 87. See also New York (State) Legislature, *Journal of the Senate of the State of New-York, . . . Twenty-ninth Session* (Albany, 1806), p. 11.

2. "Mr. Green" may have been John Green of Cortlandt, but more likely he was Benjamin Green of Stephenstown. The latter served as the town's first constable, poundkeeper, and tax collector. As of 1788, Benjamin Green also became a tavern keeper, a business which he ran from his home. Scharf, II, 471–472.

3. John Drake lived in the town of Cortlandt as of 1790. He was probably a Van Cortlandt tenant. *Heads of Families 1790* pp. 198–199.

4. John DeWitt was chosen sheriff of Dutchess County on February 28, 1789. Thomas Thomas was selected for the same position in Westchester County on March 22, 1788. Werner, pp. 284, 290.

221

Society of Tammany to Pierre, Jr. ADS
SHR

Mr. Pierre Van Cortlandt Junr.

New-York, 31 May, 1790.

Sir,

Brother Thos. Cooper,[1] having proposed you as a Candidate for Admission into the St. Tammany's Society, or Columbian Order[2] — it becomes my Duty to inform you, that you have been balloted for, and admitted a Member of the said Order; in consequence thereof, you are hereby earnestly requested to attend at our Wigwam, at Bardins[3] on Monday Evening next, at one hour after the setting of the Sun, to be initiated into our National Society.

By Order of the Grand Sachem,
Geo: Snowdon. jun.[4] Secretary

---

1. There was a Thomas Cooper practicing law in Westchester County from 1790 to 1798. Scharf, I, 539.

2. Founded on the principles of liberty and brotherhood for all, the Society of Tammany or the Columbian Order was open to all veterans of the American Revolution. The early members opposed the exclusive nature of other military organizations, with the Society of the Cincinnati being the most frequently cited example. Many men, however, were active in both fraternal organizations, Philip Van Cortlandt being one of them. Prior to the completion of Tammany Hall, members met at Bardins Tavern on Broadway or at one of several other temporary sites. Little is known of the part taken by Pierre, Jr. in the Society of Tammany. It is not likely that he spurned the organization, but his membership was evidently not an active one. Tammany Society, pp. 9–11, 22–27, 79, 99; *VCFP,* II, 260–262.

3. Edward Bardin was a long-time New York City innkeeper and former proprietor of the King's Arms, the meeting place of the Sons of Liberty. Bardin later operated Bardins in the Field, Bardins Coffee House, and the Phoenix Coffee House. Stokes, VI, 314.

4. George Snowden, Jr. was a resident of New York City and a captain of militia from 1789 until his death in 1799. *Council of Appointment, Military,* I, 154, 277, 470

222

Thomas Cooper[1] to Pierre, Jr. ALS
SHR

June 24th 1791.

Dear C

I have this instant received your's of the 20th The amount of the Damages adjudged to the Town of Cortlandt are £ 17.4.6 and the taxable costs £ 12.17.0 — The overseers of Cortlandt will not think me unreasonable when they are informed that by being concerned for them I was obliged to refuse a larger fee than they in the full extent of their Liberality after having won their cause have thought proper to allow — but that I also lost the taxable fees on the other side which were offered me if I would undertake

perhaps indeed my having this in recollection induced me to make a Proposition that to them might at first seem rather large.

The Balance of their money which is twelve Pounds four Shillings and 6d I find done over to you and Sixteen shillings over towards your costs — The Balance of your costs I will send you the next time the Boatman comes down —

I must apologize indeed to you for not finding it now but all my monies are at present out of my Hands and none payable until the Day after tomorrow —

Should the Boatman stay this long in Town I will yet pay it to him — Tell Friend Fields[2] laughingly that his friend Cooper says a fig for his Liberality —

I am Dear Sir your Sincere Friend —
P. Van Cortlandt Esqr Thomas Cooper
New York June 24th 1791

P. S.

I congratulate you upon your having arrived at the Station of a Legislator[3]

[Addressed]
Pierre Van Cortlandt Esqr
Attorney at Law
Mouth of Croton

---

1. Thomas Cooper is identified in the proceeding letter. The specific litigation involved remains unidentified.

2. There were a number of Fields' in Westchester County at this time, including Samuel, Benjamin, and Jesse Fields, all tenants of the Van Cortlandt family. *VCFP,* II, 4, 331; III, 28, 56, 210, 705.

3. Pierre, Jr. was elected as an assemblyman to the state legislature's fifteenth session, along with Samuel Haight, Elias Newman, Ebenezer Purdy, and Jonathan G. Tompkins. Werner, 414.

223

Improving Navigability of Croton River. AD
[in Philip's handwriting]

NYPL

[June 25, 1791.]

At a Meeting of a Number of Reputable I[n]habitants at the House of Major Benjamin Green[1] in May last it was Unanimously agreed that Major Jonathan Hallet[2] Charles Tead[3] John Quick Esqr.[4] Daniel Tillotson[5] should be a Committee to explore Croton River and make an Estimate of the probable Expence which would attend clearing out and making the same Navigable for Boats of at least two Tons burthen from the Mouth of the Said River to Dutchess County and that they Should advertize a time and Place of Meeting to make their Report to such Persons as wished to promote the same in consequence of which Public Notice was given and a Number of respectable Inhabitants Mett at the House of Major Jonathen Hallet in North Salem on the 25th Day of June 1791. when the above Named Committee reported the same to be very Practicable and Would be of great Service to the Public and that the probable Expence would not exceed the sum of two thousand Pounds whereupon the Gentlemen of the said Meeting after making Choice of Ebenezer Purdy Esqr.[6] Moderator did Unanimously Agree to Undertake the Clearing out the said River and appointed the following Gentlemen. Viz. Genl. Philip Van Cortlandt of Cortlandt Town. John Montross[7] and Silas Carpenter of York Town James Bailey[8] Benjamin Haight and Benjamin Green of Stephen Town Philip Petton, Colds Fields,[9] Peter Raymond, and Thitetus Phillips of Fredricks Town, John Quick, Joseph Purdy,[10] and Thomas Vait,[11] of North Salem, David Brown, and Edward Brundage[12] of Salem, Major Samuel Lyon, and William Miller.[13] of Bedford, a Committee to receive Subscriptions and report Progress on the Second Day of August next, at 10 OClock in the Morning at the House of Benjamin Haight in Stephen Town; Where the Subscribers are requested to attend to receive Said report and to make Choice of a Sufficient Number of Trustees to carry on the Work

by Order —

Ebenezer Purdy Moderator

We the Subscribers being disposed to promote the Public Advantages which must arise from the Navigation of Croton River do hereby promise and Obligate our Selves and Heirs respectively to pay in two equal Payments. Viz on the first Day of November next, and the first Day of Nov^{br} 1792, into the Hands of the Trustees, to be appointed for the Purpose, above mentioned, or any One of them such Sums of Mony or Produce at the Market Price as we have set opposite to our Names[14] —

Philip Van Cortlandt One Hundred Pounds N.Y. Cur^{cy} £ 100
Hachaliah Brown — £ 30.0.0

Silas Carpenter	20.0.0	Those Six Names
Benjn Haight	10.–.–	are Copy: from
Nathan Brown[16]	12.–.–	the originals —
Macajah Wright[17]	5.–.–	
David Brown	16.–.–	

[Endorsed] Map and Proceedings
the Navigation of
Croton River

---

1. Benjamin Green is identified in No. 220.

2. Jonathan Hallet served under Philip in the 2nd New York Regiment during the Revolution. *VCFP,* II, 289, 490.

3. Charles Teed (Tead) was a Westchester County resident and a member of the New York Assembly from 1796 to 1810. Werner, pp. 415–417.

4. John Quick, Sr. was a resident of North Salem, New York, and that town's first supervisor in 1790. Bolton, I, 474.

5. Daniel Tillotson was a Fredrickstown resident. *Heads of Families 1790,* p. 83.

6. Ebenezer Purdy is identified in *VCFP,* II, 546, 582.

7. John Montross (Montrose) was a resident of Yorktown with a family of nine, including two slaves, in 1790. *Heads of Families 1790,* p. 209.

8. James Bailey and his family of fourteen and two slaves were residents of Stephenstown in 1790. *Ibid.*, p. 206.

9. Philip Pelton was a Fredrickstown resident in 1790, with a family of nine members. His neighbor, Joseph Coles Fields, had a wife, six sons, and one daughter. *Heads of Families 1790,* pp. 82–83.

10. Joseph Purdy was a resident of North Salem, the owner of five slaves, and among the prime movers in establishing St. James's Church, which he once served as its lay delegate to the Diocesan Convention. Bolton, I, 482; *Heads of Families 1790,* p. 203.

11. Thomas Vail served as an overseer of the poor for North Salem in 1790. Bolton, I, 474.

12. David Brown was a small landowner and slave owner residing in Salem as of 1790. Edward Brundage, also of Salem, was at the head of an eight-member family in 1790. *Heads of Families 1790,* p. 205.

13. Samuel Lyon, Jr. was a Bedford resident with a family of eight, including one slave. William Miller served as chairman of the Westchester Committee of Safety during the Revolution, and figured prominently in re-establishing the Episcopal Church in Bedford after the war. *VCFP,* II, 39; Bolton, I, 25; *Heads of Families 1790,* pp. 195–196.

14. Efforts to improve navigation on the Croton River would soon meet with stiff opposition by riverside residents concerned with preserving the fishing industry. Through their lobbying efforts even the chairman of this meeting, Ebenezer Purdy, became convinced that conservation stood higher than navigation improvements. Purdy consequently submitted a bill to the legislature which stymied such improvements, and it was passed into law in March of 1795. New York (State) Assembly, *Journal of the Assembly of the State of New York, . . . Eighteenth Session, 1795* (New York, 1795), pp. 120, 127, 184.

15. A principal freeholder of Cortlandt Manor in 1768, Hachaliah Brown became one of Stephenstown's largest landowners, and served as the town's first supervisor in 1788. Scharf, II, 471, 474, 475; *VCFP,* II, 4, 9, 10.

16. Nathan Brown, most likely Hachaliah's brother, also lived in Stephenstown, with a family of six and six slaves. *Heads of Families 1790,* p. 206.

17. Macajah Wright (1763–1811) was the builder of the Mount Zion Church as well as an innkeeper. He died at the age of 48, leaving a family of four, including one son and two daughters. Scharf, II, 482; *Heads of Families 1790,* p. 206.

224

Joseph Travis[1] to Pierre. ALS
SHR

Peeks Kill Landing febry. 16th 1792.

Sir

As I was not at home in some days after your Letter come to peeks Kill is the Reason I did not send this Respecting the timber, to which I have A Conceit the Gentleman that the Govr. Refered the price to, has mistaken in his Calculation, perhaps Guided by timber after Delivered in New York, As the price at present which the Govr. sends is Almost Double of Any that has been Got at this place Since Peace, and farther as the Governor has put the timber by the frame, there will be A Number of Sticks that I shall be Obliged to Get some where Else as they cant be found on the Govr. Land so that we can draw them Out, therefore shall be glad if the Govr. will write me Once more, two prices that is by the tree, and Likewise by the tons of timber, and farther the Bounds the Govr. Sends me to Get it in, if we Understand it Right, is Almost an Impossibility to Get it to the water, I was in hopes as there is A Middling plenty of timber towards Mr Nelsons,[2] of Getting it there, On Account of Sawing it the Straight way in the Saw Mill, and as I want to know of who, and where, I am to Get the timber, shall take it very kind if the Govr. will send me Another line Explaining the bounds to Get it in if I am Districted at all, and the two prices within mentioned, as I am Desirous of knowing before I do Any thing towards it, to know upon what lay I get it, and am as is Natural with mankind to have it as Cheap as I can, when Every Circumstance is Calculated, such as price of timber and drawing likewise which Answer will be kindly Accepted by Your humble Servant —

Joseph Travis

P.S. Mr. Presher[3] Says he shall be very fond of sawing the timber the Straight way of it, if it suits —

J T

[Addressed] The Honorable Pierre V Cortlandt
Lieut. Govr.
In Senate
New York

[Endorsed] Joseph Travis
February 16th. 1792
Letter

---

1. Joseph Travis (1755–1822) was a storekeeper and prominent citizen of Peekskill, New York. In addition, he served as a sloopmaster and as the town clerk. Roebling, p. 281.

2. Possibly one of two men: Joshua Nelson, who served as a vestryman for St. Peter's Church at this time; or William Nelson, later to become postmaster of Peekskill and a distinguished national legislator. Fox, pp. 41, 128.

3. William Presher was a resident of Cortlandt in 1790. *Heads of Families 1790*, p. 197.

225

Daniel Thew[1] to Pierre, Jr. ALS
SHR

Pond March 8th 1792.

Dear Cortlandt,

I am really mortified at your and your Brother's silence. I have been induced to conclude that some unforeseen accident has tended to lessen me in your esteem. If the causes exist at present let me know them and I shall attempt to remove them. — For no consideration would tempt me to forfeit that friendship which I have ever considered sincere and have flattered myself would be permanent. I wish you to write by the Bearer and inform me of the result of your negotiations in every respect wherein your friend is the least interested —

My Father is anxious to know what success has attended his Petition.[2] — I wish to know your opinion with respect to next Election, it is really time to Electioneer —

The Country murmers at the conduct of Walter Smith in his judicial capacity and wish a Change to take place[3]; for my own part I sincerely wish it — write to me upon the subject and tell me what steps will be necessary to effect the object — I have written to the General upon the subject but have received no answer —

With my compliments to your Papa and Brother I remain your Friend
Danl. Thew

Since I saw you I have pursued the road to Hymen and find no difficulties to encounter. Attention will insure the prize. She is really a fine Girl and much admired —

D.

[Addressed]
Pierre Van Cortlandt Junr Esqr
Maiden Lane

Additional Correspondence

New York
By Mr. Clark

---

1. Daniel Thew of Pond Marsh, in Orange County, was a member of the New York Assembly in 1792–1793. Werner, p. 414.

2. The Thew petition has not been located.

3. While there was a Walter Smith living in Haverstraw, Orange County, as of 1790, no mention of his holding judicial office has been found. *Heads of Families,* p. 142.

226

William Paulding[1] to Pierre, Jr. ALS
NYPL

Tarry Town. Jany 2d 1793.

Sir,

I have got in trouble of Capt. Ackers[2] acct., and must either pay Mr. VanHorne's[3] note he has against Acker or go to Jayl[.]to pay it is impossible, and to be Confined I must suffer, With my family, as they are not able to support me, Indeed I can scarce support them when with them, It lays in your power to stop the affair, which I beg you will do, as you act for Mr Van Horne, I know Mr Van Horne would not suffer me to be Confined in Jayl on his Acct. as he is an old friend of mine and It will be no advantage to him to have me confined as I have not a friend in the world who would pay the sum for me[.]Capt. Acker is now in a fair way to be Able soon to discharge the whole as there is no doubt of his getting his Pay as Capt. of the levies in the late War, he has a years pay due. . and in the Course of two or three months he will be able to pay the whole, If I am obliged to go to Jayl I must suffer untill The Law liberates me, and it will be no advantage to Mr. Van Horne, I must once more beg the favour of you to stop the suit at present, and I will with Acker Contrive some mode to Secure Mr. Van Horne, do not fail sending me few lines by next stage to stop the suit at present as the court is near at hand your Obliging me will ever be acknowledged by yours &c

Wm. Paulding

[Addressed]
To Pierre V. Cortland Esqr. Junior N.York

---

1. William Paulding had been a prosperous shipowner and storekeeper in Tarrytown prior to the Revolution, but lost his fortune when he pledged it to obtain supplies for the American troops during the war. He was a member of the Provincial Congress and served on the Committee of Safety. His son, James Kirke Paulding, rose to literary prominence in the nineteenth century. *National Cyclopaedia,* VII, 193.

2. Captain Acker may well have been Sybout Acker (1753–1835), who served in the Westchester levies from 1775 to 1782. Grenville MacKenzie, *The Ecker–Acker Family of Philipsburgh, Westchester County, New York, 1668–1800* (Westport, Conn., 1943), p. 243; Fernow, *N.Y. in Revolution,* p. 304.

3. While there were Van Hornes in Ulster and King's counties, the man here mentioned was possibly Augustus Van Horne of New York City. The son of Cornelius G. Van Horne, he married Anne Marston and established himself as a leading New York merchant prior to the Revolution. A Loyalist during the war, he was arrested by the patriots and was later paroled. Living on Little Dock Street under British protection, Van Horne was a member of the vestry which cared for American prisoners of war. His humanitarian activities while in that office played a large part in his being allowed to remain in New York after hostilities ceased. He continued in his mercantile pursuits, and played a major role in the founding of the New York City Chamber of Commerce. John A. Stephens, Jr., *Colonial Records of the New York Chamber of Commerce, 1768–1784 with Historical and Biographical Sketches* (New York, 1867, repr. 1971), p. 166.

227

Duncan Ingraham, Jr.[1] to Pierre, Jr. ALS
SHR

Hudson[2] March 27:1793.

Piere van Cortlandt Esqr
Peekskill

Sir

I was Lately applied to by Mr Van Ness[3] for a Beaver Hat on your Account, which he inform'd me you had sold to him — it occasion'd some Surprise, because I intended to have called on you for the same thing. You cannot have forgot that the Wager, or Bet was, that Mr Clinton[4] would not have three Votes in the City of Hudson & afterwards explain'd by me, that I did not mean to include the Corporation bounds, but merely the Compact part — now Sir I have investigated the matter by enquiring of every one most likely to know the sentiments of the Inhabitants, within the City & I am persuaded you have Lost the Bet, for I sincerely believe Mr Clinton had but one Vote for Governor in the City of Hudson — I can find you the Certificates of the Judgment of Gent^{n}. here to satisfy you that I am entitled to a Beaver Hat from you & shall mark it as such. —

I am Sir:

Your most Obed: Servt
Duncan Ingraham Junr

[Addressed]
Piere van Cortlandt Esqr.
Peekskill

---

1. Duncan Ingraham, Jr. was a resident of Dutchess County in 1800.

2. Hudson, New York, was formed from Claverack and incorpo-

rated on April 22, 1785. Formerly known as Claverack Landing, it lies on the east bank of the Hudson at the head of ship navigation. Due to its advantageous location, Hudson grew rapidly as a commercial center dealing with the West Indies and Europe. For a time it even had a thriving whaling industry. French, pp. 246–247.

3. The Van Ness family was one of the most distinguished in the history of Columbia County, New York. The Van Ness in question could have been William W. or John P. William, who was born in 1776, enjoyed a large and successful law practice in Hudson until 1807, when he became a judge of the New York Supreme Court. He also served in the state Assembly in 1805, and was described by his contemporaries as "a rare genius." John P. Van Ness was born in Claverack in 1770. He was also a lawyer, having prepared for the bar under Brockholst Livingston. In 1801 he was elected to Congress. William Raymond, *Biographical Sketches of the Distinguished Men of Columbia County* (Albany, 1851), pp. 21–31, 32.

4. The results of the New York gubernatorial election of 1792 long remained in dispute. The Clintonian election canvassers, Pierre, Jr. among them, felt there was just cause to challenge the voting returns of Clinton, Tioga, and Otsego counties. By throwing out the votes of those counties, the election victory was snatched from John Jay, leaving incumbent George Clinton in office. The 1792 election became notorious for the flagrant and rampant frauds perpetrated by both leading parties. Alfred Young, *The Democratic Republicans of New York: The Origins, 1763–1797* (Chapel Hill, N.C., 1967), pp. 304–323; *VCFP, II*, 527–530.

228

Andrew Fowler[1] to Pierre, Jr. ALS

SHR

Philip's Town Febry.10.1794.

Dear Sir,

I last evening received your letter of the 7th. Instant, by which it appears that you wish to be informed of our incorporation,[2] in order to remove a difficulty, that has arisen in the house of representatives, with respect to our Petition. — The Charter of these churches was lost in the late war; and has since been renewed, according to an Act of the Legislature of this State, passed the 6th day of April, 1784, entitled "An act to enable all the religious denominations in this State to appoint Trustees, who shall be a body corporate, for the purpose of taking care of the temporalities of their respective congregations; and for other purposes therein mentioned." And in pursuance of the said Act, we have had our proceedings not only acknowledged before a judge of Common pleas, and our name and title recorded in the County Clerk's office; but we have ever since proceeded regularly in the choice [of] our trustees: the names of whom, at present in office, are William Denning[3][,]Pierre Van Cortland junr. Esquires, Messrs Sylvanus Haight,[4] James Spock,[5] Willm. Lancaster,[6] Benj. Ward,[7] Isaac Mead,[8] Caleb Morgan,[9] and Jarvis Dusenberry. The stile and name of our corporation is, "The corporation of the united protestant episcopal churches of St Peter's church in Cortlandt Town, and St Philip's chappel in Philip's Town". By this title these churches are known, and by no other, and it is to the trustees of these, that we wish to have the Farm given; to them, and to their successors in trust, for the benefit of a minister of the protestant episcopal church in these two congregations forever. The reason why we call ourselves the vestry of St Peter's Church and St Philip's chappel, is because the names of trustees is not perfectly congenial to our mode of government, and I could wish that an amendment might take place in the act above specified, and that we might be allowed to incorporate under this government, as we used to do in the former; with the prevelige of stiling ourselves the Vestry of such a church. — I am sorry, Sir, that we are obliged to give you so much trouble; but blessed is he who helpeth the poor and needy; the Lord shall reward him. — Be so kind as to inform me of the event of our affair as soon as it shall be determined, and you will oblige, dear Sir, your sincere

friend &c.
Andrew Fowler

[Addressed]
Pierre Van Cortlandt jun^{r}. Esq.
Member of the Legislature
Albany

---

1. Andrew Fowler served as the rector of both St. Peter's and St. Philip's churches from 1792 to 1794. The combined service brought him between seventy and eighty pounds per year. Born in 1760 in Guilford, Connecticut, he was descended from one of the founders of that town. Fowler became a churchman in 1779, although he did not graduate from Yale until 1783. During and after the Revolution, when the Presbyterians attempted to take control of the Westchester parishes, Fowler maintained good relations with other denominations. He later left New York and ventured to South Carolina, where he devoted the rest of his life to spreading the church to that area and to Florida. Chorley, pp. 40, 88–100.

2. At a meeting in November, 1791, the vestry took the first step toward incorporation by appointing Jarvis Dusenbury as their emissary. A royal charter had been granted in August, 1770, but was either lost or invalidated during the Revolution. Immediately after the war, circumstances were unfavorable for the re-chartering of the church due to its heavy debts, the damage incurred to the buildings and farm, and the loss of some of its major leaders into the Loyalist ranks. No vestry meeting was recorded for nearly fifteen years. *Ibid.*, pp. 22–40.

3. William Denning, senior warden of St. Peter's from 1790 to 1793, was a prominent merchant and political leader in New York City, having served in the Provincial Congress, the Senate, and on the Council of Appointment. Through his political connections he assisted in restoring the glebe farm to the parish in 1792. He personally contributed money and land to restore St. Philip's. Having bought part of the estate and the home of the attainted Beverley Robinson, he was interested in local affairs. At his death in 1819 he was interred in St. Paul's churchyard in New York City. *Ibid.*, p. 40.

4. Silvanus Haight, son of Joseph and Hannah (Wright) Haight of Rye, was a member of the vestry from 1790 to 1794 and treasurer of the united churches in 1791. A strong Tory, he had resided on the Beverley Robinson property during the war, but was imprisoned at Fort Clinton during part of the hostilities. *Ibid.*, pp. 45, 161.

5. James Spock was one of the trustees of St. Peter's Church in the 1790's. He resided in Peekskill, where he was a miller at the Robinson mill, near Continental Village. The Van Cortlandt accounts mention use of his services. He died in 1804. *Ibid.*, pp. 42, 168.

6. William Lancaster was a vestryman of St. Peter's. *Ibid.*, p. 115.

7. Benjamin Ward lived at Peekskill and served as a vestryman of St. Peter's. *Ibid.*, pp. 116, 170,

8. Isaac Mead kept a roadhouse on the Post Road, near Davenport's Corners. *Ibid.*, p. 45.

9. Caleb Morgan was a farmer of Cortlandt town who had been imprisoned as a Tory during the war. He served variously as a vestryman, warden, and trustee of St. Peter's Church. *Ibid.*, pp. 42, 162.

229

John B. Schuyler[1] to Pierre, Jr. ALS
NYPL

Saratoga Feby 19th 1794.

Dr Sir,

Cramer & Brisbean (the persons who I mentioned to you) had 800 or 1000 logs for sale, are anxious that you should come up, examine and contract with them for their logs. — I am told they have very Large logs and good stuff — and advise your coming up to agree with them, especially as very few logs can be get to the River this winter, owing to the bad Snoing — and Consequently they will increase the price towards Spring — Mrs Schuyler love to Sister Nancy, Phill & the Governor — your father I meant — Not Clinton[2] —

Yours &c &c
J.B. Schuyler

---

1. John Bradstreet Schuyler was the son of General Philip Schuyler. His father presented him with the Saratoga family estate upon his marriage to Elizabeth Van Rensselaer in 1787. Tuckerman, *Schuyler,* p. 265.

2. If bad blood existed between the Clintons and Schuylers, its origin was the result of a curious blend of political and social differences. The Schuylers considered themselves among the premier families of New York, and their aristocratic bearing naturally suited their Federalist politics. George Clinton, on the other hand, was considered by his adversaries to be several cuts below New York's finest. The Schuylers felt that Clinton's ego was a major stumbling block not only in New York's bid to ratify the Constitution, but also in developing a truly nationalistic spirit in the state. The Schuylers would continue to view Clinton as a machine politician who exploited popular issues to benefit his own career. Benson J. Lossing, *The Life and Times of Philip Schuyler* (New York, 1860), II, 441–448; Kass, p. 140.

230

Samuel Jones[1] to Pierre, Jr. ALS
SHR

Town of Cortlandt Feby 24th 1794.

Friend Cortlandt,

I wrote you some Time ago conserning a lot of Ground, I Desired an answer Immediately or as soon as convenient. my not receiving any Answer gives me reason to think you have never got my letter the Contents of it was as follows,

I am making preparations for building a House, and would rather Lease a piece of Ground of you, or the Governor than to build up the Road on my Fathers Land, I can assure you my Friend the Building shall be no Disgrace to the Corner, as I purpose to build as small as possible on acct. of Compleating it, the Lot of Ground which I should want is where the Shedd & Blacksmith shop stands, Did I think you had Recd: the other letter I should then think my proposals to you were offencive But knowing you to be a Gentleman that would not get Affrunted without some spesial offence I make bold to write to you on the subject thinking where I comit an Error in my eye'deas you will mend them, I should be happy to receive an answer from you, and hope if it is not in your power to give me a Lease you will Interceed with the Governor for me, whether it be in the Affirmative or negative Let me know by the first stage and if any ways Likely that I can get it, let me know on What conditions. Your complyance will much Oblidge thy

Humble Servant
Samuel Jones

Pierre Vn Cortlandt Junr Esqr

[Addressed] Pierre Vn Cortlandt Junr Esqr
Albany

---

1. Various Joneses resided in the town of Cortlandt at this time. As of 1790, a Samuel Jones, his wife, and one daughter lived in Mt. Pleasant. *Heads of Families 1790,* p. 200.

231

Thomas Morris[1] to Robert Morris. ALS
NYPL

Albany–March 24th–1794.

Dear Sir

I have the pleasure of introducing to your Acquaintance Mr. Pierre Van Cortlandt a Son of the Lieutenant Governor of this State & Mr DeWitt Clinton a Nephew of Governor Clintons both friends of mine. Any Attentions that you have it in your power to pay them during their stay in Philadelphia will be gratefully acknowledged by

Your Affect Son
Thomas Morris

---

1. Thomas Morris was the second of seven children of Robert Morris, the financial expert of the Revolution and of the new federal government. Thomas and his brother Robert, Jr. were sent to Europe for their educations, returning to the United States in 1788. Thomas then directed the operations of his father's land speculations in western New York, where the elder Morris acquired vast landholdings. In 1794 he sold three million acres to the Holland Land Company, while retaining a half million acre area for himself, which he hoped to settle. Ellis P. Oberholtzer, *Robert Morris: Patriot and Financier* (New York, 1903), pp. 263–265; Barbara A. Chernow, "Robert Morris: Genesee Land Speculator," *New York History*, LVIII (April, 1977), pp. 195–220.

232

Peter Jay Munro[1] to Pierre, Jr. ALS
NYPL

New York October 9th 1794.

Sir, —

Mr. Van Horne has directed me, to file a Bill against you, for improperly conducting his Suit against Mr. Brinkerhoff.[2] — I have written to you several times upon this subject without having been favored with an Answer.

I much regret the necessity of my instituting this suit against you, but unless you compromise this business by the first Day of next Term, I shall comply with the directions of my Client.

I am Sir
Your Hble Servt.
P. Jay Munro

[Addressed]
Pierre Van Cortlandt Junr. Esquire
Cortlandt
Mr Dusenbury is requested to forward this Letter immediately

---

1. Among the most respected Westchester lawyers of his day, Peter Jay Munro was a resident of Mamaroneck. He was in partnership with his cousin, Peter A. Jay, with offices located in New York City. The nature of this legal dispute remains unknown. Scharf, I, 539; Monaghan, pp. 430–431.

2. "Mr. Van Horne" was probably Augustus Van Horne, identified in No. 226. Abraham Brinckerhoff was a New York City merchant located at 10 Dock Street. *Polk's Directory* (1786), p. 23.

233

Abraham Bancker[1] to Pierre, Jr. ALS
NYPL

March 23, 1795.

Pierre Van Cortlandt Junr: Esqr. —
D^{r}: Sir.

Judge Ryerss,[2] in the course of the last Week, at a meeting of a few of his particular Friends & Connections purposely assembled on the Occasion, had himself nominated a Candidate for a Seat in the Senate of our State Legislature — In consequence of which, I have been sollicited, by a number of very respectable Inhabitants, to enter the Lists as his Opponent at the ensuing Election — The assurances I've received of being well supported, and the fervent Zeal I possess to promote the public Weal, as far as I am capable, have prompted me to listen with Attention to their Sollicitations, and have finally determined me to gratify them in their request; provided the Members of the present Legislature within this Southern District, will generally engage to promote and prosper my Election — I have in order to carry this measure into effect, thought proper to address you on this Occasion and to request, that you will be pleased, without delay, to take the Sense of the Members from your County in particular, and from the District in general with respect to the proposition now submitted to their Consideration. And, if upon Deliberation, the plan shall meet their Concurrence to have me publicly nominated as a Candidate — Being well assured of your Friendship towards me, I entertain not a doubt of your disposition to oblige me and those who are the real Friends of Liberty and the Constitution — I beg your Answer ere this week shall have elapsed —

I am, my dear Sir —

With Sentiments of Esteem & Regard,
Your most obed^{t}: h^{ble} Servt.

Richmond County

Abr^{m}: Bancker

Additional Correspondence

Castleton 23:[d] March 1795

---

1. Abraham Bancker served one term in the New York Assembly, from 1788 to 1790. In earlier years he acted as the county clerk and sheriff of Richmond County, and in 1792 as a surrogate. In 1804 he became an elector of the state of New York upon appointment by the legislature. Werner, pp. 361, 444, 463, 470.

2. Gozen Ryerss was a member of the New York Assembly from 1971 to 1797. He became a county judge in Richmond as of April, 1797, and served until February, 1802. *Ibid,* pp. 361–362, 437.

234

Commissioners of Highways
of the Town of Cortlandt. ADS
SHR

[June 9, 1795.]

We the Commissioners of Highways for the Town of Cortlandt do judge it necessary to raise the sum of Thirtyfive Pounds for the purpose of building a Bridge over PeeksKill on the Post road and to make improvements on the Public roads in the said Town. Given under our Hands this 9th. June 1795 —

Jonathan Ferris
John Haight
Richard Currey
Joseph Travis

Commissioners[1]

35
1.15.
1.8 Allowed

£36.16.8

1. Jonathan Ferris, a farmer in Cortlandt town, possessed land in the west ward assessed at £400. He would later serve as a supervisor of Cortlandt from 1817 to 1819. "Copy of a Tax list for the west ward on the Manor of Cortlandt, April 5, 1779," SHR Collections. John Haight possessed land in the west ward of Cortlandt assessed at £350. *Ibid.* Richard Currie possessed land in the west ward assessed at £300. *Ibid.* Joseph Travis is identified in No. 224.

235

Philip to Ebenezer Purdy[1]. ALS
Westchester County Historical Society

To Eb^n^. Purdy Esqr. Peeks kill
Octr. 1–1795.

Dear Sir.

You will please to remember that I consulted you about advancing Twenty five Pounds towards building the Bridge at Peeks kill[2] this Sum it seams i Already wanted to pay the men doing the Work and who have furnished the Materials and as I am now going to the Western Country and Very little Cash in my hands I beg you will pay the bearer that Sum and take his Receipt when I return I will send for you about the first of Nov^r^ — to make a final Settlement & am y^r^. Humble Servt.

Ph. V. Cortlandt

[Endorsed]
Cortlandts order to pay £20–50
paid on the order £20–

1. Ebenezer Purdy is identified in *VCFP,* II, 546, 582.

2. See preceding resolution of the Commissioners of Highways.

236

Benjamin Sneden to Philip. DS
SHR

November 21, 1795.

DISTRICT OF New York the Twenty first Day of November 1795 I, Benjamin Sneden Master Carpenter of Orange County in the State of New York do certify, That the Sloop named the Success was built under my Direction, at the mouth of Croton River during the year seventeen hundred and ninety-Five for Philip Van Cortlandt and Jacob Acker[1]

that the said Sloop is flat built, has one deck one mast is Forty two feet Keel in length, Sixteen feet Beam in breadth, and four feet, Three In= in depth, and of Twenty Nine Tons

As Witness my Hand, the Day and Year aforesaid.

Benjamin Sneden

[Endorsed] Benjn. Snedens. Certificate
as master Carpenter
of Sloop Success. 1795

---

1. Contracted by Captain Jacob Acker and Philip Van Cortlandt, the Sneden family of Orange County — including Samuel, Samuel, Jr., Lawrence, John, and Benjamin — all participated in building the sloop *Success*. Its construction took nearly six months at a labor cost which approached £200. See the following statement.

237

Benjamin, Lawrence, and Samuel Sneden to Philip. ADS
NYSHA

June–November, 1795.

Received at Croton June 22d. 1795 of Philip Van Cortlandt Seventy Dollars on Account of Self and printices work on the Vessle at Acker[2] — Samuel Sneden

£28.0.0

Received at Croton June. 22. 1795 of Philip Van Cortlandt Nine Pounds. 12/6 Infull. for 19¼ Days work at 10/ pr Day

£9.12.6 Lawrance Sneden

[Nov. 8, 1795.]

Received Novr. 8th. 1795 of Philip Van Cortlandt Five Pounds Two Shillings and Six pence Infull for my Work on the Sloop Success.

£5.2.6– Lawrance Sneden

Received Novr. 8. 1795 — of Philip Van Cortlandt Fourteen Pounds five Shillings Infull for 28½ Days Work on the Sloop Success —

£14.5.0 Samuel Sneden. Junr

Recd. Novr. 8. 1795 of Philip Van Cortlandt Thirty Two Pounds Inful for. 64. Days Work at the Sloop Success —

John Sneden Junr

£32.0.0

Received Novr. 8. 1795. of Philip Van Cortlandt Twelve Pounds Seven Shillings and Six Pence Infull for. 24¾. Days work on Sloop Success

£12.7.6 Benjamin Sneden

[Nov. 5, 1795.]

Received Novr. 5. 1795 of Philip Van Cortlandt Twenty Six Pounds Seventeen Shillings & 6d. Inful for Calking and Carpenters Work on the Sloop Success —

£26.17.6 Rich'd Steed

[Nov. 10, 1795.]

Received Novr. 10. 1795. of Philip V.Cortlandt Ten Pounds Infull for Sawing 2583=feet of Plank for Sloop Success —
£10.0.0 Benjamin McCord[2]

[Nov. 14, 1795.]

Received Novr. 14th. 1795. of Philip Van Cortlandt Twenty Five Pounds Inful for 21½ Days work of my Father and 26. Days of my Brother and my Self before the Decease of my Father —

£12.18–
13 —
£25.18.0

Benjamin Sneden

also. Received Twenty Shilling being a Ballance due on gitting the Timber —

Benjamin Sneden

---

1. The Sneden family of Orange County was headed by John Sneden, and as of 1790 consisted of his wife, six sons, and three daughters. There was also a Samuel Sneden of New York City's East Ward, with a family of five. *Heads of Families 1790,* pp. 117, 146.

2. Both Benjamin McCord and his son, Benjamin, Jr., were heads of families in Cortlandt at this time. "Federal Census, 1800," LVIII (1927), 140, 141.

238

Francis Asbury[1] to Pierre, Jr. AL [Copy]
SHR

Brunxs River Augt. 29–1797.

My much respected freind

I have a serious leisure to write to my Friends but mental and Bodily powers are weak. I am greatly obliged to you for the remembrance of me and earnest wish to see me at your mansion. It is upwards of twelve years since I began the wreak of my constitution, when I became more immediately the Superintendant of our Community in America. We have been assisted to spread our Gospel; from Freinds and Societies through the Sixteen United States, the North West Territory, Upper Canada and the other British Provinces. altho we do not number, yet we may calculate, upon One hundred thousand in the above named States in Freindship and in some degree of Fellowship with us, and perhaps ten hundred thousand that are our regular hearers. Thus hath the Lord wrought for and by us his Ministers and People; if we may even dare to call ourselves so. Many of our Preachers have suffered want, hunger, Labour[,]Lodging, Rocks, rivers, mountains, wildernesses; preaching in the Southern States night and Day, The People following to their lodgings, whenever a Preacher is in the Settlements; The Tribes of poor Africans coming in the night that cannot come in the day. The unhealthy climates, many young Men that have seldom wrought at hard labour, and tenderly brought up, where they have had Servants to do the drudgery of the plantations. These have had little less except the Clash of Arms and Encampments, many of the hardships of the American war, that you have known something of. Their zeal and indefatigable Labours wrecking their slender systems. A rehearsal of these things to Doctor Joseph Ramsay[2] in Charlestown astonished him, and that for the poor pittance of 64 Dollars, the half or one third, this made the Doctor offer and continue to our Ministers his medicines and Service Gratis. Of myself I may speak as a fool if my Journals ever pass the press, it will satisfy the Candid whether I have been labouring or Loitering, whether I have been resting on Beds of ease, or suffering night dews. I stand astonished at myself and the goodness of God that I have been kept alive and moving; during my ten months indisposition I have rode upon horseback above Two thousand miles in the worst of weather and Country south and west. And yet after all I am an unprofitable Servant, I have not done my duty.

My dear freind I feel a great Tenderness for you and the whole Family for your distinguished kindness to our

People when they were few in number. You are blest with a Godly mother, as I am also, you have a gracious Sister, whose Soul with mine, longeth for the Salvation of your Soul; and the soul of your Brother. But how hardly shall they that not only have much of this world, but are in connection with the policy and interests of this world. My dear freind you hear, you feel the Gospel, do you pray and strive? Early you have been called and are a Child of a mother's prayers and Tears, Jesus hath wept hath bled for you. from a Child God hath been at work on your heart, probably in war and Trouble saved, and perhaps you promised God, if he would spare you, you would seek him. When the Methodists came along at the first you had perhaps powerful and palpable conviction, you could not hide it, you did not wish to hide it, you cannot keep away from Methodist preaching, you would feel a great disappointment and pain not to come to hear; you cannot be happy in worldly enjoyments? You love some of the Ministry as your own Soul, yea perhaps more than your own Soul, if yet you do not love God. I should be happy to see you, and to see you love Jesus. I have been forbid reading writing and such exercises; Elder Wells that attends me, writeth my letters in general; but I would trust None with this, but myself, if ever I see you again, may it be in Jesus. Farewell —

most affectionately yours.
F. Asbury

Excuse me, I am in the Country and want paper.
With great respect remember me to the family

[Endorsed]
Copy of a Letter from Bishop Asbury to P V[n] Cortlandt Jun[r]

---

1. Francis Asbury can be credited with the successful spread of the Methodist faith in early America. As one of his biographers described him, he was "probably the greatest ecclesiastical or-

ganizer this country ever produced." He not only served as the administrator of the loyal bands of itinerant preachers, but participated as one of them, traveling on foot or on horseback over thousands of miles, reaching thousands of people with his powerful sermons. Never an imposing figure in appearance, Bishop Asbury (so consecrated on December 27, 1784) suffered from many years of exposure to all manner of inclement weather, dependent always on the hospitality of his converts for food and shelter. Among the warmest welcomes were those offered by Joanna and Pierre Van Cortlandt.

By March, 1797, he fell extremely ill and could not continue circuit riding on horseback. Friends assisted him to Baltimore, where he arrived on June 10. Although still quite ill, he attended a conference in Philadelphia in mid-August, and then set out through New Jersey for New York, where he arrived in late August. The Bishop rode as far as Kingsbridge, where he collapsed and spent two weeks in bed. Again he insisted on proceeding before he was fully recovered and forged ahead as far as New Rochelle, where he fainted and was rescued by local residents. Despite his serious illness, Bishop Asbury was spiritually driven to continue the spread of the gospel and felt guilt for every wasted moment, even though necessarily spent in a sick bed. Herbert Asbury, *A Methodist Saint* (New York, 1927), pp. 160–163, 285.

2. It is likely that Asbury meant Dr. John Ramsey of Charleston, South Carolina. William M. Clemens, ed., *North and South Carolina Marriage Records From the Earliest Colonial Days to the Civil War* (New York, 1927), p. 227.

239

Daniel D. Tompkins[1] to Philip. ALS

NYPL

New York Novmr. 24. 1797.

Dear Sir,

In pursuance of your request, I have ascertained the terms upon which Mr. Munro[2] will take my friend Mr. Vn Wyck.[3]

Two clerks who are now with him, pay him one

hundred and fifty pounds each; But upon my assuring him that Mr Van Wyck would be a more valuable Clerk to him, than either of those two, he has consented to take him upon the same terms I lived with him.

I am persuaded that it will not be arrogant for me to say that the services I rendered Mr Munro during my continuance with him, would have made it as proper for him to have abated my fee, as that of any Clerk he could have taken. But I assure you, that I paid him the whole sum agreed upon with my own hand, being one hundred pounds. I am not ignorant that it is believed by most of my friends that I ought not to have paid any fee, and they therefore conclude that none was accepted; But this is a mistake and the reason, why I have kept the thing private, is the same which will render it proper not to divulge your Nephew's terms, because his other Clerks pay him more.

I yesterday received a letter from Mr Van Wyck, expressing great anxiety to hear from me on the above subject, which I shall delay answering until I have the pleasure to hear from you.

I am, Dear Sir
with respect Your Most obt Servt.

Daniel D. Tompkins

The Honbl. Philip Vn:Cortlandt Esqr.

[Addressed] The Honbl. Philip VnCortlandt Esqr.
Philadelphia

[Endorsed]

Danl. D. Tomkins Novr.21.1794
Mr. Munro will take P.C. Van Wyck

---

1. Daniel D. Tompkins is identified in *VCFP,* III, 187. Politics soon separated the Van Cortlandts from Tompkins.

2. Peter Jay Munro, a pillar of the New York bar, was Tompkins's

legal mentor and close family friend. Irwin, pp. 14–15. See also No. 232.

3. A reference to Pierre C. Van Wyck, Philip's nephew. He is further identified in *VCFP,* III, 5, 213, 214, 366.

240

Daniel Delavan[1] to Pierre. ALS
NYPL

North Salem 22d of Jan 1798.

Dear Sir/

I was at Salem yesterday was there Invited to become a Member of a lodge to be instatuted in bedford whereof Sam yongs[2] is Master that yongs now is in New york & has Such Incoragements that they Say there is not the least danger but what a Dispensation will be obtain'd — good god has the Masonick Instatution Come to this that Such a Man as yongs who is So obnactious in his Conduct Manners so unpopular & such an infamous lyar Such a Creature Shoud now have the Confidance Placd in him as to become the father of that Sacred order[.]I Confess my Self an unworthy Member yet unless that there is a Check Post to the Progress of Such fellows I as to my Self will be a Shamed to own my Self a mason — for Supposition Suppose that Saml. yongs was not admited in to a lodge wheather he coud get admition where he is Now wheather Such fellows that gets admitions, in a Clandestine manner shoud not be kept where they are[3]

I am your 3th three
Dan. Delavan

Pyar Van Cortlandt

---

1. Daniel Delavan served as sheriff of Westchester from 1806 to

1807. Scharf, I, xx. For further details on Delavan, see *VCFP*, III, 51.

2. A Westchester lawyer and radical Republican, Samuel Young served in the state Assembly from 1776 to 1797, and again from 1808 to 1809. A valued member of the Albany Regency, Young ended his public career as a surrogate for Westchester County. Bolton, I, xxi; Werner, pp. 416, 422, 504. See also Dixon R. Fox, *The Decline of the Aristocracy in the Politics of New York, 1801–1840* (New York, 1919, repr. 1965), p. 239.

3. Pierre, Sr. was a member of Cortlandt Lodge No. 34 of the Masonic Order at this time. Within two years he would serve as Grand Master of the Lodge, only to later have his membership jeopardized as a result of his frequent absences from Lodge meetings. Joseph M. Fox, pp. 112, 171, 172.

241

Joshua Sands[1] to Pierre, Jr. ALS
NYPL

Feby 13th 1798.

Sir

Your Brother General Courtland on his way to Congress, produced to this Office a Bill of Sale for the Sloop Joanna of Courtland Town, Benjamin Salts master,[2] It is necessary before new papers can be issued, that the old ones be lodged here, you will therefore transmit them by the earliest opportunity.

I am Sir
Your Obedient Servant
Josh Sands
Collector

Custom house New York

---

1. Joshua Sands served as the collector of the port of New York in 1798. As chief port officer, he was responsible for the collection

of the custom duties. Although his lineage is not certain, he may well have been the brother of the more famous Comfort Sands of the Revolutionary era. That Joshua Sands was born October 12, 1757, the youngest of eight children of John Sands III and Elizabeth (Cornell) Sands. In 1783 the brothers embarked on a large business venture in New York City, which lasted until 1794. Joshua married Ann Ayscough, the daughter of a British army surgeon, on March 9, 1780. He died September 13, 1835. *Longworth's Directory* (1798), p. 34; Temple Prime, *Descent of Comfort Sands and His Children* (New York, 1897), pp. 10, 13–14; Malcolm Sands Wilson, *Descendants of James Sands of Block Island* (New York, 1949), pp. 23–24.

2. The captain of the Van Cortlandt sloop *Joanna* as early as 1797, Benjamin Salts (Saltz) was a Cortlandt resident with a family of five, *Heads of Families 1790*, p. 197; *VCFP*, II, 586.

242

Ann Jay to Ann Stevenson.[1] ALS
SHR

Bedford Janry. 25th. 1802.

Your kind favor dear Anne merited an earlier acknowledgement, indeed I should have thanked you before for it, had I known any thing amusing or interesting to communicate. It shall be my endeavour dearest Anne to deserve the affection & good wishes you express for me, for which I really feel grateful — Nor can my friend desire more to see me, than I long for the pleasure of seeing her, a pleasure which must be post-poned for the present — What a delightful season this has been. altho' not the most agreeable, still very pleasant. In the country tis less gay than in the City, but I am far from supposing that the winter evenings, which some think very long, can be more agreeably passed in an assembly room, than with a pleasant little circle around a comfortable fire.

Since your last, we have began a New Year; the thoughts which that naturally inspires, are to look back upon those that have gone & reflect upon the changes which time has made. How swiftly Anne time flies, & takes us with it — a few years will now deprive us of our youth, & then not many more are necessary to put an end to our career — already I can discover a vast alteration among my acquaintances, within 6 or 8 years many of them have closed their eyes upon all earthly scenes — Some families who then appeared to live in harmony & friendship are now left to mourn the loss of tender parents & affec[t]. brothers & sisters. others again that are almost all gone; as is the case of several — Fickle fortune too has made her changes, & rendered many, whom she once favored greatly, now unhappy — Indeed there is few whose situations are not very much altered. But perhaps my friend these are unwelcome reflections. your society has likewise felt the effects of time, & is now threatened with farther diminution, which Good God forbid. Pardon me, my intention was not to give pain, these considerations were chiefly awakened by receiving a letter yesterday from a friend at N.Y. who informed me that a relation of hers, whom I have often seen at school, lays at the point of death beyond all probability of recovering, & will soon follow her sister, who died a few months ago, likewise quite young. She speaks of her cousin with great tenderness & as entirely resigned to die — We too Anne in our turn will also die — Oh that we may be prepared for that aweful event, that we may deprive death of its sting — and is it dear Anne unnatural that reflecting on the death bed of a young schoolmate should give rise to serious considerations —

Adieu my dear friend, may you [torn] many happy years, but as wishing you perfect happiness here is but a vain desire, for true it is, that no age or [torn] exempt from trouble, I will extend my thoughts to the other world, where, may you enjoy forever supreme bliss — My best respects to your dear Mama, & best love to Caty, whom I wish very much to see — Again Adieu and believe me

your much attached friend
Ann Jay

Miss Stevenson

[Addressed]
Miss Stevenson
Albany

---

1. Born in Paris in 1783, Ann Jay was the daughter of John and Sarah (Livingston) Jay. She died unmarried in New York in 1856. John Jay, *Memorials of Peter A. Jay, Compiled for His Descendants* (Holland, privately printed, 1929), pp. 6, 207.
Ann Stevenson, who would become the second wife of Pierre, Jr. in 1813, is identified in *VCFP*, III, xliii.

243

Theodorus Bailey[1] and Philip to Thomas Jefferson. ALS LC

Capital 3d May 1802.

Sir,

We take the liberty to recommend the following Gentlemen as suitable persons to be appointed Commissioners of Bankruptcy in and for the District of New york, pursuant to the 14 section of the late Act amending the Judicial system of the United States — vizt Pierre C. Van Wyck, of the City of New york, and Samuel Hawkins and James Tallmadge Junior,[2] of Poughkeepsie in the County of Dutchess. All these Gentlemen are in the practice of the Law as Attornies and Counsellors — And we do not hesitate to vouch for the soundness of their morals and republican principles.

We have the honor to be, Sir, with
great Consideration and respect,
your most Obedt Servants,
Theodorus Bailey
Ph. VCortlandt

Additional Correspondence

The President of the United States

Pierre C. Van Wyck
N.Y.

Samuel Hawkins
Poughkeepsie

James Tallmadge J^{r}
Poughkeepsie

May 3, 1802

Recom^{d} for Comm^{rs} of Bankruptcy
by
Theodorus Bailey
Ph. V Cortlandt

---

1. Theodorus Bailey, a native of Poughkeepsie, was admitted to the New York bar in 1789. He attained the rank of brigadier general of the New York militia, was first elected as a congressman in 1792, and later became a U.S. Senator. At the time of this letter, Bailey was postmaster for the City of New York. He was politically and socially associated with the Tallmadge family. *Biographical Directory American Congress,* p. 540; *VCFP,* II, 593; III, 20, 495, 533.

2. Samuel Hawkins was a Poughkeepsie attorney who served in Theodorus Bailey's militia unit. He moved to Ulster County in 1801 and accepted a position as a district attorney. Werner, pp. 423, 506; *Council of Appointment, Military,* I, 564, 711.

   Another Poughkeepsie resident, James Tallmadge, Jr. studied law upon graduating from Rhode Island College. He soon became the secretary to Governor George Clinton. During his term of office as a congressman, Tallmadge became noted for the 1819 antislavery amendment that bears his name. *DAB,* XVIII, 285–286; VCFP, III, 282, 437.

   Jefferson did not act favorably upon these recommendations.

244

Philip to Thomas Jefferson ALS
LC

Washington Feby 1, 1804.

Sir,

Rufus Easton Esqr[1] who will present this has informed me that he is an Applicant for an Office under the Territory of Louisiana and has expressed a desire that I should communicate the knowledge I have respecting him —

I remember meeting Mr Easton one Morning at Oneida and was favorably impressed which produced inquiry and was informed that he resided at Rome and was a Councillor at law of respectable reputation and I have lately received a letter from M^{r}. D. Clinton giving me Similar information with a request that I shold introduce him to the members of the State and afford him every proper Attention and patronage in conjunction with them this is therefore intended as an Assurance of my Esteem for M^{r}. Easton and my concurrance with my Colleigues in sentiment.

Please to Accept the tribute of
my high Respect & Esteem
Ph. V. Cortlandt

Van Cortlandt Ph Dat Feb 02 rec^{d} Feb 6
Easton Rufus to be Atty N.O.

---

1. Rufus Easton is identified in *VCFP,* III, 400. See also No. 19.

245

Margaret Stuyvesant[1] to Ann Stevenson. ALS
SHR

Bowery House August 7th 1810.

Your requesting to be made acquainted with the particulars of the passage, and of my safe arrival here, accorded too much with my own inclination, for me to delay any longer complying with this request; be assured my dear Ann that the most lively gratitude for your kind attention & sincere regard for yourself & family will render me desirous of being remembered by you, and if an occasional letter will serve to remind you of one who finds so much pleasure in thinking of you I shall be careful to prevent your forgetting me, — you were acquainted with the circumstance of my being disappointed by Mrs: Coles not going in the Steam-boat, as I was to have been of her party; I felt a little unpleasant on the occasion, for we females are dependant beings; by the time I had reasoned on the subject, sufficiently to be reconciled to it, I was agreeably surprised, by her coming on board at Hudson. — we had a great number of passengers & more ladies than rendered it pleasant or comfortable, among the number there was one whose propensity to talking was neither sanctioned by judgment nor enlivened by wit, and who's childish prattle disturbed those whom the heat & other inconveniences would have suffered to obtain some rest. — the following morning we were much amused in attending court, there were many brought before the bar & the generality found guilty. the Capt: was among the first of the criminals, the charge alledged was his having taken sheep on board as freight, but in consideration of his being in the Employ of the Chancellor (whos sheep they were) his sentence was greatly mitigated.[2] — the principal offenders were those who had disturbed the quiet of the preceding night. — I could not restrain the wish that the talkative lady might be arrainged, but in this case I found ladies are of a privileged order. — No accident took place except the breaking of some of the machinery which was soon repaired & did not detain us more than three or four hours; we arrived at about five in the Afternoon; and I had the happiness of finding My Mother & friends in Good health, my coming was quite a surprise to them as they did not expect me until Sister Ten Broeck came,[3] she is not yet arrived but we are in hourly expectation of seeing her. — I have been to Richards (the jeweller)[4] he says he can put the inscription as you wish to have it, by placing the date on the inside. in case he makes the rings of equal weight with the one you gave me as a pattern, he will charge twelve dollars a piece, but if they are lighter they will be ten. — As I thought they would be quite as handsome for being thiner I told him not to make them until I receive further directions from you; he says it will not take him more than a fortnight to make them, & if you will have the goodness to let me know by the next steam-boat, I will send him word immediately, how they are to be done. — the hair bracelets like those of mine, are from nine to twelve dollars a pair. — he setts pearl, but has not any small enough to form a cipher. your slippers are not yet done, I will send them by the return of Capt: Boyd should Mrs: Stevenson or yourself wish to have anything done which will be in my power to Attend to, you will confer a favor in acquainting me with it. — please to offer My Affectionate regards to your Mother your brother James & Mrs: Walsh,[5] you may if so disposed offer the same to Mr: Walsh though I must acknowledge I was not quite satisfied in his refusing my invitation, as I flattered myself, he would be repaid for the trouble & fatigue in having my society & the pleasure of seeing his friends in the Bowery, who would have derived much pleasure in having him among them; my Mother sends her kind love remember me to the Children, or rather to Mr John & Miss

Walsh with the children, I suppose they will yet submit to being reckoned among them, with sincere affection & regard your friend

Margt: Stuyvesant

Should it not be convenient to you to favor me with an answer by the next Steam-boat depute your brother; as he is of the quill driving order it will not be attended with much trouble to him. — I shall however anticipate the pleasure of soon hearing from yourself. — have the goodness to let me know whether it is milk or white of egg which is to be mix'd with the lime for making a cement for mending China — M.S.

[Addressed]
Miss Stevenson
Albany Steamboat
to the care of James Stevenson Esqr.

---

1. Margaret Stuyvesant was the daughter of Petrus and Margaret (Livingston) Stuyvesant. Reynolds, III, 1015. See also No. 29.

2. Robert R. Livingston was well known for his breeding experiments with merino sheep.

3. Margaret was no doubt writing of Mrs. Cornelia (Stuyvesant) Ten Broeck, wife of Dirck Ten Broeck. Munsell, *Collections,* IV, 171.

4. Stephen Richard was a New York City jeweler and enameler located at 160 Broadway as of 1808. *Longworth's Directory* (1808), p. 268.

5. James Stevenson served as mayor of Albany from 1826 to 1828. He later helped to incorporate the Albany Gaslight Company in 1841, and served as a city water commissioner in 1850. He died in 1852. Howell and Tenney, pp. 516, 572; Werner, p. 558.

Ann Stevenson's sister married Dudley Walsh, an Irish immigrant who rose to prominence both financially and socially in Albany. He became a director of the Bank of Albany in 1795, and served as its president from 1810 to 1814. Munsell, *Annals,* I, 291; III, 129; IV, 6, 116, 304.

246

Margaret Stuyvesant to Ann Stevenson. ALS
SHR

Bowery-House August 17th 1810.

The pleasure of being thought of by those we esteem, is too satisfactory to relinquish, & I derive so much gratification in cherishing the recollection of the kind attention of yourself and family while I was your guest, that with your permission, my dear Ann, I will continue a Correspondence from which I contemplate the hope of being more actively continued in your remembrance. — had I never previously been disposed to love & regard yourself & excellent mother, it would be impossible not to do so after having witnessed the composed & Christian resignation exercised under the severe pressure of Affliction — which is evidently distinct & different in its nature from what is styled fortitude, but (what to me) appears like want of feeling. — I was as much delighted in finding my presence was no restraint, as gratified in the many instances of kindness I received & it will be my future wish to be Considered among the number of those who have claims on your friendship & love. —

I received your letter on Monday, for which I offer my thanks — Sister Ten Broeck arrived the same day, I think her health is greatly improved, she has not as yet regained her usual spirits & strength which is all that is now wanting to her being quite well — she mentioned having dined with you the day before she left Albany. — I am truly concerned to hear that you are kept in so alarming & anxious a state from the apprehension of fire; it is my earnest hope & prayer that your anxiety will soon be dissipated by the discovery of those detestable & vile perpetrators of so Nefarious a Crime.[1] —

When I was last in the City, I call'd at Richards & told him of what you mentioned respecting the rings — his answer was that if he had told the Jeweller he would make them for eight dollars, they must have been rings of a different description from the one I gave him as a pattern — as he told me it would be impossible for him to make them for less than ten dollars a piece, I have directed him to make them at that price agreeable to your order — he says they will not be done in less than four or five weeks. —

I send this by Capt: Boyed in preference to the Steam-Boat as your slippers are to go by the same opportunity. I have taken the liberty of detaining the one you gave me as a pattern, that in case you should wish to have others made the shoemaker may be the better enabled to ascertain the exact size as it is probable he might make a mistake having made only one pair, I do not recollect whether I mentioned the price in my last, which is fourteen shillings. — The two small box's which accompanies the package you will please to present to Margaret & Ann Walsh with my love — offer the affectionate regard of my mother & self to your Mama & the family — sincerely your friend M.Stuyvesant sending you the receipt for the white paint, had escaped my recollection until I had closed your letter — it is as follows

[torn out]

---

1. Between August 4 and 10, 1810, a series of destructive fires occurred in a residential area of Albany. The official verdict was arson. On the 7th, Mayor Philip S. Van Rensselaer issued a proclamation offering a $500 reward for the apprehension of "some incendiary or incendiaries." New-York *Herald,* August 11, 15, 1810.

247

Margaret Stuyvesant to Ann Stevenson. ALS
SHR

Bowery House April 1st 1811.

Although so long a period has elapsed since I have received any information from you, I flatter myself that a few lines from one who has Experienced so many proofs of your kindness and regard, will not be unwelcome, and as your brother James has promised to answer my letters in Case you should be too much occupied or not be disposed to do so, I shall at least have the satisfaction to hear particularly of yourself and family. — I inquire of Mrs: Ten Broeck whether Abraham makes any mention, and her reply is "Nothing particular"[1] . . which does not in the least Satisfy me — I wish to hear that you are well and happy, at least that you Enjoy Comparative happiness, for true piety and submission to the Will of God will not only reconcile us to the Afflictions our Natures are Constantly exposed but will with the practice of religion and resignation, produce a consciousness of the fulfilment of duty on our part, as may render us contented & happy in the humble trust of possessing the favor & love of Him who has power to Extend every benefit towards those who Serve Him in faith. — I wish also, My dear Ann to know that I am still thought of by yourself & excellent Mother, it would cause me as much pain to be forgotten by you as it gives me pleasure to bear you both in remembrance, which it will be always my desire to do with sincere friendship and affection, at present there are few circumstances would render me so happy as your society if only for a day — I think I am entitled to expect it for a longer period, for if I mistake not you promised to make a visit to Bowery in the Spring; the season as yet, promises to be fine and I trust you will not disappoint the expectations I have entertained since we parted. — the Change of air would greatly benefit the health of yourself and Mother, independant of the pleasure it would Communicate to your friends here, and your Sister will not expect you should remain at home for her twice a year . . .

You have doubtless heard of the Illness of our Good Bishop,[2] he is better than he has been, but it is not thought by his physicians that his health will ever be restored — I fear that his loss will be irreparable to the Church, at least that it will be difficult to find a Character in Every respect so adequate to supply his place. — I am told that your Clergyman is getting very much in favor and that it is the intention of the vestry to give him a permanent Call. It is a Subject of importance & if they have done so, we have reason to Conclude that they are well satisfied that he is fully capable of being useful in so large a congregation. —

There is no news worth relating & as to what is passing in the fashionable world, I do not suppose it would impart more satisfaction to you in receiving, than it would me in the relation — but to confess a truth which would be Condemned by many, I have neither taste nor Spirits to participate in the Gaiety & pleasures of the City, nor have I even visited it since last September, and what is so interesting to the Gay & fashionable is listened to by me, with an indifference which would draw upon me from them the appelation of stupidity. —

Towards the last of January I was taken ill with a violent Cold, which confined me to my room for nearly [torn] weeks, I am now quite recovered except occasionally [torn] with a pain in my breast. — the rest of the family [torn] usual health — we were much alarmed in consequence of an accident which happened to Eliza's little girl (the youngest) from having her arm fractured, it is more than a week since it happened & she is now almost recovered from it. —

Although I consent to your brother James writing when you are not inclined to, I should not wish him the trouble of perusing my letters as they are only Submitted to your indulgence & not the criticism of a Scholar — my love to him & Mrs Walsh — be so good as to offer the love of my mother to your parent & for me say whatever can express a sense of gratitude & affection which will ever be retained by your friend Marg^{t}: Stuyvesant

[Addressed]
Steam Boat
Miss Stevenson
State Street
Albany
To the care of James Stevenson Esqr.

---

1. Margaret was referring to Abraham Ten Broeck, the son of Dirck and Cornelia (Stuyvesant) Ten Broeck. Munsell, *Collections,* IV, 171.

2. Reverend Benjamin Moore, former rector of Trinity Church, was invested as the bishop of the Protestant Episcopal Church of New York in 1801. He suffered ill health in 1811, and an assistant was chosen for him, the Reverend John D. Hobart, of Trinity Church. Wilson, IV, 627.

Business, Land, and Legal Transactions

Editor's Note
Slave Sales

The ownership of slaves was quite common throughout New York during the colonial and early national periods. With a labor shortage existing in agricultural regions, the family frequently obtained slaves for work in and about the house. The Van Cortlandt slaves were used primarily in mill activities, slaughtering and butchering meat for market, and in the household. The following six documents deal with the sale of slaves in Westchester County in the period 1754–1804. Note the purchase prices for the slaves. It is to be recalled that a group of slaves possessed by Pierre, Sr. was manumitted following his death in 1814. See *VCFP, III,* 718–720, and *passim.*

248

Isaac Brinckerhoff to James G. Livingston, ADS
SHR

October 1, 1754.

TO ALL PEOPLE To whom these Presents shall Come I Isaac Brinckerhoff Esquire High Sheriff of Dutchess County Send GREETING WHEREAS a certain Writt of ffiere ffacias [fieri facias] to me Directed bearing date the Nineteenth day of October Last Issued from and out of the Inferior Court of Common Pleas for the County of Dutchess by which Writt I Was Commanded that of the goods & Chattles of Thomas Newcomb in my bailiwick I Should Cause to be made Nineteen Pounds Six Shillings and six pence Lawfull money of New York which to Henry Livingston in the said Inferior Court of Common Pleas before the judges & justices of the same court Lately held at Poghkeepsie in & for the said County, were adjudged for his Damages which he had sustained as well by Occasion of a Certain Tresspass upon the Case, to the same Henry by the Aforesaid Thomas Lately done as for his Costs & Charges by him about his suit in that behalf Appointed, whereof in the said Court said Thomas Newcomb was convicted as Appears of Record of the Aforesaid Goods & Chattles to be Levied AND that I should have those moneys before the said judge & justices at Poghkeepsie in said County on the third Tuesday in May Last to Render to the said Henry Livingston for his Damages Costs & Charges Afs[d] which said Writt of ffiere ffacias after the date & before the Return thereof was Delivered unto mee in due form of Law to be Executed By Virtue whereof and of the Statute in such Case Lately made and Provided of the Goods & Chattles of the said Thomas Newcomb in my Bailiwick I did Seize and take a Negro mulatto Girl Named Bridget Aged about fourteen years. and I did on Monday the Sixteenth day of September Last at one O Clock in the afternoon at the Court House in Poghkeepsie Expose the said Negro Girl to Sale at publick vendue after Having publickly advertized her for above Twenty days and Sold her to James G. Livingston of Poghkeepsie Gent^{m} & Barent Bond of the same place Cooper for the Sum of Twenty one pounds New York Money in Satisfaction of the Damages Costs and Charges Aforesaid and the Charges of Seizing & Exposing to sale & NOW KNOW YEE that I by virtue of the said Writt of ffiere ffacias to mee Directed as Aforesaid and by Virtue of the Statute in Such case Lately made and provided for & in Consideration of the said Sum of Twenty One Pounds New York money to mee in hand paid by the said James G. Livingston & Barent Bond to be Applyed and Rendered as Aforesaid the Receipt whereof I do hereby Acknowledge HAVE Bargained & sold and by these Presents DOE Bargain Sell Assign set over and Convey unto the Said James G. Livingston and Barent Bond their Heirs and Assigns for Ever. the said Negro Girl Named Bridget Aged about fourteen years, as the same is now in my possession and was possessed off. by the said Thomas Newcomb Together with all the Right title Interest which he the said Thomas Newcomb had of in and to the same TO HAVE AND TO HOLD the said Negro mulatto Slave unto the said James G. Livingston and Barent Bond their Heirs & Assigns to their only property benefit & behoof for Ever AS fully and Absolutely as I the said Isaac Brincherhoff might could or ought to do by force and Virtue of the said writt of ffiere ffacias and by force and Virtue of the Statute Aforesaid or Otherwise Howsoever. IN WITNESS whereof I, the said Isaac Brinckerhoff have — Hereunto Set my Hand and Seal this ffirst day of October in the Year of our Lord One Thousand Seven Hundred and fifty four —

Isaac Brinckerhoff Sheriff

Sealed & Delivered In The presence of
Thomas Newcomb Junr
Clear [Clare] Everts

249

Baltus Van Kleek to Pierre. ADS
SHR

June 13, 1758.

Know all Men by these Presents That I Baltus Van Kleek of Rumbout Precinct in Dutchess County and The Province of New York Yeoman for and in Consideration of the Sum of Ninety Pounds Current Money of the Province of New York to me in Hand Paid at and before the Ensealing and Delivery of these Presents by Pierre Van Courtlandt of Courtlandt Manor in the Province of New York the receipt whereof I do Hereby Acknowledge and My Self to be Therewith fully Satisfied Contented and Paid have Granted Bargained Sold and Released and by these Presents do fully Clearly and Absolutely Grant Bargain Sell and Release unto the Said Piere Van Courtlandt a Negro Man Slave Named Tom Aged About Twenty-four years To HAVE AND TO HOLD the Said Negro Man Slave named Tom unto the said Piere Van Courtlandt His Heirs Executors Administrators and Assigns for Ever, and I the said Baltus Van Kleek for my Self my heirs & Executors and Administrators do Covenant and agree to and with the above Named Piere Van Courtlandt his Executors Administrators and Assigns to warrant and Defend the Sale of the above Named Negro Man Slave Named Tom Against all Persons Whatsoever In-Witness Whereof I have hereunto Set my hand and Seal the Thirteenth day of June One Thousand Seven Hundred and fifty Eight.

Sealed and Delivered
In the Presence of Jacob Conklin

her
Sarah X Drake
mark

his
Baltus Van X Kleek
mark

[endorsed]
Bill of Sale
From Baltus Van Kleek
For Negro Tom
Paid Him 95–

250

John Vaile to Pierre. ADS
SHR

October 31, 1760.

Know all Men by these presents that I John Vaile of the Manor of Cortlandt In the province of New York & County of Westchester yeoman for and In Consideration of the Sum of Ninety pounds Current money of the province afores[d] — To me In hand paid at & before the Ensealing & Delivery of These present By Pierre Van Cortlandt Esq[r] of the Manor aforesaid, the Receipt whereof I Doe hereby acknowledge and myself to be Therewith fully Satisfied and Paid and thereof & Every part Thereof I do hereby Acquit and Discharge him the Said Pierre Van Cortlandt his heirs Executors administrators And Assigns. By These presents have granted Bargained and Sold. And by These presents do fully, Clearly And Absolutely grant Bargain & Sell And Release unto him the said Pierre Van Cortlandt a Certain Negro wench named Pegg with her female Child, aged about 20 years the wench & Child about Six months To have & to hold the Said Negro wench & Child Unto him the said Pierre Van Cortlandt his heirs Executors Administrators and Assigns for ever And I the Said John Vaile for my Self my heirs Executors & administrators Doe covenant promice And grant to & with the Said Pierre Van Cortlandt his heirs

Executors administrators And Assigns to warrant and the Sale of the above Named Negro wench Pegg & her Child against all persons whatsoever In witness whereof I the Said John Vaile have hereunto set my hand & Seale This 31 day of October In the Year of Our Lord 1760.
Witness, Signed Sealed and Delivered In the presents of

John Vail
Moses Knap
Phillip Van Cortlandt

[Endorsed]
Bill of Sale For Negro wench
Pegg & Child From John Vaile to —
Pierre Van Cortlandt
1760

251

Thomas Stilwell to Pierre. ADS
SHR

May 11, 1770.

Know all Men by these Presents That I Thomas Stillwell of the Manor of Cortlandt in the Province of New York Hatt maker for and in Consideration of the sum of Fifty Pounds Current money of the Province aforesaid to one in hand of Said at and before the Ensealing and Delivery of these Presents by Pierre Van Cortlandt of Cortlandt Manor in the Province aforesaid the receipt whereof I do hereby acknowledge and myself to be therewith fully satisfied contented and Said have Granted Bargained Sold & released and by these Presents do fully Clearly and Absolutely Grant Bargain Sell and Release unto the Said Pierre Van Cortlandt a Negro Girl Slave Named Elizabeth unto the said Pierre Van Cortland his heirs Executors Administrators and Assigns to Warrant and Defend the Sale of the Above Named Negro

Girl Slave Named Elizabeth Against all Persons Whatsoever In Witness whereof I have hereunto set my hand and Seal the Eleventh Day of May One Thousand Seven hundred & Seventy —

Thomas Stillwell

Sealed and Delivered In the
Presence of John Valleau
Phillip Cortlandt

[Endorsed]
Bill of Sale From
Thomas Stillwell for
Negro Girl Betty
Paid him 50.0.0

252

John Brown[1] to Philip. DS
SHR

June 4, 1787.

Know all Men by these Presents, That I John Brown of the Manor of Cortlandt and County of West Chester For and in Consideration of the Sum of Fifty Pounds. Current Money of the State of New York to me in Hand paid, at and before the Ensealing and Delivery of these Presents, by Philip Van Cortlandt Esqr the Receipt whereof I do hereby acknowledge, and myself to be therewith fully satisfied, contented and paid: Have granted, bargained, sold, released; and by these presents do fully, clearly and absolutely grant, bargain, sell and release unto the Said Philip Van Cortlandt. ~~one Neagro Boy~~[2] Two mares. five Cows. Four Heifers. Two Calves. Six Hogs and all the Household Furniture To have and to hold the said Neagro Boy. Cattle and Household Furniture unto the said Philip

Van Cortlandt his Executors Administrators and Assigns forever. And I the said John Brown for myself, my Heirs, Executors and Administrators, do covenant and agree to and with the above-named Philip Van Cortlandt his Executors, Administrators and Assigns, to warrant and defend the Sale of the above-named Neagro. Cattle & Furniture against all Persons whatsoever. In Witness whereof, I have hereunto set my Hand and Seal, this Fourth Day of June Annoq. Dom. One Thousand seven Hundred and Eighty Seven, 1787.

Signed, Sealed, and Delivered,
in the Presence of [torn]
Leonard DeKlyneshaw John [Brown]
Joseph C. Delezenne[3]

---

1. John Brown was a Cortlandt resident who served as an ensign under Philip in the 2nd New York regiment during the American Revolution. *VCFP,* II, 262, 289, 336.

2. Although the first use of the phrase "one Neagro Boy" was crossed out, the remainder of the document contains direct references to such an individual at a number of places.

3. As of 1790, Joseph C. Delezenne was a resident of the town of Cortlandt. The other witness remains unidentified.

253

Henry Churchell to Pierre. ADS
SHR

May 25, 1804.

I Henry Churchell do hereby certify that I have this day received one hundred and twenty dollars of Pierre Van Cortlandt by the hands of Isaac Cronk, which one hundred and twenty-five dollars is in full for my Negro Wench Phillis and her child Jenny (about four years old) which I have bargained and sold unto the said Pierre Van Cortlandt, and do hereby warrant the above said Wench and Child against all persons laying any claim to them. In witness whereof I Have hereunto set my hand and seal this twenty-fifth day of May 1804 —

Henry Churchell

Witness present
Frances Purdy

(endorsed)
Bill of Sale
for Phillis and
Child Jenny
May 25, 1804
Cost £50.0.0

254

Indenture between Philip [1683–1748] and Pierre. ADS SHR

[December 1, 1747.]

To all to whom these presents Shall Come I Phillip Van Cortlandt of the City of New York Esqr: send Greeting. Know ye that as Well for and in Consideration of the Naturall Love and Affection which I have & bear to my well beloved son Pierre Van Cortlandt as for and in Consideration of the Sum of Fourty Shillins of Currant money of New York to me in hand paid The Receipts whereof I acknowledge. Have given granted Bargained & Sold — And by these presents Do give Grant Bargain & Sell unto the Said Pierre Van Cortlandt his heirs and assigns for Ever. All that Certain

Farm or Parcell of Land lying in the mannor of Cortlandt In South Lott Number one Now in the Possession of John Rerick Leer.[1] Containing in all two hundred and Fifty Acres more or Less, To Have and to hold the Said farm or Parcell of Land Unto the said Pierre Van Cortlandt his heirs Executors and Assigns. To the only proper use Benefit and Behoofe of the Said Pierre Van Cortlandt his heirs and Assigns for Ever. In Witness whereof I have hereunto Set my hand & Seal This first day of December Anno Domini Seventeen hundred and fourty seven. —

Sealed and Dilivered
In the Presents of
John Livingston[2]
Rich^d: Norwood[3]

Phillip: Cortlandt

[REVERSE SIDE]

MEMORANDUM that on the Day of In the Year of our Lord one thousand Seven hundred forty nine personally Came and appeared before me Henry Holland Esqr:[4] one of his Majestys Council for the province of New York and Mayor of the Said City of New York John Livingston and of the Witnesses to the Within Written Deed poll or Instrument of Writing who being of full age and by and Duely Sworn on the holy Evangelist of Almighty God deposeth and sayeth that he the Deponant was present at the time of Executing the Said Within Written Deed and that he Saw the Within Mentioned Philip Van Cortlandt Sign Seal & Deliver the Said Deed within Written as his voluntary act and Deed to the uses therein mentioned and that the Said Richard Norwood was also present and subscribed his name as having perused and Subscribed his name as a witness thereto together with him the Deponant and I — having perused and Examined the Same and finding no Raisures or Interlineations therein Do allow the Same may be Recorded —

[Endorsed]

Deed of Gift from
my Father Philip Van
Cortlandt to My
Self for John Leers
Farm.

---

1. John Rerick Leer may have been the John Leer entered on manuscript page four in Pierre Senior's Receipt Book No. 255. His name disappears from the records after 1759–60.

2. John Livingston may have been one of two members of the Livingston family of that name. John, the youngest son of Robert L. Livingston of Albany, was baptized in March, 1709. He married Catryna Ten Broeck, the daughter of Dirck and Margarita Cuyler Ten Broeck. This John Livingston had three sons in the Revolutionary army; he died in 1791. A second possibility is John, the fourth son of Philip Livingston, second lord of the manor. He was baptized in April, 1714. In 1742 he married Catharine DePeyster, the daughter of Abraham and Margaret (Van Cortlandt) DePeyster. A Loyalist in the Revolution, he died in 1788. Edwin B. Livingston, *The Livingstons of Livingston Manor* (New York, 1910), pp. 142, 543, 563.

3. Richard Norwood received and valued the arms confiscated from disaffected persons in Westchester County during the war. New York (State) Legislature, *Journals of the Provincial Congress* . . . (Albany, 1842), II, 189.

4. Henry Holland was a New York City merchant and landowner as well as being a government official. In 1765 he was appointed as the agent to settle the boundary dispute between New York and New Jersey. He and John Van Cortlandt were masters in chancery for appraising and selling real estate. As a trustee for the late Abraham DePeyster, he entered into a lease with Isaac DePeyster and Pierre Van Cortlandt for Lot Number Three in New York. O'Callaghan, *Calendar Historical Manuscripts,* II, 756, 783, 794.

255

Pierre's Receipt Book. ADS
SHR

[1748–1762.]

Editor's Note

Pierre kept an interesting receipt book containing entries which he began in 1748 and continued intermittently until 1761–1762. It includes information on saw- and gristmill operations on Cortlandt Manor, tenant obligations and rent receipts, then-current prices, and household purchases, along with Pierre's activities as land agent for Van Cortlandt family heirs.

Among the families who had landed interests in Cortlandt Manor and whose accounts are included were Stephen and Oliver DeLancey, Peter Kemble, Sir Peter Warren, and Samuel Bayard. All had married Van Cortlandt heirs. While the female family members had received shares in the Manor upon its early division in 1734, and again in subsequent years, a married woman's real property automatically became part of her husband's estate upon the act of marriage. Therefore, Pierre maintained accounts in the names of the husbands and not of the Van Cortlandt female heirs.

Note a hiatus in the entries between December, 1749, and June 26, 1752. This was the period in which Pierre and his family relocated their permanent place of residence from New York City to the Manor house on the northern bank of the Croton River.

[on cover]

Receipt Book
Begun Octo^{r}. 31st
1738

[page one]
Received of Pierre Van Cortlandt Octo^{r}: 31.1748

Eight pounds sixteen & Six pence In full for fourty bushels & ½ of Salt.
£8 . . 16 . . 6 John Gilbert

Received of Pierre Van Cortlandt Octo^r^. ye 31.st 1748 — one pound Nine Shillins In full for baking of Ship bread for his Father some time Last Spring.
£1 . . 9 . . 0 John Van Vorst

Received of Pierre Van Cortlandt. November ye 4. 1748. the sum of four pounds & nine pence Infull for Work done for his Father at his farm & In full of all acc:^s^ to this day.
£4:0:9. P Van S:lent

[page two]

New York Novem^r^: 25. 1748 —

Then Received of Pierre Van Cortlandt the Sum of Ten pounds In part of an Account for Work done for his Father Philip Van Cortlandt Deceased.
£10:0:0 p^r^ me John Johnston

New York 5 Dec^r^: 1748 —

Then Received of Pierre Van Cortlandt Ten Shillins Infull for a p^r^: of stocking DD [delivered] Zachariah Bloom.
£0:10–0 Johanna Van Nes

New York 1 Jan^y^: 1748/9

Then Received of Pierre Van Cortlandt thirty five Shillins In full for the Making of a mourning Sute of Cloath.
£1 . . 15 . . 0 p^r^:

New York 1748/9 January 19

Received of Mr Pero Van Cortland the sum of one Pound fifteen Shillings in full of all Demands p^r^ me
£1–15–0 Jacobus Van antwerp

[page three]

New York January 21 . . 1748/9

Recieved of M^rs^. Pierre Van Cortlandt One pound Ten Shillings In full of all Accounts —
£1 . . 10 . . – James Livingston Junr.

New York 22 Jan^y^: 1748/9

Then Received of Pierre Van Cortlandt Eight Shillins & Ten pence on Zachariah Blooms acc^t^: p^r^: Johanna Van Nes
£0 . . 8 . . 10

New York Jan^{y}: 24 1748/9

Then Received of Pierre Van Cortlandt three pounds twelve shillins & 5½ pence in full for 47 lb of Wax —

£3 . . 12 . . 5½ Christopher Steymets

New York Feb^{y}: 7–1748/9

Then Received of Pierre Van Cortlandt two pounds Nine Shillins & 3^{d} in full.

£2 . . 9 . . 3 p^{r} John Lebow

[page four]

New York 9 Feb^{y}: 1748/9

Then Received of Pierre Van Cortlandt thirty two pounds In part of 100 bushels of Wheat DD at M^{r}. Phillip's Mill, —

£32 . . 0 . . 0 p^{r}. John Underhill

New York 20 Feb^{y}: 1748/9

Received of Pierre Van Cortlandt three pounds On account of John Underhill of Phillip burgh.

£3. — James Wilkes

New York 8 of March 1748/9

Received of Pierre Van Cortlandt two pounds one shilling & six pence Infull of all acc:^{ts} to this day.

£2 . . 1 . . 6 p^{r}: — Isaac Ryckman

New York 17. March 1748/9

Then Received of Pierre Van Cortlandt twenty four pounds ten shillin & 9 pence Infull for Seventy five bushels of wheat & an half Dilivered to John Leer.

£24 . . 10 . . 9 John Keats

[page five]

New York 18 March 1748/9

Then Received of Pierre Van Cortlandt the sum of Eleven Pounds Seventeen Shillins In full for 39½ bushels of Wheat DD to John Leer by John Write I Say Received In behalf of John Write by Me

his
£11 . . 17 . . 0 Abraham X Write
mark

New York 18 March 1748/9

Then Received of Pierre Van Cortlandt the Sum of one pound sixteen shillins Infull for 6 bushels of wheat DD John Leer. by me.

his
£1 . . 16 . . 0 Abraham X Write
mark

New York 18 March 1748/9

Then Received of Pierre Van Cortlandt the Sum of two pounds three Shillins & 3 pence In full for 8 bushels a half a peck & half peck. DD John Leer. by Me.

£2 . . 13 . . 3 Jacob Wrigt

[page six]

New York 29 March 1749 —

Received of Pierre Van Cortlandt Sixteen pounds & 10 pence In full for 55 bushels of Wheat DD John Leer

his
£16 . . 0 . . 10 pr Me adolph X banker
mark

New York 29 March 1749 —

Received of Pierre Van Cortlandt Seventeen pounds ten Shillins In full for 60 bushel of Wheat DD John Leer

£17 . . 10 . . 0 p^r Me Jeremiah Travis

New York 29 March 1749

Received of Pierre Van Cortlandt two pounds Eighteen Shillins & 4 pence In full for 10 bushels of Wheat DD John Leer

£2 . . 18 . . 4 p^r Me Isaac Covert

[page seven]

Crotens River 14 Aprill 1749 —

Then Received of Pierre V:Cortlandt the sum of five pounds thirteen & four pence In full for 20 bushels of wheat. DD in the store & if their be more than Mr Cortlandt is to allow Jonathan Haith for it if Less than 20 bushels than s^d Haith must allow it I say Received In behalf of Jonathan Haith by Me Philip X Travis

£5 . . 13 . . 4

Crotens River — 14 Aprill 1749 —

Then Received of Pierre Van Cortlandt the sum of Six pounds Sixteen Shillins In full for 24 bushels of Wheat. DD In Store by Nathan Witney I say Received In behalf of Nathan Witney by Me

£6 . . 16 . . 0 Philip X Travis

Crotens River 14 Aprill 1749.

Then Received of Pierre Van Cortlandt the Sum of ten pounds fifteen shillins & 6 pence In full for 37½ bushels of wheat DD himself by Me

£10 . . 15 . . 6 Phillip X Travis —

[page eight]

Crotens River 15 Aprill 1749

Then Received of Pierre Van Cortlandt the sum of Six pounds Eight shillin & 4 pence In full for 22 bushels of Wheat DD John Leer by Me.

£6 . . 8 . . 4 John Covert

Crotens River 17 Aprill 1749

Then Received of Pierre Van Cortlandt the Sum of Nine pounds Eight Shillins Infull for 30 bushels of Wheat DD John Leer

£9 . . 8 . . 0 by John Smith

Crotens River 18 Aprill 1749 —

Then Received of Pierre Van Cortlandt the Sum of Eight pounds Eleven Shillins Infull for 38½ bushels of Wheat DD In the store by Joseph Ryder I say Received by Me —

his
£8 . . 11 Richarson X Devenport.
mark

[page nine]

New York 27 May 1749.

Then Received of Pierre Van Cortlandt ten pounds Seven Shillin & 6 pence Infull for 166 boards Sold Phillip G Livingston p^{r}

£10–7–6 Jno Beeckman

New York 23.June 1749

Then Received of Pierre Van Cortlandt thirty Six Shillins In full for one tun & a half of Bread Barrels. p^{r}. me.

£1 . . 16–0 this Was Wrote for William Ellis.

New York June 23 1749 —

Then Received of Pierre Van Cortlandt.

twenty seven pounds one shillin & three & some time ago thirty two pounds ten shillins & seven pounds I gave a Receipt for making In all Sixty Six pounds Eleven Shilling & 3 d — In full for 213 bushels of Wheat.

his
£66.11 . . 3 Jeromus X Van Nester
mark

[page ten]

New York August 3–1749

Then Received of Pierre Van Cortlandt Eight pounds two shillins & 6 pence In full for Salt & all acc^{ts} —

£8–2–6 Bej. Payne

New York Decem^{r}. 1749

Then Received of Pierre Van Cortlandt Sixteen Shillins & Some time ago Six pounds Nine Shillins It being In full for plastering work done to the mannor house at Crotens River. this was wrote for

£7 . . 5–0 Thomas Ballance

Mannor of Cortlandt June 26 1752

Received of Pierre Van Cortlandt Nine pounds Eleven Shillins & four pence being Infull for 34 days work at the Saw Mill & 25½ days Work at the Grist Mill

£9–11–4 p^{r} Me William Shaw

[page eleven]

Mannor of Cortlandt Novr 3. 1752

Then Received of Pierre Van Cortlandt the Sum of twenty one Pounds sixteen Shillins being In full for 97 days work at the Saw Mill and Grist Mill.

£21 . . 16 . . 6 by Me Jonathan Whelpley

Mannor of Cortlandt Novr 3 1752

Then Received of Pierre Van Cortlandt fifteen pounds two Shillins being In full for 70½ days Work at the grist mill

£15 . . . 2.0 by Me Nathan Whelply

[page twelve]

Mannor of Cortlandt Novr 3.1752

Then Received of Pierre Van Cortlandt thirty Shillins Infull for ten days Work In gitting of Timber for ye Griss Mill

his
£1 . . 10 . . 0 Mathew X Farinton
mark

Mannor of Cortlandt Nov^r: y^e: 4–1752

Then Received of Pierre Van Cortlandt The sum of four pounds seventeen Shillins & two pence being Infull for 16½ days work at Sawing & digging & for half Sawing of 1285 feet of Planck by me

£4 . . 17 . . 2 Jacob Green

[page thirteen]

Mannor of Cortland Novr. 14, 1752

Then Receved of Pierre Van Cortlandt thirty nine Shillins in Full for the Work in getting of Timber for the Grist Mill by his tu Sons & as Like wise for the Saw mill

his
£1 . . 19 . . 0 Johannes X Snook
mark

Mannor of Cortlandt Novr 20–1752

Then Received of Pierre Van Cortlandt Three pounds thirteen shillins & Six pence being Infull for 9 days work at Sawing & 3½ days Digging & half sawing of 985 feet of Planck with Jacob Green

his
£3–13.6 by me Jacob X Banker
mark

[page fourteen]

Mannor of Cortlandt March 6 1753 —

Received of Pierre Van Cortlandt at Different times twelve pounds Seven Shillins & Nine pence and Now Receive Nine pounds Sixteen Shillings & Nine pence being In all twenty two pounds four Shilling & six pence It being In full for one hundred and twenty seven Days work at the Mill

£22.4.6 by Me Samuel Whelpley

Jonathan Whelpley p^r 2/6 Expenses

Mannor of Cortlandt March 22.1753

Then Received of Pierre Van Cortlandt the Sum of

one pound Ten Shillins being Infull for work done at the Griss Mill

Daniel Chapman

[page fifteen]

Mannor of Cortlandt March 22–1753

Then Received of Pierre Van Cortlandt Two pounds Ten Shillins It being on acc[t] of Daniel Weaton by me

£2 . . 10–0 Daniel Chapman

Mannor of Cortland March 22–1753

Then Received of Pierre Van Cortlandt the Sum of Six pounds It being on acc[t]: of Jonathan Whelpley Sen[r]: I Say Received by me —

£6 . . 0 . . 0 Daniel Chapman

[page sixteen]

Mannor of Cortlandt Aprill 15–1753

Then Received of Pierre Van Cortlandt The Value of Eleven pounds Eleven Shills & Threepence In full for work done at the Saw Mill & Griss Mill.

Benj[n]. Wood

Mannor of Cortlandt May y[e] 21–1753

Received of Pierre Van Cortlandt Two pounds Some time ago, and, this Day two pounds Seventeen & Six pence, & two Shillins & Six which was paid Jacobus Tellor. being in all five pounds It being in full for work done at the Griss Mill.

Jonathan Whelpley junior

[page seventeen]

Mannor of Cortlandt. May 22. 1753

Then Received of Pierre Van Cortland One pound Eight Shillins and Seven pence, I say Received on account of my father Jonathan Whelpley Senr. by me

Jonathan Whelpley junr.

£1.8.7

Mannor of Cortlandt October 12–1753

Then Received of Pierre Van Cortlandt Eleven pounds it being Money Recev'd for Rent from Adam Miller & Joseph Putney. By Me. the above Receipt was wrote for M[r]. Peter Kemble.

[page eighteen]

Mannor of Cortlandt. Feb. 23.1754

Then Received of Pierre Van Cortlandt Nine pounds & Six pence In full of all acc^{ts}: to this day —

his
£9 . . 0 . . 6 John X Leer
mark

Mannor of Cortlandt March 9–1754

Then Received of Pierre Van Cortlandt the Value of Eight pounds Eleven Shillins & Eight pence in Grain It being In full for Labour & all accounts to this day —

£8 . . 11 . . 8 harmen montroos

[page nineteen]

Mannor of Cortlandt Jan^{y}: 6–1756

Then Received of Pierre Van Cortlandt The Sum One Pounds Seven Teen Shillins & Ten pence being in full of all accts. To this day —

£1–17–0 p^{r} Me — Jacobes daves

Mannor of Cortlandt May y^{e}: 6–1756

Then Received of Pierre Van Cortlandt the Sum of Eight pounds five shillins and Eleven pence It being the full Ballance that was due to me for two years Tending of his mill & Infull for a Bay mare, and Infull of all acc^{ts}. to this day.

£8 . . 5 . . 11 by Me, Nicholas Brewer

[page twenty]

Mannor of Cortlandt Nov^{r}: 4–1757 —

Then Received of Pierre Van Cortlandt the Sum of Eight pounds fifteen Shillins & Six pence It being Infull for Weaving & all acc^{ts}: to this day by Me —

[unsigned]

[page twenty-one]

Fish Acc^{t}: Feb–20 1757 —

Cash of Jonathan Odell	£0	3	0
Peter Virmilyea D^{r} 3/	0	3	0
Thomas Pew Junr: D^{r}. 2/3	0	2	3
Mathias Brewer D^{r}–2/3	0	2	3
Cash of Hendrick			

	Brewer 2/3	0	2	3
Pd	Jo^s^. Conklyn D^r^. to 3/ to Cut 1 Cord of wood for it	0	3	0
	Cash of John DMilt 2/6	0	2	6
	John DMilt D^r^: to 6 pence More & 2/6 more.	0	3	0
	Cash of Walter Dobbs 3/	0	3	0
	Cash of Collards–2/	0	2	0
	Willm. Collard D^r^. to 2/6 more	0	2	6
	Tunis Snook to 2/3 sent with ye Negro D^r^.	0	2	3
	The Negro D^r^: to 1/6 Paid	0	1	6
	David Hammon D^r^. to 4/3^d^	0	4	3
	John Leer D^r^: to 3/ DD harmanus	0	3	0
	Thos. Pew Senr. D^r^. to 3/ in fish	0	3	0
	Cash 10/6	0	10	6
	Cash 5/	0	5	0
	Jonathan Odell Cash to 4/6	0	4	6
	John Huson D^r^: to 4/	0	4	0
	James Rusel 4/6 for one Bus^l^: wheat to be	0	4	6
	Walter Dobbs 6/ to Thrash	0	6	0

[page twenty two]

March 1–1757

from other side	3	14	0
Doctor Bordon D^r^ to pint of wine, Scant	0	1	0
To one fish 2/3	0	2	3
Fredrick Shaffer D^r^:			

to 3/4 fish	o	3	4
Thos. Smith Son. Tho[s]. D[r].			
to 2/3 In fish paid In Oats	o	2	3
David Hammon D[r]:			
to 3/5½	o	3	5½
Cash–12–Coppers	o	o	10
Cash from NYork March 2			
& twine	8	4	o
Cash 2/ & 12 Coppers	o	2	10
Cash 8/	o	8	o
Jacobus David D[r]. to 4/	o	4	o
Cash 22/3	1	2	3
Cash 6/3 Ap[ll] 9	o	6	3
Cash 2/	o	2	o
Cash 8/9[d] Ap[ll] 19	o	8	9
Cash 3/9	o	3	9

Ap[ll] 22

Solomon Smith D[r]: to			
100 Shad at 22/	1	2	o
Received of Solomon			
Smith 8/ in part			
Jedidiah Deen D[r]: to 25			
Shad Paid	o	5	6
John Traviss D[r]: to 25			
Shad paid	o	5	6
Cash for Shad roe	o	11	o
Cash for fish 4/	o	4	o
Cash for Fish May 25	o	o	8

[page twenty-three]

Crop of the Year 1756
Thrashed out of the 1st

Barrock — 125 — with
y[e] Seed
5–poled Barrock 64–

5–poled D°	113–
4–poled D°	105½
4–poled Barrock first	24
2 load	26
2 Bus[l]: Leonard Huff borrow'd —	2
Thrashed out of the Out Barrock	105 Bus.

[page twenty-four]

Sir Peter Warrens Lotts In Cortlandts Mannor

Lott N°: 5 — Let In Smaller Lotts to pay Rent from y[e] 1 Jan[y]. 1748/9 —

N°				
1.	David Montross	£3	5	0
2.	Symon Mabey	4	10	0
3.	Henry Montross	3	10	0
4.	Adam Griffen	3	10	0
5.	John Neal	4	0	0
6.	George Hallet	4	10	0
7.	Nathan Witney	3	10	0
8.	Justice Wheeler Sold to Mat[w]: Winter	3	10	0
9.	William Ward	4	10	0
10.	John Wright Jun[r].	4	10	0
11.	Robert Harris			
12.	John Write & Father	3	0	0
13.	Abraham Write	3	15	0
14.	Jacob Write	3	10	0

On South Lott Upon Croton River N°: 9.

N°:					
1. Jonathan Pine	£12	0	0	N.B. I put the
2. James Pearce	6	0	0	rent on S.

3. Peter Montross	6	0	0	Lott N°. 9
4. Gilbert Totten On Pelloms Place	£ 6	0	0	
On South Lott upon Croton River N^{o}: 2				
Gilbert Griffen	£ 3	10	0	
Thomas Crommel	3	10	0	

[page twenty-five]

Coppy of Receipts of Money That I have paid to Mary Hughes For Rent which money I did Received of Joseph Haight & Cornight Briggs & paid it for Their Use,

New York March 28–1758

Then Received of Joseph Haight, four pounds Ten Shillins, By the Hands of Pierre Cortlandt Infull for one years Rent for the Farm whereon he now lives.

£4.10.0 Coppy Sign'd Mary Hughes

New York May ye 10–1758

Then Received of Joseph Haight four pounds Ten Shillins It being In full for the Rent of the farm whereon he did Live I say Received by the Hands of Pierre Van Cortlandt.

£4–10–0 Coppy sign'd Mary Hughes —

[page twenty-six]

Coll Oliver DeLancey C^{r}.

by Cash Received of George Hallet as p^{r} Receipt given Dated ye 19. May 1758 £40.10.0

by cash received of Gilbert Griffen as p^{r}: Receipt given Dated may ye 20–1758 3.10.0

by a Bond Received of Jacob Griffen and Samuel Frost Conditioned to pay on the ye first of may 1759 — £20.0.0

by Cash Received of Thomas Cromell for Abrahan Van Waert as p^{r} Receipt Given dated June 9–1758 for 18.0.0

by Cash Received of Thomas Crowell as p^{r}: Receipt Dated June 9–1758 18.0.0

by a Noat of hand dated June 9–1758 payable May 1–1759 of Joshua Purdy for Rent due by Thos: Cromel for seven pounds

by Cash Receid^{d}: of James Levine 4.10.0

by Cash Received of Nathan Witney 3.10.0
Paid Coll Oliver DeLancey £88–0–0
as p^r Receipt —

[page twenty-seven]

Manor of Cortlandt. May. 19. 1758

Then Received of George Hallet by the hands of his son Joseph Hallet, The Sum of Fourty Pounds. Ten Shillins New York Currency — I say Received, on acc^t: of the Rent. for the farm whereon George Hallet Did Live On South Lott N^o: 5 I say Received by order of Coll: Oliver Delancey —

£40.10.0 Coppy by me, Pierre Van Cortlandt

Manor of Cortlandt June ye 9–1758

Coppy

Received of Thomas Cromell For Abraham Van Waert Eighteen pounds New York Currency. It being the third part of the sale of the Improvement for the farm which was sold to Thomas Crommel on the Lott N^o: 2 South of Croton River — I say Received by order of Coll: Oliver DeLancey Esqr:

p^r: Pierre Van Cortlandt

[page twenty-eight]

Manor of Cortlandt May 20–1758

Then Received of Gilbert Griffen Three pounds Ten Shillins It being On Account of Rent for a farm On the Lott N^o:2 South of Croton River I Say Received by Order of Coll Oliver DeLancey Esqr:

£3.10.6 Coppy p^r: Pierre Van Cortlandt

Manor of Cortlandt May y^e: 25–1758

Then Received of Jacob Griffen a bond dated y^e: 25 May 1758 Conditioned to pay Twenty pounds On the first day of may 1759. It being for one third part of the Sale of the Improvements, for the farm whereon adam Griffen Did Live On South Lott N^o: 5 which is now sold. to Samuel Frost, of Queens County I say Received by order of Coll. Oliver DeLancey, Esqr.

Book & Paid O.D.L. Pr Pierre Van Cortlandt

[Page Twenty-nine]

Manor of Cortlandt. June 9: 1758

Then Received of Thomas Cromell Eighteen pounds

NewYork Currency it being the third part of the sale of the Improvement for the farm which is now sold to Josuah Purdy on the Lott N°: 2 South of Croton River I say Received by Order of Coll. Oliver Delancey Esqr: by me —

Pierre Van Cortlandt Coppy —

Manor of Cortlandt June 9–1758

Then Received of Josuah Purdy a Noat of hand dated June 9–1758 For Seven pounds payable ye 1. of May–1759. To Coll Oliver Delancey Or his Order It being on acc^{t}: of Rent for the farm whereon Thomas Cromell did Live on the Lott N°: 2 South of Croton River which Said Seven pounds should have been paid by said Cromell but as Josuah Purdy has bought the Improvement of the farm So takes the Debt on him to pay I Say Received by Order of Coll Oliver Delancey Esqr: by me

Pierre Van Cortlandt

Coppy

Book & Paid M^{r}: DeLancey

[page Thirty]

Paid William Yeomans In part of his Improvements at The Generall Training at Crompond — 1760	£7.0.0
Paid William In full	10–0–0
	17.0.0

Mr Duncan. In the Army — C^{r}.

By cash Rec^{d} of William Yeomans nine pounds for 2 years rents of his farm Feby. 26–1761	£9.0.0

NB I drew an Order on John Abeel to pay Walter Rutherford Nine pounds which he paid as p^{r} Receipt so I Say

M^{r}: Duncan D^{r}.

To Cash £9. John Abeel p^{d}. Walter Rutherford as p^{r} Receipt	£9–0–0

[page thirty-one]

Willm: Yeomans Says That he has paid my Brother
First £4. for Priviledge of Settling
2^{d} £4.10 Rent
3^{d} £3.10 by Edward Smith
4th £5.0 to Jacob Pinto
And that he has 4 crops on that farm the 5th is now on the

Ground Jany 20–1758 — Coppy of what Willm: Yeomans told me at that time

beginning at the Most Easternmost Corner of Lott 3
Thence S.18 Deg:° E.142 Chain^{s}: 50 Links
N. 72 .. W. 89 C
N. 18 ... E. 70 C
N. 72 ... W. 80 C
N. 18 ... E. 42 C
S. 72 ... E. 87 C to ye place of Beginning

[page thirty-two]

Manor of Cortlandt May 15–1763

Then Received of Pierre Van Cortlandt five Shillins In full of acc^{t}: to this day. By me Nathaniel Merritt

[Pages thirty-three to thirty-nine blank]

[page Forty]

Mannor of Cortlandt Nov: 25–1757

Peter Kemble Esqr. — C^{r}.

	By Money Received from Different People as p^{r}. Acct: DD him, Date above amounting in the whole to	£69.2–3
	See the Blew Book Nov^{r}: 25–1757	
	by Cash Six pounds R^{d}: of Jeremiah Hunter for Griffin Koorey	£6.0–0
	by Cash of Adam Miller	3.0–0
	by Cash of M^{r}. Lents for Adam Miller as p^{r} Receipt	3.0–0
1759	by Cash of Edward Smith Jany 21	3.10–0
		15.10–0

[page forty-one]

Mannor of Cortlandt Novr. 25–1757

Peter Kemble Esqr. D^{r}.

To Cash paid you at Different Times to Novr. 25–1757 amounting to as p^{r}. Acc^{t}. DD in Date above £69.2.3

Peter Kemble Esqr. D^{r}.
To Cash paid M^{r}. Richard Kemble your Son In full as p^{r}. Account Dilivered of Money Received by me to Jany. 1759 £15.10.0
William Horton paid me £3–10/ for M^{r}. Watts May 25.1761 p^{d}. the above to M^{r}. Watt as p^{r} Receipt

[page forty-two]

Coll Oliver DeLancey — C^{r}:

by Cash Re^{d}: of James Cock Jan^{y}: 1	£4–10–0
by Cash Rec^{d}. of Nathan Whitney D^{o}	3–10–0
by Cash Rec^{d}: of Daniel Write D^{o}	3– 0–0
by Cash Rec^{d}: of John Vail Jan D^{o} 2	4– 0–0
by Cash Rec^{d}: of Saml: frost Jany D^{o} 2	3–10–0
NB John Vail is £4–0–6	
by Cash of Abraham Write Jan 7–	3–15–0
by Cash of Jacob Write Jany 7	3–10–0
by Cash of David Montross Jan 10	3– 5–0
by Cash of Simon Mabee Jany 10	4–10–0
by Cash of Walter Ward Jany 13	4–10–0

[page forty-three]

Jonathan Pine	
Cash 6 £ Inpart of Rents as p^{r}	
Receipt of Jan^{y}: 19–1761	£6– 0–0
William Pearce	
Cash 6 £ In part of Rent Jany 19–1761	£6– 0–0
Charles Levine May–26–1761	4–10–0
March 31–1762	
Cash of Abraham Write	£3–15–0
Cash of Jacob Write d^{o}	3–10–0
Cash of Joshua Purdy. May 7.	3–10–0

[page forty-four]

Manor of Cortlandt Jan^{y}: 28–1766
Then Received of Pierre Van Cortlandt Twenty pounds, Rec^{d}: also Jan^{y}: 10–1766 Twelve pounds Three shillins & nine pence making in all Thirty two pounds Three Shillins &

nine pence it being In part of one hundred & twenty bus[l]: of wheat fourty two whereof is Dilivered
£32 . . 3 . . 9 John Comb
Manor of Cortlandt May 29–1766
Then Received of Pierre Van Cortlandt Six pounds Eight Shillins It being In part of Acc[t] —
£6 . . 8 . . 0 John Angus

[page forty-five]

1766 Jan[y]

Jan[y]
29 Paid Rob[t] William for 24 Bus[l]. In full
27 D[o] Gilbert Griffin 20/ In part
28 D[o] Gabriel Purdy for 7 D[o] In full
29 D[o] W[m]. Mosier £18–0–0 In part of 48¼ Bus[l]–
29 Paid Henry Lowberry In full for 35½ Bus[l]. £8.17.6
Paid Zachariah Bloom Infull for 31½ D[o] 8–5–3
Paid Richarson Davenport for 20–
paid Elisha Merrit for 14–
paid Joseph Infull
paid Josh. & Jacob Turrill In full 41/–
Paid Tho[s] M[c]Daniel Infull for 5 Bus[l]: 1–10–0
p[d] Shadden & Jerreau for Infull 15–
p[d] Ab[m]: Van Veart for Infull for 4 Bus[l]–
p[d]. John Bulyea In part 4£ also 3£5
paid W[m]: Horton In part 3£5
Paid Cornelius Ryder £3–5–0
p[d] D[o] March 8–£3–15

[page forty-six]

Manor of Cortlandt June. 2. 1766–
Then Received of Pierre Van Cortlandt Twenty One pounds In part of Wheat DD for the Mill —
£21–0–0 p[r] David Montross

Paid In full
John Tomkins &
Vredenburgh–27/
Andrew Glover–7/6

Paid John Teller 5/
Due him on the Pigions

In My hands
20/ for the Petiager

[unnumbered page forty-seven]

Sam[l] Merrit	£450	
Gilbert & Tom	800	
Vredenburgh & Tomkin	250	350
Abraham Baiseley	200	
Sybout	70	
Andrew Glover	70	
	1840	
Luke Tellor	200	
John Tellor	360	
	2360	

3/ to the Carman to Sell	0	3	0
Cash In Silver	8	0	0
In pistereen 12/8	0	12	8
2/6–More	0	2	6
	8	18	2
In pence	3	17	0
Sybout Baisley	0	15	0
P[d] Philip had John Laid out for him	2	15	0
	16:5		

[page forty-eight]

Ab[m]: Merrit & Philip
John DeMilt
Nicholas Vredenburgh
Abraham Baisley
Jacob Odle
Sybout Baisley
Hdk. Davids
Gilbert — Philip, & Hdk. Williams
Philip Cortlandt Shott 400
Jonathn & Staats
Rec[d]. of John Teller — 1/6 for Tomkins
Rec[d]. of Andrew 3[d] for D[o]
D[o] Luke Teller 9 for D[o]

Mr: Cortlandt 3/o Do
Paid Jo Tomkins 1 on the Above

[Pages forty-nine to fifty-nine Blank]

[page sixty]

Coppy of an Account Of Saml Bayard which he gave me Jany: 1766 Viz

1757		
23 Dec	To selling of 8 farms as pr acct: Dilivered	£31–7–11
1758		
March 18	To Selling 2 farms	8–18–6
July 14	To Do Do	7–1–3
1759		
May 4–	To Do 100 Acres	3–3–9
		£51–11–5

NB To Enquire whether the Lands Sold at the White plains belonging to the Entails —

[page sixty-one]

Rent £5 a year

To plant 100. apple Trees — In the Year. 1761. (50) & 1762. (50)
To Clear 6 acres of meadow
To Summer all my Young Cattle & Solt Them
To Leave the Road open
To fallow the Land once In four year.
If the Soil Right Should be Sold to be paid 2/3 parts
of The Improvements That he Shall make
To be Valued by 3 Men Indifferently Chosen —
Rent to begin. Jany: 1762
This farm Lays on South Lott No: 1 being the Farm That Lays East of the Brook that Run Through the Meadow, Called Andrus Meadow
On Downings Farm Containing About 250 Acres Beginning at a heap of Stone On the S. East Corner of John Lents farm Mr: Bayards Lott and as the Brook Runs NE untill it Comes

— Lately at Poghkeepsie[.]It will Now Run Like Wild fire as A Number Want to be Concerned There; dont Neglect One moment to git it One way or the Other Secured by the Cortlandt family Write a Similar Lease Ready. if Not for 7 years than 5. or 3 So that a fair tryal may be Made if the family dont Come into it than it must Lay as it is And the Oar will be daily more proved Which Will Make it More dificult dalay is dangerous

Since I Wrote what goes before Abram Pelts has been with me And he Mr Gabriel & Grist have Executed the Leases and Deposited them in to Doc^r. Coopers hands Untill the other Persons Conserned Come down With a promice that Lafferts who is Comming down Next Saterday Shall bring the Paper I Signd at Albany with him Or they are not to proceed[.]I Expect they will bring Every thing Wanting with them they were Exceedingly well pleased with the Lease And Confessed Everything Was done to bargain[.]Pelts was Sorry that Lafferts was not here to give me up the paper it was put in his hand that Van Dyke Should have No Claim, I told them that I wod not Stand to the Lease Unless that paper was here however I hope All for the best. Now it Only Remains With You to Secure Me And As I wrote to you before Must Urge it Again to do it And if the Couz^s. dont Agree the Work must Stop which will be great dammage to those that are Concerned And Will be hurting My Interest As I did it to git a discovery for the benifit of the family this Mine was Knowing in the Year 1758, git a Lease for it if One for 3 years Only

Am yours &c Pierre Van Cortlandt

[Addressed]
General Cortlandt
Crotons

A cutaway drawing of millstones. A miller was responsible for the maintenance and operation of the gristmill. This necessitated an ability to replace wornout wooden parts and a knowledge of millstone dressing. The latter process involved chiseling grooves into the stones so that a scissor-like action could be applied to the grain. The millstones were a composite of sectional pieces cemented and bound together by an iron band. (drawing by Robert Fink).

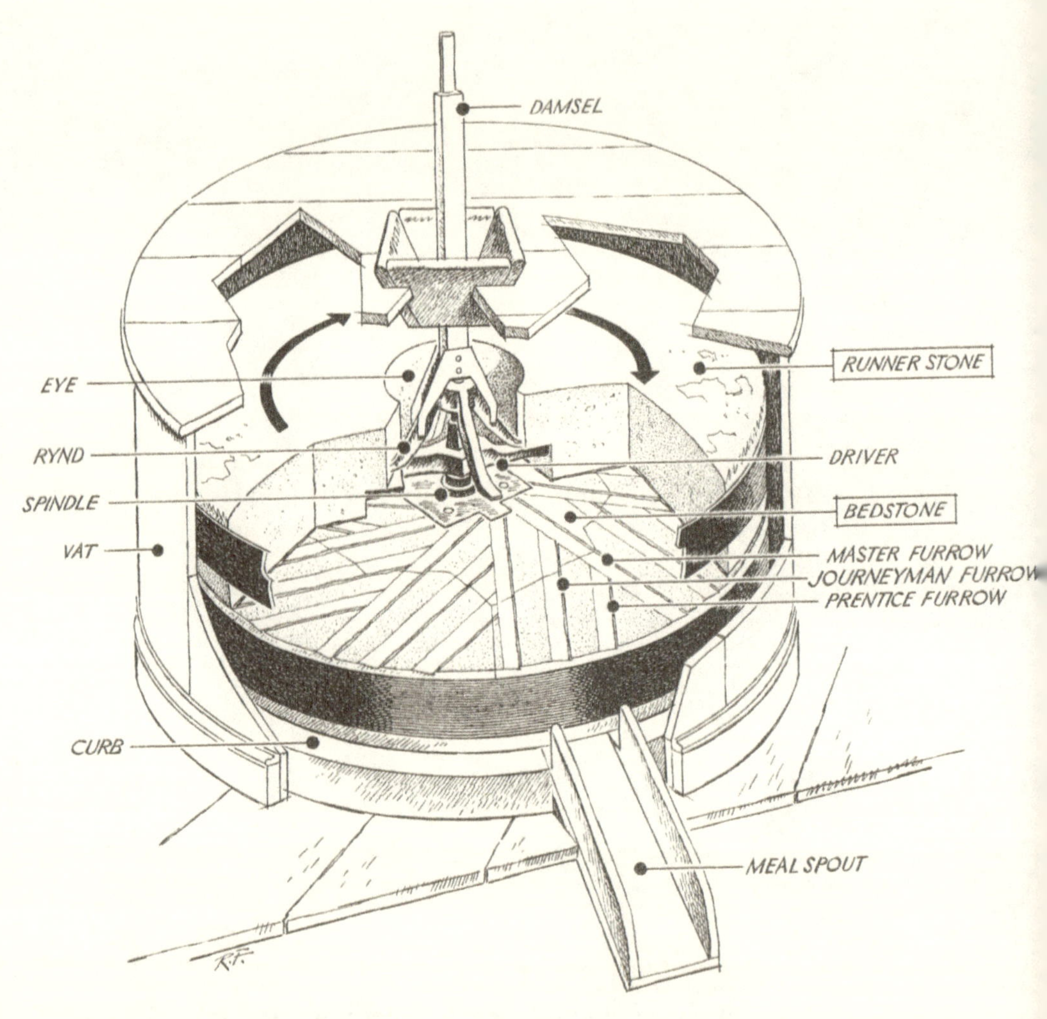
DAMSEL
RUNNER STONE
EYE
RYND
DRIVER
SPINDLE
BEDSTONE
VAT
MASTER FURROW
JOURNEYMAN FURROW
PRENTICE FURROW
CURB
MEAL SPOUT
R.F.

1. John Van Vleck was the son of Abraham and Maria (Kip) Van Vleck. He was born in 1714 and spent most of his life in New York, following the trade of a blacksmith. He also acted as a merchant dealing in tools and household equipment. He was a member of the Dutch Reformed Church, but later became interested in the Moravian movement. When the British occupied New York, Van Vleck and his family fled to Stone Arabia above Albany. After the Revolution, he returned to New York, then moved to the home of his son at Pittstown in Rensselaer County, where he died in 1803. O'Callaghan, *Documents Colonial New York,* VIII, 105, 111, 134, 135.

257

Pierre's Business Account with Elizabeth Kiersted.[1] ADS SHR

[December 10, 1754.]

1754
Dec: 10

Mr. Pearre Van Cortlandt

To Elizabeth Kiersted

To 7 yds Duffels 5/	£1	15	
4 yd swanskine 4/		16	
5 yds Checord Linen 3/3		16	3
6 hand kerchiefs		9	
1 yd fine Shalone 4/ 1 scains [skeins] silk		4	10
1 hand kerchiefe		4	9
1 scaine scarlet mohair			8
2 lb reasons [raisins]		1	8
3 lb peper		8	3
¼ lb sinment [cinnamon]		7	6
1 yd swanskine more		4	

	1 Green serge	1	16	
	1½ y^{d} Cloath		18	
	3 y^{ds} Shalone 2/9		8	3
	1 scaine Glen mohair			6
	¼ y^{d} Buckram			6
	1 scaine silk 1½ Doz Vest buttons		1	6
	5½ y^{d} Lamb skine 8/	2	4	
	1½ y^{d} shalone		4	10½
	2 scains mohair		1	
	2 Doz Coat 3 Vest buttons		2	6
	Silk			10
	4 y^{ds} swanskine		16	£11..5.
23 June 19	6 Ct 11 oz Sugar		8	5
	2 Ct tea		14	
	6 y^{ds} Checord Linnen 3/		18	
	2 Doz Vest buttons ½ oz Silk		2	3
	½ Doz Coat Buttons			7
				£2.19.3
Aug 16	1½ y^{d} flannell 3/9		4	8½
	3 Doz Vest buttons ⅜ oz. silk		3	4½
	1 y^{d} buckram ⅔ scains mohair		3	6
	1 pr Shuse		3	
		£14	19	8½
Oct 24	1½ y^{d} black Cloath 2/£1:11:6			
	3 y^{d} shalone −9−			
	1½ Doz Vest Buttons−−9			
	1 scaine Mohair −−6			
	Silk 2/ ¼ y^{d} buckram−2−6			
		£ 2	4	3
		£17	3	11½

New York Decr ye 8th 1755

Rec^{d} from Mr Pierre van Cortlandt Twelve pounds three

Shillings & 11 pence on acct in behalf of Mr[s] Elisabeth Kiersted

Pr James Livingston

[Endorsed]

Mr Kierstead Acct & Receipt for £12.3.1

---

1. Elizabeth Kiersted may have been Elizabeth (Van Dam) Kiersted, daughter of Rip Van Dam and wife of Jacob Kiersted. Her father was a native of New York of Dutch extraction who presided at the councils during English rule; he served as President of the Council after the death of Governor John Montgomerie in 1731. O'Callaghan, *Documents Colonial New York,* VI, 153.

258

Pierre's Account Book AD
SHR

[February 2, 1758–
February 27, 1766.]

[folio] 1	Laus Deo [Praise be to God] In Manor of Cortlandt	
1758	The Estate of Father Philip Van Cortlandt Deceased — Dr	
Feb 2	To Cash pd Abraham Quick as pr Receipt on his Bond Infull	£50.17.10
	To Cash paid John Killy as pr Receipt on his Bond Infull	341.12.0
	To Cash paid Catherine Parker as pr Recpt on her Bond Infull	213.11.5
Do 3	To Cash paid Mary Breastead as pr Rect on her bond Infull	057.19.4
	To Cash paid Symon Johnson as pr Rect on his Bond Infull	63. 2.6

	To Cash paid Mary Alexander as p[r] Receipt on her Bond Infull	37.13.8
	To Cash paid Peter DeLancey as p[r] Receipt on his Bond Infull	90. 1.0
	To Cash paid Peter DeLancey as p[r] Receipt on his Bond Infull	99.17.6
Feb 4	To Cash paid Mary Hughes as p[r] Receipt —	1330. 0.0
May 11	To Cash paid Mary Hughes as p[r] Receipt —	350.17.0
	To Cash paid Phillip Hughes Infull for M[r] Charleton Bond £252.10.0 as p[r] Receipt on the Bond Infull	252.10.0
May 26	To Cash paid Symon Johnson Infull for James Hudes Bond £78.10.7 as p[r] Receipt on the Bond Infull	78.10.7
	To Cash paid Soloman Brutus for his improvments & Lease which was for Life as p[r] Receipt on the Lease	80. 0.0
	To Cash paid Israel Knap to give up his possession to Henry Scoot of farm No8 North Lott No6	8. 0.0
	To Cash paid Cornight Briggs for his Lease as p[r] article of agreement Infull £160.0.0	160. 0.0
	To Cash paid Joseph Haight as p[r] article of agreement for his Lease £100.0.0	100. 0.0
	To Cash paid Samuel Field for Boards Left on the farm by Joseph Haight as p[r] agreement	2. 0.0
	To Cash I am to pay Will[m] yeomans for his possess[ions]	17.10.0

May 5	To Cash p^d Mary Hughes as p^r Receipt	5. 0.0
	To Cash p^d M^rs McPhedreas for Mary Hughes	130. 6.8
	To cash p^d Robert Crommeline Infull for Mr Hendrick Van Eiberger acc^t of Amsterdam	177. 3.6
	To Cash p^d Simon Johnson for Mrs Hughes Jany 30, 1759	110. 0.0
	To Cash paid Simon Johnson Sepr 28, 1761 by Mr Abeel	130. 0.0
	To Cash paid Abra^m DePeyster by Bond	596. 3.9
	To Cash Peter DeLancey as p^r Receipt	34.
	To Cash paid Mary Hughes as p^r Rec^t of June 19, 1761	16. 6.2½
1767 May 21	To Cash paid Simon Johnson p^r Recp^t £82.10.2	82.10.2

[folio 1 facing page]

	Laus Deo In Manor of Cortlandt	
1758	The Estate of Father Philip Van Cortlandt Deceased — c^r	
Feb 4	By Cash Received of Henry Scoot for 241 Acres of Land Sold at Vendue Master for 20/ p^r acre (conformadable to the act of assembly,) Farm N^o8 North Lott N^o6 Manor of Cortlandt Sold the 28 of Decem^r 1757	£337. 8.0
	by Cash Received of Henry Scoot for 241 acres Sold as above for 40/ p^r acre Being farm N^o9 in North Lott N^o6 Manor of Cortlandt	482. 0.0

	By Cash Received of Coll Oliver Delancey for 5 farms Containing 1219 acres being Farms — N° 1-2-3-4-&5 Sold at Vendue Decem^r^ 28, 1757	1719.07.0
May 9	By Cash Received of Coll Oliver Delancey for Interest Infull £9.18.2	9.18.2
1758	By Cash Received of John Tomkins for — 241 acres at 50/ farm N°10 Lott N°6	361.10.0
	By Cash Received of Cornight Briggs Inpart of 125 acres Sold at Vendue at Kings Briggs for 56/ p^r^ acre Being farm N°2 In South Lott N°1-In the Manor of Cortlandt Sold	200. 0.0
	By Cornight Briggs Bond Dated May 10, 1758 for 150 £ Infull for the above 125 acres	150. 0.0
D° 10	By Cash Received of Samuel Field In Part of 125 acres Sold at Kings Briggs for 56/ p^r^ acre being farm N°4 In South Lott N°1 In the Manor of Cortlandt	240. 0.0
	By Cash Received of Samuel Field Infull for his Bond principall £110.0.0 Interest £5.3.0	115. 3.0
	NB Samuel Fields Bond was dated May 10, 1758 paid it of January 14, 1759 which is 8 months and 4 days	
	By Cash Received of Cornight Infull for the Interest of his Bond, the Interest being 10 & 10/ for one year May 10, 1759	
	By 125 acres Sold to me at Vendue at 50/ p^r^ acre being	

	farm N°3 on the South Lott N°1 Manor of Cortlandt Decr 28, 1758	312.10.0
folio 2 [2 blank pages]		
[folio 3]	Laus Deo In Manor of Cortlandt Coll Oliver Delancey Esqr Dr	
1758	To Cash paid you in New York as p^r Receipt of Janu^y 12, 1759	£88. 0.0
		£88. 0.0
	Coll Oliver Delancey Esqr Dr	
	To Cash paid you in New York as p^r Receipt of May 26, 1759	£65. 1.0
		£65.01.0
	Coll Oliver Delancey Esqr Dr	
	Carried to Folio 4 on the other leaf	
[folio 3 facing page]		
	Laus Deo In Manor of Cortlandt	
1758	Coll Oliver Delancey Esqr Cr	
May 19 Lott 5	by Cash Received of George Hallet for Rent for his farm as p^r Receipt given Hallet for £40.10.0 B	40.10.0
D° 19 Lott 2	By Cash Received of Gilbert Griffen for Rent of his farm South of Croton–ODL	3.10.0
D° 19	by Cash Received of Thomas Cromell for ⅓ of the sale of Abraham Van Wert ODL	18. 0.0
Lott 2	by Cash Received of Thomas Cromell for ⅓ of the sale of Joshua Purdy ODL	18. 0.0
Lott 6 farm 3	by Cash Received of James Serine for Rent as p^r Receipt given him Decr 19, 1758 ODL	4.10.0

1759 Jany 4	by Cash Received of Nathan Whitney for Rent as p^{r} Receipt Jany 4, 1759	3.10.0
		£88. 0.0
	Coll Oliver Delancey Esqr Cr	
North Lott 6	by Cash Received of Charles Serine for Rent as p^{r} Receipt given him of Jany 23, 1759 for ODL	£4.10.0
South Lott 5	by Cash Received of Mary Ward as p^{r} Receipt given Feb 10, 1759	9. 0.0
D^{o}	by Cash Rec^{d} of Symon Mabes — D^{o} — D^{o} —	4.10.0
D^{o}	by Cash Rec^{d} of Daniel Write — D^{o} — D^{o}	5.16.0
D^{o}	by Cash Rec^{d} of John Veal — D^{o} — D^{o}	8. 0.0
D^{o}	by Cash Rec^{d} of Abraham Write — D^{o} — D^{o}	3.15.0
D^{o}	by Cash Rec^{d} of David Montross March 2, 1759	13. 0.0
North Lott 6	by Cash Rec^{d} of John Maybee — March 2, D^{o} ODL	4.10.0
Lott 2 South of Croton	by Cash Rec^{d} of Gilbert Griffen March 19, 1759 ODL	
	by Cash Rec^{d} of Mathew Winter Ap^{ll} 17, 1759 on South Lott N° 5	5. 0.0
	by Cash Received of Jacob Write Ap^{ll} 30 South Lott N°5	3.10.0
		£65. 1.0
	Coll Oliver Delancey Esqr Cr	
the Lott	by Cash Received of Silas Smith for ⅓ part of the sale of the	

N°5	Improvement of the mill farm of Robert Harris £50. 0.0 May 15, 1759	£50. 0.0
	by Cash Received of James Cock Infull for his Bond — dated May 1, 1758 with Interest to May 1, 1759 as p^r Receipt on the bond It being for ⅓ part of the sale of the Improvements for the farm whereon George Hallet did live, on South Lott N°5 — Manor of Cortlandt	64. 4.0
	[Carried to folio 4 on the other side]	
[folio] 4	Laus Deo In Manor of Cortlandt	
	Coll Oliver DeLancey Esqr Dr	
	To Cash paid you In New York as p^r Receipt of July 18, 1759 £114.04.0	£114. 4.0
	To Cash John Abeel Paid Mr Beverly Robinson as p^r his Receipt £114.0.0	114. 0.0
May 2 1760	To what you allowed me for Commis[sion] & Troble	24.15.0
		138.15.0
[folio 4 facing page]		£138.15.0
	Laus Deo In Manor of Cortlandt	
	Coll Oliver DeLancey Esqr Cr	
	Brought from folio 3	£114. 4.0
May 16 1759	By Cash Received of James Cock for one years Rent of his farm, on South Lott N°5 being the farm whereon George	

	Hallet did live	4.10.0
	by Cash Received of Josiah Purdy £7.0.0 Infull for his noat of hand Dated June 9, 1758 which was for 2 years Rent for the farm whereon Thomas Cromell did live ODL	7. 0.0
D°	by Cash Received of Josiah Purdy £3.10 for one years Rent for the farm he now lives on on Lott N°2 South of Croton River ODL	3.10.0
1759 May 24	by Cash Received of John Write Ten Pounds Inpart of Rent for the farm he now lives on on South Lott N°5	10. 0.0
June 12	by Cash Received of Sam[l] Frost £40.0.0 It being ⅓ of the sale of the Improvements of Jacob Griffens farm	40. 0.0
D°12	by Cash Received of Sam[l] Frost £3.10–In part of Rent for the farm he now Lives on Lott 5	3.10.0
June 23	by Cash Received of Richard Crab on Acc[t] of the Rent for the farm he now lives on on South Lott N°5	3.10.0
June 26	by Cash Received of Gilbert Griffen for Rent of his farm on the Lott 2–South of Croton River ODL	3.10.0
	by Cash Received of Nathan Whitney for Rent as p[r] Rec[t] Nov 22	3.10.0
1760	by Cash Received of James Cock for Rent as p[r] Rec[t] Feb 29	4.10.0
March 6	by Cash Received of David Montross for Rent as p[r] Rec[t]	

	NB	3.10.0
D^{o}	by Cash Received of John Mabee for Rent as p^{r} Rec^{t} ODL	4.10.0
18	by Cash Received of Mary Ward	4.10.0
23	by Cash Received of Daniel Write	3. 0.0
Aprill 1	by Cash Received of James Serine for Rent N^{o} Lott N°6 ODL	4.10.0
D^{o} 1	by Cash Received of Charlis Serine for Rent North Lott N°6 ODL	4.10.0
	by Cash Received of Abraham Write for Rent March 29	3.15.0
	by Cash Received of Jacob Write for Rent D^{o} 29	3.10.0
Apll 7	by Cash Received by Mathew Winter for Rent South Lott N°5	12. 0.0
D^{o} 28	by Cash Received of Simon Mabee for Rent D^{o} N°5	4.10.0
D^{o}D^{o}	by Cash Received of Samuel Frost	7. 0.0
		£138.15.0
[folio] 5	Laus Deo In Manor of Cortlandt	
	Peter Kemble Esqr Dr	
	To Cash Paid you at Different Times as p^{r} account Dilivered you Novr 25, 1757	£69. 2.3
	To Cash paid your Son Richard Kemble as p^{r} account Dilivered him Jany 1759	15.10.0
		£84.12.3
	Peter Kemble Esqr Dr	
	To Cash my wife p^{d} your Son	

	Richard Aprill 14, 1760	£3.10.0
[folio 5 facing page]		
	Laus Deo In Manor of Cortlandt	
	Peter Kemble Esqr Cr	
	By Cash Received of Different People for Rent In the manor of Cortlandt as pr acct Dilivered you Novr 25, 1757	£69. 2.0
	By Cash Received of Jerimiah Hunter for Griffen Corey six pounds Jany 6, 1758	6. 0.0
	by Cash Received of Adam Miller Jany 4, 1758	3. 0.0
Decr 23	by Cash Received of Edward Smith Jany 4, 1759	3.10.0
		£84.12.0
	Peter Kemble Esqr Cr	
	by Cash Received of Edward Smith March 7, 1760	£ 3.10.0
[folio] 6	Laus Deo In Manor of Cortlandt	
	Robert Dingee Dr	
	To an account of Rent & Sundries Dilivered you the 2 of Jany 1759, amounting In the whole the Rent of your farm included to May 1st 1759	£53. 9.11
	Their will be Due to me the 1st of May 1759 as pr the above Settlement £12.0.0	
	Joseph Putney Dr	
	To One years Rent of your Farm Due May 1758	£ 4.10.0
	To one years Rent of your Farm Due May 1759	4.10.0

	To Cash paid you at your house May 8, 1759	6.10.0
	To Cash my wife paid you May ye 5 1759 10/	0.10.0
	To one years Rent Due May 1760	4.10.0
	To one years Rent Due May 1761	4.10.0
	To one years Rent Due May 1762	4.10.0
	Samuel Dean D^{r}	
	To one years Rent of the farm you live on N^{o} Lott 6 Due the 1st of May 1759	£ 5. 0.0
	To one years Rent Due May 1760	5. 0.0

[folio 6 facing page]

Laus Deo In Manor of Cortlandt

	Robert Dingee C^{r}	
	By Cash & Sundries as p^{r} a settlement of Jany 2, 1759 Including the Noat of hand of 8£ amounting In the whole to	£41. 9.1
	See Rent Book Jany 2, 1759	
	Joseph Putney C^{r}	
	by a p^{r} of Oxen Named Buck & Goden May 3, 1759	£15. 0.0
	by cash Rec^{d} by the Hands of your wife Oct 27, 1762	10. 0.0
	Samuel Dean C^{r}	
May 26 1759	by Cash Infull for one years Rent due May 1, 1759 by the Hands of Anthony Loe £5.0.0	£ 5. 0.0
Ap^{ll} 29	by Cash Infull for one years Rent due 1760–May	5. 0.0

	by Cash Inpart of Rent as p^r Rec^{pt} of July 2, 1763	10. 0.0
[folio 7]	Laus Deo in Manor of Cortlandt	
	To Coard of wood by John Jeffers 1753–D^r	
	To 112 lb of Flower DD by Jacob Brewer at 13/ —	0.13.0
	To 53/4 of Nutwood by Tellor 1755 at 13/ p^r Coard	3.14.9
	To ¾ of Oakwood by Tellor D^o at 7/ p^r Coard	1. 2.9
	To Cash 20/ you Detailed in your hands of the money that I sent to pay Mr Walton for ye waggon	1. 0.0
	The above acc^t is Brother Stephens To 2 Barrels of Syder at 12/ 1755	1. 4.0
	Gabriel Winter D^r	
1759	To Cash 17/6 Infull for work Jany 10	£1.17.6
	George Booth at Moskoot D^r	
1759 March 19	To Cash I am to pay Jacobus Tellor for you	£0.10.8
	To Cash paid William Rogers Inpart of ye wheels	1. 4.0
	To Cash paid William Rogers Infull May 13	0.15.4
		£2.10.0
	NB I paid William Rogers 8/ for bringing down the wheels to my farm In full	
	John Roerick Leer D^r	
1759	To a Cart Iron Bound Sold him	

	for Eight pounds	£8. 0.0
Apll 7	To Cash 10/ paid Abraham Van Wert for mowing	0.10.0
Do 8	To Cash 8/ —	0. 8.0
		8.18.0

[folio 7 facing page]

Laus Deo In Manor of Cortlandt

	Brother Stephen Van Cortlandt Cr	
	By Ballance of own acct settled ye 8 of Decr 1754 Except the Wood that John Jeffers carried down the balance being In your favour 12/6, then —	£0.12.6
	by 2000 shingles at 3£ 15 1755	7.10.0
	by 3 Empty Wine pipes at 7/	1. 1.0
	the Brokade Silk paid for the 3 tickets	
	Gabriel Winter Cr	
1759	by his Receipt for 17/6 Infull of all acct to Jany 10, 1759	£0.17.6
	George Booth Cr	
	by a pr of Ox Cart wheels March 19, 1759	£2. 5.0
	allowed him 5/ more — It being a mistake	0. 5.0
		£2.10.0
1759	John Rerick Leer Cr	
Apll 7	by Labour of his son harmonus	£0.10.0
Do	by 10 Shillins In fowles	10.0
	by 6 Shillins I must pay for Albertus Turtill	0. 6.0
	by 4 bushels of wheat at 5/6	1. 2.0
	by Cash five pounds three Shillins	5. 3.0

D° 8	by 5 bushels of wheat wanting ½ peck at 5/6	£8.18.0
[folio 8]	Laus Deo In Manor Cortlandt	
	Joseph Farinton & Charles Davids Dr	
	To the Rent of the Farm whereon they now live To the 1st of May 1759 £3.10.0	£ 3.10.0
	To Cash Saml Merrit paid you at the Training	1. 4.0
	To Cash paid Annatie Apll 14, 1759 £1.16–gold	1.16.0
	To Cash paid Charles Davids Infull Apll 24	4. 3.0
		£10.13.0
	Benjamin Tillisson Dr	
	To one years Rent Due Apll 30, 1759 at £3.10.0	£ 3.10.0
	To Cash paid Benjm Tillisson Infull Apll 24, 1759	0. 6.5
		£ 3.16.5
	Abraham Van Wert Dr	
1758	To Cash over paid you for mowing at John Leers	£ 0
1759	To Cash 8 shillings	0. 8.
March	To Cash 8 shillings	0. 8.0
	To Cash 1/6 pence paid Annatie Apll 14, 1759	0. 1.6
	To One Bushel of wheat out of the mill by order of	0. 6.0
	Settled & paid Infull	
	Jonathon Odell Dr	
	To one years Rent Due May 1st 1759	£ 7. 0.0
	To 25 apple trees at 7d/ pr tree	

Apll 16, 1759	0.14.7
To Cash paid Jonathon Odell Infull May 7, 1759	30. 5.5
	£38. 0.0

[folio 8 facing page]

Laus Deo In Manor Cortlandt

Joseph Farinton & Charles Davids Cr	
by 35½ bushels of wheat at 7/ Dilivered In my mill Apll 1, 1759	£10.13.0
NB gave Charles Davids a Receipt Infull for the Rent of the Farm to the 1 of May 1759 Apll 1, 1759	

Benjamin Tillisson Cr	
by work of his Team 4/	£ 0. 4.0
by 2½ days work at 4/ pr day	0.10.0
by 1 days work at 3/6	0. 3.6
by 51 apple trees at 7d Apll, 1759	1. 9.2
	£ 3.16.5

Abraham Van Wert Cr

by Cuting of Cords of Wallnut wood at 3/6 pence pr Cord Apll 14, 1759

I have settled the above acct with Abraham Van Wert — I paid him the Ballance Infull

Jonathon Odell Cr	
by Tanning of Leather 1758	£ 1. 8.0
by his negro Caesars Tending of Carolin	0.12.0
by 120 bushels of wheat at 6/ pr	

	Bus[l] March 1759	36. 0.0
		£38. 0.0
[folio 9]	Laus Deo In Manor of Cortlandt	
	Nehemiah Travis Dr	
	To one barrel of Syder & Barrel at 11/ 1756	£ 0.11.0
	James Roussell Junior Dr	
	To Cash paid you by Cornight Briggs Infull May 1, 1759	£20. 2.0
	Henry Lownsberry Dr	
	To Cash paid you Inpart £4.0.0 March 1759	£ 4. 0.0
	To Cash paid you Infull £5.0.0 March 1759	£ 5. 0.0
		£ 9. 0.0
	William Horton Dr	
	To Cash Infull £9.0.0 March 1759	£ 9. 0.0
	Cyno Jones & Brother Dr	
	To Cash in part of wheat £5.0.0 Apll 17, 1759	£ 5. 0.0
	To Cash in part of wheat £30.0.0 May 18,	30. 0.0
	To Cash paid John Leer by your order	0.13.6
	Annanias Akerly Dr	
	To Cash paid you Infull May 15, 1759	£30.12.0
	Josuah Purdy Dr	
	To Cash £7 I must pay for your Noat of hand ODL	£ 7. 0.0
May 23	To Cash £3.10 I must pay for 1 years Rent ODL	3.10.0

1759	To Cash £1.10 I paid you Infull for the Oxen	1.10.0
		£12. 0.0
1759	Frederick Shaffer Dr	
June 20	To Cash paid Ten Dollars at 8/ Each	£ 4. 0.0
July 4	To Cash paid you Inpart £9.8.6	9. 8.6
	NB I have 50£ In hands to Change it being Jersey money To Cash paid your wife Novr 12, 1759 £50.0.0	50. 0.0
		£63. 8.6

[folio 9 facing page]

	Laus Deo In Manor of Cortlandt	
	Nehemiah Travis Cr	
	by Cash 11/ Infull for a barral of Syder Apll 14, 1759	£ 0.11.0
1759	James Russel Junior Cr	
Apll 1	by 67 bussls of wheat at 6/	£20. 2.0
	Henry Lownsberry Cr	
	by 30 bushels of wheat at 6/ pr Busl March 1759	£ 9. 0.0
	William Horton Cr	
	by 30 bushels of wheat at 6/ March 1759	£ 9. 0.0
	Cyno Jones & Brother Cr	
	by 120 bushels of wheat at 6/ March 1759	£36. 0.0
	Annanias Akerly Cr	
	by 102 bushels of wheat at 6/ Apll 30 DD In Mill	£30.12.0
May 23 1759	Josuah Purdy Cr	

	by a p^r of oxen bought this day at £12.0.0	£12. 0.0
	Frederick Shaffer Cr	
	by Cash I received of Mr Phillip Cortlandt for 210½ at 6/1d pr reducting 12/ for Cartage	£63. 8.6
[folio 10]	Laus Deo In Manor of Cortlandt	
1759	Morice De Hart Sale maker Dr	
Augt 2	To Cash Sent you with Peter Tellor Inpart of sales making for my Vessel 20£	£20. 0.0
	To Cash I paid you myself In York as pr. Receipt	10. 0.0
	To Cash Infull for making ye above sails as pr receipt	
	Peter Williams Dr	
	To one years Rent of the farm you Live on Due the 1st of May 1759 at £4.10/ pr annum	£ 4.10.0
	To Cash Infull for 74 Bushels of wheat DD Augt 10, 1759 at 6/ pr Bushel allowed	18. 7.0
		£22.17.0
	To one years Rent of the farm you Live on due May 1, 1760	£ 4.10.0
	To Cash Infull as pr Recpt 1760	22.10.0
		27. 0.0
	Cornight Briggs Dr	
	To twenty five acres of Land Next adjoining his farm on the East for which he is to have his deed at 50/ pr acre	£62.10.0
	But as I have given him a general warrantee he is to pay me three pounds the acre the	

	same that Russel gave me make it In all £75.0.0	12.10.0
		75. 0.0

[folio 10 facing page]

	Laus Deo In Manor of Cortlandt	
	Morice De Hart Sale maker Cr	
	By his acct for Sale making for my scooner Being main sail fore sail as jib as pr acct Delivered In — amounting In the whole to	£
	Peter William Cr	
	By 74. Bushels of wheat DD Augt. 10–1759 @ 6/	22. 4.0
	allowed the Over Measure 13/	0.13.0
		£22.17.0
	by 90 Bushels of Wheat DD Apll. 2. 1760 at 6/ pr Bus £27.0.0	
	Cornight Briggs Cr	
	by Cash Received of him at Different Times Amounting In the Whole to this day. being the 4th. of Augt. 1759 to	£50. 0.0
	As pr Different Receipts given him by Cash & cr In full as pr Receipts given him	25. 0.0
		£75. 0.0
[folio 11]	Laus Deo Manor of Cortlandt	
1763	Capt James DeLancey Esqr Cr	
Jan 31	By Cash Received of Nathan Bailey North Lott No9	£ 3. 0.0
Do	By Cash Recd of Robert Dederick	1. 0.0

Do	Livy Bailey	4. 0.0
Do	Ephraim Carpender	3.10.0
Do	Gilbert Thedwell	3. 0.0
Do	Christopher Hall, Inpart	2. 0.0
Do	Ephraim Baker	3. 0.0
Do	William Carpender	3. 0.0
Do	Jonathan Parmer	3. 0.0
Do	William Dicken	3. 0.0
Do	Abigail Dederick now D. Purdy	3.10.0
Do	Jehial Tyler	3. 0.0
Do	James Lockwood	3. 0.0
Do	John Purdy	3. 0.0
Do	Abraham Van Skaay & mother	3. 0.0
Do	James Bishop	3. 0.0
		£49.10.0

1763	Captn James DeLancey Esqr Cr	
Jany 31	By Cash Recd of Robert Knox North Lott No1	4. 0.0
Do	Joseph Jump	4. 0.0
	William Blumer	4. 0.0
	Timothy Delavan	3. 0.0
	Samuel Cole	3. 0.0
	Joshua Lobden	12. 0.0
	John Cole	2. 0.0
	Richard Paterick	2. 0.0
	Denton Smith	4. 0.0
	Jonah Keelar	6. 0.0
	Solomon Close	3.10.0
	Silvinus Townsend	2.10.0
	Israel Bugbus	2.10.0
		£53. 0.0

1763 Capt James Delancey Esqr Cr

March 16	by Cash Rec^{d} of Richard Patrick by J^{o} Cole	£ 1. 0.0–10	Lott
D^{o}	by Cash Rec^{d} of Joseph Cable — D^{o}	3. 0.0–10	
May 16	by Cash Rec^{d} of John Quick for Purdy & Brown	3. 0.0–9	farm
July 7	by Cash Rec^{d} of Ebinezar Purdy £3 for Secard	3. 0.0 9	
		£10. 0.0	

[folio 11 facing page]

Laus Deo Manor of Cortlandt

1763	Capt James DeLancey Esqr D^{r}	
Feb 18	To Cash paid you as p^{r} Recp^{t}	£49.10.0
1763	Capt James DeLancey Esqr D^{r}	
Feb 15	To Cash paid you at p^{r} Recp^{t}	£53. 0.0

Capt James DeLancey C^{r}	
from the other side	£10. 0.0
by Cash Rec^{d} of David Peek Octo 26 N^{o} Lott 10	3. 0.0
by Cash Rec^{d} of Jonathan Owen D^{o}–D^{o}	4.10.0
by Cash Rec^{d} of Cornelius Steanrood Oc^{t} 27 Lott N°9	3. 0.0
	£20.10.0

D^{r} to an order on
Mr John Abeel Dec^{r}
16 1763 for Twenty
pounds Ten shillins
payable to Stephen

	Delancey as p^r^ Receipt on s^d^ order £20.10.0	
[folio 12]	Laus Deo In Manor of Cortlandt	
	Land In the manor of Cortlandt belonging to the Estate of the Late Sr Peter Warren Esqr Dece^d^ Cr	
1760	By Cash Received of Richard Crab June 2	3. 0.0
	by D^o^ of John Veale Aug^st^ 26	4. 0.0
	by D^o^ of Peter Montross Augt 30	6. 0.0
1761	by D^o^ of James Cock Jany 1 1761	4.10.0
	by D^o^ of Nathan Whitney Jany 1 B	3.10.0
Jany 1	by D^o^ of Daniel Write Jany 1	3. 0.0
	by D^o^ of John Veale Jany 2	4. 0.0
	by D^o^ of Samuel Frost Jany 2	3.10.0
	by D^o^ of Abraham Write Jany 7	3.15.0
	by D^o^ of Jacob Write Jany 7	3.10.0
	by D^o^ of David Montross Jany 10	3. 5.0
	by D^o^ of Simon Mabee Jany 10	4.10.0
	by D^o^ of Walter Ward Jany 15	4.10.0
	by D^o^ of Jonathan Pine Jany 19	6. 0.0
	by D^o^ of	

	William Pearse Jany 19	6. 0.0
	by D^o^ of Richard Crab Jany 26	3.10.0
	by D^o^ of James Cock Jany 29, 1762	4.10.0
	by D^o^ of Nathan Whitney Jany 29, B	3.10.0
	by D^o^ of Samuel Frost Feb 16	3.10.0
	by D^o^ of Walter Ward Feb 16	4.10.0
	by D^o^ of Daniel Write March 19	3. 0.0
	by D^o^ of Abraham Write March 31	3.15.0
	by D^o^ of Jacob Write March 31	3.10.0
	by D^o^ of David Montross Aprill 6	3. 5.0
	by D^o^ of Simon Mabee Aprill 6	4.10.0
	by D^o^ of Richard Crab Aprill 6	3.10.0
	by D^o^ of John Veale Aprill 6	4. 0.0
	by Cash Received of Gilbert Totten on acc[t] of the ⅓ of the Sale of the Improvements From Pelham to Totten May ye 12, 1762	33. 6.8
May 19	by Cash Received of William Pearse for ⅓ of the Sale of the Improvements From Avery to Pearse	40. 0.0
May 12	by Cash Received of Gilbert Totten for Rent	24. 0.0

by Cash Received of Daniel Wolsey Inpart of the ⅓ of the Sale of the Improvements of the farm of Daniel Write May 22 — South Lott N°5	21.13.4
	£227.10.0

[folio 12 facing page]

Laus Deo Manor of Cortlandt

Lands In the manor of Cortlandt belonging to the Estate of the Late Sr Peter Warren Esqr Dec^d Dr

To Cash paid Coll^r Oliver DeLancey Esqr as p^r Receipt of July 6, 1762 Inpart £153.16.9	£153.16.9
To Cash paid Coll^r Oliver Delancey Esqr as p^r Receipt of Jany 2, 1763 with allowing me £73.2.0 for my trouble	£ 73.13.3
	£227.10.0

NB £73.13.3
34.10.0
108. 3.3

Sr P. Warrens money p^d Coll DeLancey for his own Tennan[t]s for which Sum Coll DeLancey gave me the above Receipt of Jany 2, 1762 and allow^d my Trouble

Coll Oliver DeLancey Esqr Cr

	by Cash Received of Joshuah Purdy Aprill 29, 1760	£ 3.10.0
	by Cash of Gilbert Griffen June 7	3.10.0
	by D^o of Gilbert Griffen Feb 21, 1761	3.10.0
	by D^o of John Mabee March 24	4.10.0
	by D^o of Joshua Purdy May 18	3.10.0
	by D^o of Charles Serine June 13	9. 0.0
		£34.10.0

Coll Oliver DeLancey Esqr D^r
To Cash paid you Jany 2, 1763
£34.10.0 Infull of the above
acc^t as p^r Receipt as appears
above which Is Included In the
£108. 8.3

NB £34.10.0
73.13.3
£108. 3.3

OD Lancey
Sr P. Warren

NB allowed me for my Trouble

[folio 13] Laus Deo In Manor of Cortlandt

1763 Lands In the manor of Cortlandt Belonging to the Estate of the Late Sr Peter Warren Esqr Dec^d Cr

Jany 8	By Cash Received of Nathan Whitney	£ 3.10.0
	By D^o	

	of Samuel Frost	3.10.0
	by Do	
	of James Cock	4.10.0
	by Do	
	of John Veale	4. 0.0
	by Do	
	of Walter Ward	4.10.0
	by Do	
	of David Montross	3. 5.0
	by Do	
	of Simon Mabee	4.10.0
Jany 8	by Do	
	of Richard Crab	3.10.0
Jany 17	by Do	
	of Abraham Write	3.15.0
Jany 22	by Do	
	of Mathew Winter	12.15.0
	(NB £5.15 of this was pd my wife & £7 to myself)	
Aprll 28	by Do	
	of Thomas Powell	3.10.0
Do	by Do of Thomas Powell Inpart of one third of the Sale of the Improvements of Jacob Writes farm to sd Thos Powell	15.10.0
May 4	By Cash Recd of John Write £13.12.6	13.12.6
1764	by Cash Recd	
	of Nathan Whitney Jan 9	3.10.0
	by Cash	
	of Abraham Write Jany 12	3.15.0
	by Cash	
	of Jon Veale Do 18	4. 0.0
	by Do	
	of Samuel Frost Do 18	3.10.0
	by Do	
	of David Montross Do 18	3. 5.0

	by D^o^ of James Cock D^o^ 19	4.10.0
	by D^o^ of Richard Crab Aprill 25	3. 0.0
	by D^o^ Daniel Wolsey for ⅓ of ye sale	22.15.0
Augt 12	by Cash Received of Joseph Anthony Inpart of ⅓ of the sale of John Writes farm	75. 0.0
D^o^	by Cash Rec^d^ of Joseph Anthony for Rent	12. 7.6
	by Cash Rec^d^ of Walter Ward Novr 15	4.10.0
1765	by Cash Rec^d^ of Nathan Whitney Jany 10	3.10.0
	by D^o^ of Abraham Wright Feby 12	3.15.0
	by D^o^ of Walter Ward D^o^ 12	3.10.0
	by D^o^ of Samuel Frost D^o^ 12	3.10.0
	by D^o^ of Simon Mabee corn & wheat Feb 14	9. 0.0
	by Cash & wheat of Richard Crabb Feb 20	3.10.0
	by Cash of Daniel Wolsey Feb 22	6. 0.0
	by wheat Rec^d^ of James Cock Feby 28	4.10.0
	by Cash Rec^d^ of Joseph Anthony March 1	4.10.0
	by Cash Rec^d^ of John Veale March 1	4. 0.0

[folio 13 facing page]

Lands In The Manor of

	Cortland Belonging To the Estate of the Late Sr Peter Warren Esqr Deceased Cr	
1765	Brought From the oppo[site] side	£
March 5	by Cash Recd of David Montross	3. 5.0
	by Cash Recd of Joseph Anthony Infull for ⅓ of the sale of John Wrights farm	75. 0.0
June 13	by Cash Received of William Pearse Inpart of Rent	18.10.0
1766	by Cash Recd of Joseph Anthony Jany 6	4.10.0
	by Cash Recd of Nathan Whitney Jany 7	3.10.0
	by Cash Recd of Samuel Frost Do 14	3.10.0
	by Cash Recd of David Montross	3. 5.0
	by Cash Recd of Symon Mabee Do	4.10.0
	by Cash Recd of Walter Ward Jany 29	4.10.0
	by Cash Recd of Abraham Wright Feby. 7	3.15.0

[folio 14] [1 blank page]

[folio 14 facing page]

1763	Coll Oliver Delancey Esqr Cr	
	by Cash Recd of Joshua Purdy June 10	£ 3.10.0
	by Cash Recd of Gilbert Griffen Do	3.10.0
1764	by Cash Recd of Charlis Serine Aprill 9	9. 0.0
	by Cash Recd of Gilbert Griffen	

	Aprill 17	3.10.0
	by Cash Rec^d of Joshua Purdy	
	Aprill 27	3.10.0
1765	by Cash Rec^d of Charlis Serine	
	Aprill 2	4.10.0
	by Cash Rec^d of Joshua Purdy	
	June 21	3.10.0
		£31. 0.0

Coll Oliver Delancey Esqr D^r
To Cash Infull of the above acc^t
as p^r Receipt of Feb 27, 1766
£31.0.0

259

Philip Van Cortlandt [nephew][1] to Pierre. ALS
NYPL

Jamaica 16.th Octr. 1766.

D^r. Unkle

I wrote to you about three months past relating the affair of Mr Johnson[2] but have not been favoured with an answer which surprises me as it was an affair of such consequence to the family credit, your remissness has put it in the power of that merciless man to Arrest M^r. Hughes[3] for a debt which you promis'd to settle four or five years ago & which we had reason to think was settled by your Acc^t. dated Octr. 28th 1760. The writ was this day serv'd by order of Mr Johnson who says he will not be satisfy'd unless you either pay him the Cash or give him y^r. Bond pay^d. for principal & Interest, as you know the man I beleive you will not doubt of his keeping his resolution however savage it may seem — Dr Unkle I must beg your speedy complyance in this affair as it cannot admit of any delay without the most shocking consequences, the Court sits next week —

The Treasurers Acc^t. £62 . . 3 . . 1½

Simon Johnsons Ball^{e}.	160.10 . . –	
to fulfill the Act	189 . . 9 . . 5	£412 . . 2 . . 6½

The Above sums remain still unsettled as p^{r} Acc^{t}.
I remain D^{r}Sr Your Affectionate Kinsman
Ph. V. Cortlandt

[Addressed] To Pierre Van Cortlandt Esqr
att Crotons River

---

1. The Philip Van Cortlandt who wrote this letter was the son of Stephen, Pierre's brother. He was to become an ardent Loyalist during the Revolution. See also No. 265.

2. Simon Johnson was a New York City merchant. This particular affair remains a mystery, as the earlier letter mentioned has not survived.

3. "Mr. Hughes" remains unidentified.

260

John Koopman to Pierre. ALS
SHR

Poughkeepsie. June the 19: Day 1767

Mr Peroa Cortland land Sir I do here by inform you that I shall take it has a great favour if you Will Please to Send me the Money due to me for Makeing your Waggon Which is the Sum of Fifteen Pounds and Cost me Sixteen Shillings to the Boatmen to bring it to you Which Sir I hope you Will Like wise be kind a Nough to allow me and Send the Whole by Lewis Dubois the Beare here of and you Will greatly oblige your Humble Servant

John Koopman J^{unr}

P.S.: Sir

I Hope you Will Not think much of my Writeing to you for it for I am in so great Nessetie of the Money that is the Cause of my Sending Remain Sir your Humble Servant

John Koopman Jun

[Addressed]

To
Mr
Peroa Cortland
at
Croton River

[Endorsed]

Pokeepsie. June 16. 1767
Koopmans Letter about the Waggon

[2nd Endorsement]

June 16 1767
Paid on this order Twelve Pounds Sixteen Shillings

261

Edward W. Kiers[1] to Pierre. ALS
SHR

Haverstrawe May the 4th 1770

Pirre V. Cortland Esqr

Sir

You will Gratley Oblige me if it is convenient to You to pay in to Mr George Briggs[2] the money Due for the Rey [rye] and his Receipt Shall be in full for the Same. I am Under Necessity of making Severall payment and Begg of you not to take a Miss of me Calling for the Money.

I have Settled Last Year in full with Mr. Filly [Philip] Your Sone except a few Pounds of Neals [nails] which we cane Settle aney time here after[.]Mr. & Missrs D. Noyelles[3]

joins in Compliment to Miss^{rs}. Cortland and your family and
Remain with Due Respect Sir
Your Most Humble Servant
E.W. Kiers
Manor of Cortlandt May the 9. 1770
Then Received of Pierre Van Cortlandt
Seventeen pounds Infull for 85 bus^{l} of Rey
Delivered him by Mr Kiers
p^{r} me George Briggs
his mark

[Endorsed]
Edwd. W^{m}. Kiers
Order. & Rec^{t}. for
Cash p^{d}. G. Briggs
1770

---

1. Edward William Kiers was a merchant residing in Haverstraw Precinct in Orange County. In March, 1776, Congress requested him to sell a quantity of gunpowder in his possession to Colonel Hay's regiment. Fernow, *Wills*, p. 230; Peter Force, ed., *American Archives: Fifth Series, From the Declaration of Independence . . . to the Definitive Treaty of Peace . . .* (Washington, D.C., 1848–1853), I, 344.

2. George Briggs was a farmer who served as one of the executors of Kiers's will. In 1790 he resided in Cortlandt town. Fernow, *Wills*, p. 230; *Heads of Families 1790*, p. 197.

3. "D. Noyelles" was probably John DeNoyelles of Orange County. Kiers served as one of the executors of his will. The Miss DeNoyelles was probably his daughter, Charlotte. He had land in Durham and Deerfield townships in Charlotte County, and in Tryon County and near Lake Champlain. Fernow, *Wills*, pp. 117, 230.

262

Gabriel Purdy[1] to Pierre. ADS
SHR

[June 26, 1770.]

Mr Vancort Land

Dr to 3 pr of hinges	0. 9.0
to Laying of Colten	2.6
to Shewing a horse	0. 2.6
to 2 pare of hinges and heding a plow Bolt and printing a Shear and punking colter	0. 9.0
to Sharpening plow irons and mending 2 Clevises to 2 pare of hinges	0. 6.0
To Sharpen Shear and colter	0. 1.0
to Sharpen Shear and colter mending a Clevis and one Ring and 2 boltes	0. 2.3
to 7 plow Plaights and Sharpen colter	0. 2.6
to Large Lay for colter By Thomas Derow	0. 4.0
To Shear pin 2 Colters	0. 0.6
to pint of Shear	0. 0.3
to Repairing of a bucket	0. 0.6
To Shearpen a colter	0. 0.3
to abole of todey and other Drink	0. 1.3
to a New Shew	0. 1.3
to Dozen nails for wagen	0. 1.0
to Shearpen 2 mill Pecks	0. 1.0
to Shearpen a peck ox	0. 0.1
to half pint of Genave	0. 0.8
to mending of Sythe	0. 1.3
to pint of Genave	0. 1.2
	£2.10.1

Recd: the Above June 26th, 1770

Gabriel Purdy

[Endorsed]
Gab^{l} Purdy
Acct. & Receipts
P. V. C. Esqr

[also endorsed]
Gabiel Purdy
Acc^{t}. £2.10.1

---

1. Gabriel Purdy was the sixth child of Samuel and Clorinda (Strang) Purdy of Rye. He was an ironmonger and also ran an inn in Sing Sing (Ossining) until his death in 1803. He had a son named Gabriel. MacKenzie, p. 565.

263

Pierre to William Bayard.[1] ALS
NYHS

Manor of Cortlandt Aug. 27 1771.

Dr Sir,

Your Favour of June Last in your Return from this Came Safe to my hands, the Contents have duly Considered, and have made it my Business as opportunity offered to Acquaint as many people as I Thought had the Least Inclination to purchase with the purpose thereof But find in General the Great Objection is that the price is too heigh. There are Several who waite to see at what Rate the first should be Sold at, which will verry much Regulate the Sales of the Remainder Tho at present there is No Enquiry. Suppose from the Busy Season I have Thought probably it would promote the Sales if the premises were advertised either by hand bill or in the publick prints at private Sale or otherwise as you Think best as it would make it more publickly known.

The Letter you wrote by Mr Bailey[2] he DD it me Yesterday & told me he had spoke to you About the mile Lott.

He seemed to me to be verry Indifferent, I told him he could either purchase as far as the Road & Leave the Remainder opposite the Road or Mile Lott. I could see no Difference at 5 p^{er} Acre. All the Disadvantage That I Can perceive is if the mile Lott below the Road fetches 5 that piece above the Road will hardly fetch it Tho the Mile Lott must have Timber And there is Not Enough below the Road to Support it. Bailey told me he was going to town & Then would waite on you —

I do not know his Circumstances — he has hyred the farm he now lives on from Walter Frankling[3] who Can further inform you. You may depend S^{r} my Best Endeavor Shall be used in Regard to your Interest — And am assuredly your friend and Affectionate Kindsman To Serve

Pierre VanCortlandt

[Addressed]
To
William Bayard Esqr
In New York

---

1. The Bayards inherited several tracts of land in Van Cortlandt Manor in the name of Margaret (Van Cortlandt) Bayard, daughter of Stephanus. Genealogy, *VCFP*, I, 20; see also William and Nicholas Bayard to Pierre, March 24, 1772 (No. 266).

2. Bailey was an old family name in the town of Somers, situated near the center of the northern tier of towns in Westchester County. It was carved out of the old Cortlandt Manor and was first called Stephenstown. The Bailey in question may have been Lewis Bailey, who received farm No. 9 in the west range of Lot No. 7 from the devisees of Andrew Johnston. A James Bailey owned a farm lying one mile south of the village. Scharf, I, 471, 479–480.

3. Probably Walter Franklin, who was active in land acquisition from 1769 to 1772. Both in 1769 and in 1770, he and a number of associates surveyed and petitioned for grants

amounting to over 20,000 acres in the area surrounding Albany. In September, 1771, he and associates petitioned for a grant of the Burlington tract of 23,000 acres on Onion River, formerly granted under New Hampshire. New York, *Calendar of Land Papers*, pp. 482, 500, 543, 551.

264

Robert G. Livingston Jr. to Philip. AD
SHR

1771 Mr. Philip Van Cortland
Octr. 18 Bought of Rob G Livingston Junr

To 1 ps mixt broad Cloth. 19¼	9/6	£ 9. 2.10½
15½ Gro Coat binding	9/6	6.19.6
2 ps Cambletees 26 yds	52/	5. 4. .
1 ps Chints		5.
1 doz black Worsted Mills		1.
1 black Vest Pattern		16
1 doz Chyit Hatts		13
1 doz bonnet Paper		4
1 ps thread Lace 8½ yds	3/4	1. 6.4
1 doz Sett Pletania buckles		1. 5. .
1 Gro Lettd. Garters		10
1 Gro Laces		7
½ lb Darning thread	21/	10.6
12 bags bask buttons	5/6	[torn]
2 bags Do	14/	1. 8. .
1 doz Ivory Combs		13
1 doz Worsted Hose		2
1 doz Checkd handkerchiefs		6.6
2 Packs Pins	6/6	13
1 ps Shalloon		3. 6
1 ps Cotton Check 17½ Ells	2/6	2. 3.9
		£46.14.5½

Errors Excepted
R G L Junr

[Endorsed] R.G.Livingston Acc^{t}. 1771 —

265

Pierre to Philip Van Cortlandt [nephew]. ALS
SHR

New-York Feby 20. 1772.

Dear Couz^{n}.

Your Letter I Received Just after that I Returned from the Manor, Since Which I have Wrote up to my Son Philip Who I have Expected to have been Here Last Week With the acc^{t}. that Stands Open In my Books. Agst. my Brother Estate.[1] he is not as yet Come down Suppose Occasioned by the Verry heigh fresshes that have Lately been by which have Sustained great dammage. I have this day Wrote to him again, and you may Depend as soon as he Comes down Will Send him to you or go my self to you if if I possibly Can; Couz^{n}. Philip be so good and Convince your Self how that Conveyance is by Which My Brother and my self Enter Into Covenant to Sell Such Lands as are there in Mentioned and for what purposes. I dare say you will Render me an acc^{t}. how the monies have been appropriated. it is better that that affair is Settled In my Time or it probably will Create Disputes. My Respect to Your Self Cous^{n}. Cortlandt and the Couzens. am Your

Affectionate Unkle
Pierre Van Cortlandt

---

1. According to the last will and testament of Philip Van Cortlandt, his four sons were made both executors and heirs to Cortlandt Manor. As Pierre, Sr. was the sole survivor upon the

death of his brother, Stephen, in 1756, all shares in the Manor reverted to his care. In writing to his Uncle Pierre, Stephen's son, Philip, had asked for clarification of his entitled share in the estate. As a consequence of Philip's subsequent Loyalism and flight to Nova Scotia, he and his heirs were virtually ignored by their New York kinsmen and their property claims were unfulfilled. New York *Mercury,* March 1, 1762; Scharf, I, 137; see also No. 259.

266

William and Nicholas Bayard to Pierre. ALS
Rutgers University Library

Greenwich March 24th 177.2.

D Sir

In Consequence of the Conferrence that We had with you Yesterday Under the Hall relative to the Sale of our Lands in the Mannor[1] which by the News Papers, as well as by Advertiziments struck up thro Ye. Country, you will observe We have Directed such persons as Choose to become purchasers, to Call upon you or ourselves Therefoure the Thing Next to be Done, is to Ascertain ye Value of Each Lott, how to do it, We cannot Say, but by the Value Old Mr Ver Plank[2] put it when he Laid it Out, which you now have the Original Inclosed to you, as also two other Estimates that you Aided us in Making, when we Intended It for Publick Sale, but these last two we do not expect — they will Sell for, but have only sent them to give you all the Information we had, perhaps some Lotts may fetch some of them prices, & some not, but upon the Whole, Mr Ver Planks is the Lowest Estimation by much. Therefore as It will not suite us to Let it Lay in the Manner it now does, we beg it as a very singular favour, you will Dispose of it for us as you would do If your own Under be same Circumstances, & your Agreement shall be

Confirmed by us, We hope on your return home you will find Your family Equal to your own & our Wishes & are Dr Sir

Your Obliged & Affection Kinsmen
Wm Bayard
N^{s} Bayard

To P Van Cortlandt Esqr

[Endorsed]
Copy Letter to PV Cortlandt Esqr
24 March 1772 & 2 Estimates of Lotts of Land

---

1. The land in question, which was first advertised in the New York *Journal or the Weekly Advertizer* on March 12, 1772, comprised ten lots carved out of the former plot known as Lot No. 5, the home of Hendrick and William Lent. The property was described as "good land and well timbered, and very conveniently situated near the north-river." The advertisement read in full:

   To Be Sold
   On the Manor of Cortlandt

   The following lots of land in said manor being parts of the Lot No. 5, whereon Hendrick and William Lent lived, and are now laid out in the following manner, Lot No. 1 adjoins to Hudson's River, and the public road that leads to Albany, containing 211 acres, has a good stream for mills of any sort, and is well supplied with timber. Lot No. 2 contains 103 acres of choice land, and fronts the East side of the before-mentioned road. Lot No. 3 binds upon said road, to the Eastward of Lot No. 2, is equally good, and contains 100 acres and three rods. Lot No. 4 contains 103 acres, and lies in the rear of the before mentioned lots. Lot No. 5 contains 103 acres, and lies in the rear of Lot No. 4. Lot No. 6 contains 103 acres and lies in the rear of Lot No. 5. Lot No. 7 contains 103 acres, and lies in the rear of Lot. No. 6. Lot No. 8 contains 103 acres, and lies in the rear of Lot. No. 7; This Lot No. 8 has on it a good fall for a mill or mills. Lot No. 9 contains 103 acres and lies on the rear of Lot. No. 8. Lot No. 10 contains 101 acres, and lies in the rear of Lot. No. 9. All the before mentioned lots, are good land and well timbered, and very conveniently situated near the north-river; a plan of the lots as they are here mentioned, may be seen by applying to Pier Van Courtlandt Esq; living on said manor, or to William Bayard, living at Greenwich, or Nicholas Bayard in Bowry Lane, who will inform them of the condition of sale and give a good title to such as choose to purchase.

William Bayard
Nicholas Bayard

N.B. a plan of the above lots may likewise be seen in the hands of Doctor Graham, at the White Plains, and Doctor Haviland at Rye.

The advertisement was repeated on March 19 and 26, and also was carried in the New York *Gazette and Weekly Mercury* on March 16, 23, and 30.

2. Philip Verplanck, the son of Jacobus and Margaret (Schuyler) Verplanck, married Gertrude Van Cortlandt, daughter of Johannes, the eldest son of Stephanus Van Cortlandt. He followed the career of a surveyor and in that capacity performed several surveys of Cortlandt Manor. He was a party to the 1731 division of the Manor, and appraised the lots at that time. Ver-Planck, pp. 114–137; *VCFP,* II, xli–xlii, 9.

267

Robert C. Livingston Jr. to Philip. AD
SHR

New York May 25th, 1773.

Mr. Phil Cortlandt

Bought of Rob. G. Livingston Junr

To 3 doz frinze	9/	£	1. 7. .
" 3 Handkerchiefs	4/		.12. .
" 7 doz Kives	4/4		1.10.4
" 11 Fans	13d		.11.11
" 3 ps Shalloon	56/		7. 8. .
" 3 doz Fringe	7/6		1. 2.6

" 30 yds. Cotton Holland	2/5	3.12..
9 warting 1½ doz. H.C. Hinges	18/	1. 7..
" 1 ps Tammy	45/	2. 5..
" 4 Gauze Aprons	8/	1.12..
" 8 Handkerchiefs	4/4	.18.8
" 12 yds. Black Spotted Garose	4/	2. 8..
" 2 doz Scalping Knives	8/	.16..
" 10 yds. Black Catgut	3/6	1.15..
		£27. 5.5

[Endorsed] Phil Cortlandt Account

[Further endorsed] Robert G. Livingston Acct. 1773

268

Samuel Drake[1] to Pierre. AD
SHR

[1772–1773.]

1772	Peair Van Cortland detor unito	Samuel Drake —
January	To 3 Cogwheals arms & carting	£0. 8.0
21	116 futt of inch Bords	
	Delivered to Hillites	0. 7.6
1773		
October	for 3 wortherwheals arms	0.13.0
30	3 Cog wheel arms	0. 8–
	for a tree for the cants	0. 6.0
	for Drawing of the cants	0.12.0
	the carpendor work & luckin	1. 6–
	for sawing	0. 6.0
	for carting to the Landing	0. 8–
	46 futt of inch for Buckets	0. 3 —
		£4.19.6

March 26. 1773
Rec^d the above by order and for
Saml Drake Esqr by John Mc Creery[2]

[Endorsed] Saml Drake Esqr
Acct & Receipt
1773

---

1. Samuel Drake was a resident of Eastchester who in 1768 was located on farm No. 2, north lot No. 1, west of Lake Mohegan. He was a colonel in the local militia and in June, 1779, commanded a unit at the Yorktown Presbyterian Church near Crompond. He later served in the Assembly. Scharf, I, 441.

2. Perhaps John McKready, a resident of the Middle Ward with land assessed at £320. "Tax List for the Middle Ward, April, 1779," SHR Collections.

269

Philip's Business Account with William Penyar. AD
SHR

[May 26, 1774–September 16, 1776.]

William Penyar to Philip Dr May 26th 1774

May 26	To ¼ C^t of Fine Flower		0. 5.0
Octo^r 8	To 1 Q^rt of Rum		0. 1.2
1775	To Fish		0. 8.0
March 27	2¼ yd' of Check	@3/9	0. 8.5
	1 lb of Chocolate		0. 2.0
	103 lb Pork	@5	2. 2.11
	22 lb Hogs fat	@7	0.12.10
Ap^l 19	To 1 p^r Sissors		0. 1.0
D^o 22	To 1 yd' Check		0. 2.9
	7 lb Sugar		0. 5.0

May 3	To ½ C^{t} of Rye Flower		o. 6.0
	1 p^{r} ½ Soles		o. 1.0
	1 Peck Pease		o. 2.0
	7 y^{d}. Check	@2/9	o.19.3
	1 gal^{n} Mol^{s}		o. 2.8
	7 y^{d}. Linning	@2/7	o.18.1
D^{o} 29	To 1 lb Ginger & ½ Pepper		o. 2.9
June 10	To 1 Gal^{n} Rum		o. 5.6
	1 Gal^{n} & 1 Q^{rt} Mol^{s}		o. 3.4
	1 Pint Rum		o. 0.9
	1⅛ y^{d} of Check	@2/9	o. 3.1
	1 4 lb Sugar		o.10.6
	1¾ y^{d} Sheeting	@3/7	o. 6.2
	1 lb Chocolate		o. 2.0
			£ 8.12.2
May 11	To Tobacco		o. 1.0
D^{o} 29	To 2 y^{d}' Check	@3/9	o. 7.6
June 30	To 1 Gal^{n} Rum		o. 5.6
	2 Oz Indigo		o. 2.0
	1 Sickle		o. 2.6
	1 Sissars		o. 2.6
July 23	To 1 Gal^{n} Spirits		o. 5.6
29	2 y^{d}' Cloth	@4/3	o. 8.6
	To ¾ y^{d} Stuff	@2/	o. 1.6
	1 y^{d} & ⅛ of Shalloon	@3/	o. 3.4½
	2 Sk^{s} Silk	@9^{d}	o. 1.6
	½ y^{d} Stuff	@2/	o. 1.0
	1 Stick Hair		o. 0.9
Sepr 16	To 1 File		o. 0.9
	Awls & Thimble		o. 0.6
			£10.16.6½

[Endorsed] Wm Penyar Sep^{t} 16, 1776
Acct

270

Indenture between Richard Varick[1] and Pierre. ADS
SHR

[January 4, 1775.]

THIS INDENTURE made this fourth Day of January in the Year of our Lord one thousand seven hundred and seventy five Between Richard Varick Esqr. of the City of New York attorney at Law of the one Part and Pierre Van Cortlandt of the Manor of Cortlandt in the County of West Chester in the Province of New York Esqr. of the other Part WITNESSETH that the said Richard Varick for and in Consideration of the Sum of five Shillings lawful Money of New York to him in hand paid by the said Pierre Van Cortlandt at or before the Ensealing and Delivery of these Presents the Receipt whereof is hereby acknowledged HATH granted bargained and sold and by these Presents — DOTH hereby grant bargain and sell unto the said Pierre Van Cortlandt All that certain House and Lot Tract Piece or Parcel of Land scituate lying and being in the Outward of the City of New York on the East Side of the Bowry Lane[2] and described in the Letters Patent thereof bearing Date at Fort James[3] in New York the nineteenth Day of October anno Dom. one thousand six hundred and sixty seven granted to Fransisco a free Negroe[4] by Richard Nicoll Esqr. Governor of the Province of New York[5] as follows to wit A certain Parcel of Land lying and being upon the Island Manhatans to the East of the High Way[6] or Waggon Path having to the North Gerard Hendricks and to the South Anthony Congo's the Negroe[7] containing in Length alongst the said Waggon Path two hundred Paces and in Breadth three hundred thirty three Paces Together with all and singular the Houses, Outhouses, Kitchens stables, Buildings, Yards, Wells, Walls, Ways Paths, Passages, Waters Water Courses, Rivers Riverlets and Streams of Water, Feedings Pastures, Meadows, Marshes, Woods, Underwoods, Easements, Profits, Commodities Advantages, Emoluments, Hereditaments and appurtenances whatsoever to the same House and Lot Tract Piece or Parcel of Land & Premisses belonging or in any wise

Appertaining AND the Reversion & Reversions Remainder and Remainders Rents Issues and Profits thereof and of every Part & Parcel thereof with the Appurtenances TO HAVE & TO HOLD the said House Lot Tract, Piece or Parcel of Land and Premisses above particularly mentioned and discribed with the appurtenances unto the said Pierre Van Cortlandt his Executors administrators & Assigns from the Day next before the Day of the Date of these Presents for and during and unto the full End and Term of one whole Year from thence next ensueing and fully to be compleat & ended Yielding and Paying therefor unto the said Richard Varick his Heirs and Assigns the Rent of one Pepper Corn on the last Day of the said Term if the same be lawfully demanded to the Intent and Purpose that by Virtue of these Presents and by force of the statute for transferring of Uses into Possession the said Pierre Van Cortlandt may be in the actual Possession of all and singular the said Premisses and be thereby enabled to accept and take a Grant & Release of the Reversion & Inheritance thereof to him his Heirs & Assigns to his & their only proper Use Benefit & Behoof for ever By Indenture intended to be made Between the said Richard Varick of the one Part and the said Pierre Van Cortlandt of the other Part & to bear Date the Day next after the Day of the Date of these Presents In Witness whereof the Parties to these Presents have hereunto interchangably set their Hands & Seals the Day & Year first above written

Sealed & Delivered
in the Presence of Us. Rich^d^. Varick
the Words (Paces and in Breadth three
hundred) between the sixth & seventh
Lines of the second Side being interlined
before Execution
Nich^s^ Fish
Solomon Simson

[Endorsed] Rich^d^. Varick to Pierre Van Cortlandt
Lease[8]

---

1. Abandoning a successful law practice in New York, Richard Varick entered the army in 1776 and served as a military secretary to General Philip Schuyler and aide-de-camp to Benedict Arnold. Suspicions aroused because of his relations with the traitor Arnold were silenced when Washington chose Varick to classify and copy all correspondence of the headquarters of the Continental Army. His postwar career was no less impressive: Recorder of the City of New York, 1783–1789; Speaker of the New York Assembly, 1787–1788; New York Attorney General, 1788–1789; Mayor of New York, 1791–1801; and president of the New York Society of the Cincinnati, 1806–1831. *DAB*, X, 226–227; McAdam, I, 510.

2. When Governor Peter Minuit divided the lower part of Manhattan Island into farms (called "bouweries"), the road that led through these farms was called Bouwerie Lane, later shortened to Bowery. Hemstreet, p. 21.

3. After the English took control of New York, Fort Amsterdam was renamed Fort James, in honor of the English king. It was bounded by State, Whitehall, and Bright streets and by Bowling Green. Originally erected in 1626, it contained such diverse structures as the Dutch Reformed Church of St. Nicholas, the governor's house, and military barracks. The earthwork was demolished in 1787. John A. Kouwenhoven, *The Columbia Historical Portrait of New York* (New York, 1953), p. 41; Hemstreet, p. 54.

4. A slave named Francisco was first recorded in New Amsterdam in 1658. Peter Stuyvesant, the last Dutch governor of New Netherland, followed the procedure of manumitting slaves who had served the West India Company. O'Callaghan, *Documents Colonial New York,* I, 425; II, 31.

5. After defeating the Dutch, the Duke of York placed Colonel Richard Nicholls in command of the English troops in New York. Nicholls served as the colony's first governor (1664–1668). Hemstreet, p. 55.

6. The King's Highway commenced at Fort James and proceeded northward to where Bouwerie Lane diverged to the northeast,

then ran through the Common and public cow pasture. Townsend MacCoun, *Amsterdam in the New Netherlands, 1653–1664* (New York, 1909).

7. A Gerrett Hendricks was listed as a property owner in the West Ward in New York City from 1695 to 1699. *Collections of the New-York Historical Society for the Year 1910* (New York, 1911), p. 15. The family named Congo, free Negroes, can be traced back to 1696 in the city. *Collections of the New-York Historical Society for the Year 1885* (New York, 1886), p. 569.

8. The described tract of land belonging to Pierre Van Cortlandt encompassed an area east of the King's Highway, north of Stanton Street, south of North or Houston Street, and west of Fourth (now Allen) Street. J.B. Holmes, "Map of Part of the Stuyvesant Property" (New York, 1867).

Editor's Note
Beekman Estate

Throughout this series devoted to the Van Cortlandt family correspondence, passing references are made to the controversies surrounding the estate of Gertrude (Van Cortlandt) Beekman. Gertrude, who married the extremely wealthy widower Henry Beekman, was the daughter of Stephanus and Gertrude (Schuyler) Van Cortlandt. She was a sister to Philip, Pierre, Sr.'s father, and therefore Pierre Jr.'s great-aunt.

Henry Beekman's first wife was Janet Livingston, daughter of Robert Livingston. She died in 1724, leaving two children. Henry married Gertrude two years later. There was no issue from this marriage. To add to the confusion of relationships, Pierre, Sr.'s wife, Joanna, was Henry Beekman's niece. Henry died in 1776, his widow in March, 1777. Pierre, Sr., along with his cousin, John Van Cortlandt, were named co-executors of Gertrude's will.

The complications that arose over the settlement of

the estate stemmed from the extent of Gertrude Van Cortlandt's personal possessions at the time of her marriage, for she had been a wealthy woman in her own right. According to Van Cortlandt sources, Gertrude and Henry allegedly entered into an ante-nuptial arrangement whereby she would retain sole rights to any monies she voluntarily commingled with those of her husband. Such a document was diligently searched for during and after the American Revolution on both sides of the Atlantic, but was never found. The executors argued that Gertrude had given Henry £500 sterling for him to keep for her, which was supposed to have been deposited in the Bank of England. After Henry died and his will was read, no reference to such monies was found, and the complications began. In addition, a second document was said to exist in which Henry declared that he had deposited monies belonging to his wife in the Bank of England.

The executors, at first both John and Pierre Van Cortlandt, and then Pierre alone following John's death in 1786, requested the only direct heir to Henry Beekman's estate, his surviving daughter, Margaret, to provide the Van Cortlandts with an equivalent sum in dollars, amounting to $13,333.33. Margaret Beekman was then the wife of the extremely influential Robert R. Livingston. It is to be remembered that Pierre's wife, Joanna, also was a Livingston. The monetary entanglement soon became an internecine family affair.

In recent years, an individual brought a sheaf of manuscripts, found in the attic of a building in upstate New York about to undergo extensive renovation, to the attention of the Rhinebeck (New York) Historical Society. Among those papers, now in the possession of Clermont State Historic Park in Germantown, New York, are documents having a direct bearing upon Gertrude Beekman's estate.

The seven following documents, when added to those found in *Van Cortlandt Family Papers,* I, 99–106; II, 37–38, 498–500, 582–583, 584–586, 588–590, 600–601, 616; III,

3–6, 30–31, 42–44, 54–55, 381–383, 704; and No. 6 in this volume help to complete the Gertrude Beekman story.

A brief synopsis of court suits filed and counterfiled would show:

January 15, 1801	Pierre filed suit against Livingstons in New York Supreme Court for payment of $13,333.33.
October, 1801	Jury summoned. Case postponed twelve times until June 18, 1804.
February 24, 1802	Countersuit filed by Edward Livingston.
December 13, 1802	Pierre answered bill of complaint.
December 7, 1803	Edward Livingston filed a second bill of complaint.
June 14, 1804	Pierre filed answer to above bill.
October 1, 1804	Judgment recorded in Pierre's favor. Livingstons were to pay him $13,333.33 plus court costs.
May 31, 1805	Bill of complaint dismissed.
May, 1806	Pierre complained of Livingston non-compliance.
July 22, 1807	Edward Livingston claimed legal harassment by Pierre.
December 23, 1807	Edward Livingston fled New York for new life in New Orleans. Robert R. Livingston guaranteed payment of court costs.
January 18, 1809	Judgment of October 1, 1804, set aside.
February 6, 1809	Edward Livingston requested an injunction against Pierre.
October 31, 1809	Pierre filed answer.
January 15, 1811	Demurrers filed by group of Livingston relatives claiming that Gertrude Beekman left two wills, the

	first one providing for payment of £500 to Pierre, John Van Cortlandt, and to Robert R. Livingston.
April 24, 1811	Subpoena issued for court appearance of Margaret B. Livingston.

The case disappeared from court records after September, 1811. It appears that Pierre never obtained the $13,333.33 he claimed was due him from the Livingston relations.

Gertrude (Van Cortlandt) Beekman Estate

271

Henry Beekman: Statement Concerning Bank Accounts. ADS

Clermont State Historic Park

[July 25, 1760.]

Whereas I Henry Beekman in the Years 1758. & 1759 Remitted in the hands by Bills of Exchange to Mr William Baker marcht. in London above Two thousand pounds sterling to be put in Banck, for saffity, to be Draw out by occasion, which accordingly by Mr. Baker was don, and by his letter of advise Bundled up and posted at large in my Ladger. Nomr. D. fos. 80. & 83. Now this is to Certify that one quarter part thereof as £500: sterling money was productive occasionally of my wife Gertruyds money of which, I declare hereby; that she shall have free Liberty to Dispose there of with the Interest thereon accruing in her Life time, or by her last will & Testiment as Shee shall be pleased to Doe; to which I Consent. And AGreetoo as being her Shaere and right there in; and I injoin & abjure my Heirs Executrs. Administrs. or Assisgns to Abbide there to above,

Wittness my hand in Rinebeck this 25. July 1760

Henry Beekman

272

Vendue of the Estate of Gertrude (Van Cortlandt) Beekman. AD

Clermont State Historical Park

[Post March, 1777.]

List of Sundries Sold at Publick
Vendue belonging to the Estate of
the Late Mrs Gertruyd Beekman Decd.

Eight leather chairs to Pierre Cortlandt £7- 0-0

One Tilt Table with drawers to Mrs.

	Radlieft	1– 6–0
	One Table to Mrs Radlieft	1– 0–0
	One Round Leaf Table to Gilbert Cortlandt	3– 5–0
Paid	1 Picture to Admiral Greaves	1– 1–0
	11 Pictures to Mr Radlieft	6– 3–0
	7 Gelly Glasses Mrs Van Wyck	1–18–0
	5 Small D^o^ Mrs Van Wyck	0–15–0
	2 large & 1 small D^o^ Mrs Van Wyck	1– 5–0
	2 large Pictures Mrs Van Wyck	0–16–0
	1 pewter old Bason & 4 pewter old plates P.V:C	1–12–0
Paid	2 Pewter Dishes Admiral Greaves	2– 4–0
Paid	2 d^o^ d^o^ Mrs Hardenbarrack	1– 9–0
	1 Large Pewter Cheese Dish Mr Van Cortlandt	2–10–0
Paid	1 D^o^ D^o^ Admiral Greaves	1–12–0
Paid	1 D^o^ D^o^ Mrs Cowenhoven	2– 0–0
Paid	1 Cullender Mrs Howe	1–11–0
Paid	1 Large Pewter Dish Admiral Greaves	2– 6–0
	1 bulliabiesie [bouillabasse] Pan Mrs Radlieft	0–19–0
	1 Glass to Admiral Greaves	3–15–0
	2 black Sconces to Mrs Hardenburgh	4–10–0
	1 Copper Plate Warmer PV. Cortlandt	3–10–0
	1 large looking Glass PVCortlandt	14–15–0
	1 large Copper kettle PV Cortlandt	17–10–0
	1 D^o^ D^o^ Admiral Grieves	17– 0–0
	1 Brass Kettle P VCortlandt	6– 0–0
	1 double Brass Candle Stick Willm Radlieft	2– 4
		88– 1–6
	2 Gilt Looking Glasses Willm Radlieft	£15–10–0
	1 large looking glass P Van Cortlandt	10– 0–0
	1 Bead bolster & pillow Johannes Van	

Wagener	14– 5–0
1 cabinet Pierre V Cortlandt	31– –
1 Cubberd Ab^{m} Van Wyck	4–15–0
1 Chest Pierre V Cortlandt	2– 5
1 Desk	
1 large Dining Table Gilb^{t} V Cortlandt	
1 Small Tin Chest & Cannisters PV Cortlandt	2–16
2 dutch books Joannis V Wagenner	0–10–0
1 Large Bible Jno. Moffett	7– 0–0
	88– 1–6
	109–16–0
	197–17–6

[Endorsed]
Vendue List
Mrs Beekmans Estate —

273

Pierre to Philip Van Rensselaer. ALS [Copy]
NYPL

[Post April, 1777.]

Dear Coll.

You will be pleased to Hand this Letter to My Couzin M^{rs}. Renselaer to whom I Should have Wrote before this about the Bureau had Couz^{n}. John Stopt'd here In his passing Who I Should have been Verry glad to have Seen[.][1] Couz^{n}. Rensselaer Can have the Bureau at any Time when Ever She will please to Send for it for Couz^{n}. Hanah Or Send me her Order what She will have done with it It Stands here In the front Room In one of the best places in this House, It is pritty much Shackled as She will Know; Gilbert Tells me the Reason Why he wrote as he did was that Couz^{n}. Rensse-

laer Some Time ago[2] — Shortly after that I acquainted her that I had bought the bureau for her Told him that as it was old & wod Cost more that [than] it was worth to move it to Couz^{n}. Hannah was the Reason of his Writing as he did — as my Caty[3] had a mind for it I Also Sent to Couz^{n}. Livingston at that Time & made her the offer of it but She absolutely Refused it, Said what So Much; And after that Sent word with Mrs Lawrence that She did not want it. M^{rs}. Montgomery wanted it. Mrs Tellitson[4] was anctious for it, M^{rs} [?] bid £38 And as it Was an old piece of furniture of Aunt Beekman[5] I Choose Reather to Keep it for Caty more than any Stranger Should have[.] However as Cousin Hannah has a Mind for it She Is heartily Welcome to take it When ever it Sutes It was Struck of In Vendue at thirty One pounds Ten Shillings Which I Shall place to Your & Couz^{n}. Hannahs Acc^{t}. The whole amount of the Vendue List is about Two Hundred pounds. I have paid M^{rs}. Cockran[6] & Mrs Livingston their proportion am With the Greatest Regard to you Couz^{n}.
Renssalaer and the Couzins

Dear Couz^{n}. Your most Obedient & Verry hum^{e}.
Ser^{t}. Pierre Van Cortlandt

P.S.
Aunt Beekmans
Picture is here
Mrs Livingston Says
it was given M^{rs}. Parker[7]
I Could wish you wod
Send for it When you Send
for the Bureau.

[Endorsed] Coppy of a Letter to Couz Renselaer
Relative
the Bureau &c^{r}

---

1. "Cousin Rensselaer" was Elizabeth Van Rensselaer (1765–1841), the only daughter of Stephen II and Catherine (Livingston) Van Rensselaer. Elizabeth was married twice, first to John B. Schuyler in 1787, and then to John Bleecker in 1800. *VCFP,* II, 23.

   "Cousin John" was John Van Cortlandt (1721–1786), the son of Stephen and Catalina (Staats) Van Cortlandt. A sugar refiner with both his business and residence on New York's Broadway, he married Hester Bayard, the daughter of Nicholas Bayard. During the disastrous September 20, 1776, fire in New York City, his property escaped the flames even though most of Broadway's west side was reduced to ashes. The John Van Cortlandt house was later commandeered by the British for the use of royal Attorney General John Tabor Kempe. *VCFP,* II, 499; Stephen and John Van Cortlandt to Philip, July 10, 1789 (No. 218); *Pennsylvania Gazette,* October 2, 1776.

2. "Cousin Hannah" is a reference to Hannah Van Cortlandt. Gilbert Van Cortlandt (1757–1786) was Pierre's son.

3. Catharine Van Cortlandt (1751–1829) was Pierre's eldest daughter and the wife of Abraham Van Wyck.

4. Mrs. Thomas Tillotson was the former Margaret Livingston, daughter of Robert R. and Margaret (Beekman) Livingston. *VCFP,* II, 500.

5. Gertrude (Van Cortlandt) Beekman, wife of Colonel Henry Beekman.

6. Dr. John Cockran's wife was a direct heir of Mrs. Gertrude Beekman.

7. Most likely Mrs. James Parker, the niece of Colonel Henry and Gertrude (Van Cortlandt) Beekman.

274

Pierre: Statement Concerning the Gertrude (Van Cortlandt) Beekman Estate. ADf

Clermont State Historic Park

[post 1777.]

Some time in the beginning of the Year 1777 And in the Life time of Gertruyd Beekman I Rented the Mantion House and farm at Rinebeck of the late Coll Henry Beekman of the Proprietor M[rs] Margaret Livingston, Without Any Hesitation Or Reservation Whatever Mentioned or made with Respect to M[rs] Beekman the widow of the Late Coll Beekman who then Lived in the Said House —

In Sep[r]. 1773 At Rinebeck Aunt Beekman gave me in Charge a parcel of Gold to the Amount of the Whole being seven hundred and Eighty Eight pounds Eleven Shillings[.] M[rs]. Montgomery will Recollect it This money I paid to the Legatees agreeable to Aunt Beekman's Will

In the year 1755 I applyed to my Aunt and Coll Beekman to lend me some money the Coll Told me My Aunt would Let me have what I wanted She Let me then have Eighty pound I gave her my Obligation to be paid to her Order — after her decease without Interest, She ordered it to be paid to General Schuylers Two brothers Stephen and Cortlandt I gave the obligation to him and paid him the money for them the General will remember it, I paid the money 1777 —

Just before Aunt Beekman made her will Coll Beekman sent for me to Come to Town On Some necessary business[.]while Wee were speaking about her Will, which I was anxious to have done, and mentioned if Aunt Should die without a will That then the Estate would go to the heir at Law (The Coll Jocosely said if the Heir knew there was no will he might give me five or six thousand pounds for my dissenting and I should only forfeit the Two Thousand pounds and still be a great gainer)

[Document ends here]

275

Andrew Billings[1] to Pierre. AD
Albany Institute of History and Art

[July 25, 1778.]

Honbl Pier Vancortlandt Esq B^{t}
of And^{w} Billings

1778	
July 25	
16 Ennamelled Rings death and age	
Mrs Beekman @32/	25 .. 12 .. 0
12 Plaine D^{o} D^{o} @20/	12 .. 0 .. 0
	37 .. 12 .. 0
Credit by 6 halfe Johannase @64/	19 .. 4 .. 0
	[20] .. 4 .. 0
Ballance	18 .. 8 .. 0

Poughkeepsie October
y[e] . . . 3d . . 1778.
Received of the Honbl Pier Vancortlandt Esq Eighteen pounds Eight Shilling in full for the above account for p^{r}

And^{w} . . Billings

---

1. Andrew Billings was a Revolutionary War patriot and silversmith. *VCFP*, III, 227–228, 503.

276

John Van Cortlandt to John Watts. LBC
NYPL

New York Octo^r^ 1784.

Dear Sir

Mr Pierre Van Cortlandt & Self are Appointed Executors of Aunt Beekmans Estate — M^rs^. Judge Livingston we are Informed has drawn for the money that Aunt had in the Banck of England, & appropriated to her own private Use, & refuses Paying it to the Family Aunt has devised it to — but says she has reassumed it, some of the Legatees Insist upon the Executors Commencing a Suit in Equity for the recovery of it — knowing you have transacted some Matters respecting Aunt's money in Banck Mr Pierre Van Cortlandt & Self request the favour that you will be so kind as to Advise us of Every matter you know respecting Aunt's money that she put in the Banck of England; I am Extreamly unhappy that a Controversy between the Family's should be Occasioned by M^rs^: Livingston's tenaciousness; your favour of advising the Executors respecting the Matter will be grately Acknowledged, I am Sincerely Your

friend & Most Ob^t^ Hum Servt
John V Cortlandt

John Watts Esqr

277

John Van Cortlandt to William Smith. LBC
NYPL

New York Octo^r^:1784.

Dear Sir

When I last saw you at New York you Offered Every Servise in your Power to Oblidge me & famely: which I Acknowledged with every Mark of respect, I am verry Sorry the

Connection of so Good Friends should be separated by the Means of a Cruel War of one Nation, I am now with the Remains of my Famely in my Old Mantion House — after the Expence of £ 300 to put it in the Situation I left it; Unhappy I am to be destitute of my Old Acquaintance; In short I am Almost a Stranger to the People that Inhabit this City — Mr. Pierre Van Cortlandt & Self are Appointed Executors of Aunt Beekmans Estate; we Applyed to Mrs. Widow Livingston respecting the money Aunt Beekman had in the Banck of England she refuses Every Matter of our Application, she persisting that her Father & She had reassumed it; after Our repeated Applications she still persevers, the Legatees Insist upon the Executors filing a Bill for the recovery of the Money; Mr Cortlandt & I must Comply with these requisitions & as you are know'n to some of the Transactions beg you will be so kind as to make some Enquiry if Mrs: Livingston has draw'n upon the Banck for Aunts' Money & the Time when & give us Every Inteligence you know Concerning the Matter Everything in my Power I Can Serve you samely you may freely Command, believe me to be your Sincear Friend &

Most Obt: Hum Sert:

John V Cortlandt

William Smith Esqr: —

278

Gilbert to Pierre. ALS

SHR

[March 27, 1781.]

You'l be pleased to Observe the Diference of Grain is all Calculated according to the Continental prises fixed — The Buckwheat, at three fifths of a Dallar — 3/5 Should we want Hay (which I am sure we shall as I was Disappointed in getting Straw) Mr. Johnston can furnish us with as much as we will want, and have agree'd with him for £ 3.10–pr. Ton — I likewise have apply'd to M^{r}. Everson who asks the same prise — I first ask'd Sherif Smith the Prise of Hay before I would engage, he told me he had Sold for £4.0 and if I could get it under that prise by all means to take it, that Hay was rising, and not much to be had under £4.0.0 what I have done was for the best — Tomorrow set out for PeeksKill in order to set out an Orchard, and as there will not be Trees enough at Croton It will take up some time in collecting them is a Reason why I leave this before You come home, and for other reason I refer Papa to mamma who can enform — From P.Kill shall write by every Opportunity. In the interim I remain Your Dutiful

Son to Command —

March 27th. 1781 Gilb^{t}. V Cortlandt

March 28th —

Badness of the weather prevented my setting out this Morning. Sent Tite over the Mountain for Brand and Rec^{d}. in part 37½ Bus^{ls}. now their still remains due 48½ Bus^{ls}.

March 11. Philis took 2½ to and half quartes of Clean Flax to Spin at the farm House —

March 16th. 1781 then agreed with Joseph S. Mabbitt to take 50 Bus^{ls}. of Brand which is at Thomas Jenks Mill, He is to exchange 6½ Bus^{ls}. of Brand for One bus^{l}. of Wheat —

I have Rec^{d} of the above Brand in part . . . 36 Bus^{ls}.

Agreed with Noah Gale to take 18 Bus^{ls}. of Brand for which I am to allow him 3 Bus^{ls}. of Wheat. and have Rec^{d}. of the above in part 17 Bus^{ls}.

There remains dew on the Horse Lion sold belonging to

Brother Pierre. . 20 Bus^{ls}. of Wheat which is to be good and Merchantable according to the Agreement

---

The above acc^{ts}. are wrote for my Fathers Parusal that he may know how the accounts Stand in my Absence and what has been done in his —

Gilb^{t}. V Cortlandt

Dr Sherif Melancton .... Smith C^{or}

To 90 Bus^{ls}. of Corn	@6/	£27.0.0	By 40 Bus^{ls}. of Corn	@6/	£12. 0.0
To 50 D^{o}. Bwheat	@3/5	12.0.0			
		£39.0.0			
			By 10 D^{o}. B.Wheat	@3/5	2. 8.0
			By 80 D^{o}. of Oats	@4/	0.0
			By 86 D^{o}. of Brand	@2/	8.12.0
					£39. 0.0

N.B — The following number Bus^{ls}. of Brand is yet to be Delivered My Father to complete the above account. (Viz) 40 Bus^{ls}. at the first Mill over the Mountain the Miller has the Sherifs Orders for the Delivery of the same; and 46 Bus^{ls}. to recive perhaps at M^{r}. Thomas Jenks Mill, if not, then to receive it at the first mentioned Mill These 86 Bus^{ls}. of Brand when Deliver'd will account for the Last mentioned artikle on the credid side of the above acc^{t}.

279

John Van Cortlandt to Mary Miller. ADS
SHR

Mannor of Cortlandt 12th June 1781.

Received from Mrs: Mary Miller a Bay horse of the Value of twenty one pounds on account of Rent for the farm She lives upon.

£21.0.0 John V.Cortlandt

[Endorsed]
John V.Cortlandt
1781
Mrs.Miller

280

Samuel Jones[1] to Pierre. ADS
SHR

[June 14, 1782.]

May 10th. 1780 His Excellency Governor V:Cortland: his Bill —

To: 9 pounds of steel at 3 pr pound	2	7	0
To: laying a Shear & pointing a coulter	0	6	0
To: Laying a shear	0	10	0
To One plow Bolt	0	1	6
To: Shoeing two Horses	0	4	6
To: laying a coulter	0	3	6
To: Shoeing a Horse Round	0	4	0
To Shoeing Two Horses	0	6	9
To a large Clabbis	0	8	0
To Fixing Plowplates and Nails	0	2	6
To: mending Hooks	0	1	6

To: 4 & ½ pounds of Steel at 3 p^r pound	0	13	6
To: 12 & ¼ pounds of Iron at 7 p^r pound	0	7	2
To: Shoeing a Horse	0	2	3
To: Fixing Whipple-Trees	0	1	6
To: pointing a coulter & sharpening a Shear	0	2	6
To: Sharpening two Shears	0	1	6
To: Sharpening a Coulter & Fixing a shear	0	1	6
To: Laying a Shear & Coulter	0	10	0
To: Shoeing three Horses	0	9	0
To Shoeing a Horse all Round	0	6	0
To: 1 Horse 1 Shoe & 1 Toe'd	0	2	0
To: Shoeing 1 Horse all Round	0	6	0
To: Sharpening a Shear and Coulter	0	1	6
To 6 new Shoes and 2 Removes	0	12	0
To: 2 New Shoes	0	3	6
To; 8 Bolts for a Waggon	0	6	0
To: 8 Staples to a Waggon	0	4	0
To: Sharpening & pointing a coulter	0	3	6
To: 2 New Shoes	0	3	0
To: upsetting an ax	0	1	6
To laying of a hoe	0	5	0
To: 4 New Shoes	0	6	0
Brought forward	£ 9	18	2
Brought over	9	18	2
To: 2 New Shoes	0	3	0
To 4 New Shoes	0	6	0
To: 4 linc pins to the Waggon	0	4	0
To: 2 New shoes	0	3	0
To: 2 Removes	0	1	6
To: 4 Removes	0	3	0
	£10	18	8
To 1 Bushel of Salt	2	0	0
To: pasturing 2 Stears through My latter feed	0	8	0
To Wintering a stear a part of ye Winter	0	8	0

£13 14 8

Ro Mr VanWycks Acc^t
To 2 half Joes May 1 1780
To lb of Veal sent you
To Cash p^d Mr Roger Gale 3
To ye keeping your Ox

Received of Pierre Van Cortlandt June 14 1782 three pounds by order of Samuel Jones on this account.

Roger Gale

£3.0.0

[Endorsed]
Saml Ferris
Acc^t Nine Partners

---

1. Blacksmith Samuel Jones resided with his wife and one daughter in Mt. Pleasant as of 1790. *Heads of Families 1790,* p. 200.

281

Rent Account of Philip Van Cortlandt [nephew].[1] AD SHR

[1782.]

The Rents Paid by Alexander Bridges to Philip Cortlandt for the house at the Corner of Beekmans Slip & formerly James Thompsons

	£ S d
For the Year 77	18.0.0
For the Year 78	18.0.0
For D^o D^o 79	20.0.0
For D^o D^o 80	34.0.0
~~For D^o D^o 81~~	~~34.0.0~~

Only for the Shop

	£ S d
For the year 81 house and all	78.10.0
For the year 82 D° D°	120. 0.0
Rents of Mr Bridges.	£298.10.0

The Rents of Thomas Whiting who is [torn] to Nova Scotia, Paid to Ph: Cortlandt

	£
For the years 77 . . 78 . . 79 . . 80 — about in all	200.0.0
For the years 81 . . 82 . . about 100 a year	200.0.0
	400.0.0

This house formerly accupied by Mr Bassett

The house of James Thompson

	£ S d
For the year 77–78 . . 79 . . 80 . . — 28 pr an.	108.0.0
For the year 81 . . 82 — £30 p^r^ An.	60.0.0
	£168.0.0

This paid by Jacob Lewis who is gone to the West Indies —

1. Philip Van Cortlandt, the Loyalist, collected rents on several Bowery Lane properties during the Revolutionary War years. These dwellings were Van Cortlandt family possessions. Pierre, Sr. claimed that the value of the rents received by Philip, his nephew, offset any later claims Philip may have had to family properties in Westchester County. In figuring receipts for Bridges's property, Pierre, Sr. made an error of £10.

282

Pierre to Lewis Delavergne.[1] ADS
SHR

[April 22, 1783.]

This day I bought a P^{r}. of Oxen of Lewis Delavergne Esqr for fourty pounds and have paid him In part Thirty pounds Two Shillins and four pence Remains nine pounds Seventeen Shillins and Eight pence to be paid unto him or his order Some time between this and harvest Next by me

Pierre Van Cortlandt

Nine Partners
April. 22 1783

[on reverse side]
Peeks Kill Novr 11, 1783 —

Then Rec^{d}. of the $Hono^{e}$. Pierre Van Cortlandt the within Sum of Nine pounds Seventeen Shillins & Eight Infull In Behalf of Lewis Delaverge Esqr

Thomas Patterson

£9.17.8

[Endorsed]

Paid Infull Nov 11. 1783

---

1. Lewis Delavergne was a lieutenant in the Amenia Precinct militia. New York (State) Legislature, *Journals of the Provincial Congress* . . . (Albany, 1842), II, 93.

283

John Cape[1] to Philip. ADS
NYHS

[November 29, 1783.]

1783	General Cortland to John Cape	D^r
$Novem^r$ 28th	To am^t of and furnish'd	1.16.0
	To 3 Days hay and Oats for 2 horses at 6^sP Horse p a day	1.16.0
		3.12.0

Rec^d the Contents in full
for John Cape
Hugh Montogomery[2]

---

1. John Cape was the owner and proprietor of Cape's Tavern, a watering establishment of enduring popularity. It opened in 1754 as the Province Arms; while called the City Arms it was a favorite spot for British officers. During Cape's tenure, the tavern was a popular meeting place for gentlemen subscribers to the dancing assembly, which was the social feature of the winter of 1783. Wilson, II, 556; Maud W. Goodwin, et. al., *Historic New York,* II, Half Moon Papers, Series Two, p. 269.

2. Hugh Montgomery may have been the man of that name who served as a first lieutenant in the 4th New York regiment of militia in 1778. Fernow, *N.Y. in Revolution,* p. 281.

284

Pierre's Business Account with Justus Wescott. AD
SHR

[1775–1783.]

1775	To a Cow when you settled with Son Philip in 7th year 1773	£6. 0. 0

March 2^{d}	To Cash 60/		3. 0. 0
	To 50 lb of Beef	@/4^{d}	16. 8
Apr^{l} 10	To Cash 40/		2. 0. 0
	To D^{o} 40/ for Fish		2. 0. 0
	To Cash a half Joe and Cash 8/		3.13. 3
D^{o} 22^{d}	To 1 Gammon 19½ lb	@6½	10. 7
May 3^{d}	To 1212 lb of Rye flour		11.10
	To 1 Buss^{l} of Wheat		7. 0
11	To 1 Bus^{l} of Potatoes		2. 0
21	To 1:3:1 h Rye flour & ye Bar^{l}		1. 1. 0
June 13	To 1 C^{t} Rye flour		10. 0
D^{o} 26	To 1 C^{t} D^{o} D^{o}		10. 0
	To 18½ lb of Wool	@2/	1.17. 0
	To Cash 4/		4. 0
	To half a Side of Sole Leather 5½ lb		9. 2
	To 1 p^{r} of Shoes		10. 0
July 21	To Bus^{l} of Wheat		6. 6
Augt 2^{d}	To 2Bus^{l} of Wheat	@6/6	13. 0
	To 1 p^{r} o Shoes		10. 0
Sep^{t} 5	To 2 Bus^{l} of Wheat	@6/6	13. 0
	To 2 D^{o} D^{o} from P.kill		12. 0
	To 27 lb of Lamb	@4^{d}	9. 0
	To 3 Lambs	@8/	1. 4. 0
	To 2 Sheep	@14/	1. 8. 0
	To 2 Pails of Butter each 2@1		2.12. 0
	To 1 Pail of Butter 25 lb from Philips Store	10^{d}	1. 0.10
	To 1 Piggon of Butter 8 lb	11	7. 4
	To 12 lb of Tobacco	8	8. 0
	To Cash 1/ at the White Plains		1. 0
	To Cash p^{r} Staats De Groit		2.13. 4

Novr 14	To Cash p^r John Levinus or Mr Beekman		10. 0
	To 29¼ lb Butter	1/	1. 9. 3
	To 1 Cheese from Meeds 8¼ lb		6. 0
			£39. 5.11
1775	To Amo^t Bro^t Over		39. 5.11
Novr 14th	To 1 Bus^l of Salt p^r John Levinus		4. 0
	To 1¼ acres of Meadow	7/	10. 6
	To 1 Bus^l of Corn		3. 6
	To ½ D^o D^o	3/6	1. 9
	To 1 Gal^n Vinegar & 1 Bus^l of Corn		4. 6
	To 13½ lb of Veal 3/11 & 36 lb of Beef	3½	14. 5
	To 44 lb of Beef and head and Pluck	3½	14.10
	To the Cart and Team One Day		8. 8
	To 7 Bus^l of Corn	3/6	1. 4. 6
	To 171 lb of Beef and 7 head and Pluck		1.17. 7
	To 1 Bus^l of Wheat 6/ & 1 Hog w^t 128 lb 3½^d		2. 3. 4
	To 1 Bus^l of Wheat and 1 Bar^l of Cider		18. 0
Decr 12	To Cash 2/		2. 0
27	To 1 p^r of Shoes		10. 0
	To a Beef from Zachariah's W^t 382 lb 3		4.15. 6
	To a Cow in 1775		6. 0. 0
	To the pasturage of a Cow		16. 0
	To 1 p^r of Shoes in Aug^t		10. 0
	To an Order Dated March 23 1776 For Six		

Date	Entry	Amount
	pounds 2/DD by Joseph Legget	6. 2. 0
1776 Feb[y] 16th	To Cash Paid you at P. Kill	6. 0. 0
	To Cash P[d] Jonathan Chatterton for you	4. 0. 0
Ar[l] 4	To 2 lb of Butter 1/	2. 0
13	To 1 p[r] of Pumps (best sort)	10. 0
	to ½ C' of Rye flour	5. 3
	To your acct to my Son Philip amounting to	20.17. 0
22[d]	To Cash paid you at P. Kill 80/ of M[r] Blagg present	4. 0. 0
July 2	To Cash 4/	4. 0
24	To D[o] 4/ to go to y[e] Training	4. 0
	To 2 Hogs from Zacharians W[t] 305½ lb	6. 2. 0
	To Sundries delivered by Staats De Groit as to Sdy	~~6. 4. 6~~
1783 May	To Cash paid you 8 Crowns & 1 Dol:	4. 0. 0
	To the Rent of the House and privoledge of Wood 2 Years	12. 0. 0
	To Sundries had out the Mill as p[r] James Spocks acct 1776	1.18. 4
	To Sundries DD delivered you by Staats De Groit as p[r] his acct 1776	6. 4. 6
	To 305½ lb of Pork Zachariah Bloom DD you 1776	6. 2. 0
		£145.19. 5

Justus Wescott Cr 1775

	By Getting of Cogs and Rounds		2.18. 0
	By 123 Days work	@6/	36.18. 0
	By 67 Days work of Abrahams	@3/	10. 1. 6
	By Boarding of Saml Williams 19 Weeks & 2 Days		7.14. 8
	By Boarding of Ian Merritt 16 Weeks & 3 Days		6.12. 0
	By Boarding Luther Kenicut 10 Weeks		4. 0. 0
	By Boarding Saml Haviland 7 Weeks		2.16. 8
	By Boarding himself 19 Weeks & 1 Day		7.13. 4
	By Boarding Abraham Wescott 11 Weeks & 1 Day		4. 9. 4
	By 34 lb of Veal	@/4d	11. 4
	By ½ Busl of Potatoes		1. 6
	By 3½ lb of Loaf Sugar		0. 4. 8
	By his part of the Filling Mill		12.10. 0
			£96. 9.10
1776	By 61 Days work	@6/	18. 9. 0
	By 13 Days work of Abraham Wescott	@3/	1.18. 0
	By Boarding himself 10 Weeks & 1½ Days		4. 2. 0
	By Boarding of Abraham Wescott 2 Weeks & 1 Day		0.17. 4
	By his part of the lump work		8.15. 3

By 4 Gal^{n} of Rum	0.18. 0
By 107 W^{t} of Rye flour	
Saml Williams is D^{r} for	1.10. 8
	£132. 1. 1
By 1 p^{r} of Shoes a mistake	
in Aug^{t}	0.10. 0
By 1 Sheep from Zachariah	
Blooms DD to	0.14. 0
By 1 Lamb	0. 8. 0
By 18 lb of Butter	0.18. 0
By 6 lb of Tobacco 8^{d}	0. 4. 0
	£134.15.10

285

Abraham P. Lott[1] to Pierre. AD
SHR

May 14, 1784.

Govr. Pirre Van Cortland
To Ab^{m} P. Lott D^{r}.

		£	s	d
May 14th				
1784	To 4 pear Shoes at 8/	£1	12	0
	To 6 hactches at 1/	0	6	0
	To 7 Jacketts & briches a 3/3	1	2	9
	To 3 Nap sacks at 9^{d}	0	2	3
	To 6 Pear Jackets & briches •			
	a 3/3	0	19	6
		£4	2	6

Paid Alderman Lott £4.2–6
May 14. In full.

[Endorsed]
Abram P. Lott
Acc^{t} p^{d} Infull

1. Abraham P. Lott, a New York City merchant, was alderman for the North Ward of the city. As of 1790, he was a resident of the North Ward and had a family of four with four slaves. *Polk's Directory* (1786), pp. 37, 185; *Heads of Families 1790*, p. 125; see also Nos. 305 and 306.

286

[Unknown] to Pierre. AD

NYSHA

New York July 15 1784.

Govenner Cortlan An a Count

To Five Hundred and fifty feet of Gice and Board	
Att three hapence Per foot	£3. 9.1
To Teen Boards Att 2 PD	1. 0.0
To Riding two Loads of Boards and Gice	0.10.0
To Fore Days and a half Work att 12 P D	2.14.0
	£7.13.1
the August 10 1784	
To Riding three Loads of Shingels Att	£0.18.0
To Riding two Loads of Boards	0.12.0
To Riding two Loads of Boards and Gice	0.12.0
To Riding two Loads Stores	0.12.0
To Riding one Load Lath and gice	0. 6.0
To Riding one Load Plank	0. 6.0
To Riding two Loads Plank and gice	0.12.0
To Riding 2 Loads Timber	0. 2.6
To 2 Pare hinges Att 4 P	0. 8.0
To Making 2 Gats	1. 4.0
To 1 Day Work att the Sellor	0. 6.0
To 1 Day Work att the Barron	0. 9.0
To hook and hasses for the Doores And Windours	£6. 78.6
	£6.15.6

287

Henry G. Livingston to Philip. ADS
SHR

July 25, 1784.

Sir —

Please pay M^r. Gilbert Van Cortlandt Seventeen pounds Seventeen Shillings for a p^r. Pistols and four years Interest and charge the same to his

To Genl. Philip Cortlandt Y^r. hum Servt.
H. G. Livingston

New York 25th. July 1784

Pistols — £ 14.0.0
4 y^r. Int^t. — 3.17
£17.17.0

[Endorsed] Orders and Recd
of Henry. G. Livingston
for. £17.17 —

288

Pierre's Business Account with "Mrs. Moore." AD
SHR

[1784–October, 1787.]

1784	Mrs Moore D^r			
Augt 29 —				
	To 2 bus^l of wheat and one bus^l of Corn	£1	0	0
	To 2 bus^l of Rye Sep^t 29 and One Crown	0	19	0
	To 2 bus^l of Rye Octo^r 28	0	10	0
	¾ of Mutton W^t 7 lb Novr 17			

at 4^{d}	o	2	8
2½ bus^{l} of bockwheat Decr 1	o	7	6
2 bus^{l} of Rye Decr 16 and one lb. of Candles	o	10	4
1 bus^{l} of Rye April 12 1784	o	4	6
5½ lb of beef at 4^{d}	o	1	10
1 bus^{l} of Corn & 1¼ of Cheese	o	5	o
2 bus^{l} of Corn June 26	o	8	o
5½ lb of Pork & 1¾ lb hog cheek July 5	o	5	5
2 bus^{l} of Rye Aug 1	o	9	o
2 bus^{l} of Rye Aug 24	o	9	o
½ bus^{l} of Wheat & 1 bus^{l} of Rye	o	8	o
1 bus^{l} of Rye & ½ bus^{l} of Corn	o	6	3
2 bus^{l} of Rye Sep^{t} 30	o	9	o
3¾ of Wool	o	11	3
1 bus^{l} of Corn Oct 12	o	4	o
1 bus^{l} of Corn & 1 bus^{l} of Rye Novr 7	o	8	o
4½ lb of Wool & 1 p^{r} of Shoes D^{o}	1	1	6
½ bus^{l} of wheat 2 bus^{l} of Corn & 1 lb Candles	o	12	1
1 bus Corn Decr 25	o	4	o
1 bus Corn Jany 1787	o	4	o
2 bus^{l} of bockwheat Jany 27	o	5	o
1 bus of Corn & 1 bus^{l} of bockwheat Feb:13	o	6	6
1 bus of Rye & ½ bus of wheat Feb 27	o	9	o
2 bus of Rye & ½ bus of bockwheat March 23	o	11	3
1 bus^{l} of Rye April 12	o	5	o

2 bus^{l} of Rye April 21	0	10	0
1 bus of Rye & 1 bus^{l} of Corn May 2	0	9	0
1 bus of Rye May 9 & ½ bus of Corn	0	7	0
1½ bus of Corn & 3¾ lb of Smoak beef	0	8	6
Cash 2/2 bus of Rye & ½ bus of Corn Aug 31	0	14	0
2½ lb of wool Sep^{t} 6	0	7	6
2 bus of Corn Sep^{t} 22 & 2 bus Rye Novr 1	0	16	0
1½ lb of Tallow. Some time ago	0	1	6
	15:	11:	7
half Souls for Henry	0	1	0
1 p^{r} of Shoes Your Daughter Patty	0	8	0
	16	0	7
Mrs Moore D^{r}			
Brought over from otherside	16	0	7
1 bus of Salt	0	4	6
	16	5	1
Deduct on the Grain	1	0	0
	15	5	1
Mrs Moores acc^{t}: the amount	15	16	6½
my acc^{t}	£15	5	1
Due to M^{rs}			

½

15 16 6½

M^{rs}. Moore ...... C^{r}.

by a ballance due to you on Settlement of Aug^{t}: 29–1784	£1	15	6

Sep 29.	by Spinning 1 lb & ½ & half a ¼ of thread @3/6	o	5	8½
Octo. 12	Spinning 1 lb of Wool for Nancys stocking	o	3	o
Novr. 12	D^{o} 1 lb & ½ and half a ¼ @ 2/6	o	4	1
Novr. 17	by ¾ of lb by Ismael @ 2/	o	1	6
Decr 1	by Knitting 2 p^{r} Stock:^{g} for Martin	o	6	o
Decr. 16	by D^{o} 1 p^{r} Mrs Moore brought	o	4	6
	by 1 p^{r} for my self	o	4	6
	by Spinning 8 lb worp wool @ 2	o	16	o
Ap^{ll} 12	by D^{o} 4 lb and ½ and ½ a ¼ of Toe @ 1/6	o	6	11½
	by 4½ lb at 1/6	o	6	9
	by 4½ and ½ a ¼ of Toe @ 1/6	o	6	11
	by 1½ lb of filling @ 1/6	o	2	3
Aug^{t}	by 10 lb of filling @ 1/6 Wool	o	15	o
	by 6½ and ½ a ¼ worp @ 2	o	13	3
Novr 7	by 3 lb Cotton Stocking yarn @ 4/6	o	13	6
Nov 24	by 1 lb of Wool Stocking yarn 3/	o	3	o
	by 2 lb wanting ½ of ¼ @ 2/	o	3	9
	by ½ lb of Cotton Candle Wick 1/6	o	o	9
Decr 15	by nitting 1 p^{r} of Stockins 3/	o	3	o
	by 1¾ lb stocking yarn @ 3	o	5	3
	by 1¾ D^{o} @ 2/6	o	4	4½
	by nitting 1 pr for my self	o	4	6
	by D^{o} 1 pr for Marting	o	3	o
	by 17 lb at 1/6 March 23	1	5	6
	by 10 lb at 1/ Toe	o	10	o

	by 3¼ & ½ a ¼ @ 2/	o	6	9
Ap^ll	by 3¼ @ 1/9	o	5	8
	by 4¼ @ 1/9	o	7	5½
	by 6 lb at 1/9	o	10	6
	8¼ & ½ @ ¼ 1/9	o	14	8
		£12	13	7½

Brought over		£12	13	7½
	Spinning half a lb of CandleWick	o	o	9
	hatcheling 56 lb of flex @ 1^d	o	4	8
	3 lb of yarn @ 2/ Sep^t 1787	o	6	o
	Nitting 2 p^r at 2/6	1	5	o
	D^o of 2 p^r @ 2/	o	4	o
	6 lb & ¾ at 2/	o	12	9
		£14	6	9½
Octo^r 11	6½ filling at 1/6. wooling yard taken out of Lents book	o	9	9
	by nitting 4 p^r Stockings @ 5/ P^r p^r for my self	1	o	o
		£15	16	6½

[Endorsed:] Mrs Moore Acc^t. Settled.

289

Joseph DeGroot[1] to Pierre. ALS
SHR

Loningburgh Decem^b 29th 1784 — .

Sir I Embrace this opportunity to Acquaint you of my ill Success Concerning the Collecting of my money I Exspected to Received A Consederabel Sum of money this fall but I fell far short in my Exspecttation for money I could not git from them as yet thay keep me off From time to time which gives me great Consarn[.]I have sent you A littel money by the Barer of my letter to Ten Dollars which was all I had I must Still Ly at your mercy till I can collect my money which I hope will be in A Short time[.]I must confest you have been Very Favourabel with me for which I Return you my Senseer thanks for it has been out of my Power to make you proper Satisfaction as yet my Business has been Very Slack till Now of Late.

I Remain with due Respect your friend and Very humbel Servant

Joseph Degroot.

[Addressed]
Mr Perie Van Coartlandt
Living at Peeks Kill or at Crotan River
This with Care.

[Endorsed]
Joseph DeGroots
Letter with Ten Dollars on
Acct of his Bond.

---

1. Joseph DeGroot may have been a resident of "Loonenburgh," an early name for Athens, in Greene County. French, pp. 247, 331.

Pierre to Philip. AL
SHR

Fryday Noon Feby. 18 1785.

Dr. Philip

Several People Lately have applyed to me for the Ferry Among the many Mrs. Warran.[1] She will Sute the place better than any one that I Know of She is Cleanly and Industrious. And will not be Troblesome She will have Some fit Person with her to Keep the Ferry. Dont Engage the House or Ferry to any one Untill you See me. this from Your Loving Father, Pierre Van Cortlandt P.S. If you have Not Settled your Acc[t]. with John Merret, I have found a Mistake in my favour

---

1. A ferry across the Croton River had been under a Van Cortlandt leasehold as early as 1746. The ferry provided an important link for those traveling the Albany Post Road. Since its operator lived adjacent to the Manor house, the Van Cortlandts were especially concerned as to the leaseholder's character. While Mrs. Warren remains unidentified, a widow by that name was living in Dutchess County at this time.

291

Pierre to Philip Schuyler. ALS
Cornell University Library

March 8, 1785.

Dear Sir

Mrs. Brewer was with me here yesterday and Desires to Know Wether you Will take her Lease for the farm She holds of you Inpart of the first payment of the farm She is to have of you whereon Doc[r]. Perry now Lives And that you would Send her your answer as Soon as possible. Or wether She Might Sell the Lease So as to have the Money Ready In order to make you the first payment agreable to your Letter, She Says She Can have two hundred pounds for it in Cash Or Can Now Rent it for twenty pounds a year for five years to Come, and if you would bring the deed with you or Send it to Coll Hamilton It wo'd oblidge her much and that She will punctually attend So as to fulfill the agreement.

Am D[r] S[r] with great Respect

Your Kindsman & Verry huml
Sert. Pierre Van Cortlandt

Peeks Kill
March. 8. 1785
Genl. Schuyler

292

Samuel Verplanck to Pierre. ALS
SHR

Marchye 9, 1785.

Dear Sir

Mr. Dykman has just now delivered your Letter, which informs me of the agreement you have in part made with him by the joint concurrence of General Schuyler and Mr. Beekman for the hire of the farm at the point. I take it for granted that Mr. Rooney has informed you of an intention to quit the place and that you are apprised that a Mr. Dusenbury and Isaac Lane have severally applied for it,

You are so well acquainted with the value of the farm that I dare not hazard an Opinion Upon the Terms; farther then I think we cannot with any propriety rent it for longer then five years; at which period the heirs to the estate will be of age. The terms then will be as follows —

Five years at the Yearly Rent of fifty pounds in specie at the rate it now passes paid in half yearly payments, and the Tenant to pay all Taxes. —

Not to plough more then fifty Acres yearly, nor to sow the same land with Winter Grain oftner than Once in three Years — To fence with Old Timber either standing or lying and not to make waste of any young Timber — to suffer no wood to be removed from the premisses — to plant out and surround with a sufficient fence on the second year two hundred Apple Trees and as Many more on the third year for which he is to be allowed at the expiration of the term for every thriving Tree the sum of two shillings; and all such buildings, fences &c &c as he shall find it convenient to erect to revert to the Landlord at the expiration of the Lease.

He is to allow pasture for one horse during the summer season —

Shou'd this Agreement be carried into Effect I must beg you wou'd be so kind to direct a lease to be drawn up Accordingly. With respectfull comp^{l}. from the family to Mrs Cortland and family, I am with regard

Dear Sir. Your Most humble Ser^{t}
Samuel Verplanck

Fishkills March y^{e}. 9. 1785

[Addressed]
The Hon:^{bl} Pierre Van Cortland Esq.
in New York

[Endorsed]
Sam:^{l} Ver Planck
Relative
the Point

293

John and Henry Van Pelt to Pierre. AD
SHR

Newyork March 24th 1785.

Mr Van Cortlandt to John van pelt D^{r} for mason work Done in the year one thousand Seven hundred & Eighty two from September 25th untill December 2th at the rate of one bushel wheat or 7/p^{r} day

John to 37 — ½ Days
Henry to 30 — ½ Days £ 23.16.0

68 at 7/
7
———
476
———
23–16

[Endorsed]
Van Pelts
Receipt
INFULL

294

Gilbert to Pierre. ALS
NYHS

New York April 1st 1785.

Dr Papa,

I received yours by Jno. Livinus — & Mr. Van Wyck will take charge of the Flour and dispose of it to the best advantage as soon as possible[1] —

I have been to all the Iron Mongers I could think of to get your Cart Tire, its the scarcest article in Town (Money excepted) and could not light of as much as you wrote for[2] — I have sent by Capt Hitchcock[3] 8 Barrs. Six of which are bent the other two Streight. Wt 2.0.10 at 38 p. ct. not quite 3 inches wide and something better than half Inch thick, its all I could come across, and have been enquiring these Eight Days —

I am very glad to hear Gramma is better, give my best love to her. I hope this may find her perfectly recovered and All the Family Well —

I am your loving Son

Gilbert VanCortlandt

10 lb. 20d Nails omitted in the within actt 10d½.£0.8.9

[Addressed]
Pierre VanCortlandt Esqr
Peckskill

---

1. A Westchester sloopmaster often employed by the Van Cortlandts, John Levinus was a Cortlandt resident with a family of three in 1790. *Heads of Families 1790,* p. 198.
"Mr. Van Wyck" was most likely Abraham Van Wyck, the husband of Catharine Van Cortlandt, and Gilbert's brother-in-law.

2. Gilbert Van Cortlandt was involved in the ironmonger's trade at this time, with offices located at 42 Dock Street in New York. *Polk's Directory* (1786), p. 24.

3. Possibly Abraham Hitchcock of Mt. Pleasant, New York. *Heads of Families 1790,* p. 201.

295

Samuel Verplanck to Sampson Dyckman. ALS
SHR

June 4, 1785.

Sir.

As the Executors of Mr Verplanck have placed his Son Philip in Town, at a considerable expence, there will be a necessity for your being punctual in the discharge of your rent. I shall therefore expect to hear that it has been paid to the Order of Governor Cortland. — Our chief dependance is upon the rent of the Point; for which reason I hope you will exert yourself to Oblige.

Sir Your Most humble Ser^{t}.
Saml: Verplanck

Fish kills 4 June 1785
Mr Sampson Dyckman

[Addressed]
To
Mr Sampson Dykman
Manor of Cortland

296

Samuel Verplanck to Pierre. ALS
SHR

Fish kills June ye 4th. 1785.

Dear Sir

I have just time to acknowledge your favour of yesterday agreable to which I have entered the agreements made with Ellis and Capt. Lilly.[1] inclosed is a letter for Dykman, who I hope will be able to discharge his rent;[2] as the sum is considerable if he be suffered to run in Arrears there may be some difficulty in obtaining payment.

Such rents as you may receive I Judge it advisable to remit to Mr. Beekman, for the support of Philip,[3] who I am happy to find he has placed with a person of a Good repute in the City. With respects of All the family to Mrs & Miss Cortland. I am With Esteem Dr Sir. Your Most humble Sert.

Saml: Verplanck

[Addressed]
To
The Honbl: Pierre Van Cortland Esqr.
Peekskill

---

1. Joseph Ellis, of Cortlandt, is most likely the individual referred to here. *Heads of Families 1790*, p. 197.

"Capt. Lilly" was possibly James Lilly of Cortlandt. *Ibid.*, pp. 73, 198.

2. Sampson Dyckman had rented Verplanck's Point from Samuel Verplanck prior to 1784. He made extensive alterations to the structures on the Point. Samuel Dyckman to Samuel Verplanck, May 23, 1784, SHR Collections.

3. Philip Verplanck, Jr. (1768–1828) was the son of Philip and Aefje (Beekman) Verplanck. He became a merchant with offices in New York City. In 1796 he married Sally Arden, daughter of Thomas Arden, and by her had five children.

297

Joseph Travis[1] to Pierre. ADS
SHR

June 23, 1785.

half Plate Tax	£1. 8. 8
Poor tax for the year 1783 — Peekskill	0.10. 5
Poor tax & Incidental Charges	3. 8. 1
Harmanus Liers tax 1784	1. 3. 9
Poor tax 1783 Croton	0. 2.10
Poor Tax wood place 1783	1. 6. 3
	7. 0. 0

1785		
	14 bus[l]: Wheat 6/2	£4. 6. 4
June 23		
	Cash in full	2.13. 8
		7. 0. 0

Received of Pierre Van Cortlandt the above Seven pounds In Wheat and money In full.

Jo[s] Travis —

June 23. 1785

[Endorsed]
Receipt for Tax p[d] Joseph Travis Collector June 23–1785

1. Joseph Travis is identified in No. 224.

298

Philip's Business Account with Hercules Mulligan[1]. AD SHR

New York [July, 1785.]

General Philip V. Cortlandt
To Hercules Mulligan Dr.

th 26		
To makeing a Vest & Breeches @ 16/	£ 1.12	
1½ yd Cloth @ 40¼ yd Rattinet 5/	3. 6. 3	
1 yd Cotton 4/6 1yd Linen 3/9	8. 3	
3 doz 2 Buttons 5/ Silk twist thread 10/	1. 5.10	6.12.4
ditt the 26 To makeing a Pr. drawres Compleat 10/6		10. 6
1784 January th6		
To makeing a Regimental Coat 40/	£ 2.	
4½ yds Cassimeer 22/ ⅝ yds Buff. 18/	5.10. 3	
Pocktes & Sleve lineings 6/3 doz 8 Buttons 5/	1. 4. 4	
Silk twist thread Buckram stays &c 10/	.10.	9. 4.7
ditto 28		
makeing a silk Vest 18/	£ .18.	

To a Gold Embroiderd Satten Vest Pattern 80/		4.	
1½ yd Cotton 5/ Buttons Pockte's silk twist &c 5/		.12. 6	
1½ yd serge de roy 14/		1. 1.	6.11.6
March th3			
makeing a Pr. Breeches 16/	£	.16. 0	
2½ yds White sattin 18/		2. 5	
Pocktes Buttons silk twist thread &c 12/		.12.	3.13
ditto 8th			
makeing a Vest 16/	£	.16	
1½ yd Cassimeer 18/ 1yd Cotton 5/		1.12	
½ yd Rattinet 5/ 1 doz 6 Buttons 3/		7	
Pocktes silk twist thread stays &c 5/		5	3
April 14th			
To 2½ yds Florentine 24/	£		3
May 7			
Makeing a Leppeld Coat 34/	£	1.14	
2½ yds blue Cloth 42/		5. 5	
Pocktes & Sleve lineings 6/		6	
2 doz Buttons 10/		1 –	
Silk twist thread Buckram stays &c 10/		10	8.15
June 30th			
makeing 2 Pr. Breeches 14/	£	1. 8	
2 yds linen 2/6		5	
Buttons Pocktes silk twist thread &c 8/		8	2. 1
September 20th			
makeing a Coat	£	1.10	

2yds Green Cloth 40/ 3yds Rattinet' 5/	4.15	
Pocktes & Sleve lineings 6/	6	
1 doz 8 Buttons 2/	3. 4	
Silk twist thread stays Buckram &c 10/	10	7. 4.4
October 29th		
makeing a Vest 12/	12	
Vest Pattirn 20/ Backs 3/6	1. 3. 6	
1¾ yds Flannel 5/	8. 9	
Pocktes Buttons Silk twist thread &c 5/	5	2. 9.3
November 16th		
makeing a Vest 12/	£ 12	
¼ yd Rattinet 5/ 1½ yd Flannel 5/	8. 9	
¼ yd Coating 16/ Pocktes silk twist thread 5/	9	1. 9. 9
December 20th		
makeing a Coat 26/	£ 1. 6	
2¼ yds Cloth 42/ Pocktes & Sleve lineings 6/.	5 6	
1 doz 8 Buttons 18/ Coller 9/	1.19	
Silk twist thread Hooks Eyes stays &c 10/	10	8.15.6
		£63. 6.9
Carried Over		
1785 Amount brought Forward	£63. 6. 9	
January 30th		
makeing a Vest & Breeches @ 12/	£ 1. 4	
1½ yd Satten 30/ 1 yd Rattinet 5/	2.10	
1 yd Linen 3/9 2 yds		

Fustian 4/6	12. 9	
1 doz 6 Buttons ½ doz ditto 9/	19. 6	
½ yd serge de roy 14/	7	
Silk twist thread stays &c 10/	10	6. 3. 3
February 26th		
makeing a Vest & Breeches 12/	£ 1. 4	
2⅝ yds Corderoy 6/6	17 ¾	
¾ yds Rattinet 5/ 1yd Flannel 4/6	8. 3	
¼ yd White Coating 16/ 1 yd linen 3/6	7. 6	
3 doz 10 Buttons 3/	11. 6	
Silk twist thread stays Buckram 10/	10	3.18.3¾
March 6th		
makeing a Great Coat 20/	£ 1	
1 yd Green Beize 6/6 1 yd linen 3/6	10	
1 doz ½ Buttons 8/	12	
Silk twist thread stays &c 6/	6	2. 8
May 10th		
makeing 2 Pr. Breeches 12/	£ 1. 4	
1 piece nankeen 20/ 1 yd ditto 3/6	1. 3. 6	
2 yds linen 3/9	7. 6	
Buttons silk twist thread &c 8/	8	3. 3
ditto 16th		
Ripping & makeing a Coat 28/	£ 1. 8	
Velvet Coller 10/ 1 doz ½		

Buttons 10/	1.5	
Silk twist thread Pocktes & Sleve lineings 14/	14	3. 7
		£82. 6.3¾

[Addressed] General V. Cortlandt

[Endorsed] Hercules Mulligan
Acct. July. 1785
Tailor

---

1. Hercules Mulligan was a merchant and tailor residing at 23 Queen Street in New York in 1786. By 1790 he had removed to 30 Golden Hill. Noah Webster, ed., *The New York Directory for 1786* (New York, 1786), p. 38; Duncan (1790), p. 30. See also No. 326.

299

Gilbert to Pierre. ALS
NYHS

New York Sepr 8. 1785.

Dr Papa

I now send you pr Levinus your Cloth and all the Trimmings except the Silk. 1 P. Superfine Blankets cost 50/. There was a mistake in the price of the Cloth — its charg'd 35/pr yd.

Last Tuesday evening TenBroek was married[1] — nobody present except General TenBroek,[2] his Lady and Daughters. — and Miss VanRenssaler, her Brother Phill[3] — Sister Nancy, & Self. They begin to see company this afternoon. I now am going out. Sister Nancy, and Cousin Betsey VanRenssaler who were the Brides Maids. look'd supirb.

That is vastly better than —. If they should look as much better this afternoon, I know who it will, & likewise know who it will not please. — I have no time to get the patern of her gownd. It was made from home. Bo^{t} of Ten Broeks cost 9/6 p. yard a light pink. This day she will put it on. The first Evening they all appeared in White — Nancy says Mrs Ten Broek insists on her going to Albany. I have not seen her to deliver your message, Nancy will not be neglected. I think she appears as well as the best —

We are all well, my Brother Grooms man Philip Van Renssaler is here at my Elbow and desires me to present his compliments.

In great haste I am your affec^{t} Son

Gilb^{t} V.Cortlandt

Pierre Van Cortlandt Esqr.

---

1. Gilbert and his sister, Ann (Nancy), who served as a bridesmaid, attended the September 6, 1785, marriage of General Abraham Ten Broeck's only son, Dirck (1765–1832), to Cornelia Stuyvesant (1768–1825), the daughter of Petrus and Margaret (Livingston) Stuyvesant. Dirck later served as Speaker of the New York Assembly (1798) and practiced law in New York City. Emma Ten Broeck Runck, comp., *The Ten Broeck Genealogy: Being the Records and Annals of Dirck Wesselse Ten Broeck of Albany and His Descendants* (New York, 1897), p. 98.

2. The brother-in-law of Philip Livingston, Abraham Ten Broeck (1734–1810) served in the colonial legislature, was appointed a brigadier general of New York militia during the Revolution, and later acted as a county judge and mayor of Albany from 1779 to 1783, and again from 1796 to 1799. *DAB,* XVIII, 365.

3. Elizabeth Van Rensselaer would marry John B. Schuyler in 1787. Her brother, Philip S. (1767–1824), married Ann Van Cortlandt, the daughter of Pierre, Sr. See *VCFP,* II, 507; III, *passim.*

300

Indenture between Pierre, Jr. and Commissioners of Forfeiture. DS

SHR

[October 10, 1785.]

This Indenture made the Tenth Day of October in the Tenth Year of the Independence of the State of New York, and in the Year of Our Lord One Thousand Seven Hundred and Eighty Five Between Isaac Stoutenburgh[1] and Philip Van Cortlandt, Esquires, Commissioners of Forfeitures for the Southern District of the said State, appointed in Pursuance of an Act of the Legislature of the said State, entitled, "An Act for the Speedy Sale of the confiscated and forfeited Estates, within this State, and for other Purposes therein mentioned," passed the Twelfth Day of May, One Thousand Seven Hundred and Eighty-four, of the one Part, and Pierre Van Cortlandt Junior of the other Part, WITNESSETH, That the said Isaac Stoutenburgh and Philip Van Cortlandt, Commissioners as aforesaid, by Virtue of the Power and Authority to them in and by the said Act granted[2]; and for and in Consideration of the Sum of Thirteen hundred and ninety six pounds fifteen shillings Lawful Money of the said State to them in Hand paid by the said Pierre Van Cortlandt Junior the Receipt whereof is hereby acknowledged, HAVE Granted, Bargained, Sold, Enfeoffed and Confirmed, and by these Presents Do Grant, Bargain, Sell, Enfeoff and Confirm unto the said Pierre Van Cortlandt Junior and to his Heirs and Assigns, ALL That certain Farm of Land situate lying and being in the Manor of Philipsburgh and County of West Chester Bounded Southerly by Land now or late in the possession of Albert Orser[3] Westerly partly by Hudsons River and partly by the Mouth of Croton River Northerly by

Land late in the possession of John Basley[4] and Easterly partly by Land late in the possession of Elisha Merrit and partly by Land late in the possession of John Storm[5] Containing One hundred and fifty one Acres more or less as the same was formerly possessed by John Bulyea[6] Forfeited to the people of the said State by the Attainder of Frederick Philipse late of the said County Esquire And all and singular the Estate, Right, Title and Interest, whether in Possession, Reversion or Remainder of, in or to the said Premises, which in Consequence of any Conviction or Attainder is become forfeited[7], or attached to, or vested in the People of the said State, TO HAVE and to HOLD all and singular the said Premises hereby Granted, Bargained, Sold, Enfeoffed and Confirmed, with the Appurtenances unto the said Pierre Van Cortlandt Junior and to his Heirs and Assigns, to the only proper Use, Benefit and Behoof of the said Pierre Van Cortlandt Junior and his Heirs and Assigns forever.[8] IN WITNESS WHEREOF, the Parties to these Presents have hereunto interchangeably set their Hands and Seals, the Day and Year first above written.

Sealed and Delivered
in the Presence of us
The Word, Acres in the
thirteenth being first
Wrote upon an Erazure
John Stoutenburgh
Isaac Stoutenburgh
Junr[9]

Be it Remembered,
That on the __________
Day of ________
One Thousand Seven
Hundred and __________
personally came and
appeared before me

____

the above-named
Isaac Stoutenburgh and
Philip Van Cortlandt,
Esquires, and each of
them respectively
acknowledged that he had

executed the above
Indenture, by sealing and
delivering thereof as his
voluntary Act and Deed, for
the Uses and Purposes
therein mentioned; and I
haveing examined the said
Indenture, and found no
material Erazures or
Interlineations therein

Isaac Stoutenburgh
Ph. V.Cortlandt

---

1. Isaac Stoutenburgh served in the Provincial Congress 1776–1777, in the state Senate 1778–1783, and was a member of the Council of Appointment in 1781. Werner, pp. 367, 371, 372, 408.

2. Appointed by an act of the legislature on this date, the commissioners of forfeiture were charged with arranging the sale of Loyalist property confiscated during the Revolution.

3. Albert Orsor was a Mt. Pleasant farmer who purchased 164 acres of the Philipse estate on December 6, 1785. *Heads of Families 1790,* p. 200; Yoshpe, p. 144.

4. There was a John Baseley living in Brooklyn at this time. *Heads of Families 1790,* p. 97.

5. Among the Storm family members residing in Cortlandt were Gerritt, who served as highway master in 1788; David, who was a tenant farmer mentioned in the sale of the Philipse estate in 1785; and John, apparently David's father. Bolton, I, 61; II, 428–429.

6. A tenant farmer on the Manor of Philipsburgh prior to the Revolution, John Bulyea adopted a Loyalist stance during the war and lost his property as a result. After removing to King's

County, New Brunswick, he petitioned for compensation in the loss of his home, cider mill, personal property, notes, and book debts totaling £847.2s currency. As a settlement of this claim he was awarded £110 sterling. Yoshpe, p. 191; Lorenzo Sabine, *Biographical Sketches of Loyalists of the American Revolution* (Boston, 1864), I, 274–275.

7. After breaking parole by refusing to return to his Yonkers home under house arrest in 1779, Colonel Frederick Philipse (1746–1785) was declared an enemy of the state and his properties were confiscated. Frederick, Jr. later claimed that his father's losses totaled £155,328 sterling, and that this figure was a conservative estimate. After considering the compensation question, the Claims Commissioners awarded the younger Philipse £62,075, one of the largest amounts granted to an American Loyalist. Of the estate itself, it was auctioned off in parcels to nearly sixty individuals. Bolton, II, 428–429; Yoshpe, p. 202; Beatrice Reubens, "Pre-emptive Rights in the Disposition of a Confiscated Estate, Philipsburgh Manor, New York," *William and Mary Quarterly,* 3rd Ser., XXII (1965), pp. 435–456.

8. Upon the break-up of the Philipse estate, tenants unable to purchase their farms were subjected to having them sold to the highest bidder. Consequently, Pierre, Jr. purchased a number of these farms, including those of Benjamin and William Underhill. He bought 314 acres on October 10, 1785, in three lots of 150, 151, and 13 acres, and purchased three more lots, of 100, 131, and 7.5 acres, on the following December 22. While he kept some of the property, he sold two of the largest parcels at a profit in August, 1787. Yoshpe, p. 146; Deeds, Westchester County, Lib. L, p. 426.

9. Both John Stoutenburgh and Isaac Stoutenburgh, Jr. lived with their father in New York City's West Ward as of 1790. *Heads of Families 1790,* p. 134.

301

Samuel Verplanck to Pierre. ALS
SHR

Fishkills the 3^d. May 1786.

Dear Sir

Walter Dobbs informs me that he has understood M^r. Lane was about to leave the farm he had hired, and express'd a strong desire that he may be permitted to return to his former possession — If it be any ways practicable to comply with his wishes, we will hope that he may be reinstated & permitted to enjoy the farm he has improv'd upon reasonable terms. With respects of the family to Mrs Cortland & Miss Ann I am Dear Sir:

Your most h^b. $Serv^t$.
Saml: Verplanck

Pierre to Samuel Verplanck. ALS [attached to above letter]
SHR

Dr Sir

Just after That I Returned from New York Ap^{ll}: 13. Stephen Horton Came to me and acquainted me that $Abra^m$: Lane had Left the farm that he had hired the Last Year. And that he Stephen Horton had agreed with $Abra^m$: Lane to pay the Last years Rent. being £ 10 — And that he would take the farm on the same Conditions that $Abra^m$: Lane had it Provided the family Consented. I told him I made No doubt but that he Could have it as he was one of the Tennants that Dully paid his Rent and that I would acquaint you & the $Couz^{ns}$ with it, whenever he would Let me Know when he went up to pay his Rent.

Since which I have Rec^d: your favor of the 3^d Instant Relative to Walter Dobbs. I have therefore advised Stephen

Horton to go up to you and Inform you & the Couz^{n}: what has been done So that he may Know what he may depend on. his son Is in Possession of the farm & has made Considerable Improvement thereon. Our Respects attend you & the Couz^{s}: I am Dr Sr Your

Verry hum^{l}: Sert.
P.V.C.

D^{r}

[Addresed]
Honble: Pierre Van Cortland Esqr
Peeks kill

302

Talmadge Hall to Philip. ADS
SHR

[1786.]

M^{r}. Talmadge Hall To Ph.V.Cortlandt. D^{r}.	
1785 — To Stabling 4. Horses 6.Nights —	£ 1. 4.–
Novr. To Drawing a Load of Hay —	12.–
Decr 31 To 11. Bus^{h}. Corn up to this month	2. 4.–
To ferrage of 29. Passengers before Cutter came	9.8
1786	
Jany. To. 1900 W^{t}. of Hay & Riding [word lost]	3.17.–
Feby. To. 1 Stack of Hay and Drawing	4. –.–
To 7. Bus^{h}. Corn up to the End of Feb^{y}	1. 8.–
March.10 112.lb Hay	3.6
To Horse Hire with the Male	4–
To 21½ Bus^{h}. Corn to last of april	4. 6.–
To Grinding Corn	–2–

1786

	18.10.2
To Cash paid Cutter	24.17.6
Ap^{l}. 26	
To d^{o}. p^{d}. Mason	4.12.2
To d^{o}. Masons Ac^{t}.	1.17.6
To Salt Hay	4–
To 1 Bus^{h}. Corn omitted	
To 1 Horse in the Stage Two Days	8.–
	£50. 9.4

[Endorsed] Talmadge Hall
Acc^{t}. 1786.

Received of M^{r}. Talmadge Hall by the hands of Philip Van Cortlandt the Sum of Twenty Four Pounds Seventeen Shillings and Eight pence it being Infull for Sundry Accounts of Ferrage Horse and boarding the Stage Driver up to the first of may last and in full of all Acc^{ts}. to this Day — Rec^{d}. by me

Ebenezer Cutter

[Endorsed] Eb. Cutters. Acc^{t}.
and Receipt to
Talmadge Hall
1786

1786

first acc^{t} in march	£17. –.–
ap^{l}.25.–	7. 4.2
cash	13.6
	£24.17.8

303

Talmadge Hall to Philip. ADS
SHR

[1786.]

1785 General Cortlandt in $^{a}/_{c}$ with Talmage Hall -- D^{r}	
Novr 8th To a seat 31 Miles 13sh Dinner & Club 10sh	£ 1.13. 0
To Cash paid Farrier 11/6 in Keeping horse 10 days. 20sh	1.11. 6
To Dinner & Club for two	16. 4
1786	
Ap^{ll} To a seat 2 breakfeast	15. 4
14 To a seat & Club	10. 8
To a seat 19 Miles	4. 9
27 To a seat 2 Breakfeast	12. 0
June 6 To a Seat 19 Miles Tea Supper Lodging & Club	13. 3
To a seat 9 Miles breakfeast & 3 Ladies at Tea	10. 3
12 To 2 seats and Breakfeasts	1. 3. 6
17 To 3 seats 39 Miles 4 d^{o} 40 Miles 2 1 at Tea	3.10. 9
26 To a seat & Breakfeast fr Mr Bateman	9. 6
29 To a Seat & Punch	10. 9
July To 2 Seats fr M^{rs}. Cortland 8 Miles ea is 16 Miles	4. 0
18 To a seat & Club	11. 6
To seat & Punch f^{r} Your Brother	10. 6
To 1 Horse Price Agreed	£44. 0. 0
	£57.12. 7
April 21 To a seat & breakfeast Omitted	15. 4
Errors Excepted	
	£58. 7.11
Augt 14 To a seat 30 Miles & breakfeast	9. 6
	£58.17. 5

304

Pierre's Business Account with John Dusenbury. ADS SHR

[1786–1787.]

1786	John Dusenbury D^{r}			
	To one bus^{l} of Wheat July 4	£ 0	8	0
	To two bus^{l} of Corn of Isaac Odell	0	8	0
	To one bus^{l} of Rye by Mrs Van Cortlandts Order	0	5	0
	To two bus^{l} of Rye Augst 25	0	10	0
	To one & a half bus^{l}. of Rye Sept 11	0	7	6
	To one bus^{l} of Wheat & 1 bus^{l} of Rye Sept. 12	0	13	0
	To two bus^{l} of Rye Octo^{r} 14	0	10	0
	To two bus^{l} of Corn Novr 20	0	8	0
	To two bus^{l} of Buckwheat Novr 24	0	5	0
	To one and a half bus^{l} of Corn Decr 8	0	6	0
	To one and a half bus^{l} Rye Decr 16	0	7	6
	To two bus^{l} of Corn & 2 bus^{l} of buckwheat Decr 29		13	0
	To one bus of Rye and one & a half Bus Corn Jan 16	0	11	0
	To two bus^{l} of Rye and two bus of buckwheat Feb 26	0	15	0
	To Six & Sixpence in Grain			

	March 4	0	6	6
	To one bus of Rye and one bus of Corn March 7	0	9	0
	To half a bus[l] of wheat & half a bus of Rye & 1 bus Corn March 19	0	10	6
	To two bus of Rye and 1 bus of Corn Aprill 8	0	14	0
	To Six & a half pound of Beef May 3	0	2	8½
	To 1 bus[l] of Rye and 14½ lb of Veal May 22	0	9	10
	To 1 bus of Wheat June 8	0	8	0
	To one & an half bus[l] of Rye July 2	0	7	6
	To one bus[l] of Rye July 17	0	5	0
	To one bus[l] of Corn July 24	0	4	0
		10	1	1½
	To Cash due M[r] Beekman	1	10	0
		£11	11	0½
Sep[t] 8	1 bus[l] of Rye DD John Week	0	5	5
		11	16	0½

John Dusenbury C[r]			
by 2 Tables DD	4	0	0
Due to him on the Saw 8/	0	8	0
Setting my Saw & making a buck	0	4	0
one days work 7/Dec[r] 1787 in the Mill	0	7	0
Mending my Slay & Stuff 10/	0	10	0
by a press 3 DD	3	0	0
3 days work at 8/	1	4	0
4 days work at 8/	1	12	0

1½ days work at 8/	0	12	0
	£11	17	0

John Dusenbury Dr

Brought from the other Side		£11	16	0½
1787 Sept 7	To 4½ busl Rye & half a busl Wheat	0	10	0
	To a Cow & Calf at 6.0.0	6	0	0
	To Cash at Ten Shillings bill	0	10	0
		£18	16	0½

John Dusenbury Credit

From the other side	£11	17	0
By an order from my son Philip for 5.0.0	5	0	0
	£16	17	0

[Endorsed]
1786
John Dusenbury
Carpenter
Acct Dr £11.11.0½
6
Cr £11.17.0

NB What money did I pay him, it was a Ten Shilling Bill & Grain out of the Mill by Philips order. how much.

Also a Cow & Calf £6.0.0

305

Abraham P. Lott[1] to Philip. ALS
NYPL

New York October 26th 1787.

Sir

By Mr. P. Livingston,[2] who I requested to wait on you in my behalf, as I could draw no answer from you either Verbally or in writing, I am given to understand that you say

First, that you cannot think of Allowing me Interest on your Debt during the War.

Secondly, that some of the goods charged to you ought to be charged to James Abell

Thirdly, that you have overpaid, and owe me nothing — And

Fourthly, that you neither called upon me, or answered my Letters, for fear of hurting my Sensibility — This I think is the substance of his Report; and to which I briefly answer —[3]

First, you must surely remember that all goods you bought of me were at the ready money price, and that Interest was to be charged thereupon from the date of the Bill of Parcels 'till paid? — You must likewise remember that I pressed you hard for payment before the War, and that you did not pay me? — If then you did not pay me according to Contract before the war, it was your fault and not mine — And therefore you ought to Allow Interest during the War, as you had all that time the use of my Money; and the more so as I have been obliged to allow and pay such Interest.

Secondly I know nothing of your Second Objection — The goods in my Books are charged to you. — The Invoice was made out in your name — you own the Receipt of the goods — and therefore you are liable to pay. —

Thirdly, the account I have rendered you will prove, that so far from overpaying me, there was due to me on the 1st October 1786 the sum of £59.1–

Fourthly, as to hurting my sensibility, you could not have done it in a more effectual manner, than you have done by the silent contempt with which you have treated Several of my late letters to you

I have only to add that I have requested Mr P. Livingston to deliver this, and that I hope and expect you will not leave this City before you liquidate your Account with

Sir

Your very humble serv^{t}
Abr^{m}. Lott

Genl. Ph.V.Cortlandt

[Addressed]
Genl. Philip V. Cortlandt
Present

---

1. Abraham P. Lott is identified in No. 285.

2. There were a number of Livingstons at the time bearing this initial: Philip and Philip P. of New York City; Philip of Greenburgh; and the most likely candidate, Philip J. Livingston of Westchester Town in 1790. *Heads of Familes 1790,* pp. 126, 133.

3. Prior to the Revolution, Philip operated a general store on the Manor. This longstanding unsettled account dates from that time. See Philip's *Memoir* in *VCFP,* I, 33, and the following letter.

306

Philip to Abraham P. Lott. DFS
NYPL

Croton Novr 6 1787.

Sir,

Permit me to lay before you the Amount of Cash paid Since the late war as Appears by your Receipts and Orders[.] the first Sum was Thirty Pounds paid the 20th Novr 1784. Twenty five Pounds to Robt. Manly[1] the 10th June 1785. Fifteen Pounds the 21st of June 1786. and Three Pounds four Shillings the 6th Decr. 1786 paid to Jacob Trimper[2] Making in all Seventy Three Pounds four Shillings —

It also appears by Your Account Current rendered me the 15th August 1775. that the Ballance in Your Favour was One Hundred and Twenty Two pounds Thirteen Shillings at which time I paid you as p^{r}. Your Receipt On the Back of Said Acc^{t}. & Seventy Pounds in part payment so that the ballance remaining was Fifty Two Pounds Thirteen Shillings and you will find by substracting the Said ballance from the Sum paid Since the war that there is Twenty Pounds Eleven Shillings Over paid which Sum I had Conceived to be Sufficient for Interest, I therefore beg you will please to reconsider the acc^{t}. and I make not the least doubt but you will be of my Opinion

I am Sir, Your Hum^{l} Ser^{t}

A Lott Esqr Ph.V. Cortlandt

[Endorsed]
Copy to A^{m}. Lott Nov^{r}.6.1787

---

1. A coachmaker with his shop located on Broadway in New York City, Robert Manley lived in the West Ward with his thirteen-member family and three slaves. *Polk's Directory* (1786), p. 38; *Heads of Families 1790*, p. 134.

2. Jacob Trimper was a Dutchess County resident who served as a lieutenant of militia in the 6th New York regiment during the Revolution. Roberts, I, 144.

307

John Cumbo[1] to Pierre. ADS
SHR

Manor of Cortlandt Jan^{y}: 2–1788.

I John Cumbo. of Peeks Kill Laborer Do hereby promise to pay Unto Pierre Van Cortlandt Esqr: or Order on demand Three pounds two shill–and Six pence It being for Value Received
Witness by me.
P.J. Van Rensselaer[2]

his
John X Cumbo
mark

C^{r}: John Cumbo

by 4 days diggin Ended June ye 9–1788[3]

[Endorsed]
John Cumbo
note for
£3–2–
1788
Peekskill
Laborer

1. A Peekskill resident, John Cumbo was an employee of the Van Cortlandt family.

2. Philip S. Van Rensselaer, identified in *VCFP*, II, 23, was Pierre's son-in-law.

3. Cumbo was remunerated at the rate of 15 shillings, 7½ pence per day for his labor.

308

Stephen DeLancey[1] to Pierre, Jr. ALS
SHR

Fredericksburgh precinct January ye 14th 1788.

2 years Rent	£4 . . 14
paid 9 Bushils of Rye	£1 . . 16
Rent Due	£2 . . 18

January 5 1788

Dear Cousen

I am able at last, blessed be God: once more to hold A pen: Baker was with me to Day & will Deliver you this, he Says to morrow: he has been twice to see you to settle about Browns Note: he came to me some time ago, & wanted me to Settle with him but I Refer'd him to you: however. as he Cou'd not see you, I Sent for him; to Come to me; & told him: I would take ye Money for the Note, & the Interest; if he wou'd give me A bond of twenty pound to pay you your Demands; but he Refused: so I send him once more to you; & since he is so much afraid he will be hurt; Do you Deal with him accordingly: I wrote you in my letters I sent you: before I hurt my Arm: that I had of Jacob Brown;[2] by Abraham Knox;[3] Six Bushels of Rye: for which I was to give him what the price was In January: it was then 3/10: but I am willing to allow him 4/ p^r Bushel: I had also 9 Bushels, I gave Timothy Ryan[4] an Order for on the same Condition: which makes in all £1.16^s: his Jacob Brown's Rent is £2 . . 7^s p^r year; so there was due to me the 5th day of January 1787 besides the Rye 11s/ which added as above makes £2 . . 18s Due for Rent; I think the Note was £18 . . 18 at 7 pr Cent for two years, makes in all £23:12:5: taking in 9 for the Interest of the [torn] Due on January first 1787: & since he is so very much afraid of me; that I will wrong him: Dont let him wrong me: I tell him he must give you £5 for me: for taking him: in Browns Room: & that if he dont settle with you: you will put him: to more than that in Costs: I wou'd rather deal with five other men: than one Quaker: they are so Obstinate:[5] I wish to hear from you what you have done in Regard of Jonathan Bayles affair[6]; is he taken, or not. my arm is still very lame, I am forced to write on a book, and often to lay down my pen: I wish to let me know what you have done about that lease, I put into your hands: Gilbert Bayley[7] has a Lease; of One hundred & Thirty Acres of it: Abel Nicols[8] has possession of 70 Acres; the Rest is in the possession of Peter Ferris: hired out at present to Stephen Williams: Gilbert Bailys Rent is £4 and & I want to know what you have done about the place leased to Ebenezer Purdy: sold first without my consent to Jeremiah Warren;[9] by him, without leave, to Ichabod Williams by Williams to Crossman[10]. I wish much to see you: I must try to get up to poughkeepsie this week if possible: as I want to see your father: if I Return, hope you will come & see me after Court: I shall send you a small note: I got a man to write for me to you by Baker[11] when he went before: I am afraid you cou'd not read it, I write badly, but I hope you can find it out. the farm Crossman is in possession of has been set on fire: & above a hundred pound Damage done to the timber, besides 20 families get their wood from off it: I shall go to your father & try to get something Done: perhaps I may meet you at poughkeepsie: if I cant return here: I shall stay near Mr Carmans[12] in Beekman's precinct; where I hope to see you; I inclose you A bond against Ebenezer Purdy: I wish you to get John Strang[13] to take it: & give me Credit on my Note: & let him Send me word by you how much more I am in his Debt which I wish get out of: if

John Strang wont take it: take out a writt for Purdy & collect the money for me: Do pray Inclose me the Money, Baker pays you: as I want it to Send to New York: I would come and see you, but I fear at present to do it, of which I will let you know when I see you: do write very particularly, make Baker Settle all off: I believe he is honest: but an Obstinate fool: my Arm akes: I must finish yours

Affectionately
Stephen Delancey

take up the little Note Strang
has & endorse the Rest on the
Large Note —

Brown's Note	£18 . . 18^{s} . . 0^{d}
Interest for One Year	£ 0 . . 6 . . 10
Ditto	0 . . 6 . . 10
Rent due	£ 2 . . 10 . . 0
Interest on 11/ one year	9
Due to me	£24 . . 10 . . 5

[Addressed]
Pierre Van Cortlandt Junr. Esquire
Attorney at Law
Croton River

---

1. Stephen DeLancey is identified in No. 202.

2. Jacob Brown was a resident of Bedford with a five-member family in 1790. *Heads of Families 1790,* p. 196.

3. For Abraham Knox, see No. 216.

4. Little is known of Timothy Ryan beyond his service in the 4th Regiment of Westchester militia during the Revolution. Roberts, p. 216.

5. A large portion of Crum Elbow Precinct was settled by Quakers at an early date. Many of the families came from New England and Long Island, and there were sufficient numbers of them to warrant the construction of a meeting house by 1774. Among the representative families of this persuasion were the Marshalls, Bakers, Briggs, Hoags, Halsteads, Moshers, Nelsons, Stringhams, Walters, Lamborees, and Williams. *Historical and Genealogical Record, Dutchess and Putnam Counties New York* (Poughkeepsie, 1912), p. 34.

6. Jonathan Bayles is identified in No. 216.

7. Gilbert Bayley (Bailey) of North Salem served as a town fence-viewer in 1790. Bolton, II, 475.

8. Abel Nichols was a resident of Rensselaer County as of 1800.

9. Ebenezer Purdy is identified in *VCFP,* II, 546, 582. Jeremiah Warren and his son, Jeremiah, Jr., were both heads of households in North Salem at this time. *Heads of Families 1790,* p. 203.

10. Both Ichabad Williams and John Crossman were residents of North Salem. In 1790, Williams had a family of four, while Crossman had a seven-member family. *Ibid.,* p. 203.

11. Possibily a reference to Stephen Baker of North Salem. He acted as a trustee for the town's poor and served as a fence-viewer in 1790. Bolton, II, 474–475.

12. John Carman was a resident of Beekman Precinct and the father-in-law of John H. Sleght, the New York City merchant. *VCFP,* II, 412–413.

13. John Strang (1744–1809) of Yorktown married Drusilla Oakley (1751–1794) and by her had nine children. Yet another contemporary John Strang lived in Bedford at this time, with a five-member family. Roebling, pp. 236–237; *Heads of Families 1790,* pp. 178, 209.

309

Pierre to Philip. ALS
SHR

Sepr. 9–1789.

Dr Son Philip.

Solomon Palmer[1] Was With me and Said You wanted to Know my acct with him It Stands thus Viz.

Solomon Palmer -- Dr

1786

Augst: To Cash 2sh. An Order for		£0. 2.0
1 busl. of Rye & ½ busl of wheat		0. 8.0
Aug 22 ½ busl of wheat & 1 busl of Rye		0. 8.0
To a Milks Cow £5.10.0 if he had taken the fenikan Cow. it was £5. only he took the other		5.10.0

1789

Apll. 2	To 2 busl of Rye @ 4/6	0. 9.0
do 20	To 1 busl of Rye @ 4/6	0. 4.6
do 30	To ½ bus of Rye	0. 2.6
	To 2 busl of wheat John Miller, June	0.16.0
May 1	To ½ pd of Rye flour 1789	0. 8.0
	To 1 busl of Rye March 6. 1787	0. 4.6
	To 2 busl of My Wheat May 7. 1787	0.13.0
		9. 5.6

Cr

by Making 4. Waggon Wheels	£ 5. 4.0
by Making a Low Wheel Cart	4.10.0
by 5½ days Work @ 5sh —	1. 7.6
	11. 1.6

Yours &cr Pierre Van Cortlandt

[Endorsed] Pierre V. Cortlandt Esqr. and Solomon Palmer acc^t.

---

1. Solomon Palmer was a resident of North Salem and the head of a four-member household in 1790. He may have been the son of Samuel Palmer of Mangopson Neck. Bolton, II, 68; *Heads of Families 1790,* p. 203.

310

Pierre, Jr. to Philip Schuyler.[1] ALS
NYPL

Jan^r. 3, 1791.

Sir

Israel Underhill[2] a tenant of yours in the manor of Cortlandt wishes to purchase the soil of the farm which he has in possession and requested me to write to you to know how much you would ask and what terms of payment you would allow.

I am sir with Esteem your
most Ob^t servant
P.V^n. Cortlandt Junr
Cortlandt Jan^r. 3. 1791 —
The Honble. Philip Schuyler Esqr.

---

1. Philip Schuyler is identified in *VCFP,* II, 25–26.

2. The son of Nathaniel and Mary (Hunt) Underhill, Israel Underhill (1732–1806) married Abigail Lispenard (1738–1806), daughter of Anthony and Maria (Milbourne) Lispenard. In 1790 they were residents of Westchester Town and communicants of St. Peter's Church, where Israel served as warden. The couple bore eight children and owned six slaves as of 1790. Four years later, Israel unsuccessfully challenged

Pierre, Jr. for the Assembly. *VCFP,* II, 546–547; *Heads of Families 1790,* p. 206. See also Josephine C. Frost, ed., *Underhill Genealogy: Descendants of Captain John Underhill* (Brooklyn, N.Y., 1932), II, 119–120.

311

Henry Adams[1] to Pierre. ADS
SHR

Town of Cortlandt April 27, 1791.

Then Received of Pierre Van Cortlandt Esqr. Eight Spanaish dollars on Doctor Henry Adams Account and by his order
John Mandiville[2]

£3.4–

[Endorsed]
Docter Adams for enoculating Stephen D Beekman[3] 1791 paid £3.4.

[2nd endorsement]
John Mandivile Receipt for Doctor Adams for Enoculating

---

1. Dr. Henry Adams is identified in No. 203.

2. John Mandiville (Manavile) is previously noted in *VCFP,* II, 32.

3. The son of Gerard G., Jr. and Cornelia (Van Cortlandt) Beekman, Stephen D. Beekman was eleven years old at the time of this letter. He was later to become a physician and is further identified in *VCFP,* III, 92.

312

Pierre to John Levinus.[1] ALS
SHR

June 21, 1791.

Mr John Levinus

I Send Inclosed a Three pound bill, you will be so good and bring me a cag with good West India Rum
One cag of Milk buisket for M^{rs}. Cortlandt
two doz^{n}. of Large Mohair buttons
one doz of Vest buttons and
three yards of bottle green Shallon
two skains of twist. and
one skains of Silk all the articles
above of bottle green Colour,
bring the account with you
Am Yours to Serve
Pierre Van Cortlandt

Town of Cortlandt
June 21–1791

[Addressed] $Capt^{n}$ John Levinus
Onboard of the Scooner at Peeks Kill

[Endorsed] Paid John Livinuss acc^{t} of Infull frait Etc & ^{cr}. frait of 2500 shingles 20/

	John Levinus	C^{r}
	by frait of 32 board 3^{d}	£0. 8.0
	flour Cloth & box	0. 1.6
	Servants passage	0. 6.0
	To Mrs Cortlandts passage	0. 3.0
	To 1 Waggon	0.10.0
Dec^{r}	To 30 boards frait	0. 7.6
1785		
ap^{ll}	10 bb^{s} of flour fraits	0.15.0
	1 Table	0. 1.6

June	1 Cag of Wine & hog[u] of salt ------------	o. 6.6
Octo[r]	1 p[r] of mill stones ---------------------------	1.12.0
	To frait of 1½ Cords of Wood -----------	1. 1.0
		5.12.0

1½ D[r] Cords Wood £3.12.0
To pasturage of a Cow.

---

1. John Levinus is identified in No. 294.

313

Timothy Benedict to Philip. ALS
NYPL

March 21, 1792.

Sir

I Rec[d] by the post last week six pounds two Shillings from you, he Told me that you Expected me in Town. I should have been in Town before this Time but the Travling is such that it has been the means of my Not Coming. If you Can Conveniently I wish you would send the Ballance on the Right of Deans as I have Engaged some money on the account of Expecting to have Rec[d]. it from You. as for the other two Rights you can determin wheather you will have them or not in case you do not mean to have them you will pleas to send them by the post other ways you can send the Blanks to Have Executed by me and my wife to you which shall be done by Next week post the Conveyanns from the soldiers I have sent to the war official for the warrants for the other Hundred acres but as soon as I Reade them you shall have them immediately[1] —

I am Sir your Humble
Serv[t]. Timothy Benedict

21st of March 1792
P. Van Cortlandt Esqr.

[Endorsed]
Timothy Benedict acknowledging the Rec^{t}. of
£6.2–0 — 1792

---

1. It appears that Philip was already deeply involved in the mania of land speculation that swept through New York in the early 1790's. While all New York Revolutionary War veterans were entitled to land as a bonus for enlistment, most opted to liquidate their holdings for cash. Throughout 1792–1794, Philip made a concerted effort to buy as many of these parcels as possible, with the intent of owning much of the "lands between the military townships and the ten townships ceded to Massacheusetts," which accounted for thousands of acres largely situated in Onondaga County, New York. New York, *Calendar of Land Papers,* pp. 907, 938, 949, 959. For further details on military bounties, see *VCFP,* II, 260, 380–381, 493, 501.

314

Pierre to Silvanus Tomkins.[1] ADS
SHR

[April 30, 1792.]

This day the 30th of April 1792 I Pierre Van Cortland have Let Silvenas Tomkins have a Large P^{r}. of Oxen to Keep for me untill the first day of August next and work them to git out Saw Loggs. to be Sawed In Ship planck and when the plank is Sawed he is to Let me have them if he does not git out the Loggs. by the Time above & the Plank Sawed if there is water to Saw, That Then he the said Tomkings is to DD me the Oxen again and to pay me the damage for Working of S^{d} Oxen. The price of the oxen is Twenty pounds to be paid by the first of Augst. next In planck or money In Testimony whereof we Both parties have hereunto Set our hands & Seal

the day above written
Sealed & Dilivered
In the Presents of
William Turner
Sam[l]. Jones

Pierre Van Cortlandt
Silvanes Tomkins

[Endorsed]
Silvanus Tompkins
Note of hand
For a p[r] of Oxen
£20 in shipplank
to be paid by 1st of August
1792

---

1. Silvanus Tompkins and his eleven-member family were residents of Cortlandt in 1800. During the War of 1812, Tompkins served on the local committee to construct fascines for the defense of New York. "Federal Census, 1800," *New York Genealogical and Biographical Record,* LVIII (1927), 137; *VCFP,* III, 718.

315

Philip: Rates on Croton River Ferry. ADS
SHR

May 1, 1792.

Rate of Ferrage,[1] from the first day of May to the first day of November for a man and Horse — 4[d]: a One Horse Sulkey or Chair. 1/.
a Waggon With 2 Horses and Load — 2/–
a Cart and Oxen ~~with or Without Horses~~ 2/
a Pheaton and pair ---------------------------- 2/
all four wheal Carriages with 2. Horses. 2/
if four Horses the Carriage 3/
foot Passingers — 2[d] —

Chariots. or Coaches —

from the first of November to the first of May the ferrage of a man and horse to be. 6^{d}: but no alteration as to any other Unless to Carry a foot Passenger to the foot of the hill which is at all times to be four Pence — given under my Hand May. 1. 1792

Ph. V. Cortlandt

[Endorsed] Rate of Ferrage
1792–

---

1. The ferry across the Croton River was operated by a tenant farmer who rented the adjacent farm, ferry house and the ferry rights from the Van Cortlandts. What is of special interest is the fact that Philip established the rates and did not leave it to the ferrymaster to do so. See references to the Croton River ferry in *VCFP*, III, 31–32, 37–38, 44–45, 57.

316

Pierre to Gould John Selleck.[1] ADS
SHR

May 14. 1792.

This day I Pierre Van Cortlandt Sold a Red Cow. Called Cherry Unto Gold John Sillick for Seven hundred feet of White Oak Plank one half to be two Intch and the other half to be Intch an half, making in the whole Seven hundred feet as above to be Delivered as soon as Convenient at John Levinus's Landing. and Should the Cow do other wise then well in Calving it is at my Risqe and will allow the Dammages the above is agreed'd on by Both Parties, as witness Owr hands date above

Pierre Van Cortlandt
Gould John Selleck

[Endorsed]
Gold John Sillicks Note Settled & P^{d}.

To Diliver 700 feet of Plank for a Cow Sold him & DD^{r}.
May 14. 1792

---

1. Gould John Selleck (1760–1812) and his wife Elizabeth (1755–1847) were residents of Peekskill Hollow, located just south of Adam's Corner. As members of the Reverend Silas Constant's Presbyterian Church, their home served as a preaching station on numerous occasions. Roebling, p. 334.

317

[On reverse of previous letter]
Pierre to Andrew Barton.[1] ADS
SHR

Cortlandt Town May ye 30th 1792.

This day I Pierre Van Cortlandt Let Andrew Barton Son of Andrew B have a milks Cow Called blossem for Six hundred and fifty foot of Inch & half White oak plank to be good & merchantable the plank are to be delivered at John Levines's Landing by the Last of August next and if Not Delivered then to pay the dammages — In Witness. whereof I the Said Andrew Barton have hereunto Set my hand & Seal date above —

Sealed & dilivered
In the Presents of
Jarvis Dusenbery
W^{m}. Dusenbery[2]

Andrew Barton

June 14, 1792 then
Let Andrew Barton have fourty One Shillins for Plank he is to Diliver me at John Levinus's Landing
P.V.C.

[Endorsed]
Silvanus Tomkins[3]

Note of hand For a Pr of Oxen
£ 20 in shipplank
to be paid by 1st of August 1792

---

1. Andrew Barton was a Westchester County resident who served as an ensign of militia as of 1793. *Council of Appointment, Military,* I, 241.

2. The son of Henry Dusenbury, William Dusenbury was a resident of Rye, New York, at this time. Theresa H. Bristol, "Descendants of Henry Fowler of Roxbury, Mass., Providence, R.I., Eastchester and Mamaroneck, N.Y.," *New York Genealogical and Biographical Record,* LIX (1928), 330, 331.

3. Silvanus Tompkins is identified in No. 314.

318

Pierre's Business Account with Joseph Conklin.[1] ADS
SHR

[1792.]

1787	Joseph Conklyn Dr			
June 1	To 2 busl of Rye at 4/	£ 0	8	0
Augt 14	To 1 busl of Rye	0	4	0
1788				
Apll. 21	To 2 busl of My Rye	0	8	0
May 9	Cash 5/ to pay your fine	0	5	0
May 31	1 busl of Crib Corn 4/	0	4	0
June 18	1 Sythe 8/	0	8	0
Augt 6	1½ busl of Rye at 4/	0	6	0
Novr 18	1 busl of Mill Rye at 4/	0	4	0
1789 Apll 13	1 busl of Rye dd 4/	0	4	0
Augt 8	Cash 12/ worth from Mr. Birdsall[2]	0	12	0

Sept 12	1 lb & 2 Oz of Steal	0	1	3
1790 March 6	1 Ct of Rye flour at 12/	0	14	0
July 9	a Cow at £5. Three pounds to be pd Infull	5	0	0
Do	¼ of a Ct of Rye flour	0	3	6
Augt 3	1 bus of Crib Corn & 20 lb of Rye flour	0	7	6
Do 18	28 lb of Cornel 4/	0	4	0
Do 26	1 busl of Corn of mrs Cortlandt	0	4	0
Sept 2	28 lb of Rye flour 4/	0	4	0
Decr 28	1 busl of Wheat	0	8	0
1791 Augt 24	½ Ct of Rye flour 7/6	0	7	0
1792	5½ lb of Side pork at 3/	0	3	0
May 4 Do 25	½ Ct of Rye flour at 6/	0	6	0
	1.6 lb of Side pork at 8/	0	10	8
	15/ to pay Isaac Kronk[2]	0	15	0
	My part of the Loggs Sold Birdsall	0	10	0
		£13	1	7

Joseph Conklyn Cr.

by 25½ days work Gittin hay at 5/	£ 3	17	6
Team & Cradling	0	18	0
2½ days work along the Road	0	7	6
23 days other work at 3/	3	9	0
6½ days work Different work	0	19	6
On the Mowing work 20/ due	1	0	0
Drawing out the Rails	1	8	0
Gitting 50 post Gilbert howled [hauled]	0	3	0
	£12	2	6
2 days work for the Sythe	0	8	0
	£12	10	6

				1792
My acc^{t} from the other side £13.1.7			11	1
		13	01	7

1792				
June 21	Due to Ballance	£ 0	11	1
D^{o} 21	To ¼ C^{t} of Rye flour	0	6	0
Augt 20	10 lb of side pork	0	7	6
Sep^{t} 8	¼ C^{t} of Rye flour	0	3	0
	2 acres meadow	0	12	0
	to straw	0	4	0
		2	0	4
	Rum		4	4
	Due to Conklyn	2	4	10
		1	2	8

[Endorsed] Joseph Conklyn Acc^{t} 1792

1. A Yorktown native, Joseph Conklin was the father of John, Joseph, Jr., Caroline, and Jane Conklin. Bristol, "Abstracts of Wills," p. 204.

2. The Birdsall family was among the first to settle Peekskill, New York. Its founder, Daniel Birdsall (1734–1800), was a storekeeper, with his home located on the corner of Main and Division streets. His son, Daniel W. Birdsall, later became supervisor and town clerk for Cortlandt from 1816 to 1822. He was married twice, first to Phoebe Brown and then to Letitia Lewis. His brother, Samuel Birdsall, was also married twice, first to Nancy Haws, and upon her death to a Miss Spock, possibly the daughter of John Spock. Bolton, II, 502; Scharf, II, 375, 389, 422, 423.

3. Isaac Cronk is identified in *VCFP,* III, 472.

319

Moses Cantine[1] to Pierre. ADS
SHR

[March 18, 1794.]

Pierre Van cortlandt Esqr
To Moses Cantine D^{r}

1779 July 10th	To one p^{r} Buchskin Brichers	
	For your Overseer	2.8
	To ferrages of 3 horses	6
	To 6 ferrages a foot	6
	To Gilbert ~~a foot~~ with a horse	2
	To Perrie with a horse	2
1781	Gilbert a foot	1
1783	D^{o} — D^{o}	1
		£3.6
	To Interest for 10 years	2.6
		£5.12

plan to pay the above Amount to Jacob Radcliff Esqr and Oblige you Humble

Ser^{t}
Moses Cantine

Rhinebeck Landing
March 18th 1794
To Perrie Van Cortlandt Esqr

[Endorsed] Moses Cantine
March 18 1794
Acc^{t}

---

1. Moses Cantine, a ferryman, had served as a captain in the New York militia in 1780. Heitman (1914), p. 143. For the settlement of this long-standing account, see No. 327.

320

Pierre's Business Account with Smith Jones.[1] ADS

SHR

[1789–July 26, 1794.]

Smith Jones Cr				
By 96½ days work at the store house and gitting some timber and hewing and fraiming the Store house at the Landing of Heny: Mathewes[2] and a few days work for Mr Beekman making fence, Barrock &Cr In all 96½ days as above at 6/6 pr day	£	31	7	3
by his son Zophar[3] at all the above places 100½ at 3/6		17	11	9
by 76 days of himself at 6/		22	16	
by 86½ days of Zophar at 4/		16	18	0
by 50½ days of himself at 6/		15	3	0
by 75½ days work of Zophar at 4/		15	2	0
by making Some Work for the Saw and 6 shash [sash] lights		0	6	0
		119	4	0

1789	Smith Jones Dr.				
Aug 18	To a hind ¼ of Veal Wt 20 lb @ 4d	£	0	6	8
Sept 2	To 7½ busl of Seed at 2/		3	0	0
	To an order on Mr Birdsall[4] for 35/		1	15	0
	To 4£ an order on Mr Birdsall & Cash		12	0	0
	To 8½ lb of sole leather at 2/		0	17	0
Jany 1790	To beef hide & Tallow Wt: 387 @ 3.	£	4	16	0
	Deduct the hide		0	13	4

		£	s	d
		4	3	5
	Deduct 5/3 short weight	0	5	3
		3	18	5
		3	18	5
	To 4½ lb of Steal and Iron 2/6	0	2	6
Ap[ll]	To 2 bus[l] of Crib Corn	0	8	0
May 4	To 1 C[t] of Rey flour 14/	0	14	0
D[o] 7	To 1½ C[t] of Rey flour & ½ bus[l] of Corn	1	3	0
	To £5.5./p[d] Dusenbury	5	5	0
	To Cash £5	5	0	0
	To a hide and 10 bus[l] of Wheat £4.5.6	4	5	6
Dec[r]	To 10 bus[l] of Rey out of the Mill at 4/	2	0	0
792 May 1	To Cash in bank Notes 25 dollars	10	0	0
May 8	To Cash in gold and silver	15	0	0
	To a horse £12	12	0	0
1763 Ap[ll]	To a heafer at £5–10	5	10	0
May 6	To cash £20. And May [ye] 22 £21.10	41	10	0
	Your Wifes goun[d] 31/	1	11	0
	Boards from the Saw Mill			

Smith Jones's Acc[t]: Stands thus in my Book —

		£	s	d
1789 D[r]	To a hind ¼ Veal W[t]. 20 lb at 4[d] Aug[t]	£ 0	6	8
Sep[t]	To 7½ bushels of Seed Wheat at 8/	3	0	0
	To an Order on M[r] Birdsall for 35/	1	15	0
	To 4.£ an order on M[r] Birdsall and	4	0	0
	Cash 8£	8	0	0

		£	s	d
	To 8½ lb of Sole Leather at 2/	0	17	0
	To beef hide and Tallow Wt 327. lb. at 3d £4.16.0 deduct 0.13.4 for the hide 4. 3.5 deduct 5.7 short Wt. 3.18.5	3.	18	5
1790	To 4½ lb Steel & Iron 2/6	0	2	6
Apll	To 2 Busl of Crib Corn at 4/	0	8	0
May 4	To a Ct of Rey flour at 14/	0	14	0
May 7	To 1½ Ct of Rey flour & ½ busl of Corn	1	3	0
	To £5–5/ paid Dusenbury	5	5	0
	To Cash 5£	5	0	0
Decr	To a hide and Ten Busl of Wheat 4–5:6	4	5	6
1792	To 10 busl of Rey at different times. One Order for it	2	0	0
May 1	To Cash in bank notes 25 dollars	10	0	0
May 8	To Cash in gold and silver £15	15	0	0
	To a horse at £12	12	0	0
1793	To a heafer at 5.10£	5	10	0
May 6	To Cash £20. And May 22 Cash £21–10	41	10	0
	Calico your wife had £1.11	1	11	0
		£126	6	1
1794	Boards from the Saw Mill No Charge			
July 26	Omissions and Errors Excepted cash	4		
		130	6	1

Pierre Van Cortlandt

[Endorsed]
Smith Jones

---

1. Smith Jones was the son of John and Rachel Jones and a Cortlandt resident at this time. Bristol, "Abstracts of Wills", p. 146.

2. A Cortlandt resident, Henry Matthews was the head of a nine-member family in 1800. "Federal Census, 1800," LVIII (1927), 139.

3. The son of Smith Jones, Zophar Jones would later become a second lieutenant of Westchester militia under Colonel David Hobby, Jr.'s command in 1810. *Council of Appointment, Military,* II, 1168.

4. Members of the Birdsall family are identified in No. 318.

321

Pierre to George W. Tompkins[1]. AD
SHR

Aprill 18–1795.

This day I have Agreed with George Tomkins to build and Compleat the Mill house which is to be built at the New dam on Peeks Kill for which I am to pay him two hundred pounds And he is to Live in the New house One year, for Nothing and to have the pasture for two Cows he is to find his own fire wood but has the Liberty to pick up the Chips and any dry wood. and is to find himself and work men with provisions and <u>board</u> the Out Side boards of the Mill are to be plain and the Shingles are to be dressed by him fit for Laying on the Roof And he is to make the place for the Mill. but no Other thing for the Mill itself. And I am to have all the Timber and Materials Ready for him But Should he go into the Wood to git any timber that Should be wanted if he gits it with his hands he then is to be paid for his Labour, I must have the foundation of the Mill house made at my Cost

[Endorsed]
George Tomkins
Saw Mill days
work &c —

---

1. George Washington Tompkins was a resident of Scarsdale. He had a family of four and one slave in 1800, and served as an officer in the county militia as of 1803. "Federal Census, 1800," LVII (1926), 259; *Council of Appointment, Military,* I, 653.

322

Staats William's[1] Account. AD
NYSHA

[1795–1796?]

Staats Williams Acct — is thus
7 Days work at Spocks House[2]
2 Days at the old mill
1 Day Getting Timber with Mill Eight
Days at Burling House
5 Days now
59 rods Stone fence on Peeks Kill
10 Along the road
50 rods heretofore given an Acct of —
1 Day putting up Gaps in Stone wall

---

1. Staats William was a Cortlandt resident with a wife and two

children in 1800. "Federal Census, 1800," LVIII (1927), 138.

2. James Spock is identified in No. 228.

323

Pierre to William Bates. ADS
SHR

Peeks Kill Oco^{r}. 21, 1796.

This day I bought of William Bates[,]Miller; three Burr Stones two of which are now in the mill, Called Corneys mill, the other Lays out, for fifty-seven pounds, and One boulting Cloath for five pounds twelve Shillins and Six making in the whole Sixty two pounds twelve Shillins and Six pence which Said money Is payable the 25 of decem^{r}. next and In Case the money is not then paid I am to allow him the Interest untill I pay it which is to be on the first of May following being May 1797 as witness my
hand the date above
Pierre Van Cortlandt

attestd
George Tomkins
[on reverse]
Pay the within to James Devin or order
Bates & Randall

April 27th. 1797

Recd July 8. 1797 the within infull
James Devin

[Endorsed]
Bates & Randall
April 27 1797
Order in favour of James Devin
paid

324

Pierre's Business Account with George Tompkins.[1] AD
SHR

[May, 1795–January, 1797.]

(I)

1795	George Tomkins Acct —	£	S	D
May 24th	To Two Bushels of Rye	0	14	0
	1 bushel of Potatoes		3	6
	bushels of Do from the General			
	16½ lb of Veal at /5d		6	10
June 30th	½ bushel Corn & 14½ lb of Veal at /5d		9	0
	two Dollars to pay for the Grindstone		16	
July 22	11 lb Veal		4	7
31	Cash ten Dollars	4	0	0
Augt 1	½ bushel Corn at 6/ prbushl	0	3	0
	To Burlings Acct. £5.4.0[2]	5	4	0
14	To Cash 12½ Dollars & August 15 7½ Dollars making	8	0	0
Sepr 28	7 lb of Beef . . Pierre let you have at /4d		2	4
Octr 8	10 Dollars & 11½ lb of Beef	4	3	10
Novr 2	28 lb of Beef at /5d and ½ bushel potatoes	0	13	7
Decr 5	½ bushel of Potatoes at 3/6		1	9
	1 bushel Corn		6	0
11	Cash 16/ & 2 bushels of Buckwheat at 6/6	1	9	0
13	1 bushel of Potatoes 3/6		3	6
27	Cash five dollars Pierre paid you	2	0	0
28	1 bushel potatoes Saturday		3	6
30	Cash a Ten Dollar Bill by Crommel[3]	4	0	0
	1 pair of half soles for Forbes		1	6

			£	S	D
Decr.	1	2 bushels of Hyats[4] buckwheat at 6/6		13	0
	3	Cash 5 dollars by Pierre	2	0	0
	9	Cash 6 Crowns & 30 two shilling pieces by Sibbey	5	13	0
	10	1 bushel of potatoes 3/6		3	6
	12	1 bushel of Corn		6	0
	14	1 hand Saw 14/ Pierre bought for you		14	0
	16	27 lb of Beef at /5d		11	3
	19	one hind Qr. Beef Wt 96 lb at /5d	2	0	0
	22	1 Bushel of Hyats Buckwheat at 6/6		6	6
		medicine Huson[5] brought up 8/		8	0
1796					
Janr.	8	1 pair of Shoes for Jasper		10	0
	8	1 bushel of Hyats buckwheat		6	6
	15	1 pr of half Soles	0	1	6
	24	Cash 4 Dollars	1	12	0
	25	one hind Qr. Veal Wt. 14½ lb at /5d		6	0
	26	1 bushel of Potatoes		3	6
Febr.	2	Cash 50 Dollars	20	0	0
	5	One fore Qr. Veal Wt. 14 lb at /4½		5	3
	10	1 Bushel of Potatoes	0	3	6
	25	25 Dollars to Account for	10	0	0
	27	1 bushel of Potatoes		3	6
			£ 79	12	11

(2)

1796	Account brought over	£	S	D
		79	12	11

March 11	Paid Mr James Diven £100 by your Order	100	0	0
12	1 bushel of Potatoes		3	6
	One Qr. Veal Wt. 15 lb. at /5d	0	6	3
23	1 bushel of Potatoes	0	3	6
	Cash when you was in New York £21.9	21	9	0
April 6	1 bushel of Potatoes at 3/6		3	6
8	1 bushel of Corn 8/		8	0
14	Cash £6.0.0 to account for	6	0	0
16	1 bushel of Potatoes by Tom		3	6
	1 Ct of Rey flour from Jones 34/	1	14	0
22	24 Wt of Veal at /5d		10	0
23	1 bushel Corn		8	0
	Leather for your wife Shoes &c.		6	0
26	1 bushel of red potatoes		3	6
	Cash 8/ to buy butter		8	0
27	1 hind Qr. of Veal Wt. 15½ lb		6	3
May 2	3 Bushels of Potatoes & planting potatoes 4/		12	0
3	One hind Qr Veal Wt 13½ lb at /6		6	9
4	One fore Qr Veal Wt. 12 at /5		5	0
	one bushel of Corn Sibbey measured		8	0
9	Cash 30 Dollars	12	0	0
	1 Ct. & ¾ of Rey flour from Saml Jones[6] £2.19.6	2	19	6
N.B.	Cash £5.8.5 & £3.0.0 making £8.8.5 to pay for 2 Spindles, 2 drivers & 2 bales had of James Brewster[7] May 17. 1796			
	Cash £16.0.0 out of Which he is to pay Chapman for making the Shasses [sashes] £7.10.0	17	0	0

25	Cash 30 dollars to buy pork	12	0	0
June 4	Cash 20 dollars. Haver[8] wanted part of it	8	0	0
6	Leather for a pair of Shoes for Fergus		8	0
10	½ bushel Corn		4	0
11	Cash 10 Dollars Pierre let you have	4	0	0
20	Cash 20 Dollars Pierre let you have	8	0	0
July 1	1 Qr. Ct. Rye flour Pierre's order		8	6
2	Cash Ten Dollars Pierre Let you have	4	0	0
6	2 Qrs. Lamb		6	0
9	Cash by Jesse 17 Dollars & 1 bank note 3 dollars	8	0	0
15	1 hind Qr. Veal Wt. lb. by Philips	0	12	0
18	1 fore Qr. of Lamb 3/		3	0
22	Cash 7 Dollars by Jesse	2	16	0
	½ a Cheese Wt 18 lb at ½		19	6
		294	13	11
	Carried over			

		£	S	D
1796	Account brought over	294	13	11
July				
22	To Cash 5 Dollars by Jesse	2	0	0
30	1 bushel Wheat out old mill Pierre's Order		13	0
Augst 6	Cash £3.0.0 Pierre sent you by Jesse	3	0	0
17	Cash two Crowns Pierre let you have		17	8
22	Cash 20 Dollars	8	0	0

Sepr 9	Cash 6/ for butter		6	0
10	Cash 20 dollars	8	0	0
10	11 lb of Beef at 6/		5	6
Octr 4	Cash ten dollars	4	0	0
	1 pair of half Soles for Jesse		1	6
8	Cash 8 dollars & 2 Crowns by Jesse	4	1	8
14	An Ax 10/		10	0
14	Cash sent by Fanny. 40/	2	0	0
	1 pair of half Soles for Forbes		1	6
22	Cash 5 dollars	2	0	0
25	20½ lb beef at /6		10	3
	Cash 2 dollars by Jesse		16	0
Novr 3	1 hind Qr. Mutton Wt. 9 lb. 4/6		4	6
	Cash 30/ by Jesse	1	10	0
5	1 hind Qr. Mutton sent by Mr Carman[9] Wt. 10 lb.		5	0
7	Cash 3/6		3	6
7	22 lb of fresh pork & Gammon at /9		16	6
12	Cash by Jesse five Dollars	2	0	0
21	¼ Mutton 8 lbs		4	0
24	3¼ Yards of Cloth at 6/		19	6
	3 Qrs. of Beef Wt. 78.75.81 at 36/pr hundred	4	7	0
	½ bushel Salt 3/3		3	3
30	358 lb of pork at 70/ pr Hundred	12	10	0
	½ bushel Salt 3/3		3	3
	To Sundries on Thorn's[10] Account brought you	3	15	5
	To ditto on do do at another time		9	0
Decr. 14	To One bushel of Potatoes		5	0
18	1 pair of half Soles for Forbes		1	6

	12	1 d^o d^o d^o d^o for Jesse	1	6
1797				
Jan^r.	5	1 Q^r Veal W^t. 12½ lb at /6	6	3
	15	1 bushel Potatoes	5	0
	17	1 hind Q^r Veal W^t 16 lb at /6	8	0
	27	a pair of half Soles for Forbes	1	6
			£360 17	7

[Endorsed]
N^o: 1 —
£360–17–7

---

1. George Tompkins is identified in No. 321.

2. Thomas Burling and his family of nine were residents of Harrison in 1800. "Federal Census, 1800," LVII (1926), 118.

3. Possibly a reference to another Harrison family, John and Hannah Cromwell, who had five sons and three daughters. Bristol, "Abstracts of Wills," p. 252.

4. Among the Hyatts of Cortlandt were John, James, and Joshua, all Van Cortlandt leaseholders. *VCFP*, II, 380, 563; III, 96.

5. Members of the Huson family are identified in *VCFP*, II, 553.

6. Samuel Jones is identified in No. 280.

7. For James Brewster, see *VCFP*, II, 419.

8. The census of 1790 lists thirteen Haver families, most of whom were residents of Dutchess County. *Heads of Families 1790*, pp. 62, 69, 71, 77, 86.

9. John Carman is identified in No. 308.

10. Justus Thorn and his seven-member family were residents of Cortlandt. "Federal Census, 1800," *New York Genealogical and Biographical Record*, LVIII (1927), 142.

325

Pierre's Business Account with George Tompkins and John Titus.[1] AD

SHR

[March 13, 1797.]

1797				
March 2,	Memorandum for George Tomkins			
	Bolting Cloaths of John Titus	23	16	10
	Sides of Leather for the Elivators			
	at 25/Pence Pound	4	16	8
	Tin plates of ox D°	0	18	10
	lb of 20 penny Nails	0	3	0
	28, lb Sugar Best Muscovado	1	16	0
	a Jug of Lamp Oyl	0	10	0
	7:lb of Sugar for Mrs Mangle[2]	0	8	0
	2 Overhalls			
	Tobacco One dollars Worth	0	8	6
	6 lb of Flour Cask Nails — 4,lb	0	7	6
	100 Oysters	0	5	0
	a high Pot to hold about a pale			
	2 or 3 Skains of Twine	0	3	0
	Say 30 lb, of Flax 1/3	1	17	6
	6 yards of Linnen for the bolts,	0	16	9
	6 saw mill files	0	10	6
	1 barr of steel	0	9	6
	1 Viol. of Balsom Capivi[3]	0	2	0
	1 Ounce Good Silk for the bolts	0	3	9
	1 Bar of iron	0	15	8
	1 Bolter of Est	0	0	6
		14	13	2

Cash 5 dollars

Tomkins Received In New York

	£20– 7–9	
Laid out	14–13–2	March–13–1797
	5:14:7	

[Endorsed]
G. Tomkins
and
John Titus

---

1. John Titus was a North Salem resident. He married Esther Huggerford, the daughter of Dr. Peter Huggerford, and after her death he married the widow of George J. Brinkerhoff of Fishkill. Roebling, pp. 207, 332; "Federal Census, 1800," LVII (1926), 351.

2. The widow Hannah Mangle and her two young daughters were residents of Philipstown, Dutchess County, in 1790. *Heads of Families 1790,* p. 89.

3. Possibly balsam copaiba, which was used as a stimulant, diaphoretic, and expectorant. Originally this semi-fluid compound was also thought to relieve symptoms of gonorrhea. Normand L. Hoerr and Arthur Osel, eds., *Blakiston's New Gould Medical Dictionary* . . . (New York, 2nd ed., 1956), p. 281.

326

Pierre's Business Account with Hercules Mulligan.[1] ADS SHR

[September, 1799.]

	Mr. Peir Van Cortland To H Mulligan Dr	£	£
1784 June 20th	To Making a Suit Cloaths	2.16.0	

	" 2 y^{ds} Cloth/ @ 40/	4.0. .0	
	" 2½ y florentine @ 24/	3. 5.0	
	" ½ y Silk mantles @ 16/	1. 4.0	
	" 1½ y^{ds} Rattinet @ 5/	0. 7.6	
	" 4 y^{d} Linen @ 3/6	0.14.0	
	" 1½ doz buttons @ 1/	0. 1.6	
	" Silk, twist &c	1. 0.0	
	" 2 doz, Buttons @ 10/	1.10.0	
29th	To making a Bree^{s}:	0.14.0	14.18.0
	" 2½ y^{d} princess stuff @ 16/	2. 0.0	
	" Buttons, Pockets Silk &c	0.10.0	
1785	To making a Coat	1. 4.0	3. 4.0
Augt 23^{d}			
	" 2 y^{ds} Garnet Cloth @ 42/	4. 4.0	
	" 3 y^{ds} Rattinet @ 5/	0.15.0	
	" Pockets & slevelinings	0. 6.0	
	" 1½ doz buttons @ 8/	0.12.0	
	" Silk twist &c	0.10.0	
Sepr 24			
	To ripping & turning a Coat	1. 8.0	7.11.0
	" Pockets & Slevlinings	0. 6.0	
	" 1½ doz butt^{s}. @ 10/ Silk &c 10/	1. 5.0	
Decr 19			
	To Making a surtout Coat	1. 4.0	2.19.0
	" 3¾ y^{d} Coating @ 16/	3. 0.0	
	" 1½ y green baize @ 6/	0. 9.0	
	" Pockets and Slevelinings	0. 6.0	
	" 1 doz 13 buttons @ 2/ Silk &c 10/	0.13.8	
1786			
Feby 10th			
	To making a Breeches	0.12.0	
	" 2¾ y^{d} Sattinet @ 10/	1. 7.6	
	" Buttons, pockets Silk &c 10/	0.10.0	

April 1th	To making a Vest & Brees	1. 4.0	8. 2.6
	" Buttons &c 10/ 1 yd Linen 3/	0.13.0	
May 3	To Making a Coat	1. 4.0	1.17.0
	" 2¼ yds Cloth @ 40/	4.10.0	
	" 2½ yds serge du roy @ 12/	1.10.0	
	" 1½ dozen butts. @ 4/6. Silk @ 10/	0.16.9	
19th July	To making a pare overhals	0.11.0	8. 0.9
	" 1 pice Nankeen 18/8. Trim @ 6/	1. 4 8	
4th Novr.	To Making a peir Brees	0.11.0	1.15.8
	" 2¾ yd Silk Sattinet @ 12/	1.13.0	
	Linen, Silk, twist &c	0. 8.0	
			2.12.0
New York 3d Sepr 1799			£~~44.18.9~~
			£50.19.7

H.M.

The above account was paid me in full by Beekman, Son & Goold[2] —   -N-

H: Mulligan

Sworn Before me
this 12th. Sept 1799
Gabriel Furman[3]

[Addressed] Mr Peir V. Cortlandt
acct. £50.19.7

[Endorsed] G.G. Beekman accounts against Pierre Van Cortlandt Decd. handed to me in Novr. 1815 —
Book F.42 —

It is Entred in

Fathers Book
Page 132 —
— 132 —

---

1. Hercules Mulligan is identified in No. 298.

2. For Beekman, Son and Gould, see *VCFP,* III, 65.

3. Gabriel Furman was the proprietor of a boardinghouse, Sign of the Free American, located at 111 Queen Street in New York City. He served in the state Assembly in 1796, and was returned in 1814. *Polk's Directory* (1786), p. 87; Werner, pp. 415, 424.

4. Gerard G. Beekman, Jr. was the son of Gerard and Anna (Van Horne) Beekman and the husband of Cornelia Van Cortlandt, Pierre's daughter. Philip L. White, *The Beekmans of New York in Politics and Commerce, 1647–1877* (New York, 1956), p. 214.

327

Moses Cantine[1] to Pierre. ADS
SHR

[June 25, 1800.]

Perrie Van Cortland Esqr
To Moses Cantine Dr.

1779 Augt. 16 To 1 p^r buckskin brichers for your overseer @ 6 Do^ll	2. 8.0
Your Negro Man Tite[2] to ferrage with 3 horses @ 2/	6–
Yourself to ferrage 6 times @1/	6
Gilbert to ferrage with a horse	2–
Perrie to D' with a horse	2
1781 Gilbert to ferrage a foot	1

1783 D' — D' — D' — D' — D' — D' [Ditto]	1
	3. 6.0
Interest from 1783	3. 6.0
	£6.12.0

Sir please to pay this Acc[t]. to Maj[r]. Radcliff and his Recep[t] shall be your Discharge
with due respect Your
Most Humble Ser.[t]
Moses Cantine
Kingston Ferry June 21st 1800
To Perrie Van Cortland Esq[r].

[Endorsed] Beekmans Mills June 25–1800
Received of Pierre Van Cortland Esq[r].
(by Compromise) Three pounds Six Shillins in Cash
Infull for the Within Acc[t].
In behalf of Moses Contine
by me W[m] Radclift[3]

[Further Endorsed]
Moses Contines Acc[t].
Paid Infull to
William Radclift
June 25–1800 —
£3.6.0–

---

1. Moses Cantine is identified in No. 319, his earlier billing for this account.

2. "Tite" was the nickname for Pierre's favorite slave Titus. *VCFP*, III, 592.

3. A Dutchess County native, William Radclift served in the state Assembly in 1792–1793. Werner, p. 414.

328

Pierre's Business Account with James Forsyth.[1] ADS
SHR

[Aug. 16, 1800.]

1786	Pierre Van Cortlandt Esqr. To James Forsyth D^{r}.			
14 Dec^{r}.	To 2 Doz. Pipes	£0	1	8
	1 do. Shirt Buttons			6
	1 oz. Thread		2	10
28	Two Wine Goblets		4	
	1 Milk pot		1	
	½ Doz. pipes			5
	16½ Y^{ds}. Blk. Durant @ 3/	2	9	6
			2.19.11	
1787				
Feby. 10	To 1 Skine Silk 1 do Twist		1	6
	1 Wine Goblet		2	
22	1 Bowl		2	
	1 oz. Thread N. 40		4	6
	1 do. 34		3	6
	1 do. 31		2	10
March 5	1 pint Bowl		1	
22	1 piece Tape		2	
	3 Gill Glasses		3	
	1 Black Mugg			10
May 11	1 Doz. Pipes			10
Augt. 16	2 do shirt Buttons		1	
Octo^{r} 26	8 Wine Goblets		16	
1788	1 oz Thread N. 60		5	6
	1 do. 34		3	6
June 2	1 Quart Bowl		2	
July 30	1 tb Pepper		4	6
		2	16	6
		£5	16	5

Peeks Kill Augt. 16 1800
Rec^{d}. the above Acc^{t}. in full
James Forsyth

[Endorsed]
This account is Settled and paid
In full by Discount On the old
barn,
Octo^{r}–6–1800 as p^{r} my
receipt to James Forsight

[2nd Endorsement]
Receipt of James Forsyth
Acct Settled and paid

---

1. James Forsyth resided in Cortlandt with his wife and their family of two sons and one daughter as of 1800. "Federal Census, 1800," *New York Genealogical and Biographical Record,* LVIII (1927), 140.

329

Seth Miller[1] to Pierre. ADS
SHR

[March, 1802]

Govr. Van Courtlandt
to Seth Miller Dr.

1802		
24 Oct^{r}.	to Visit & Med. for Your Lady	£0.12.0
Nov. 2^{d}	to d^{o} d^{o}	0.12.0
10	to d^{o} d^{o}	0.12.0
24	to Vis. & Dircitions	0. 8.0
6 March	to Gum Arabic	0. 2.0
		£2. 6.0

Rec[d] the above in full Seth Miller

[Endorsed]
Seth Miller March 1802
Acc[t] paid
Gov[r]. Van Courtlandt acc[t]. 2.6.0
Doc[r] Miller Acc[t].
P[d] In full

---

1. Dr. Seth Miller, originally of Ossining, later moved to North Castle, where he became the first practising physician in that town. Scharf, II, 573.

330

John Cregier to Pierre. ADS
SHR

[undated]

The Hon[ble]. Pierre V. Cortlandt Dr.
To John Cregier

To Sundry Visits, Medecines, and Attendance, for your Family in the Malignant Sore Throat Distempor	£8. 0.0
To Cash in part A half Johannes	3. 4.0
Ballance Due	£4.16.0
P[d]. 1 Guinea & a half on this Acc[t]. to Doctor	2.16.0
Cragin, and took his Receipt — Remains due the Doctor	£1.19.6

[Endorsed]
Doctor Cragiers
Acc[t]. against Papa

Glossary

awl	pointed instrument for punching holes.
axletree	a bar fixed crosswise under the body of a vehicle, with rounded ends for wheel fittings.
bailiwick	the jurisdiction of a bailiff.
barl	barrel
battinett	small sheets of cotton used in making quilts.
beize	woolen fabric left in its natural color.
bolt	a roll of cloth normally containing 40 yards.
bouillabaisse	fish stew
bolster	a long under-pillow for a bed or couch.
buckram	fine linen or cotton fabric which is stiffened.
buff	buffalo leather with a nap to one side, used in making belts, pouches, and coats.
calico	initially, the name given cotton cloth from India.
camblet	woven fabric made of camel's hair, wool, cotton, or goat's hair.
cant	iron ring around a carriage wheel.
cask	wooden container made of curved staves and iron hoops, usually larger and stronger than a barrel.
chain	unit of measurement in surveying: 66 feet.
check	fabric with a checkered pattern.
chint	the singular form of chintz, a painted or stained calico from India.
clevis	a piece of U-shaped metal with a pin or bolt passing through holes at the two ends for attaching a draft-chain for plowing.

colter	iron blade at the front of a plow.
crib corn	unshucked Indian corn.
curb bit	chain passing under a horse's lower jaw and fastened to the branches of a restraining bit.
c[t]	one hundredweight.
damsel	an attachment to a millstone spindle for shaking the hopper.
DD	delivered
demurrer	a legal pleading intended to stop an action.
duffel	coarse woolen cloth with a nap.
durant	stout cloth in imitation of buff, used in clothing.
elevator	a mechanical device, usually an endless belt with a series of scoops or baskets, used in milling.
entail	to limit the inheritance of an estate to a specified line of heirs.
farrier	a blacksmith or veterinarian.
firkin	one quarter barrel or 9 imperial gallons.
flanning	the internal splay of a window jam.
florentine	a type of silk.
frieze	woolen cloth with a shaggy or tufted nap to one side.
fustian	stout cotton or flax fabric with a short pile.
gammon	the buttock or thigh of a hog, usually smoked or salted for bacon.
garnet cloth	a deep-red-colored fabric.
geneva	an alcoholic beverage flavored with juniper berries, also called Holland gin.
gr[o]	gross
gudgeon	a metal pin used in milling to keep grinding stones in place.
guinea	a coin, first struck in 1663 for use in the

	African trade, made of gold from Guinea.
gum arabic	a gum, yielded by several species of acacia growing in Africa and Asia, used as a medicinal mucilage.
half Joe	a Portuguese gold coin.
hatcheling	the process of combing flax or hemp.
hog cheek	the side of a pig.
iron dog	a mechanical device for gripping or holding something.
kip	the hide of a young or small calf.
kive	a mashing vat.
lath	a thin strip of wood used to form supports for plastering and roofing.
Laus Deo	Praise be to God.
link	unit of measurement in surveying: 7.92 inches.
luckin	a varying form of lucken; meaning to gather up.
lump work	the process of loading or unloading a vessel.
mace	a spice made of nutmeg.
mantle	a loose, sleeveless cloak.
middlings	a combination of the coarser parts of ground wheat with the finest bran separated from flour in bolting; usually an animal feed.
mol^{s}	molasses
muscovado sugar	raw or unrefined sugar.
nankeen	firm yellow or buff fabric made of natural-color Chinese cotton.
ozenbrig	a material used for lining.
piggin	a small wooden pail or tub.
peck	one quarter of a bushel.
pipe of wine	one-half ton, two hogsheads, or four barrels.

pistareen	Spanish silver coin.
pluck	heart, liver, and lungs of an animal used for food.
punking	the process of firing metal and then shaping it with forcible blows.
q[rt]	quart
rattinett	a woolen cloth, thinner than ratten.
rod	measure of length: 16.5 feet.
rynd	a piece of iron, crossing the hole in the upper millstone, by which the stone is supported on the spindle.
scant	a measured size of small quantity.
serge	originally a silken fabric, but also a woolen cloth used in clothing.
shaloon	a light woolen material used for linings.
sheeting	a linen or cotton cloth used for bed linen.
sattinet	a thin kind of satin or cotton used in making trousers.
sinnet	a cordage made of several strands of yarn.
skein	a quantity of thread or yarn wound on a reel.
staple	a U-shaped metal bar or rod.
stuff	a woven textile, mainly of wool without a nap.
princess stuff	a worsted material used in making a lady's close-fitting dress or robe.
superfine	over-refined grain.
surtout	overcoat
swanskin(e)	a soft flannel material.
tallow	harder types of fat used for candles and soap.
tammy	fine worsted wool.
tierce	one third of a pipe, or 42 gallons; also the name of a cask of this size.
trammel	a shackle for training horses.

trunnils	iron supports of equal length.
twist	thread or silk usually used for buttonholes.
warting	a type of cloth.
whippletree	the pivoted or swinging bar to which a harness is fastened.
wings	appendages put in wing-like motion by the action of the air, as a fan or vane for winnowing grain.
warp wool	a type of cloth in which the lengthwise strands are twisted harder than the crosswise.
worsted	firmly-twisted thread for ornamental tailoring.
writ of fieri facias	a legal term meaning to institute the process for executing a judgment.

Bibliography

MANUSCRIPT COLLECTIONS

Albany Institute of History and Art

VAN CORTLANDT FAMILY

Boston Public Library

BENJAMIN WALKER

PHILIP VAN CORTLANDT

Brown University Library

JOHN BARCLAY

Columbia University Special Collections

NICHOLAS FISH

ALEXANDER HAMILTON

PETER JAY

JOHN JAY

VAN CORTLANDT FAMILY

Cornell University

PIERRE VAN CORTLANDT

Harvard University

VAN CORTLANDT FAMILY

Historical Society of Pennsylvania

CORNELIUS RAY

VAN CORTLANDT FAMILY

The Henry E. Huntington Library and Art Gallery

VAN CORTLANDT FAMILY

MISCELLANEOUS MANUSCRIPTS

Kingston (New York) Senate House Museum

PIERRE VAN CORTLANDT

Library of Congress

JAMES CLINTON

GEORGE CLINTON

PETER FORCE COLLECTION

ROBERT MORRIS LETTERBOOK

Massachusetts Historical Society

VAN CORTLANDT FAMILY

National Archives

FIRST CENSUS OF THE U.S. (1790) 3 ROLLS.

SECOND CENSUS OF THE U.S. (1800) 52 ROLLS.
THIRD CENSUS OF THE U.S. (1810) 71 ROLLS.
FOURTH CENSUS OF THE U.S. (1820) 142 ROLLS.
PAPERS OF THE CONTINENTAL CONGRESS

New York County Clerk's Office

CHANCERY COURT RECORDS
MAYOR'S COURT RECORDS
SUPREME COURT RECORDS

The New-York Historical Society

DEWITT CLINTON
GEORGE CLINTON
JAMES CLINTON
DEPEYSTER FAMILY
WILLIAM DUER
JOHN JAY
JOHN TABOR KEMPE

The New York Public Library

DEWITT CLINTON
GEORGE CLINTON
GEORGE WASHINGTON CLINTON
JAMES CLINTON
EMMETT COLLECTION
JOHN JAY
ROBERT R. LIVINGSTON
DANIEL MORGAN
PHILIP SCHUYLER
PIERRE VAN CORTLANDT, JR.
VAN CORTLANDT-VAN WYCK FAMILY
RICHARD VARICK

New York State Historical Association

VAN CORTLANDT FAMILY

New York State Library

JAMES CLINTON
GEORGE CLINTON
COUNCIL OF APPOINTMENT, CIVIL, FOR THE YEARS 1801–1815.
JABEZ HAMMOND
JOHN JAY
REVOLUTIONARY WAR MANUSCRIPTS
VAN CORTLANDT FAMILY
MARQUIS DE LAFAYETTE

ALEXANDER McDOUGALL
McKESSON PAPERS
REVOLUTIONARY WAR: NEW YORK STATE REVOLUTIONARY WAR COMMITTEES AND COMMISSIONS
SOCIETY OF THE CINCINNATI
BARNARDUS SWARTWOUT
VAN CORTLANDT FAMILY
PIERRE CORTLANDT VAN WYCK
VERPLANCK FAMILY

The Pierpont Morgan Library
MISCELLANEOUS MANUSCRIPTS

Queens College, City University of New York, Paul Klapper Library
NEW YORK PREROGATIVE COURT RECORDS
NEW YORK WILLS

Franklin D. Roosevelt Library
LIVINGSTON-REDMOND FAMILY

Sleepy Hollow Restorations
BEEKMAN FAMILY
VAN CORTLANDT FAMILY
MISCELLANEOUS MANUSCRIPTS

State Historical Society of Wisconsin
PIERRE VAN CORTLANDT

Syracuse University, George Arents Research Library
PHILIP VAN CORTLANDT

University of Michigan, William E. Clements Library
PHILIP VAN CORTLANDT

Yale University
PHILIP VAN CORTLANDT
MISCELLANEOUS MANUSCRIPTS

PRINTED SOURCES

Alexander, DeAlva S. *A Political History of the State of New York* (New York, 1906–1909; Reprint, Port Washington, NY, 1969), 4 vols.

[Annals of Congress]. *The Debates and Proceedings in the Congress of the United States, 1789–1824* (Washington, D.C., 1834–1856), 42 vols.

Belknap, Waldron P., Jr. *The De Peyster Genealogy* (Boston, 1956).

Bolton, Robert. *The History of the Several Towns, Manors, and Patents of the County of Westchester, from Its First Settlement to the Present Time* (New York, 1881), 2 vols.

Bonney, Catherina V.R. *A Legacy of Historical Gleanings* (Albany, NY, 1875), 2 vols.

Bristol, Theresa H. "Abstracts of Wills Recorded at White Plains, New York, Subsequent to May 1, 1787." *New York Genealogical and Biographical Record,* LVIII (January, 1927).

Chorley, Edward. *History of St. Philip's Church in the Highlands, Garrison, New York; Including, up to 1840, St. Peter's Church, on the Manor of Cortlandt* (New York, 1912).

DeForest, L. Effingham. *The Van Cortlandt Family* (New York, 1930).

Duncan, William. *The New-York Directory, and Register* (New York, 1791–1795).

"Federal Census, 1800 — Westchester County, New York." *New York Genealogical and Biographical Record,* LVII–LIX (1926–1928).

Fernow, Berthold, comp. *Calendar of Wills on File and Recorded in the Offices of the Clerk of the Court of Appeals, of the County Clerk at Albany and of the Secretary of State, 1626–1836* (New York, 1896).

———. *New York in the Revolution* (Albany, NY, 1887).

Flick, Alexander C., ed. *History of the State of New York* (New York, 1933), 10 vols.

Fox, Joseph M. *The Story of Early Peekskill, 1609–1876* (Peekskill, NY, 1947).

French, John H., ed. *Gazetteer of the State of New York: Embracing a Comprehensive View of the Geography, Geology, and General History of the State* (Syracuse, NY, 1860).

Hammond, Jabez D. *The History of Political Parties in the State of New York, From the Ratification of the Federal Constitution to December 1840* (Albany, NY, 1842), 2 vols.

Hasbrouck, Frank, ed. *The History of Dutchess County, New York* (Poughkeepsie, NY, 1909).

Heitman, Francis B. *Historical Register and Dictionary of the United States Army* (Washington, D.C., 1903), 2 vols.

———. *Historical Register of Officers of the Continental Army During the War of the Revolution, April, 1775 to December, 1783* (Washington, D.C., 2nd edition, 1914).

Hemstreet, Charles. *The Story of Manhattan* (New York, 1901).

Hibbard, B.[illy]. *Memoirs of the Life and Travels of B. Hibbard, Minister of the Gospel . . .* (New York, 1843).

Horton, Stephen D. *Sixteen Nine to Eighteen Seventy: Glimpses from the Past in Connection with the Early History of the Manor of Cortlandt and the Village of Peekskill* (Peekskill, NY, 1912).

Hough, Franklin B., comp. *The New York Civil List, Containing the Names and Origin of the Civil Divisions, and the Names and Dates of Election or Appointment of the Principal State and County Officers* (Albany, NY, 1855–1860).

Howell, George R. and Jonathan Tenny. *History of the County of Albany, New York, from 1609 to 1886* (New York, 1886).

Irwin, Ray W. *Daniel D. Tompkins: Governor of New York and Vice President of the United States* (New York, 1968).

Kass, Alvin. *Politics in New York State 1800–1830* (Syracuse, NY, 1965).

Longworth, David. *American Almanac, New-York Register, and City Directory* (New York, various years).

McAdam, David, and Bishoff H. McAdam, et al., eds. *History of the Bench and Bar of New York* (New York, 1897–1899), 2 vols.

McCormick, Richard P. *The Second American Party System: Party Formation in the Jacksonian Era* (New York, 1973).

MacKenzie, Grenville. *Ten English Families of Philipse Manor in Westchester County, New York . . .* (New York, 1942).

Monaghan, Frank. *John Jay: Defender of Liberty Against Kings and People* (New York, 1935).

Munsell, Joel. *Annals of Albany* (Albany, NY, 1850–1859), 10 vols.

———. *Collections on the History of Albany, From Its Discovery to the Present Time* (Albany, NY, 1871), 4 vols.

The National Cyclopaedia of American Biography, Being the History of the United States (New York, 1892–1971), 53 vols.

New York, Secretary of State. *Calendar of New York Colonial Manuscripts, Indorsed Land Papers in the Office of the Secretary of State of New York, 1643–1803* (Albany, NY, 1864).

O'Callaghan, Edmund B., ed. *Calendar of Historical Manuscripts Relating to the War of the Revolution in the Office of the Secretary of State* (Albany, NY, 1868), 2 vols.

———. *The Documentary History of the State of New-York* (Albany, 1849–1851), 4 vols.

———. *Documents Relative to the Colonial History of the State of New-*

York (Albany, NY, 1853–1887), 15 vols.

Polk's New York City Directory (New York, various years).

Reed, Harriet A., ed. *Autobiography of Thurlow Reed* (Boston, 1884), 2 vols.

Remini, Robert V. *Andrew Jackson and the Course of American Empire, 1767–1821* (New York, 1977).

Reynolds, Cuyler. *Genealogical and Family History of Southern New York and the Hudson River Valley* (New York, 1914), 3 vols.

Roberts, James A., ed. *New York in the Revolution as Colony and State* (Albany, NY, 1901–1904), 2 vols.

Roebling, Emily W., ed. *The Journal of the Reverend Silas Constant, Pastor of the Presbyterian Church at Yorktown, New York* (Philadelphia, 1903).

Ruttenber, Edward M. *History of the County of Orange: With a History of the Town and City of Newburgh* (Newburgh, NY, 1875).

Schuyler, John. *Institution of the Society of the Cincinnati, 1783, with Extracts, from the Proceedings of its General Meetings and from the Transactions of the New York State Society* (New York, 1886).

Sharf, John T., ed. *History of Westchester County, New York, Including Morrisania, Kings Bridge, and West Farms, Which Have Been Annexed to New York City* (Philadelphia, 1886), 2 vols.

Shonnard, Frederick, and William W. Spooner. *History of Westchester County, New York, from its Earliest Settlement to the Year 1900* (New York, 1900).

Stokes, Isaac N. Phelps, ed. *The Iconography of Manhattan Island, 1498–1909* (New York, 1915–1928), 6 vols.

Tammany Society, or Columbian Order. *150th Anniversary Celebration, 1786, July 4, 1936* (New York, 1936).

Tuckerman, Bayard, ed. *The Diary of Philip Hone 1828–1851* (New York, 1889), 2 vols.

———. *Life of General Philip Schuyler 1733–1804* (New York, 1904).

VerPlanck, William E. *The History of Abraham Isaacse VerPlanck, and His Male Descendants in America* (Fishkill Landing, NY, 1892).

Werner, Edgar A., comp. *Civil List and Constitutional History of the Colony and State of New York* (Albany, NY, 1889).

Wilson, James G., ed. *The Memorial History of the City of New York, from its First Settlement to the Year 1892* (New York, 1892–1893), 4 vols.

Yoshpe, Harry B. *The Disposition of Loyalist Estates in the Southern District of New York* (New York, 1937).

Index

Sleepy Hollow Restorations, Incorporated, is a non-profit educational institution chartered by the *Board of Regents of the University of the State of New York.* Established under an endowment provided, in large part, by the late John D. Rockefeller, Jr., Sleepy Hollow Restorations owns and maintains *Sunnyside,* Washington Irving's picturesque home in Tarrytown; *Philipsburg Manor, Upper Mills,* in North Tarrytown, an impressive example of a colonial commercial mill complex and *Van Cortlandt Manor,* in Croton-on-Hudson, a distinguished eighteenth-century family estate.

www.ingramcontent.com/pod-product-compliance
Lightning Source LLC
Chambersburg PA
CBHW030813310726
48980CB00006B/486/J

9780912882413